T0271389

This book presents a fresh view of crucial processes of change, offering through an interdisciplinary analysis new insights into both the history and literature of the land in early modern England. In the period 1500 to 1660 the practices and values of rural England were exposed to unprecedented challenges. Within this context a wide variety of commentators examined and debated the changing conditions, a process documented in the pages of sermons, pamphlets, satiric verse and drama, husbandry and surveying manuals, chorographical tracts and rural poetry. The analysis of these texts in *God speed the plough* explores changing patterns of representation. The book argues that important movements revised preexistent assumptions about agrarian England and shaped bold new appreciations of rural life. While Tudor moralists responded to social crises by asserting ideals of rural stability and community, by the seventeenth century a discourse of improvement promoted vitally divergent notions of thrift and property.

Past and Present Publications

God speed the plough

Past and Present Publications

General Editor: JOANNA INNES, *Somerville College, Oxford*

Past and Present Publications comprise books similar in character to the articles in the journal *Past and Present*. Whether the volumes in the series are collections of essays – some previously published, others new studies – or monographs, they encompass a wide variety of scholarly and original works primarily concerned with social, economic and cultural changes, and their causes and consequences. They will appeal to both specialists and non-specialists and will endeavour to communicate the results of historical and allied research in the most readable and lively form.

For a list of titles in Past and Present Publications, see end of book.

God speed the plough

The representation of agrarian England, 1500–1660

ANDREW McRAE

University of Sydney

CAMBRIDGE
UNIVERSITY PRESS

PUBLISHED BY THE PRESS SYNDICATE OF THE UNIVERSITY OF CAMBRIDGE
The Pitt Building, Trumpington Street, Cambridge, United Kingdom

CAMBRIDGE UNIVERSITY PRESS
The Edinburgh Building, Cambridge CB2 2RU, UK
40 West 20th Street, New York NY 10011–4211, USA
477 Williamstown Road, Port Melbourne, VIC 3207, Australia
Ruiz de Alarcón 13, 28014 Madrid, Spain
Dock House, The Waterfront, Cape Town 8001, South Africa

http://www.cambridge.org

First published 1996
First paperback edition 2002

A catalogue record for this book is available from the British Library

Library of Congress Cataloguing in Publication data
McRae, Andrew.
God speed the plough: the representation of agrarian England,
1500–1660 / Andrew McRae.
        p.   cm. (Past and Present Publications)
Includes bibliographical references (p.   )
ISBN 0 521 45379 8 (hc)
1. English literature – Early modern, 1500–1700 – History and
criticism.   2. Pastoral literature, English – History and criticism.
3. Agriculture – England – History – 16th century – Historiography.
4. Agriculture – England – History – 17th century – Historiography.
5. Literature and society – England – History – 16th century.
6. Literature and society – England – History – 17th century.
7. Rural conditions in literature.   8. Country life in literature.
9. Agriculture in literature.   10. Farm life in literature.
11. England – In literature.   I. Title.
PR428.P36M38   1995
820.9′321734–dc20   95–14940   CIP

ISBN 0 521 45379 8   hardback
ISBN 0 521 52466 0   paperback

Transferred to digital printing 2005

For my mother and in memory of my father

Contents

Illustrations

Acknowledgements

As this study has lurched its way from early postgraduate research into pastoral literature, through interdisciplinary enthusiasms, toward its final form, I have received invaluable support from a great many individuals and institutions. I could not have wished for two more tireless and acute critics than Marie Axton and Stephen Bending, each of whom has read more versions of more chapters than either would care to remember. As a doctoral student I also benefited from the supervision of John Rathmell, supplemented by valuable spells with Richard Axton, Patrick Collinson and Geoffrey Hiller. Joan Thirsk offered encouragement at a crucial time, and was instrumental in bringing the study to the Past and Present series. Among the many other scholars to have generously offered comments on drafts of the work are: Sarah Bendall, Brendan Bradshaw, Bradin Cormack, Elizabeth Freidberg, John Dixon Hunt, Philippa Kelly, Claire McEachern, Anthony Miller, Timothy Raylor, David Rollison, Helen Small, Michael Wilding, Janet Williams and Keith Wrightson. The careful reading of Kristin Hammett and my Cambridge University Press copy-editor, Karen Anderson Howes, prompted numerous late amendments.

Financing research into early modern culture from an Australian base is rarely easy, exacerbated as it is by the tyranny of distance and the realpolitik of funding applications. My own patchwork of assistance has come from: the Australian Academy of the Humanities; the Cambridge Commonwealth Trust; the Commonwealth Scholarship and Fellowship Plan; Dumbarton Oaks; the Huntington Library; the Barbara A. Macrae Trust; the Monash University English Department; Pembroke College, Cambridge; and the University of Sydney. The University of Cambridge, Dumbarton Oaks and the Huntington Library provided wonderful research resources and stimulating environments at various stages. The Sydney University English Department was consistently supportive toward a colleague in the early stages of a research and teaching career.

Acknowledgements   xiii

Earlier versions of chapters 5, 6 and 9, respectively, have been published in *Culture and Cultivation in Early Modern England: Writing and the Land*, ed. Michael Leslie and Timothy Raylor (Leicester, 1992); *Huntington Library Quarterly*, 56 (1993); and *Sydney Studies in English*, 20 (1994–5).

Conventions

This study is based on a reading of a broad range of material relating in various ways to contemporary agrarian conditions and practices. The analysis is often supported by bibliographical evidence regarding the distribution and contemporary popularity of a text: most notably, details of dates and numbers of editions are given where this information may have some bearing upon the analysis. These details are derived from *A Short Title Catalogue of Books Printed in England, Scotland, and Ireland . . . 1475–1640*, compiled by A. W. Pollard and G. R. Redgrave, 2nd edn (3 vols., London, 1976–91); and *Short-Title Catalogue of Books Printed in England, Scotland, Ireland, Wales, and British America and of English Books Printed in Other Countries 1641–1700*, compiled by Donald Wing (3 vols., New York, 1972–88). Where a text may be difficult to trace, I include reference numbers to 'STC' and/or 'Wing'. Unless otherwise stated, the place of publication of all primary texts is London and references are to the first edition.

In accordance with the aim for breadth of coverage, I have compiled a bibliography of primary sources, which it is hoped will provide a useful resource for further scholarship in the area. Since manuscript sources were only used selectively, the bibliography breaks with the convention for historical studies, by listing these where possible under author and title. This system is also intended to facilitate further research along thematic lines. Given the eclectic range of secondary material drawn upon, and the already lengthy list of primary sources, it was decided to restrict secondary references to footnotes.

Original spelling and punctuation in primary material is retained, except in cases where a reliable modern edition has been preferred to the original text. Contemporary uses of u/v and long 's', however, are standardized; and conventional verbal contractions are expanded.

Abbreviations

AHEW IV	*The Agrarian History of England and Wales, Volume IV 1500–1640*, ed. Joan Thirsk (Cambridge, 1967)
AHEW Vii	*The Agrarian History of England and Wales, Volume Vii 1640–1750: Agrarian Change*, ed. Joan Thirsk (Cambridge, 1985)
BL	British Library
CUL	Cambridge University Library
DNB	*The Dictionary of National Biography*, ed. Sir Leslie Stephen and Sir Sidney Lee (22 vols., London, 1917)
OED	*The Oxford English Dictionary*, 2nd edn, prepared by J. A. Simpson and E. S. C. Weiner (20 vols., Oxford, 1989)
PRO	Public Record Office, London
STC	*A Short Title Catalogue of Books Printed in England, Scotland, and Ireland . . . 1475–1640*, compiled by A. W. Pollard and G. R. Redgrave, 2nd edn (3 vols., London, 1976–91)
Wing	*Short-Title Catalogue of Books Printed in England, Scotland, Ireland, Wales, and British America and of English Books Printed in Other Countries 1641–1700*, compiled by Donald Wing (3 vols., New York, 1972–88)

Introduction

'I do not dwell in the Country, I am not acquainted with the Plough:
But I think that whosoever doth not maintain the Plough, destroys this
Kingdom.'

(Robert Cecil, House of Commons, 1601)

The plough was upheld, throughout the early modern period, as a central
symbol of agricultural activity and rural life. Its perceived value within
political debate at the turn of the seventeenth century highlights the
complex range of significance it could evoke, as contemporary writers
sought to represent the practices and values of agrarian England. The
ballad 'God spede the Plough', written around 1500, eulogizes the
struggles of a husbandman crippled by the demands of the clergy, tax-
collectors, purveyors and others.[1] Subsequently the plough was claimed
as an emblem of traditional structures of rural society, in a stream of
complaint decrying the effects of depopulating enclosure. Equally,
though, the plough could symbolize the expansive energies of a farmer
improving his land. John Fitzherbert's 1523? *Boke of Husbandrye*,
concerned to educate 'a yonge gentylman that entendeth to thryve',
begins with a series of chapters on ploughs.[2] In the words of one
landowner, 'The Plowghe is the Lords penne', with which he can
inscribe his ideals of labour and productivity onto the land.[3] Others
would extend this argument to fashion sweeping visions of national

[1] BL Lansdowne MS 762, fol. 5ᵃ; printed in *Pierce the Ploughmans Crede, to which is
appended God spede the Plough*, ed. Walter W. Skeat (London, 1867), pp. 69–72.
There was also a play of this name, of which no text survives, performed in London in
1593 (*Henslowe's Diary*, ed. R. A. Foakes and R. T. Ricket (Cambridge, 1961), p. 20),
while an anonymous writer used the phrase as the title for a pamphlet of 1601 which
defended traditional systems of ploughing and sowing against the recent innovation of
corn setting.
[2] *Boke of Husbandrye*, chs. 2–6; the quotation is from fol. 47ᵃ (1530 edn).
[3] John Kay of Woodsome, 'the Plowghe'; Folger Shakespeare Library MS W.b.483,
p. 1.

1

profits and pleasures generated out of the countryside. 'The Kingdoms portion', declared the poet Robert Herrick, '*is the Plow.*'[4] The figure of the labourer at his plough attained a similar resonance; yet here too disparate texts reveal an ongoing struggle over the identity of a cultural icon. For conservative critics of rural change, the ploughman typified the stable community of the manorial estate. In a wave of mid-Tudor publications that combined traditional social morality with Protestant agitation, the honest labourer emerged as a powerful spokesman for complaint. *The Praier and Complaynte of the Ploweman unto Christ* (1531?) and *Pyers plowmans exhortation unto the lordes knightes and burgoysses of the Parlyamenthouse* (1550?) are but two examples of this tradition. Following generations, however, were more sceptical. In the eyes of the Elizabethan satirist, not even the ploughman was immune to the pernicious lure of 'Lady Pecunia',[5] while for those seeking to improve agricultural yields, the customary practices of ploughmen were clogs to progress, 'poor silly shifts . . . to preserve themselves ignorant and unserviceable'.[6] The movement toward aesthetic celebrations of the English landscape in the seventeenth century effected a further metamorphosis of the figure. In John Milton's 'L'Allegro', which participates in an influential poetic project to merge naturalistic detail with the values of a classical pastoral tradition, the native ploughman 'Whistles o'er the furrowed land' at the break of day.[7]

The apparent contention over the significance of both plough and ploughman draws attention to crucial questions concerning the representation of the land. Was the plough a symbol of manorial community and self-sufficiency, or an instrument of national expansion through a competitive market economy? Was the ploughman a roughly eloquent spokesman for the downtrodden, or a decorative figure in a pastoralized landscape of enamelled fields? At stake was the very meaning of rural England, and the attendant contests over meaning are documented in the pages of ballads, sermons, pamphlets, satiric verse and drama, husbandry and surveying manuals, chorographies and rural poetry. As these various texts shape images of rural life, broader questions crystallize. Was the English countryside to be envisaged as a patchwork of stable and self-contained estates, a site of agricultural innovation and economic

4 'The Country life' (1648); *Poetical Works*, ed. L. C. Martin (Oxford, 1956), p. 230.
5 Richard Barnfield, *The encomion of lady Pecunia* (1598); *The Complete Poems*, ed. George Klawitter (Selinsgrove, 1990), p. 155.
6 Walter Blith, *The English Improver Improved* (1652), p. 196.
7 Published 1645; *Complete Shorter Poems*, ed. John Carey (Harlow, 1968), p. 135.

competition, or a scene of natural beauty and bounty? Were the interests of the country best served by the humble ploughman, the thrifty yeoman, the entrepreneurial innovator or the retired lord? The representation of the land in the early modern period requires interpretation. Confronted by the rich plurality of images and arguments, one must attend to 'the processes by which meaning is constructed' in earlier periods.[8] This book will thus be concerned with the various and changing ways in which English men and women of the early modern period sought to ascribe meaning and order to the economy and society of their native countryside. At a time of considerable uncertainty and upheaval in rural England, the impetus to fashion authoritative representations of agrarian practice and change assumed a heightened significance. The Tudor moralists' cries of complaint in the face of change and the agrarian improvers' calls for progressive reform are equally urgent, yet utterly opposed in their definitions of social and economic values. In order to appreciate such confrontations, this study will focus on the discourses of agrarian England. For the representation of the land should be seen less as an unproblematic reflection of material conditions than as the site of a struggle over signs and discursive knowledge. Discourse constructs meaning by working upon the infinitely diverse and mutable circumstances of economic practice, social relations and topographic situation. The process of representation is aptly exemplified by the plough, at once a pivotal signifier in rival discourses of agrarian order and an essential instrument in the labours of rural survival, the currency of political rhetoric and the primary lesson of a husbandman's education.

Whereas an interest in the textual construction of meaning is shared by both historians and literary critics, my central concern to survey signifying practices throughout a wide range of texts departs from the strategies most frequently employed by the latter. The characteristic methods of analysis associated with the literary movements of the new historicism and cultural materialism aim to situate a particular literary work within its contemporary milieu.[9] By comparison, while I will

8 Roger Chartier, *Cultural History: Between Practices and Representations*, translated from the French by Lydia G. Cochrane (Cambridge, 1988), p. 14. See also, in relation to changing approaches to 'cultural history', *The New Cultural History*, ed. Lynn Hunt (Berkeley, 1989); and Catherine Belsey, 'Towards Cultural History – In Theory and Practice', *Textual Practice*, 3 (1989), pp. 159–72.
9 The best introduction to the earlier phases of these movements is Jean E. Howard, 'The New Historicism in Renaissance Studies', *English Literary Renaissance*, 16 (1986), pp. 13–43. See also *The New Historicism*, ed. H. Aram Veeser (New York, 1989).

occasionally focus on particular texts, the governing aim of such analysis will be to illuminate the representational fields within which those texts operate. If a poet such as Herrick demands attention for his rural poetry, the attention accorded will not privilege his works over those of contemporary pamphleteers or politicians. More consistently, however, I will argue that the role of literature as an 'agent in constructing a culture's sense of reality' may valuably be explored through attention to literary modes.[10] Hence the unashamedly earthbound tracts of improvement to be considered in chapter 5 might usefully be set alongside the contemporaneous poetic initiative toward georgic celebrations of labour and productivity. Similarly, the changing structures of agrarian complaint may be explored through a study of the textual strategies adopted by Renaissance satirists. In each case the development of a literary tradition is embedded in broader social, economic and ideological movements, yet at the same time literature itself asserts a significant cultural force as it performs its distinctive labours of representation.

The broad parameters of investigation are nonetheless qualified by a decision to pursue printed texts in preference to the vast range of manuscript material that might well command attention. Court records of enclosure disputes, manorial documents outlining tenurial practices and state papers concerning agrarian reform all offer to further our appreciation of rural discourse. But such sources will be employed only selectively, whereas my consideration of printed works aims for a comprehensive coverage of publications concerned with the land. Indeed, *God Speed the Plough*'s concerns with structures of discourse and processes of cultural change across a period of 160 years are perhaps best accommodated by a concentration on the printed word. It is reasonable to expect, from works prepared for the press, attention to the construction of authoritative discourses of rural order. Print facilitates the formation of textual conventions, and prompts writers to pursue nascent conceptions of national identity. These imperatives become immediately apparent in chapter 1, which will be drawn, by the sheer outpouring of printed matter, to the mid-Tudor reign of Edward VI, when preachers, poets and pamphleteers realized the potential of the press for the promotion of religious and social reform. Throughout the following hundred years print was established as the principal medium for cultural exchange, and the steady stream of works concerned with rural issues

---

10 Howard, 'New Historicism', p. 25.

demonstrates at once the breadth and vitality of the gathering dialogue. Moreover, the relatively low cost of books and changing patterns in literacy ensured that the emergent print culture touched all socio-economic groups.[11] Even among agricultural labourers there was a small proportion who could read; 'everywhere', Margaret Spufford observes, 'illiteracy was . . . face to face with literacy, and the oral with the printed word'.[12]

In fact, the possibilities afforded by the medium of print had a significant impact upon several of the textual traditions to be considered, and consequently the analysis will frequently be extended by a consideration of bibliographical issues.[13] Details of the number of editions printed offer valuable evidence of the currency of texts and discourses. In an extreme case, such as Thomas Tusser's phenomenally successful *Five Hundred Points of Good Husbandry*, such information literally thrusts a work to the forefront of the study.[14] Further, attention to the physical form of a text promises insight into the 'assumed public', or cultural status the author or printer desired for a work.[15] The mid-Tudor complaint tracts reinforce their claims to be speaking in the voice of the people by conforming to cheap pamphlet formats and a stark black-letter page embellished only by marginal references to biblical texts. Reynolde

[11] Tessa Watt argues persuasively for the spread of print culture, especially through ephemeral textual forms, throughout the social order. The movement was facilitated in part by the low cost of the printed page; from 1560 to 1635 'book prices remained steady . . . when other commodities more than doubled in price and wages rose by half to two-thirds' (*Cheap Print and Popular Piety 1550–1640* (Cambridge, 1991), p. 261).
[12] *Small Books and Pleasant Histories: Popular Fiction and Its Readership in Seventeenth-Century England* (London, 1981), p. 32. Spufford here interprets the available evidence about literacy rates among labourers between 1580 and 1700 in a manner which contrasts with the view of David Cressy, whose research produced the figures. See Cressy's *Literacy and the Social Order: Reading and Writing in Tudor and Stuart England* (Cambridge, 1980).
[13] See D. F. McKenzie's programme for a study of 'texts as social products', in *Bibliography and the Sociology of Texts* (London, 1986), p. 52. Roger Chartier's studies in cultural history adopt similar strategies: see especially *The Cultural Uses of Print in Early Modern France*, trans. Lydia G. Cochrane (Princeton, 1987); and *The Culture of Print: Power and the Uses of Print in Early Modern Europe*, ed. Chartier, trans. Cochrane (Cambridge, 1989). Jerome McGann develops similar arguments, from the perspective of a literary scholar, in *The Textual Condition* (Princeton, 1991).
[14] Tusser's husbandry manual went through twenty-three editions in eighty-one years, after its first publication in 1557 as *A hundreth good pointes of husbandrie*.
[15] See Elizabeth L. Eisenstein, who distinguishes between 'audiences', as 'actual readership as determined by library catalogues, subscription lists and other objective data', and 'publics', 'the more hypothetical targets envisaged by authors and publishers, to whom they address their works' (*The Printing Press as an Agent of Change* (Cambridge, 1979), p. 64).

Scot makes a similar claim to a broad appeal by including in his husbandry manual detailed woodcut illustrations, for the education of 'him that cannot reade at all'.[16] By contrast, the tradition of chorography adheres to weighty and decorative forms of presentation, signalling its intent to appeal solely to the landowning elite.

The national structure of the publishing trade in England further influenced the dissemination of broad and coherent structures of discourse throughout the country. As the tentacles of a print culture spread outward from London, published representations of the land regularly formulated generalized images of rural order. The complaint tradition consistently insists upon a socio-economic model relevant across the country; specific details, if considered at all, are claimed as typical of nationwide problems. Similarly the Digger Gerrard Winstanley, who was driven more by a revolutionary vision than by any notable knowledge of agricultural and tenurial practice, saw no reason why the communist experiment at St George's Hill should not be multiplied across the country. The attention here to practices of representation which aspired to a national perspective should thus be distanced from the recent emphasis in social history on the local study. Although early modern England was unquestionably fractured by regional interests and identities, generations of writers fashioned vital new forms of nationhood.[17] While discourse has important local dimensions, attention here will consistently be drawn to the universalizing, naturalizing imperative so characteristic of the ideologically motivated statement.[18]

The wealth of texts that fall within the parameters of the study demonstrates the vigorous range of attention directed toward the land between 1500 and 1660. The representations of agrarian conditions and practices evidence at once cultural diversity and underlying ideological conflict. Discourses take form as mutable and plural, rather than oppressively monolithic. Nonetheless, important developments throughout the period challenge and remould predominant assumptions about

---

[16] *Perfite platforme of a Hoppe Garden* (1574), sig. B3b.

[17] The applicability of the concept of nationhood to early modern England remains contentious. Richard Helgerson, however, has ably explored a range of movements toward the fashioning of national identity, in *Forms of Nationhood: The Elizabethan Writing of England* (Chicago and London, 1992).

[18] For a stimulating analysis of local structures of discourse, see David Rollison's study of 'proverbial culture' in the Vale of Berkeley, Gloucestershire (*The Local Origins of Modern Society: Gloucestershire 1500–1800* (London and New York, 1992), ch. 3).

rural England, and the scrutiny of these movements is my central purpose. I will argue that discursive change progressed through constant interaction with processes of social and economic upheaval. Over the past century historians have maintained fierce debate over the nature and pace of these developments; the transition from feudalism to capitalism in the countryside, the pace and character of the enclosure movement, and the 'revolution' in agricultural practices all remain points of contention.[19] Although I do not intend to engage directly with such debates, my analysis is grounded in a belief that practices of representation are enmeshed with processes of material change. Discourse at once responds to and enables shifts in social and economic practice. Consequently, while the origins of English individualism might well be traced back to the Middle Ages,[20] the effects of a discourse which offered to legitimate and promote such practices and attitudes could be profound. As the individualist farmer was metamorphosed from a covetous canker on the body politic into a godly man of thrift and industry, the meaning of agrarian England shifted accordingly from a site of manorial community and moral economy toward a modern landscape of capitalist enterprise.[21]

The central contests over the representation of the land may be illustrated through a brief analysis of debates in the House of Commons in 1597

[19] Arguments over a shift from feudalism to capitalism date back to Karl Marx's précis of English agrarian development in *Das Kapital*, vol. 1, chs. 27–8. R. H. Tawney developed a more expansive analysis of structural change, in *The Agrarian Problem in the Sixteenth Century*, first published in 1912, while Eric Kerridge constructed his *Agrarian Problems in the Sixteenth Century and After* (London, 1969) as a direct response to Tawney. More recently, see *The Brenner Debate: Agrarian Class Structure and Economic Development in Pre-Industrial Europe*, ed. T. H. Aston and C. H. E. Philpin (Cambridge, 1985); and John E. Martin, *Feudalism to Capitalism: Peasant and Landlord in English Agrarian Development* (London, 1983). On the changes in agricultural practice, see Kerridge, *The Agricultural Revolution* (London, 1967); and Mark Overton's historiographical review of arguments in this field, 'Agricultural Revolution? Development of the Agrarian Economy in Early Modern England', in *Explorations in Historical Geography: Interpretative Essays*, ed. Alan R. H. Baker and Derek Gregory (Cambridge, 1984), pp. 118–39. I will outline below some of the principal factors influencing rural change in the period.
[20] See Alan Macfarlane, *The Origins of English Individualism* (Oxford, 1978).
[21] It must be acknowledged that the vast majority of texts represent agrarian England as a field of predominantly masculine labour and responsibility. Although *God Speed the Plough* is necessarily directed by the gendered perspectives of early modern writers, I begin with a belief that such an approach need not perpetuate their apparent gender biases. I aim instead to work within a context of scholarship which is continuing to broaden our appreciation of the status and activities of contemporary English women.

and 1601, over two bills intended to prevent depopulating enclosure and maintain existing rates of tillage.[22] These debates responded to one of the most intense rural crises of the early modern era. The years of dearth and famine around 1596–8 had markedly different effects in different regions; however, many communities, such as the parish of Whickham, four miles from Newcastle, suffered devastating increases in mortality rates in the wake of harvest failures.[23] As the legislators sought to comprehend and respond to the situation, they fashioned divergent representations of agrarian order, which at once highlight central ideals in agrarian discourse, and suggest the influence of certain rhetorical and representational conventions within contemporary society.[24]

Robert Cecil's Commons speech of 1601 appealed to a fundamentally agrarian sense of national identity. The secretary of state proclaimed to the House: 'I do not dwell in the Country, I am not acquainted with the Plough: But I think that whosoever doth not maintain the Plough, destroys this Kingdom.'[25] The basic logic of the argument should not be discounted, especially in the light of historical evidence documenting the dangers for rural communities of specialization in pastoral farming.[26] But Cecil's statement should also be considered within a wider cultural context. Speaking without 'acquaintance' with the countryside, Cecil

[22] The 1597 debates resulted in the enactment of two statutes: 'An Act against the decaying of towns and houses of husbandry' (39 Eliz. c. 1), and 'An Acte for the maintenance of Husbandrie & Tillage', or 'The Tillage Act' (39 Eliz. c. 2). Fragments of the debates may be pieced together from journals and manuscript sources.

[23] Recent studies have demonstrated the significant influence that local factors – including farming conditions and practices, integration within regional marketing networks and levels of communal and interpersonal support – could have upon the impact of dearth in early modern England (see especially Andrew B. Appleby, *Famine in Tudor and Stuart England* (Liverpool, 1978); John Walter and Roger Schofield, 'Famine, Disease and Crisis Mortality in Early Modern Society', in *Famine, Disease and the Social Order in Early Modern Society*, ed. Walter and Schofield (Cambridge, 1989), pp. 1–73; and Walter, 'The Social Economy of Dearth in Early Modern England', in *Famine, Disease and the Social Order*, pp. 75–128). On Whickham, see Keith Wrightson and David Levine, 'Death in Whickham', in *Famine, Disease and the Social Order*, pp. 143–5; and more generally on the crisis in these years, Appleby, *Famine*, pp. 109–21.

[24] The value of the language of parliamentary debates has been recognized, similarly, by Joyce Oldham Appleby, who comments that 'Traditional rhetorical themes mixed with pungent descriptions of commercial realities' in the parliaments of James I (*Economic Thought and Ideology in Seventeenth-Century England* (Princeton, 1978), p. 34).

[25] Sir Simonds D'Ewes, ed., *The Journals of All the Parliaments during the Reign of Queen Elizabeth* (London, 1682), p. 674.

[26] See Walter and Schofield on Appleby's '"thesis of the two Englands", the one vulnerable to famine, the other resistant to it' ('Famine, Disease and Crisis', pp. 21–5); and their assessment of sixteenth-century mortality crises in the north-west (p. 32).

relies upon – and expects his audience to accept – a particular representation of agrarian conditions. In this respect, his symbolic use of the plough draws upon its conventional association not only with grain production, but also with an entire socio-economic model based around the national primacy of arable farming and the ideal of a stable manorial structure.

In the parliament of 1597, Francis Bacon introduced the bills with the claim that they are 'not drawne with a pollished pene, but with a polished harte free from affeccion'. He argues that although

it maie be thought ill and verie predudiciall to Lordes, that have inclosed great groundes and pulled downe even whole Townes, and Converted them to Sheepe pastures, yett Considering the increase of people and the benefitt of the Common wealth – I doubt not but everie Man will deeme the Rivall [i.e. revival] of former Motheetten lawes in this poynt a prayse-worthy thing . . . for inclosures of groundes bringes Depopulacion, which bringes .1. Idlenes. 2 decay of Tillage, 3. Subversion of howses and decrease of Charitie, and charges to the poores mayntenance. 4. the Impoverishing of the State of the Realme . . . And I would be sorrie to see within this kingdome the peece of *Ovids* verse prove true. *Iam seges est ubi Troia fuit,* soe in England instead of a whole Towne full of people, nought but Greenefeildes a Shepheard and his Dogg.[27]

Bacon develops a conventional attack on covetousness into an extended criticism of the processes of agrarian change. His construction of a strict logical progression charts an inexorable development from enclosure to depopulation, which undermines at once the moral basis of society (causing idleness and a decrease in charity) and the economic success of the commonwealth. His final complaint of towns being replaced by 'nought but Greenefeildes a Shepheard and his Dogg', assumes an essential morality inherent in arable farming within a common-field system, which can only be undermined by the conversion of land into the barren fields of sheep-farming.

Bacon propels his argument with a distinctive tone of complaint, directed against those who are perceived to be subverting the traditional order. A later, anonymous speaker underlines the significance of this rhetorical approach when he reflects upon Bacon's 'first motion that sounded in this place in a kinde of lamentacion', before exploiting this rhetorical potential himself:

[27] Hayward Townshend, 'Hayward Townshend's Journals', ed. A. F. Pollard and Marjorie Blatcher, *Bulletin of the Institute of Historical Research*, 12 (1934–5), p. 10.

it is strange that men can be so unnaturall as to shake off the poore as if they were not parte of the bodye, and because we live not in a savage land, where wolfes can devoure sheepe, therefore we shalbe knowne to live in a more brutishe land, where shepe shall devoure men.[28]

His representation of an 'unnaturall' threat to the traditional order is based on the image of the body politic. Within this model of organic unity, the aspirations of enclosers are inevitably dangerous, analogous to a callous amputation of a 'parte of the bodye'. The image of sheep devouring men reinforces the vision of an agrarian world turned upside down, with a commonplace of agrarian complaint which dates back at least as far as Sir Thomas More's *Utopia*.[29] Later in the speech the speaker offers contrasting images of 'The eares of the greate sheepmasters' which 'hang at the doores of this House', hoping to exploit any leniency in the law, and the 'eyes of the poore' which 'are upon this Parliament . . . and sad for the want they yet suffer'. Parliament, therefore, must protect the passive 'poor' from the devious aggression of the enclosing 'sheepmasters'. He concludes with the declaration: 'We sit now in judgement over ourselves . . . therefore, as this bill entered at first with a short prayer God speed the plough: so I wish it may end with such success as the plough may speed the poore.' Within the order established by God, the land will always have the capacity to sustain the poor; the bills are nothing more nor less than an opportunity to place the force of national law behind that order.

In the same speech, the anonymous supporter of the bills draws attention to an oppositional discourse, focused around 'the Law of propertie, whereby men could say, (This is mine)'. This statement epitomizes the ideological conflict at the heart of the Commons debates. His identification of a 'Law of propertie' highlights the threat posed to moral economics by a discourse that embraces individual economic aspirations. The imperative that every person should 'know one's own', as chapter 6 will demonstrate, promotes radically new representations of the agrarian economy and social order. As many a moralist commented in the course of the period, the legal logic of 'meum and tuum' effectively shatters corporate notions of rural order. The 'law of property' champions the rights of individuals to develop and expand

---

[28] Hatfield MSS, vol. 176 (11); BL microfilm M485 (47). See also J. E. Neale, *Elizabeth I and Her Parliaments 1584–1601* (London, 1957), p. 340.

[29] *Utopia: The Complete Works of St Thomas More, Volume Four*, ed. Edward Surtz and J. H. Hexter (New Haven and London, 1965), pp. 65–7.

their own resources, free of the social duties and restraints that dominate the traditional order.

Henry Jackman, who opposed the bills in 1597, was at once a likely advocate of the 'law of property', and a particularly vulnerable target for the proponents of the legislation. J. E. Neale describes him as 'an independent type of man, resistant to mass emotion'; yet through his occupation as a London cloth-merchant and his representation of Wiltshire boroughs, he was also directly linked to the interests of the 'great sheepmasters'.[30] Indeed, it is perhaps partly a self-consciousness about these vested interests, coupled with an awareness of the cultural orthodoxy of his opponents' arguments, that causes Jackman to adopt a stiflingly defensive tone in his speech. He protests that, 'this Bill cannot without suspicion of impietye, cruelty and partialitye be impugned as thoughe the contradicts therof went about to take the use of the ploughe from the bowells of the earth, or the nourishment of bred from the bellyes of the poore'.[31] Despite his readiness to be counted among the reviled 'contradicts' of the bills, however, Jackman appears almost unable to enunciate his argument for want of an accepted oppositional language. His most clearly polemical statement exists only in the bold simplicity of his notes, where he writes, 'Men are not to be compelled by penalties but allured by profite to any good exercise.'[32] Here his belief in self-interest as a positive force signals an allegiance to an individualist ethic. Further, his use of the phrase 'good exercise' carries a crucial ambiguity, as it echoes language traditionally used to argue the moral value of labour within a subsistence economy, yet also prepares the way for a new ideology, within which 'good exercise' would suggest a more flexible concept of agrarian practice – for the 'good' of both individual and nation.

The contributions of Sir Walter Raleigh in 1601 present the most coherent and strident opposition to the bills. In fact Raleigh was particularly active on agrarian issues in 1601, as he took up the theme of regional specialization in another debate, declaring, 'I do not like the Constraining of Men to Manure, or use their Grounds at our Wills; but rather, let every Man use his Ground to that which it is most fit for, and therein use his own Discretion.'[33] In relation to the Tillage Act he focuses

---

[30] Neale, *Elizabeth I and Her Parliaments*, p. 341.
[31] BL Lansdowne MS 105, fol. 202ª.   [32] BL Lansdowne MS 83, fol. 198ᵇ.
[33] The debate is over 'an act touching the Sowing of Hemp' (Hayward Townshend, *Historical Collections: or, An exact Account of the Proceedings of the Four last Parliaments of Q. Elizabeth* (London, 1680), p. 188).

more particularly on the individual farmer:

> I think this Law fit to be repealed; for many poor men are not able to find seed to sow so much as they are bound to plough, which they must do, or incur the Penalty of the Law. Besides, all Nations abound with Corn. *France* offered the Queen to serve *Ireland* with Corn for sixteen shillings a quarter, which is but two shillings the bushel; if we should sell it so here, the Ploughman would be beggered. The *Low-Country* man and the *Hollander,* which never soweth Corn, hath by his industry such plenty that they will serve other Nations. The *Spaniard* who often wanteth Corn, had we never so much plenty, will not be beholding to the *English* man for it, neither to the *Low-Country* men, nor to *France,* but will fetch it even of the very Barbarian. And therefore I think the best course is to set it at liberty, and leave every man free, which is the desire of a true *English* man.[34]

Raleigh begins with the tropes of the poor farmer and the plough, but overturns their traditional associations as he represents the legislation as a clumsy imposition on independent producers. Consequently the plough becomes symbolic of poverty rather than sustenance, and the ploughman an economic agent requiring only a free market in which to prosper. His concern with an international economy extends this process, placing English agrarian production in a broader context in an attempt to undermine his opponents' insistence on the nation as an insular, self-sufficient unit. His final, climactic sentence proffers a construction of national identity radically different from that of Cecil. Raleigh has struck the keynote of English capitalism, which would reverberate through the centuries to come.

The parliamentary debates aptly demonstrate the anxiety aroused throughout English society by the pressing realities of rural change. Given the importance of these processes for this study, it will be useful to review here the principal features which produced a period of sustained and often disturbing upheaval.[35] Arguably the single most important social development of the period was an explosion in the English population, which grew from a little over two million in 1500 to around five million in 1660.[36] Regional variations and the influence of

---

[34] D'Ewes, *Journals*, p. 674.

[35] The following outline of social and economic change is intended merely to introduce the field to non-specialists. It is principally indebted to C. G. A. Clay's *Economic Expansion and Social Change: England 1500–1700* (2 vols., Cambridge, 1984).

[36] Clay, *Economic Expansion*, vol. 1, p. 1; E. A. Wrigley and R. S. Schofield, *The Population History of England 1541–1871: A Reconstruction* (London, 1981), pp. 208–9.

internal migration meant that some areas experienced a rise considerably greater than the national average; the population of Leicestershire, for example, increased by 31 per cent between 1524 and 1563, and a further 58 per cent between 1563 and 1603.[37] Largely as a result of the greater pressure on existing resources, prices of basic commodities soared. Again, significant local differentiations and marked short-term fluctuations distort any attempt to generalize; however, the sheer magnitude of average price rises is impossible to ignore. C. G. A. Clay estimates that by the middle of the seventeenth century, agricultural products had risen approximately 600 per cent on the rates of 1500. The average wages for an agricultural labourer throughout the same period rose only by around 300 per cent.[38] These trends created a pressing need for increased agricultural productivity. Across the countryside, farmers moved to bring into cultivation unused or lightly used land; 'in the sixteenth and early seventeenth centuries', Joan Thirsk writes, 'men made war upon the forests, moors, and fens with a zeal which they had not felt for some three hundred years'.[39] Further improvements in productivity, on both arable and pastoral land, were brought about by the introduction of new crops, stock, fertilizers and equipment, and by the spread of innovations such as up-and-down husbandry and the floating of watermeadows.[40] The financial incentives provided by an expanding market economy stimulated a concurrent trend toward increased regional specialization. Differences in soil and climate had long divided England into pastoral regions in the north and west, and mixed farming regions in the south and east. This broad distinction was reinforced by the economic developments of the sixteenth century, while certain regions also developed more particular local specialities, such as pig-keeping, horse-breeding or fruit cultivation.[41] A claim in the 1597 Commons debates that Shropshire might serve as 'the Dayrie howse to the whole Realme' remains firmly in the realm of rhetorical exaggeration; however, commercial farming, especially in areas with access to London, inevitably encouraged farmers to concentrate their efforts on produce best suited to their regions.[42]

[37] Clay, *Economic Expansion*, vol. 1, p. 26.
[38] Clay, *Economic Expansion*, vol. 1, pp. 43–5, 50.
[39] Thirsk, 'The Farming Regions of England', in *AHEW IV*, p. 2.
[40] See Kerridge, *Agricultural Revolution*.
[41] Thirsk, 'Farming Regions', pp. 2–5.
[42] 'Hayward Townshend's Journals', p. 16; Clay, *Economic Expansion*, vol. 1, pp. 116–25; Thirsk, 'Farming Regions'.

Associated developments in property holdings and tenurial relations affected the very foundations of agrarian life. Whether or not one might interpret these trends as evidence of a movement from feudalism to capitalism, this study must recognize from the outset their undeniable impact on contemporary observers. The rate of land transfers was a particularly noticeable phenomenon; John Norden remarked in the early seventeenth century that lands are being 'posted from one to another, more in these latter daies then ever before'.[43] The market in rural property had indeed assumed a recognizably modern shape over the preceding century, a development fuelled by massive sales of Church and Crown land from the middle of the sixteenth century.[44] As some families lost their lands under the weight of financial pressures, others were accumulating the necessary capital to purchase for themselves a place in the country.[45] Especially during the early seventeenth century, an increasing number of landed fortunes were built at least partly on the profits of office, profession or trade,[46] while productive and innovative yeomen were often able to exploit a time lag between rising prices and rents in order to secure a place within the ranks of the landed.[47] Women too, despite the patriarchal assumptions of the vast majority of contemporary commentators, were engaged in the transfer and management of property, and might equally perceive the importance of knowing one's own.[48] Moreover, the increased activity and competition in the property market caused both ownership and occupancy of land to be concentrated in fewer hands.[49] It has been estimated that between the middle of the fifteenth century and the late seventeenth century the percentage of cultivated land in England owned by the 'middling and lesser gentry' increased from 25 per cent to 45–50 per cent; and the share of 'yeomen, family farmers and other small owners' lifted from 20 to 25–33 per cent.[50]

---

[43] *The Surveiors Dialogue* (1610 edn), p. 216.

[44] Joyce Youings, *Sixteenth-Century England* (London, 1984), ch. 7.

[45] Clay, *Economic Expansion*, vol. 1, p. 146.

[46] Gordon Batho, 'Landlords in England', in *AHEW IV*, p. 285.

[47] Batho, 'Landlords', p. 305.

[48] See Amy Louise Erickson, *Women and Property in Early Modern England* (London, 1993).

[49] Clay, *Economic Expansion*, vol. 1, p. 97. R. B. Outhwaite has argued, however, that as cultivation was extended into forests and other 'marginal lands' – especially in the north and west – 'there was a veritable explosion of small holdings' ('Progress and Backwardness in English Agriculture, 1500–1650', *Economic History Review*, 2nd series, 39 (1986), p. 9).

[50] Clay, *Economic Expansion*, vol. 1, p. 143.

Prospects for tenant farmers were less promising. Generalizations
about conditions for tenants are inevitably problematic, due to regional
differences, the unpredictable nature of any landlord's attitudes toward
estate management and the wide variety of tenurial systems employed
throughout the country. However, a broad survey of the main types of
tenure might encompass four categories: freehold, which was clearly the
most advantageous for the tenant; copyhold, which generally involved
the payment of a substantial 'fine' on admittance to the land and a lower
annual rent; leasehold, for terms up to twenty-one years; and tenancy at
will, based on an annual lease.[51] Although some forms of tenure were
resistant to change, the majority of tenant farmers were exposed to
significant increases in financial exactions during the period covered
here. In particular, copyhold tenants – who made up an estimated
two-thirds of the landholding population – were generally liable to
'arbitrary' increases of their entry fine on the succession of an heir.[52]
'Taking the country as a whole', Clay estimates, 'increases of four or five
fold between the middle of the sixteenth and middle of the seventeenth
centuries were commonplace.'[53] Another strategy available to the
ambitious landlord in many areas was the substitution of the more
remunerative form of leasehold tenure for copyhold. In fact, Raleigh,
around the time of his contribution to the agrarian debates of 1601, was
actively pursuing this policy on his estates in Dorset, in a process that
forced several tenants from the land.[54]

Tenurial structures could also be affected by contemporary movements

[51] Peter Bowden, 'Agricultural Prices, Farm Profits, and Rents', in *AHEW IV*, pp. 684–7;
David Grigg, *Population Growth and Agrarian Change: An Historical Perspective*
(Cambridge, 1990), pp. 86–7. See also Kerridge's discussion of tenures and estates, in
Agrarian Problems, pp. 32–64.

[52] The estimate of the proportion of copyholders is made by Clay, *Economic Expansion*,
vol. 1, p. 87. An important distinction in this respect, however, must be made between
copyholders of inheritance, whose fines were fixed, and copyholders for one or more
lives, or generations. The economic status and security of the latter – who, Bowden
estimates, outnumbered copyholders of inheritance by about two to one in Tudor times
– has been a cause of fierce debate among historians, and remains one of the prime
testing grounds for any argument over the Marxist interpretation of agrarian change in
England. Bowden follows Tawney's argument in *The Agrarian Problem* by stressing
the arbitrary nature of fines ('Agricultural Prices', p. 685); however, Kerridge has
argued that the changes were 'arbitrary *but reasonable*', and that the Court of Chancery
regularly enforced restrictions on excessive demands by landlords (*Agrarian Problems*,
pp. 54–64; my italic).

[53] Clay, *Economic Expansion*, vol. 1, p. 89.

[54] J. H. Bettey, 'Agriculture and Rural Society in Dorset 1570–1670' (unpublished Ph.D
dissertation, University of Bristol, 1976), p. 209.

toward enclosure and engrossing. Enclosure, which involved the abolition of common rights over land, occurred on wastes and commons or in the village fields, where arable strips could be exchanged and consolidated in the hands of individual landholders.[55] Engrossing, which was not necessarily carried out in association with enclosure, 'signified the amalgamation of two or more farms into one'.[56] Each process extended the rights of individuals over those of a community; and in many instances, each could lead to depopulation and an abandonment of traditional methods of husbandry. The actual pace of these movements remains a point of conjecture among historians.[57] Perceptions that enclosure necessarily caused social upheaval must also be tempered by our knowledge that many instances were carried out by 'agreement' amongst the inhabitants of a manor, in an attempt by landlord and tenants alike to increase their productivity.[58] Nevertheless enclosure and engrossing remained, without doubt, the most prominent and potentially disturbing manifestations of agrarian change. In consequence both practices were consistently drawn to the centre of agrarian debate, and the conflicting attitudes of contemporary commentators serve to highlight ideological differences about rural order.

Much of that debate also focused attention on the plight of those at the lowest end of the socio-economic scale, who were especially vulnerable to the fluctuating forces of change. It has been estimated that landless labourers and servants in husbandry constituted about a quarter to a third of the rural population in the Tudor and early Stuart periods, and their number was increasing.[59] The rising costs of living, which left the labourer of 1660 with roughly half the purchasing power of his ancestor

[55] Joan Thirsk, 'Enclosing and Engrossing', in *AHEW IV*, p. 200.
[56] Thirsk, 'Enclosing and Engrossing', p. 201.
[57] Among the more important recent contributions to this debate are: Thirsk, 'Enclosing and Engrossing'; J. A. Yelling, *Common Field and Enclosure in England 1450–1850* (London, 1977); J. R. Wordie, 'The Chronology of English Enclosure, 1500–1914', *Economic History Review*, 2nd series, 36 (1983), pp. 483–505; and Robert C. Allen, *Enclosure and the Yeoman* (Oxford, 1992).
[58] Maurice Beresford, 'Habitation Versus Improvement: The Debate on Enclosure by Agreement', in *Essays in the Economic and Social History of Tudor and Stuart England, in Honour of R. H. Tawney*, ed. F. J. Fisher (Cambridge, 1961), pp. 40–69. Roger B. Manning, however, argues that Beresford exaggerates the extent of true agreement, and overlooks much coercion by landlords (*Village Revolts: Social Protest and Popular Disturbances in England, 1509–1640* (Oxford, 1988), ch. 5).
[59] Alan Everitt, 'Farm Labourers', in *AHEW IV*, p. 398; Clay, *Economic Expansion*, vol. 1, p. 17. On servants in husbandry, see Ann Kussmaul, *Servants in Husbandry in Early Modern England* (Cambridge, 1981).

of 1500, have already been noted, while a family's livelihood could be further eroded by the loss of rights of common attendant upon enclosure. General patterns suggest that many adapted to the changing conditions. As the structures of commercial farming spread, labourers increasingly tended to specialize in certain tasks; the Kentish farms of Nicholas Toke, for example, employed carters, shepherds, haywards, ploughmen, gardeners, thatchers, carpenters, hopmen and overseers of the orchards.[60] By-employments also became increasingly important, especially in pastoral and forest regions, where the cloth industry and woodland crafts flourished from a base in labourers' cottages.[61] Despite these general trends, however, the concurrent rises in population and inflation led inexorably to problems of unemployment, poverty and vagrancy. As is evident in the parliamentary debates, the plight of the poor rural labourer is regularly drawn to the centre of arguments over – and representations of – agrarian England.

Of course the path of rural change was not an even process. Underlying movements could be exacerbated or distorted by periods of crisis, as may be seen in the years surrounding the Commons session of 1597. The argument of *God Speed the Plough*, however, is grounded upon the supposition that significant long-term processes of change in the representation of the land might be distinguished between 1500 and 1660. The three parts of the book are intended to encompass the predominant discursive developments. The first part examines the codes of moral economics, which maintained a status of cultural orthodoxy in the sixteenth century, and continued to exert a significant influence throughout the early modern era.[62] My purpose is not to eulogize this ideological structure as a site of ontological moral value; indeed, one might well argue that these codes were as much instruments of oppression as anything erected by a dominant socio-economic group before or since.[63] Yet the immense cultural authority accrued in the name of Christian morality signals the need for analysis. In chapter 1, then, I examine the contours of moral economics through a study of a discourse

[60] Everitt, 'Farm Labourers', pp. 432–3.
[61] Everitt, 'Farm Labourers', pp. 425–9.
[62] See, for example, E. P. Thompson's important arguments about patterns of popular protest, in 'The Moral Economy of the English Crowd in the Eighteenth Century', *Past and Present*, 50 (1971), pp. 76–136.
[63] Elizabeth Fox Genovese makes this salient point in 'The Many Faces of Moral Economy: A Contribution to a Debate', *Past and Present*, 58 (1973), pp. 161–8.

18   *Introduction*

of agrarian complaint, developed out of medieval practice and freshly impelled by the socio-political turmoil of the mid-Tudor years. Complaint sets the simple values of the downtrodden labourer against the expansive desires of the 'great possessioners', decries processes of socio-economic change as manifestations of the sin of covetousness, and calls for sweeping moral regeneration to parallel the religious reform of the age. But, from the reign of Elizabeth, agrarian complaint was undermined by emergent movements in religious thought and literary practice. Chapters 2 and 3 trace the transformations of the discourse of complaint effected by these curiously intertwined developments, which prompt crucial revisions of many of the old verities. Agrarian communism might be seen simply as a particularly radical version of moral economics; however, my analysis in chapter 4 reveals communism as a consistently shadowy and subversive force in relation to traditional moral codes. The insight of Winstanley is most striking in his declaration of the fraudulence of such codes, and it is from this position that he formulates his vision of a land in which the earth is 'a common treasury for all'.

The discourse of improvement not only challenged the orthodoxies of moral economics, but itself erected a powerful new set of values, which would underpin the consolidation of capitalism in both country and city. 'Improvement' overturns traditional constructions of individual endeavour, agrarian production and rural change; indeed, its association from the early sixteenth century with enclosure strikes at the very foundation of moral economics, confronting the doctrine of manorial stewardship with the logic of absolute property. But developments of this magnitude rarely proceed either swiftly or simply. In chapters 5 to 7 I examine the often awkward and hesitant fashioning of this discourse, while also stressing the bold potential realized by the end of the period. Chapter 5 investigates the development of English husbandry manuals, from the early Renaissance discovery of classical tracts on the subject, through the proselytizing work of Tusser, to the Baconian 'new science' movement of the middle of the seventeenth century. The subsequent chapter considers surveying manuals, which developed in parallel with husbandry manuals in the wake of Fitzherbert's twin volumes on the practices.[64] The surveyor's strictly legalistic appreciation of tenures and new geometric methods of land measurement effectively strip away

[64] *The Boke of Surveying and Improvements* was published with *The Boke of Husbandrye* in 1523.

moral concerns, and establish instead a representation of the land as a field open to the improving intents of its owner. Finally, my study of georgic in chapter 7 investigates the interaction between agrarian discourse and literary mode. I argue that the resultant blend of 'georgic economics' provided a significant impetus and cultural credibility to the emergent ethics of improvement.

Whereas parts I and II are concerned to delineate the principal confrontations over the representation of the land, part III turns to discourses of rural description and celebration ordered around the interests of the landed gentry and nobility. These movements will be traced firstly through the 'discovery of England' inscribed in the wave of chorographical texts of the latter sixteenth and early seventeenth centuries, and secondly in the development of a tradition of poetry concerned with rural England. Both traditions proceed upon assumptions of social stability and timeless country pleasures, thereby admitting literary debts to the pastoral mode. But in each case the central attention to the place of the propertied in the rural landscape effectively elides considerations of a landlord's moral duties and responsibilities. Consequently the textual forms of chorography and the seventeenth-century rural poem provide a conceptual space within which writers can reassess the status of the rural landowner. My interpretation in each chapter will stress the ways in which these texts articulate an awareness of wider debates over rural order; and I will argue that by the seventeenth century, chorographer and poet alike were invigorating their representations of the land by subtly accommodating the arguments of the improvers. Herrick combines a panegyric on 'enameld Meads' with an appreciation of the 'wise Master' supervising his estate in the interests of both his family and his nation. 'The Kingdoms portion *is the Plow.*'

Part I

Versions of moral economy

1. Covetousness in the countryside: agrarian complaint and mid-Tudor reform

'Wo unto them that joyne one house to another, and bring one lande so nygh unto another, that the poore can get no grounde, & that ye maye dwel upon the earth alone'

(Isaiah 5.8, 'Great Bible')

Sir Thomas More's social criticism, voiced by Hythlodaeus in the first book of *Utopia*, includes perhaps the single most influential complaint about agrarian change ever published in England. The lengthy passage begins:

> your shepe that were wont to be so myke and tame, and so smal eaters, now ... be become so greate devowerers and so wylde, that they eate up and swallow down the very men them selfes. They consume destroy and devoure hole fieldes howses and cities. Ffor looke in what partes of the realme doth growe the fynyst, and therfore dearest woll, there noble men, and gentlemen: yea and certeyn Abbottes, holy men god wote, not contenting them selfes with the yearely revennues and profyttes that were wont to grow to theyr forefathers and predecessours of their landes, nor beynge content that they live in rest and pleasure nothyng profytyng ye muche noyinge the weale publique: leave no grounde for tyllage: they inclose all in pastures: they throw downe houses: they plucke downe townes, and leave nothing stondynge but only the churche to make of it a shepehowse.[1]

More's vision of an agrarian world turned upside down focuses on the phenomenon of depopulating enclosure. Underpinning his polemic is a powerful ideal of socio-economic order in the countryside, in which sheep-rearing is universally subordinated to the production of grain, and landlords acknowledge a moral duty toward their tenants. The corrosive force, motivating the 'insatiable gluttons', is simply and forcefully identified as the sin of covetousness.

---

[1] Trans. Ralphe Robynson (1551); facsimile edn (Amsterdam, 1969), sigs. C6ᵇ–C7ᵃ.

More wrote *Utopia* for an assumed public of humanist intellectuals stretching throughout Europe. Hence Hythlodaeus's claim that principles of Christian morality should 'be proclaymed in open houses' (sig. F7ª), so as to reach the widest possible audience, is in fact carefully restrained by the author within the language of scholars. Moreover, in 1533, faced by the spectre of religious upheaval, More declared that he would rather burn his book than see it translated into the vernacular and applied to the English problems of the day.[2] The English translation of 1551 (sixteen years after More's death), however, claimed a life and relevance for the book in terms that would no doubt have appalled the author. The translator, Ralphe Robynson, not only struck a popular idiom (as evidenced by the above quotation), but also added a dedication to William Cecil which related the publication to the contemporary trend for 'learned men' to 'dayly [put] forth in writing newe inventions, & devises' in the interests of 'the common wealthes affaires' (sig. +3ª). In the reign of Edward VI (1547–53), when radical Protestants combined strident social criticism with their agenda for religious reformation, More was posthumously enlisted for the cause of remodelling the Christian 'commonwealth'.

The appropriation of More by the Edwardian reformers marks the trajectory of this chapter. Agrarian complaint was hardly new to the sixteenth century; indeed both More and the Edwardian Protestants had well-established religious, literary and legal traditions upon which to draw. In the sixteenth century, however, the cultural forces of Protestantism and print, applied to particularly turbulent social and economic conditions, produced a vitally new and widely influential discourse of agrarian complaint. Protestant preachers and pamphleteers at this time formulated a coherent conception at once of an ideal agrarian socio-economic order and of the perceived corruption threatening that ideal. Yet for all its accrued authority, the vision of mid-Tudor complaint was also fragile. The bold application of traditional morality produced statements of tenuous relevance within the rapidly changing circumstances of the early sixteenth century, while the uncertain status of complaint in relation to the 1549 revolts prompted an authoritarian backlash against its rhetorical excesses. I will pursue an ongoing consideration of such limitations of and reactions to the mid-Tudor discourse into the final section of the chapter, in which I will read Sir

[2] David Norbrook, *Poetry and Politics in the English Renaissance* (London, 1984), pp. 30–1, 32.

Thomas Smith's contemporary *Discourse of the Commonweal* as a critical reflection upon complaint. The text – like Smith's long career of government service – will direct the study out of the heady years of Edward's reign, toward the new cultural climate of the Elizabethan era. The Edwardians' vision of moral economics in the countryside stood for subsequent generations as a culturally authoritative orthodoxy in the representation of agrarian conditions and practice – an orthodoxy which later writers reshaped or rejected, but which they could rarely afford to ignore.

AGRARIAN COMPLAINT: FORM AND FORMATION

Strategies of social and economic complaint were etched into medieval culture. Traditions of Christian populism drew support from both the Old Testament prophets and the social mission of Christ, 'to preach the gospel to the poor . . . to heal the broken-hearted, to preach deliverance to the captives, and recovering of sight to the blind, to set at liberty them that are bruised' (Luke 4.18). The effects of this powerful impetus toward social criticism can be traced throughout a wide range of medieval texts and contexts, including sermons, poetry and political discourse. Indeed, the significance of Christian social doctrine was reinforced in the fifteenth century by the foundation of the Court of Chancery (to which aggrieved parties would submit documents of 'complaint'), which aimed to fix the demands of 'conscience' into the law.[3] Chancery thus endorsed complaint as a mode for mediating relations between state and subject, and for preserving traditional values of social and economic order. Its status in this context as a licensed mode, ostensibly conservative but potentially subversive, provided a model widely adopted and adapted throughout the Middle Ages and into the early modern period.

The force of medieval Christian ethics, which underpinned traditions of complaint, helped to shape coherent and influential representations of rural society. The crucial issue for the Church in this regard was the relation between worldly wealth and covetousness. Even a conservative position on this question leads to attacks on the excesses of landlords, merchants and employers, while more extreme arguments could verge on

---

[3] See J. H. Baker, *An Introduction to English Legal History*, 3rd edn (London, 1990), ch. 6.

the revolutionary (as evidenced by the Peasants' Revolt of 1381).[4] The orthodox position, consolidated through centuries of sermons and social theory, was carefully negotiated around the often conflicting interests of moral invective and social control. The vast majority of the medieval clergy, indeed, accepted and endorsed social distinctions which separated labourers from landowners. Even the religious radical John Wycliffe struck a more measured tone when he turned from his attacks on monastic 'possessioners' to consider the distribution of wealth in secular society. Like the majority of contemporary preachers, Wycliffe depicted a strictly hierarchical socio-economic structure, in which the different degrees were bound together within a rubric of reciprocal obligation. In his treatise *Of Servants and Lords*, he wrote: 'Lordis schullen traveile als faste to kunne Holi Writt and do treuthe and equité and mayntene right of pore men, and reste and pees, as pore men bisi to labore for here owene liflode and to paye here rentis to lordis.'[5] Wycliffe's conventional model claimed the late feudal estate as an ideal structure of social and economic order, which embodies Christian principles of 'truth' and 'equity'. In accordance with this vision, contemporary agrarian complaints principally focused on practices and attitudes which might challenge the ideal of manorial community. In fact change of almost any kind was feared: rising rents were represented as oppressive upon the poor; economic expansion by either landlords or tenants inevitably courted censure; and the profits of merchants were always held in suspicion. The desire of the encloser to 'join land to land' (attacked on the authority of Isaiah 5.8) occasionally attracted attention, but was by no means the defining issue it would become for Tudor complainants.[6]

Medieval poetry of social criticism also flourished within this context.

---

[4] Traditions of medieval agrarian communism will be considered further in chapter 4.

[5] Quoted in Helen C. White, *Social Criticism in Popular Religious Literature of the Sixteenth Century* (New York, 1944), p. 18. Modernized, the quote reads: 'Lords must work as diligently to learn holy scripture and to do what is right and just, and maintain the rights of poor men and their happiness and peace, as poor men intent upon working.' (I am grateful to Geraldine Barnes for assistance with the translation.)

[6] G. R. Owst, *Literature and the Pulpit in Medieval England*, 2nd edn (Oxford, 1961), p. 318. This impression aligns with Roger Manning's argument that while enclosure was not a new phenomenon in the sixteenth century, it did not cause significant social disturbances in the Middle Ages because of the relatively low population density. Manning argues that enclosure disputes 'were primarily a response to the pressure of expanding population upon available land resources after 1530' (*Village Revolts: Social Protest and Popular Disturbances in England, 1509–1640* (Oxford, 1988), p. 27).

Indeed, the interconnectedness of poetry and preaching is highlighted by the occasional use of verse within prose sermons, a strategy which has caused one critic to claim that 'the work of preachers formed . . . a generative centre for the production of English lyrics'.[7] Such 'complaint verses' tend to operate on a level of generalized vices and virtues, without developing detailed representations of socio-economic practice. Longer medieval poems, by comparison, apply the orthodox moral principles to a particularly earthy rural life. The crucial text in this loose but important tradition is William Langland's late fourteenth-century *The Vision of William concerning Piers the Plowman*.[8] The thought and doctrine of *Piers Plowman* aligns with contemporary Christian social criticism; as G. R. Owst writes, the poem provides 'a perfect echo in every respect of the Church's message to the world'.[9] Although Langland consistently intertwines literal and allegorical levels of signification, a rural vision nonetheless underpins the poem. The landlords, labourers and merchants of manorial society people the poem; the title-figure is set in a world in which, 'for profit of al the peple Plowmen [are] ordeyned / To tilie and to travaille as trewe lif asketh' (Prol. 119–20). The ploughman's role as the primary producer of food places him at the foundation of a corporate conception of social order, bound together by a network of reciprocal rights and responsibilities.

From this perspective, the poem identifies poverty as the central problem in English society. In a manner consistent with the preachers' strategies of complaint, Langland isolates a moral cause of this problem: the deadly sin of avarice. The poem's attack on this force is centred around the figure of the lady Mede, who represents the desire for monetary reward and social advancement. Mede's significance is highlighted allegorically when she is offered to Conscience as a bride, and the latter denounces her as a woman who 'maketh men mysdo many score tymes' (iii.124). Through 'trust of hire tresor', Mede corrupts the Church, law and government; in the country she makes 'men lese hire lond and hire lif bothe' (iii.123–4, 168). Consequently, Langland's solution to the social problems he identifies is grounded in moral and spiritual rectitude: in individual regeneration, rather than social reformation. The figure of Holy Church defines the path for the true

[7] Siegfried Wenzel, *Preachers, Poets, and the Early English Lyric* (Princeton, 1986), p. 13.
[8] *Piers Plowman: The B Version*, ed. G. Kane and E. Talbot Donaldson (London, 1975).
[9] Owst, *Literature and the Pulpit*, pp. 548–9.

Christian at the beginning of the poem, as she proclaims the importance of love and truth. And the moral doctrine for a member of the Christian community is concentrated in the figures of Dowel and Dobet. To 'Dowel', the reader is told, 'is to doon as lawe techeth. / To love . . . thi frend and thi foo – leve me, that is Dobet' (ix.200–1). In the face of the powers of lady Mede, the social order must be held together by a reassertion of the bonds of Christian love and charity.

A vital 'Piers Plowman tradition' of social and religious complaint developed in the wake of Langland's poem, and provides the most significant link between the Middle Ages and the material at the heart of the current chapter.[10] 'Plowman' texts published during the first half of the sixteenth century include *The Praier and Complaynte of the Ploweman unto Christ, A Lytell Geste howe the Plowman lerned his Pater Noster* and *The Plowmans Tale* (apocryphally attributed to Chaucer).[11] Perhaps the most striking aspect of this burgeoning tradition, however, is the consistent lack of reliance upon the *Vision*. Despite Langland's often ambiguous theological and political positions, later writers appear to have associated him with Wycliffe in a movement of radical religious reform; the persona of the ploughman, in consequence, was appropriated as a mouthpiece for a Lollard or Protestant cause.[12] As Anne Hudson has tentatively suggested, he became 'a proverbial model of the upright, honest labourer, and . . . of the plain man with somewhat radical notions about the church and its role in society'.[13] The ploughman provided a focal point around which the early Protestant polemicists selectively appropriated for their cause the authority of medieval Catholic traditions of religious and social criticism.

The attention of sixteenth-century religious reformers was freshly focused on social – and specifically agrarian – issues by the dissolution of the monasteries. Earlier plowman texts lack consistency on questions of rural order: some merely ignore the potential of the humble labourer as a spokesman for anything other than religious criticism; others present

---

[10] See White's delineation of 'The Piers Plowman Tradition', in *Social Criticism*, ch. 1; Anne Hudson, 'The Legacy of *Piers Plowman*', in *A Companion to 'Piers Plowman'*, ed. John A. Alford (Berkeley, 1988), pp. 251–66; and Myrta Ethel McGinnis, '"Piers the Plowman" in England, 1362–1625: A Study in Popularity and Influence' (unpublished Ph.D dissertation, Yale University, 1932).

[11] Two edns (1531?, 1532); (1510; STC 20034); 3 edns (c.1535, 1548?, 1606).

[12] On the publication of Wycliffite works in the early years of the Reformation, see Anne Hudson, *Lollards and Their Books* (London, 1985), pp. 227–48.

[13] Hudson, *Lollards and Their Books*, p. 258.

radical – albeit idiosyncratic – proposals for reform.[14] The dissolution, however, concentrated religious, moral, social and economic issues, and hence served to galvanize the reformers' agrarian vision. Protestant leaders initially promoted the scheme in the hope that it might lead to a redirection of resources into charity and education. Hugh Latimer and Thomas Cranmer were notable supporters of the dissolution legislation of the mid-1530s, and each preached at the important forum of Paul's Cross on several occasions in favour of the government line and against rebels involved in the pro-monastic Pilgrimage of Grace.[15] But the subsequent dispersal of monastic lands was directed more by a concern for government revenue than by any social ideals, and became the focus of rising discontent among the reformers at the policies of the Henrician regime.[16] As they perceived a gathering threat to both their religious principles and their social ideals, the radical Protestants were prompted to adopt an attitude of outraged reaction.

In the later Henrician state the rising wave of complaint was rigorously suppressed, as the reformers lacked both access to the press and any significant sense of involvement in the processes of power. Nevertheless the perspectives and textual strategies which would characterize mid-Tudor complaint are presaged in two important pamphlets which evaded the censors by being printed on the Continent. Henry Brinkelow's *The Complaynt of Roderyck Mors* was published anonymously in Strasburg in 1542?;[17] and a text variously attributed to either Brinkelow or Robert Crowley, *A supplication of the poore commons*, was perhaps first printed in the Netherlands in 1546.[18] Each of these texts attempts a wide-ranging critique of religious, social and economic practice, expressed in the legal language of supplication and addressed to sources of authority: the former to the parliament and the latter to Henry VIII. Both also anticipate the Edwardian works'

---

[14] See, for example, White's discussion of the 'radical version of the stewardship theory of possession' in *The Praier and Complaynte of the Ploweman* (*Social Criticism*, pp. 27–8).

[15] See Allan Chester, *Hugh Latimer: Apostle to the English* (Philadelphia, 1954), ch. 17. The significance attached by contemporaries to a sermon delivered at Paul's Cross is established in Millar Maclure's study, *The Paul's Cross Sermons 1534–1642* (Toronto, 1958).

[16] See Joyce Youings, *The Dissolution of the Monasteries* (London, 1971), pp. 117–30.

[17] Reprinted twice in 1548? and again in 1560?.

[18] (STC 23435.5); a second edition was published the same year in London (STC 10884), in a volume with Simon Fish's anti-monastic *Supplication for the Beggers*, first printed in 1529.

conventions of physical presentation, and thereby herald the potential significance of print in the formation of a discourse of complaint. They are published in cheap octavo formats, while the use of title-page biblical texts, in English, invokes from the outset the authority of the vernacular Bible. Brinkelow chooses the solicitous Psalm 54.2, 'Oh Lord God, heare my prayer, & despyse not my complaynte: looke uppon me and heare me'; the author of the *supplication* preaches the moral authority of the poor from Proverbs 21.13, 'Who so stoppeth hys eare at the cryeng of the poore, he shall crye hymselfe, and shall not be herde.'[19] Such cries of complaint, voiced in the name of the oppressed, boldly demanded a Protestant commitment to values of moral economy. The climate of religious upheaval generated a profound and widespread sense of the potential for reform in other spheres.

During the brief reign of Edward VI, preachers, poets and pamphleteers revitalized and reshaped preexistent traditions of social complaint. Latimer, whose reformist views and polemical style drew him to the forefront of this movement, applied the weight of tradition to the new context in his 'Sermon of the Plough', preached at Paul's Cross in 1548.[20] He declared,

And now I shall tell you who be the plowers, for Gods worde is a seede to be sowne in Gods field, that is the faithfull congregation, and the preacher is the sower. And it is in the gospel: *Exivit qui seminat seminare semen suum.* He that soweth, the husbandman, the ploughman went forth to sow his seede. (fol. 12ª)

Latimer actually has to stretch the Latin to accommodate his metaphor; 'qui seminat' is more concisely rendered, in contemporary translations, simply as 'sower'.[21] His insistence on the figure of the ploughman, however, draws attention to its rhetorical potential, at a time when the government of Edward Seymour, Protector Somerset, was giving new impetus to Protestant reform. The emphasis on the preacher's labour draws upon traditions of Christian georgic, aligning his efforts in the

[19] Both biblical texts are quoted as they appear in the pamphlets.
[20] Published as *A notable Sermon of the reverende father Maister Hughe Latemer*, 2 edns (both 1548). All references to Latimer's sermons are to *27 sermons*, ed. Augustine Bernher, 2nd edn (1571).
[21] This translation of the text (Luke 8.5) is followed consistently in Miles Coverdale's translation (1535), the 'Geneva' Bible (1560), the 'Great Bible' (1539) and the Authorized Version (1611).

pulpit with the biblical injunction of Genesis 3.19,[22] while England becomes 'Gods field', in which the preacher must fulfil the lesson of the parable of the sower (Matthew 13.19–23), and plant the seed of the true religion. The sermon, one of Latimer's first during the reign of Edward VI, thus heralds the brief period of intense Protestant activity which followed the death of Henry VIII. In a movement which incorporated textual forms ranging from sermons and prose tracts to poetry and dramatic dialogues, the Protestants forcefully declared a new vision for the 'fields' of the nation.

Paradoxically, Latimer's use of the ploughman conflates a radical religious agenda with an essentially conservative socio-economic vision. This may be seen in a later reference in the 'Sermon of the Plough' to enclosure:

> But there be two kindes of inclosing to let or hynder both these kindes of ploughing. The one is an inclosing to let or hynder the bodely ploughing, and the other to let or hynder the holy day ploughing, the church ploughing. The bodely ploughing, is taken in and enclosed thorow singular commodity. For what man will let go or diminish his private commodity, for a commune wealth? and who will susteine any damage for the respect of a publique commodity? (fol. 16ᵃ)

The ploughman, whose 'bodely ploughing' is equally important to the Christian commonwealth as the 'church ploughing' of the reformist preacher, becomes a symbol for the Protestants' social values. But while Latimer argues for the active propagation of a new religion, his social doctrine depends upon an ideal vision – grounded in late feudal theory – of a common-field manorial estate. His ploughman is placed at the base of a strictly hierarchical social and economic structure, organized around the imperatives of a traditional Christian morality. This attitude toward the figure is epitomized in a statement from another of Latimer's Edwardian sermons, that 'The poorest plowman is in Christ equall with the greatest Prince that is' (fol. 108ᵇ).[23] While he stresses the moral value of the poor labourer, Latimer's concern with a static social order demands certain restrictions on the doctrine of 'equality'. Therefore the declaration turns on the phrase 'in Christ'. This one vital qualification allows him to assert a religious and moral equality while simultaneously

---

[22] 'In the sweat of thy face shalt thou eat bread, till thou return unto the ground; for out of it wast thou taken: for dust thou art, and unto dust shalt thou return.'

[23] 'Last Sermon Before King Edward VI', published as *A Moste faithfull Sermon*, 2 edns (1550, 1553?).

upholding the principle of social hierarchy. It strengthens the authority of grievances expressed through representatives of the lower orders, yet leaves them powerless substantially to affect or improve their positions. This paradox is central to the Edwardian texts of concern here. Simply, the various writers and ploughmen-preachers reacted against the strengthening social and economic pressures of the sixteenth century, and insisted upon a profoundly conservative model of national order. As R. H. Tawney writes, 'doctrinal radicalism marched hand in hand with social conservatism', as the religious reformers 'saw in economic individualism but another expression of the laxity and licence which had degraded the purity of religion'.[24] The prevailing sense of urgency in their discourse, furthermore, was reinforced by conditions of severe socio-economic instability in the 1540s. Harvest fluctuations and government monetary policies combined during these mid-Tudor years to produce a highly volatile economy, though also one in which the omnipresent forces of inflation pushed grain prices at the end of the decade to almost double their 1540 levels.[25] A growing population and an increasingly active property market compounded the instability, and led to problems of poverty and vagrancy. C. G. A. Clay identifies the mid-1540s as a time when 'the problem of the able bodied poor and vagrancy' assumed 'terrifying proportions'.[26] And although one recent study has argued that the rate of enclosure in the sixteenth century has to date been vastly overestimated, others have shown the potentially devastating impact of harvest failure in regions newly converted to pastoral farming.[27] The almost overpowering contemporary anxiety about such manifestations of agrarian change was not without foundation.

The expression and dissemination of social polemic borne out of such anxieties was given fresh impetus in the mid-Tudor years by the crucial

[24] *Religion and the Rise of Capitalism* (London, 1984 edn), p. 146.
[25] Peter Bowden, 'Agricultural Prices, Farm Profits, and Rents', in *AHEW IV*, p. 630. Bowden also notes, however, that the harvests of 1546, 1547 and 1548 were exceptionally good; indeed, the paradoxical conditions of dearth in a time of bountiful crops appears to have injected a sense of urgency into the search for causes conducted by the Edwardian commentators. See also Whitney R. D. Jones, *The Mid-Tudor Crisis 1539–1563* (London, 1973), ch. 5.
[26] *Economic Expansion and Social Change: England 1500–1700* (2 vols., Cambridge, 1984), vol. 1, p. 222.
[27] J. R. Wordie, 'The Chronology of English Enclosure, 1500–1914', *Economic History Review*, 2nd series, 36 (1983), p. 494; John Walter and Roger Schofield, 'Famine, Disease and Crisis Mortality in Early Modern Society', in *Famine, Disease and the Social Order in Early Modern Society*, ed. Walter and Schofield (Cambridge, 1989), pp. 21–5.

– though not always comfortable – convergence of radical Protestantism and state power. Under the regime of Seymour, outspoken Protestants such as Latimer, Thomas Lever and Robert Crowley were given access to both the court and the press; for a brief period it appeared to many that the state would embrace unprecedented programmes of religious and social reform. This position helps to explain Latimer's approach to complaint, informed at once by moral indignation and a sense of involvement in ongoing processes of change. In the earlier development of the Piers Plowman tradition, by comparison, the rhetorical structure of complaint had been consistent and straightforward. Through the persona of the ploughman, authors presented statements from one at the base of the social order, directed to an individual or class at the top of that order. The ploughman was the embodiment of powerlessness, humbly appealing to the better judgement of the powerful. Moreover, the leading Protestant preachers and writers of the middle of the sixteenth century had forged their sense of personal and communal identities in their struggles with the Henrician regime, which was rarely more than an ambivalent partner in religious reform. Throughout these experiences, the Protestants derived their direction and purpose not from any allegiance to a state, but from the Bible.[28] As Patrick Collinson comments about the emerging Protestant perspective, they 'were living, in a sense, in the pages of the Bible',[29] an approach to religious, political and socio-economic life which earned the mid-Tudor Protestants the title of 'gospellers'. That Seymour's regime actively identified itself with the Protestant reformers, and sanctioned their publications, thus raised crucial questions about the representation of the country and its problems. Was England to be equated with the oppressive state of Babylon or the troubled but elect nation of Israel?[30] Were the Protestants

---

[28] See Stephen Greenblatt's analysis of the cultural significance of the vernacular Bible, in *Renaissance Self-Fashioning: From More to Shakespeare* (Chicago and London, 1980), ch. 2.

[29] *The Birthpangs of Protestant England: Religious and Cultural Change in the Sixteenth and Seventeenth Centuries* (London, 1988), p. 10. Interestingly, given the practices of representation which I will trace in the following chapters, Collinson continues, 'Theirs was a mode of discovering a shared identity which was indirect and is somewhat mysterious to us, but it was as meaningful as those other processes of England's self-discovery which involved chroniclers, antiquarians, topographers, surveyors and mapmakers' (pp. 10–11).

[30] Richard Helgerson, in a stimulating analysis of Protestantism and discourses of nationhood in Tudor England, argues the significance of exile (under both Henry and Mary)

a 'poor persecuted little flock' or a 'commonwealth of Christians'?[31] Indeed the alliance between the gospellers and Seymour's government in these vital few years must be seen as a crucial influence in the construction of a Protestant national identity. The spirit of this milieu is captured in the woodcut of Latimer preaching to Edward VI – the latter flanked by Seymour and the former surrounded by a crowd including a woman scanning her Bible – which was later published with both Latimer's *27 sermons* and John Foxe's *Actes and Monumentes* (illustration 1.1).

The very social and economic order of the nation was perceived to be at stake, and the state itself directly participated in the processes of critical redefinition. Ultimately, as I will argue below, the authoritarian reaction to the 1549 rebellions rejected much of the gospellers' socioeconomic discourse. Yet the remarkable and lasting achievement of the Edwardian years lies in the creative turmoil of preachers, poets, printers and statesmen striving to redefine their society and its values.

The nature of that achievement was bound to the medium of the printed word. Indeed the sheer magnitude of the Edwardian publishing boom is immediately striking: it has been estimated that the volume of publications between 1548 and 1550 was roughly equivalent to 'the average mid-Tudor decade'; and 'approximately three-eighths of all editions printed under Seymour could not have been published legally during the reign of Henry VIII because of their association with radical protestantism'.[32] The output eased in the wake of the 1549 rebellions and Seymour's demise, but was not fully stemmed until the death of the Protestant king. Alongside contemporary pamphlets, and sermons rushed from pulpit to press, publishers also helped to construct a sense of tradition by printing preexistent texts. The English translation of More's *Utopia* was noted above. Of still greater significance was the first printed

---

to the self-perception of the early Protestants; and he draws attention to Revelation 18.4 as a text which lent authority to a belief that exile from a Babylon-like state could be 'a divinely appointed vocation' (*Forms of Nationhood: The Elizabethan Writing of England* (Chicago and London, 1992), pp. 258–9).

[31] See Catharine Davies, '"Poor Persecuted Little Flock" or "Commonwealth of Christians"; Edwardian Protestant Concepts of the Church', in *Protestantism and the National Church in Sixteenth-Century England*, ed. Peter Lake and Maria Dowling (London, 1987), pp. 78–102.

[32] John N. King, *English Reformation Literature: The Tudor Origins of the Protestant Tradition* (Princeton, 1982), p. 88; and 'Freedom of the Press, Protestant Propaganda, and Protector Somerset', *Huntington Library Quarterly*, 40 (1976), p. 3. See also King's arguments about the links between Seymour's regime and publishing in 'Protector Somerset, Patron of the English Renaissance', *Papers of the Bibliographical Society of America*, 70 (1976), pp. 307–31.

1.1 Hugh Latimer preaching before Edward VI: woodcut illustration from Latimer, *27 sermons*, 1571 edn.

text of *Piers Plowman*, in an edition by Robert Crowley which employed marginal notes and textual summaries in an attempt to reshape the poem as a proto-Protestant prophecy.[33] The cultural status Crowley claimed for the text was reinforced by the contemporaneous publication of other texts aligned with the Piers Plowman tradition, such as *Pierce the Ploughmans Crede* and *I playne Piers*, while the tradition was applied specifically to the Edwardian context in the anonymous pamphlet, *Pyers plowmans exhortation unto the lordes knightes and burgoysses of the Parlyamenthouse*.[34]

The man whose work most clearly typifies the period was Crowley

---

[33] Three editions in 1550, and a fourth in 1561; John N. King, 'Robert Crowley's Editions of *Piers Plowman*: A Tudor Apocalypse', *Modern Philology*, 73 (1975–6), pp. 342–52; and King, *English Reformation Literature*, pp. 322–39.

[34] *I playne Piers* (1550?; STC 19903a) has been dated as from the final years of the reign of Henry VIII (Anne Hudson, 'Legacy of *Piers Plowman*', p. 258); *Pierce the Ploughmans crede*, a poem probably of the late fifteenth century, was first printed in 1553 (STC 19904); *Pyers plowmans exhortation* is a contemporary work (1550?; STC 19905). See also Luke Shepherd's figure of John Bon, in *John Bon and Mast person* (1548?).

himself, a prolific author and publisher involved in the production of at least nineteen works of Protestant polemic between 1549 and 1551.[35] His own texts include prose tracts, didactic verse and dramatic dialogues, almost all of which are directed by the characteristic purpose and tone of complaint. Crowley's publications also helped to mould strategies of physical presentation calculated to reinforce the author's perspective and arguments. Complaint tracts of the period were regularly printed in octavo formats, and conformed to a stark, undecorated presentation of the printed word. Dedications in the standard contemporary form of complimentary addresses to prospective patrons were rarely used, although a popular modification of this convention was an epistolary address to the king, Seymour, the Privy Council, parliament or any combination of these authorities. This device allowed the author to reinforce the fundamental complaint form, by constructing himself as a powerless representative of the 'poor commons', rather than an individual seeking to establish a relationship based on counsel or patronage. The only sort of textual embellishments regularly embraced were title-page biblical texts and further biblical citations in marginal notes – a strategy which at once celebrates the vernacular repossession of the Word, and involves the instrument of religious change in an associated programme for social reform.

These publications consistently identify a disparity between moral ideals and socio-economic practice within the Christian nation. Latimer's attack on enclosure in the 'Sermon of the Plough' (quoted above) focuses specifically on the relation between self-interest and the good of the country, as he asks, 'For what man will let go or diminish his private commodity, for a commune wealth?' The rhetorical question implicitly claims the term 'commonwealth' as a conception which draws together the various moral and ethical ideals which underpin the sermon. In a true commonwealth, people work in harmony toward the good of the whole; they abandon their selfish desires in the interests of a fundamentally *common* wealth. Latimer's use of the 'commonwealth' ideal draws upon a tradition of reformist discourse which stretches throughout the Tudor period.[36] The 'very and true commonweal' was, as Arthur

---

[35] King, *English Reformation Literature*, p. 96.
[36] The heritage of the term is the subject of debate among historians. David Starkey, in an attempt to challenge Sir Geoffrey Elton's claims about a 'revolution in government' in the 1530s, argues that 'commonweal' emerged as the centrepiece of a new language of government as early as the middle of the fifteenth century ('Which Age of Reform?', in *Revolution Reassessed: Revisions in the History of Tudor Government and*

Ferguson states, a 'touchstone of all early Tudor social and political thought'.[37] Yet the frequency of the word's occurrence also suggests a certain malleability in its signification; and the fears expressed by Sir Thomas Elyot in 1531, that 'common wealth' implied communal property, were a constant source of anxiety.[38] While always wary of such fears, the Protestant reformers of the Edwardian period adopted the term as an ideal sanctioned by tradition yet sufficiently vague that it could be refashioned to accommodate their own attitudes and agenda.

The extent to which the idea of the 'commonwealth' also became associated with strategies of complaint during the reign of Edward is suggested in a letter sent by Sir Anthony Auchar to William Cecil in 1549, to express concern at Seymour's social policy. He writes, 'Sir as a pore man maye requier you, be playne with my Lords grace that undar the pretence of Symplyssetie and povertie ther maye rest mouche myschyffe. So doe I feare ther dothe in these men called common welthes and there Adherents.'[39] Whether or not this document can be used as reliable historical evidence for the existence of a 'commonwealth party' operating under Seymour, its value in the current context is considerable.[40] For Auchar focuses on the tone adopted by the 'men called common welthes'. His description of the reformers' 'pretence of Symplyssetie and povertie' identifies their plain style and controlling sympathies with the poor and oppressed. From this perspective, Auchar fears, an attack on the motivations of 'private commodity' will assume a potentially subversive force, as any manifestations of economic individualism may be identified with the sin of covetousness. The characteristic claims of the complainant to conservatism and humility would always be met with such suspicion among many of the economically and politically powerful. The 'gentilmen', Auchar writes, 'ar in souche dowte that allmost they dare touche none of them'.

Administration, ed. Christopher Coleman and David Starkey (Oxford, 1986), pp. 19–27). Elton countered with a convincing attack on the adequacy of Starkey's evidence ('A New Age of Reform', *Historical Journal*, 30 (1987), pp. 715–16).

[37] Arthur B. Ferguson, *The Articulate Citizen and the English Renaissance* (Durham, N. C., 1965), p. 244.

[38] See Norbrook, *Poetry and Politics*, pp. 49–50.

[39] Dated 10 September 1549; PRO SP Dom, Edward VI, vol. 8, no. 56.

[40] See Sir Geoffrey Elton's criticism of the common use of this letter to demonstrate the existence of a coordinated 'party' of 'commonwealth men' ('Reform and the "Commonwealth Men" of Edward VI's Reign', in *The English Commonwealth 1547–1640: Essays in Politics and Society Presented to Joel Hurstfield*, ed. Peter Clark, Alan G. R. Smith and Nicholas Tyacke (Leicester, 1979), pp. 23–38).

The impact of the strategies identified by Auchar on the representation of the nation becomes apparent in Crowley's 1548 prose pamphlet, *An informacion and Peticion agaynst the oppressours of the pore Commons of this Realme.*[41] Like many of the complaint writers, Crowley draws heavily for scriptural support upon the Book of Isaiah. He chooses for his title-page text Isaiah 58.9: 'When you suffre none oppression to bee amongst you, and leave of youre idle talkes then shal you cal upon the Lord and he shal hear you, you shal crie, and he shal say, Behold I am at hand.'[42] The apocalyptic tone insists at once on the need for fundamental change and the very real opportunity of salvation for the reformed commonwealth. Later in the text Crowley reinforces this position by placing himself more explicitly in the prophetic tradition:

> For even the same spirit that sayd unto Esaie, crye and sease not, declare unto my people theyr wyckednes: cryeth also in my conscience, bydyng me not spare to tell the possessioners of this realme, that unlesse they repente the oppression wherewyth they vexe the pore commons, and shew themselves through love to be brothers of one father & membres of one body wyth them: they shal not at the laste daye enherite wyth them the kyngdom of Christe. (sig. A5b)

Crowley draws the authority of the Old Testament prophecy to bear upon the perceived 'oppression' of the 'pore commons' of England. Like Isaiah, he is impelled by a Christian 'spirit' to speak out as an unpopular voice within a maelstrom of evil, in an attempt to purge the sins of the nation in preparation for the 'laste daye' of national judgement.[43]

Crowley's reference to rich and poor alike being 'membres of one body' relies upon the conception of society as an organic unit, or 'body politic'. This essentially conservative representation of national order, informed at once by medieval political thought and the biblical authority of 1 Corinthians 12, regularly underpins the Edwardian texts.[44] In a subsequent expansion of the figure, Crowley emphasizes the interdepen-

---

41 Two edns (both 1548); references are to the second edition.
42 Crowley's translation is noteworthy for its elaboration. The 'Great Bible' is both more accurate and more typical of contemporary translations, with its rendering of the verse: 'Then yf thou callest, the Lorde shall answere the: yf thou cryest, he shall saye: here I am.'
43 Compare Davies's discussion of Latimer's self-representation in his 1548–50 sermons ('"Poor Persecuted Little Flock"', p. 84).
44 See David George Hale's survey, *The Body Politic: A Political Metaphor in English Renaissance Literature* (The Hague, 1971). On the use of the metaphor in the middle of the sixteenth century, see also Ferguson, *Articulate Citizen*, especially ch. 8.

dence of all parts of the body. He asks,

> For what discommoditie is it to the heade, shoulders, the armes, and other
> the upper membres of the body, beynge all redy sufficiently clothed: to put
> on the legges & feete a peare of hose and shoes, to defende them also from
> the injuries of the wether and other hurtes that might chaunce unto them
> in theyr travaylynge to cary the body from place to place, for hys
> commoditie and pleasure? Verily in myne opinion, that body is far
> unworthy to have either legges or feete: that wyll lette them goe bare,
> haveynge wherwyth to cover them. (sig. B2b)

For the purposes of complaint, Crowley focuses his attention on the
labours and interests of the lower 'members' of the body. His use of the
image reinforces the notion of reciprocal bonds of rights and responsibilities which link the 'heade, shoulders, [and] armes' to the 'legges &
feete'. Consequently, any individual aspirations of the 'upper membres'
will distract them from their appointed role within the social 'body', and
upset the organic harmony of the true commonwealth.

When applied to the agrarian economy, this vision of the nation
imposes a strict moral code upon the 'upper membres of the body'. The
predominant doctrine of the time is that possession of land constitutes a
position of stewardship, sanctioned by God. In *A Prymmer or boke of
private prayer nedeful to be used of al faythfull Christianes*, this
argument is infused with the orthodoxy of a pronouncement 'auctorysed
and set fourth' by the Protestant king.[45] In fact the book's prayer 'For
Landlordes' presents one of the most extensive statements of the doctrine
of stewardship extant from the Edwardian years. It states:

> The earthe is thyne (O Lorde) and al that is contayned therein,
> notwythstandynge thou haste geven the possession therof unto the
> chyldren of men, to passe over the tyme of theyr shorte pylgremage in thys
> vale of misery: We heartlye pray thee to sende thy holye spirite into the
> heartes of theym that possesse the groundes, pastures, and dwellynge
> places of the earthe, that they remembryng them selves to be thy tenauntes,
> may not racke and stretche oute the rentes of their houses and landes, nor
> yet take unreasonable fines and incoms after the maner of covetous
> worldelynges, but so lette theym oute to other, that the inhabitauntes
> thereof maye bothe be able to paye the rentes, and also honestly to lyve, to
> nourishe their familye, and to relief the poore: geve theym grace also to
> consider, that they are but straungers & pylgremes in thys world havyng
> here no dwellyng place, but sekynge one to come, that they remembrynge

45 (1553; STC 20373).

the shorte continuaunce of theyr lyfe, maye be content, with that that is sufficient, and not joyne house to house, nor couple lande to lande, to the impovryshment of other, but so behave them selves in lettinge out theyr tenementes, landes, and pastures, that after thys lyfe they maye be receaved into everlastyng dwellynge places: Through Jesus Christ our Lorde, Amen. (sigs. P5ᵃ–P6ᵃ)

As the opening words assert, in this vision there can be no absolute rights of property in the land, beyond those held by God. Hence the 'landlords' to whom the prayer is addressed become 'thy tenauntes', restricted themselves within networks of responsibility and deference stretching far beyond 'thys vale of misery'; and any desire for personal economic improvement is identified as the sinful 'maner of covetous worldelynges'. As a godly steward, the landlord's primary responsibility is for the lives of his tenants.

The very existence of God, therefore, imposes absolute standards of fair dealing and charity upon those involved in the agrarian economy. Crowley writes in the *informacion and Peticion* that,

> If ther were no God, then would I think it leafull for men to use their possessions as thei lyste . . . But forasmuch as we have a God, and he hath declared unto us by the scripturs, that he hath made the possessioners but Stuardes of his ryches . . . I thynke no Christian ears can abyde to heare that more then Turkysh opinion. (sig. A4ᵇ)

The use of the word 'possessioners' draws upon a tradition of complaint at monastic wealth which stretches back to Wycliffe.[46] In an important extension of this tradition, impelled by the prevailing reformist disenchantment after the dissolution of the monasteries, the Protestant texts insist that the doctrine of stewardship is also being rejected by private landowners throughout the country. As Crowley declares in the opening lines of the *Peticion*, the most 'weyghty' matter in the realm is 'the great oppression of the pore communes, by the possessioners as wel of Clergie as of the Laitie' (sig. A2ᵃ). The dissolution, he suggests, has simply replaced one type of 'possessioner' with another; and now a gulf of oppression splits the entire country between covetous 'possessioners' and defenceless 'poor commons'.

The practical applications of this attack on 'possessioners' revolve around a strict adherence to traditional manorial structures of property relations. Crowley's *One and thyrtye Epigrammes*, for example, isolate

---

[46] White, *Social Criticism*, p. 14.

a variety of evils which threaten the harmony of the commonwealth.[47] A prefatory verse declares the aim to reprove 'the faultes of all menne'. In the prophetical tradition of Isaiah, the book will 'tell the Lordes people / of their iniquitie' (sig. A3ᵃ). As he works through a range of moral and socio-economic abuses – in a methodical alphabetical order – Crowley touches upon the activities within the agrarian economy of 'forestallars', 'Idle persons', 'Leasemongars', 'Marchauntes', 'Unsaciable Purchaysars' and 'Usurars'. In 'Of Rente Raysers' he focuses his narrative on a particular piece of land:

> A Manne that had landes
> of tenne pounde by yere
> Surveyed the same
> and lette it out deare. (sig. E1ᵇ)

In accordance with his assumption of a static model of socio-economic order underlying the practices of the countryside, Crowley states the economic value of the land as an inherent quality; the desire to increase that value, linked with the activity of surveying, is represented as an overt attempt to upset the established order.[48] Eventually the poem turns upon a confrontation between the doctrine of stewardship and motivations of economic individualism:

> But when he was tolde
> whan daunger it was
> To oppresse his tenauntes
> he sayed he did not passe.
> For thys thynge he sayde,
> full certayne he wyste
> That wyth hys owne he myghte
> alwayes do as he lyste
> But immediatlye I trowe
> thys oppressoure fyl sicke:
> Of a voyce that he harde
> geve accountes of thy Baliwicke. (sig. E1ᵇ)

The debate about a landlord's rights over 'his own' would shape rival representations of agrarian England throughout the following hundred years. Crowley's fable prefigures this confrontation, as he emphasizes

---

[47] *One and thyrtye Epigrammes, wherein are bryefly touched so many Abuses, that maye and ought to be put away*, 3 edns (1550, 1550, 1573); references are to the first edition.
[48] Crowley's attacks on surveyors and surveying will be discussed further in chapter 6.

the distance between his landlord's statement of an unfettered right of property, and the ideal standards of accounting demanded by God. Within the latter model, interests of individual expansion and economic improvement become the motives of the 'oppressoure'; the rent-raiser's distance from the Christian ideal is neatly reinforced by a marginal citation of Luke 16, the parable of the unjust steward.

Throughout the various Edwardian statements of agrarian complaint, it is undoubtedly enclosure that emerges as the preeminent manifestation of covetousness in the countryside. Arguments against the practice are regularly supported by Isaiah 5.8, translated in the 'Great Bible' as: 'Wo unto them that joyne one house to another, and bring one lande so nygh unto another, that the poore can get no grounde, & that ye maye dwel upon the earth alone.' The utter conventionality of this text, which is used in almost every significant enclosure complaint of the period, highlights the fundamental significance for the gospellers of this particular aspect of agrarian improvement.[49] To a certain extent 'enclosure' became a catch-all phrase, which covered a wide range of agrarian abuses; as Roger Manning writes, in the sixteenth century, the term was used

> as shorthand for a variety of agricultural practices that resulted in depopulation, the decay of tillage, engrossing, encroachment upon wastes or overcharging common pastures, or the assertion of absolute rights of private property that led to the extinction of common use-rights – whether or not the land was actually hedged or ditched.[50]

The common factor in all these forms of 'enclosure' is a threat to traditional conceptions of social and economic order on the manorial estate. Whether it is conducted unilaterally by the landlord in a manner which leads to depopulation, or by agreement amongst the landlord and his tenants, the guiding principle of enclosure is the rational apportionment of rights of property over any given piece of land. Its strict distribution of common and waste land privileges individual interests over communal relations, and thus facilitates the gradual formulation of a modern conception of property, as a right 'to exclude others from some use or benefit of something'.[51] The notion of the manorial land as a

---

[49] See, for example, the prayer 'For Landlordes', quoted above, pp. 39–40, in which the reference to Isaiah 5.8 is reinforced on the printed page by marginal citation.
[50] *Village Revolts*, p. 33.
[51] C. B. Macpherson, 'Capitalism and the Changing Concept of Property', in *Feudalism, Capitalism and Beyond*, ed. Eugene Kamenka and R. S. Neale (London, 1975), p. 106.

resource over which each member of the community would own a particular 'bundle of rights', is confronted by a structure which promotes absolute rights and autonomous action.[52] While it need not spell the end for a manor as a social and economic unit, enclosure inevitably undermines traditional concepts of landholding within a moral economy. Consequently the anti-enclosure tirade became something of an independent subgenre of agrarian complaint, impelled by widespread anxiety surrounding the rise of great sheepmasters in the early decades of the sixteenth century.[53] For example, Thomas Becon's 1550? dialogue *The Jewell of Joy* (a work which otherwise devotes little consideration to agrarian issues) includes a passage which stands as a *tour de force* even in the rich field of the Edwardian texts.[54] In the tradition of More's *Utopia*, Becon depicts an agrarian world in which 'Those beastes which were created of God for the nouryshment of man doe nowe devoure man' (fol. 16b). He declares:

> If ever heretofore in this our tyme specyallye in [sic] thys saiynge of the Prophet found true, From the lest unto the most they hange upon covetousnes, and from the prophet unto the pryest they go all aboute wyth falshead and lies. Howe joyne they Lordeshyp to Lordeshyppe, manner to manner, ferme to ferme, land to lande, pasture to pasture, house to house, and house for a vantage? Howe do the rych men, and specielly suche as be shepemongers oppresse the kynges lyege people by devourynge theyr commune pastures wyth theyr shepe, so that the poore people, ar not able to kepe a cowe for the conforte of them and of theyr poore famylye, but are lyke to starve and peryshe for honger, yf there be not provisyon made shortly? What shepe ground scapeth these caterpyllers of the commune weale? Howe swarme they wyth aboundaunce of flockes of shepe? . . . If these shepemongers go forthe as they begyn, the people shall both miserablye dye for colde, and wretchedly peryshe for honger. For these gredy woulves and comberous cormerauntes, wyll eyther sell theyr woll and theyr shepe at theyr owne pryce or els they wyll sell none.

> (fol. 15a-b)

Like many other commentators, Becon recognized the spread of sheep-farming in the 1540s, and saw it as a movement antithetical to the

---

52 F. M. L. Thompson, *Chartered Surveyors: The Growth of a Profession* (London, 1968), p. 3; see also below, chapter 6.
53 See, for example, C. E. Moreton, *The Townshends and Their World: Gentry, Law, and Land in Norfolk c. 1450–1551* (Oxford, 1992), ch. 5.
54 References are to *Worckes* (3 vols., 1564), vol. 2.

interests of the commonweal.[55] Hence his passage, driven by the moral imperative of complaint, shapes bold, generalized representations of the countryside. The rich are first defined by their exploitation of the wool market, as 'shepemongers';[56] and subsequently they are misshapen – through their association with essentially unnatural practices – as predatory 'gredy woulves and comberous cormerauntes', and parasitic 'caterpyllers of the commune weale'. The 'poore', meanwhile, remain passive and helpless, overwhelmed by the decimation of the commons, upon which they depend for their livelihood.

Significantly, Becon also assumes a problem of similar proportions throughout the nation. While *The Jewell of Joy* considers in some detail the particular difficulties involved in spreading the new religion into such dark regions as Derbyshire, Becon's socio-economic perspective relies on a traditional image of England as a patchwork of manorial estates. One major reason for this perhaps lies in the literal application of Old Testament doctrine such as that of Isaiah 5.8. As Patrick Collinson writes, the Bible knew nothing of counties or regions, 'it knew only of a nation, Israel, and of a city, Jerusalem'.[57] When the Protestant author turned to the land, then, any appreciation of regional difference typically gave way under the weight of a driving biblical fundamentalism. Indeed the complaint texts rarely admit the possibility that in certain instances enclosure may actually improve conditions for tenants, or that in many places – on manors enclosed for over a century, or in the disparate economies of the forests and fens – it will be an irrelevant issue. Throughout the nation, the only possible solution perceived for complex socio-economic problems is a simple imposition of the idealized manorial model, within which the 'shepemongers' will accept their role as God's stewards, and the manor will become a self-sufficient unit of agricultural productivity, devoid of any association with a market economy.

---

[55] As Bowden suggests, the expansion of sheep-farming in the 1540s helps to explain the prevalent conditions of dearth, even in the years of bountiful harvests at the end of the decade ('Agricultural Prices', pp. 630, 638). The point provides a salient reminder of the material circumstances within which – and upon which – discourse works.

[56] 'Sheepmonger' may have been a morally neutral term until the early sixteenth century; however, the vigour of the mid-century attack on market practices appears to have altered the signification of 'monger', when used either alone or in compounds. The OED notes that, 'In formations dating from the middle of the 16th c. onwards -*monger* nearly always implies one who carries on a contemptible or discreditable "trade" or "traffic"' (OED 2).

[57] Collinson, *Birthpangs*, p. 8.

Other texts pursue this logic to develop more detailed analyses of the rural economy. Latimer's Edwardian sermons, for example, regularly elaborate upon the conventions of agrarian complaint by incorporating a specific appreciation of contemporary issues. This characteristic conflation of moral imperative and attention to detail is particularly apparent in the sermon he preached on his return to court after the 1549 unrest. Generally known as his 'Last Sermon Before King Edward VI', it is based on Luke 12.15, and begins: 'Take heede & beware of covetousnes. take heede & beware of covetousnes: take heede & beware of covetousnes: take heede & beware of covetousnes. And what and if I should say nothing els these three or fower houres' (fol. 103^b). From this stark moral basis, he calls on England's preachers to 'strike at the roote' of evil, 'and feare not these Giauntes of England, these great men and men of power, these men that are oppressours of the poore' (fol. 107^b).[58] Subsequently the sermon focuses on enclosure. In the wake of the 1549 uprisings, and in response to widespread suspicions that government action and rhetoric directed against enclosure had incited or lent a certain legitimacy to the rebels, Seymour's anti-enclosure policy had temporarily been reversed and the Statute of Merton re-enacted.[59] Latimer derides these changes, and seizes especially on the statutory provision that in any enclosure 'sufficient' land should be left for the tenants. 'But who shoulde be the judge to limite what was sufficient for them? Or who shall now judge what is sufficient?' (fol. 108^a–b). The rhetorical questions appeal to an assumed identity between the process of enclosure and the sin of covetousness; the only way for the tenants to obtain 'sufficient' land is within the traditional structure.

Latimer compounds this argument with one of his famous descriptions of rural life, focusing on the interests of the humble tenants and labourers:

> Let them therefore have sufficient to maintayne them, and to finde them their necessaries. A plow land must have sheepe, yea, they most [sic] have sheepe to dunge their grounde for bearing of corne (for if they have no sheepe to helpe to fat the grounde they shal have but bare corne and thinne.) They must have swine for their foode to make their veneries or bacon of . . . They must have other catteles, as horses to draw their plough

---

[58] Conventionally, the 'unnatural' aspirations of such men are reflected in their unnatural size. Crowley constructs an entire narrative poem around this conceit (*The Fable of Philargyrie The Great Gigant* (1551); facsimile edn (London, 1931)).

[59] Whitney R. D. Jones, *The Tudor Commonwealth 1529–1559* (London, 1970), p. 40.

and for cariage of things to the markets, and kine for their milke and chese, which they must live upon and pay their rentes. These cattell must have pasture, which pasture if they lacke, the rest must needes faile them. And pasture they cannot have if the land be taken in and enclosed from them.

(fol. 108ᵇ)

The passage appeals to the authority of the common-field system.[60] The notion that the manorial estate can be subdivided into 'sufficient' portions is thus challenged by the countryman's appreciation of the multiple and interrelated uses made of the same land in a system which treats it as a communal resource. From this position Latimer perceives even a regulated introduction of enclosure as a threat to traditional ideals of manorial and national identity. Only the common-field system will ensure that the tenant farmer will achieve true self-sufficiency, that the manor will remain a site of stable community, and that the common-wealth will retain the common directions assumed by the figure of the body politic.

Despite his detailed appreciation of the common-field system, Latimer's sermon is nonetheless typical of its age in its representation of a moral economy corrupted by the forces of covetousness. For agrarian complaint relies on stark images of oppression committed by manorial lords. It represents economic power in simple binary terms, and thus places all hopes for reform in the hands of the landed. In this respect complaint clearly offered an inadequate model for a critique of an emergent market society, in which power was more fluid and dispersed than the gospellers could ever admit. (This was one of Sir Thomas Smith's insights about the limitations of complaint, as will be seen below.) Moreover, the complaint structure, which sets poor ploughman against powerful landlord, frequently works against the interests of analysing the complex and uncertain effects of agrarian change upon the lower orders. Indeed the complaints regularly ignore the significant socio-economic differentiations across the broad spectrum of tenant farmers, cottagers, labourers and servants in husbandry, who operated within a variety of tenurial structures throughout the country. In effect they tend to collapse all the particular – and potentially conflicting – interests of these groups into a concentration on the landlord–tenant relationship. Even the ploughman, in texts of the middle of the sixteenth century, frequently serves as a figure of a small tenant farmer, rather than

---

[60] See Joan Thirsk, 'The Common Fields', in *The Rural Economy of England: Collected Essays* (London, 1984), pp. 35–6.

a worker of lower socio-economic status. In contemporary terms these tenant farmers would be known for legal and administrative purposes as 'husbandmen' or lesser 'yeomen', whereas by the sixteenth century 'ploughmen' appear only rarely in estate records as specialist labourers.[61] Consequently the discourse of complaint offers little of direct relevance for the interests of a large proportion of those it ostensibly claims to support. At a time when social and economic turmoil was producing an unprecedented number of 'masterless' and placeless people in the countryside, the complaints only rarely formulate policies which grapple with the manifold realities of rural change.[62]

These limitations are apparent in Crowley's reworking of the literary tradition of estates satire, in *The Voyce of the laste trumpet . . . callynge al the estates of menne to the right path of theyr vocation*.[63] As the title suggests, the text conflates a medieval doctrine of estates with the nascent Protestant concept of a 'vocation' or 'calling'. Later in the century, Puritan theologians would insist that a person's vocation is determined by an individual contract with God.[64] Crowley's text, however, consists of twelve verse 'lessons', all but one directed toward a static and pre-ordained socio-economic or occupational group. (The exception is the closing 'Womans Lesson', which briefly shifts attention to gender relations. In accordance with the patriarchal assumptions of moral economics, Crowley denies women economic agency, and places them firmly behind figures of masculine authority.) The vision of social harmony presented within the poem clearly depends upon the figure of the gentleman, to whom Crowley teaches the virtues of knowledge, justice, moderation and charity (sigs. C6ª–C8ᵇ). Beneath the gentleman, in the countryside, he has lessons for the yeoman and the servant, each of whom is fixed in place by his relationship with his lord. The definition of

---

61 I owe this specific observation to Keith Wrightson, drawn from his extensive and continuing work on descriptions of the social order in early modern England. (See, for example, 'The Social Order of Early Modern England: Three Approaches', in *The World We Have Gained: Histories of Population and Social Structure*, ed. Lloyd Bonfield, Richard M. Smith and Keith Wrightson (Oxford, 1986), pp. 177–202.) A more symbolic use of the plough for self-definition is noted by David Cressy, who finds records of husbandmen or labourers unable to sign their names drawing instead crude images of a plough (*Literacy and the Social Order: Reading and Writing in Tudor and Stuart England* (Cambridge, 1980), p. 59).
62 See A. L. Beier, *Masterless Men: The Vagrancy Problem in England 1560–1640* (London, 1985).
63 Two edns (1549, 1550); references are to the second edition.
64 See also below, pp. 68–9.

the yeoman as 'Thou that arte borne the ground to tyll' insists upon
his labour rather than his status (sig. A5ᵇ); however, it perhaps suits
Crowley's purposes to focus on a category generally recognized for a
certain level of stability and independence, and consequently to ignore
the 'husbandman', who was more likely to be affected by economic
pressures.[65] Crowley teaches the yeoman to be satisfied 'within the
bondes of thy degre', by at once acting as a godly 'stuarde' in regard to
the poor and behaving with suitable obedience toward his landlord
(sigs. A5ᵇ–B1ᵇ). He is warned, in closing, that any attempt to 'change thy
vocation' will result in 'thy soules damnation' (sig. B1ᵇ).

The servant's calling is also defined by reference to his master, whom
he must serve 'as faythfully, / As he were thy Lord, and thy God' (sig.
A4ᵃ). Again, the lesson insists upon a strictly hierarchical social order,
ultimately dependent upon the directions of the godly steward. But while
the lessons for yeoman and servant are principally notable for their
bold simplicity, the arresting shortcomings of the doctrine of passive
obedience are most clearly manifest in Crowley's glance beyond the
manor in 'The Beggers lesson'. This begins:

> If God have laied hys hande on the,
> And made the low in al mens sighte:
> Content thy selfe with that degre,
> And se thou walke therin upright.   (sig. A2ᵃ)

The 'lesson' assumes poverty as a divinely ordained state, with which the
beggar must be content. In a manner characteristic of much of the
gospellers' social doctrine, Crowley's hopes for reform are principally
based on the medieval ideal of charity.[66] While the authors of complaint
tracts consistently cry out against the 'covetousness' which they believe
causes massive social displacement and poverty in the countryside, their
doctrine of Christian quietism can offer little practical advice for the
lower orders.

> Yea though thou shouldest perishe for fode,
> Yet beare thy crosse patiently:

---

65 As Peter Laslett writes, 'All yeomen were husbandmen, because they worked the land,
but not all husbandmen were yeomen by any means, because most of them had neither
the qualifications nor the status' (*The World We Have Lost: Further Explored* (London,
1983), p. 44).
66 See, for example, Elton's comments on the preacher Thomas Lever, in 'Reform and the
"Commonwealth Men"', p. 31.

> For the ende shall turne to thy good,
> Though thou lye in the streates & dye.   (sig. A3ᵃ)

Crowley's ultimate recourse is to the moral standards and strict judgements of God. The beggar's reward will come – like the punishment of the 'rent raiser' in the *Epigrammes* – when he moves beyond the trials of his earthly vocation. 'Doubtles at thy last endynge', Crowley concludes, 'Thou shalt be crowned at Gods hand' (sig. A3ᵇ).[67]

Given their consistent emphasis on social control and Christian quietism, the rebellions of 1549 (and particularly Kett's uprising in Norfolk, which was specifically focused on socio-economic issues) understandably shocked the gospellers. Kett's rebellion, as Diarmaid MacCulloch has shown, was hardly a rising of the dispossessed, nor did it present a threat to the central government of the magnitude feared by many at the time.[68] Yet perhaps the most troubling aspect about the events of 1549, for those who had propelled a discourse of complaint, was the language the rebels threw back at the government. The list of grievances in Norfolk was presented to the king as 'the compleynt of your pore comons', and depicts landowners acting 'to ther gret advaunchment & to the undoyng of your pore subjectes'.[69] Framed in the terms of a Chancery 'complaint', and drawing also upon the rhetorical strategies adopted from the contemporary pulpit, the document highlights the malleable nature of the gospellers' discourse. Whereas complaint is a mode grounded upon an assumption of powerlessness and humility, the massed force of the Norfolk complainants gave their document a menacing edge, which lent some credence to the fears of Sir Anthony Auchar about the policies of the 'men called common welthes'.

The rebels' approach also directs attention to the government's curious degree of complicitness with the language of complaint. For,

---

67 The frequently arresting gulf between reformist rhetoric and repressive social policy at this time is perhaps best illustrated by the short-lived statutory imposition of slavery as a punishment for the refusal to work. See C. S. L. Davies, 'Slavery and Protector Somerset; the Vagrancy Act of 1547', *Economic History Review*, 2nd series, 19 (1966), pp. 533–49.

68 'Kett's Rebellion in Context', *Past and Present*, 84 (1979), pp. 36–59. MacCulloch notes, in particular, that Sir Thomas Smith was 'beside himself with worry' at the height of the rebellion (p. 44), a reaction which helps to contextualize Smith's treatment of socio-economic complaint in his *Discourse of the Commonweal*, to be considered below.

69 BL Harleian MS 304, fol. 78; printed in F. W. Russell, *Kett's Rebellion in Norfolk* (London, 1859), pp. 48–56.

whatever the actual political influence of individuals such as Latimer and Crowley within Seymour's regime, their distinctive representations of agrarian conditions were a pervasive presence within government rhetoric in the years immediately preceding the revolts. In particular, this interaction between complaint and policy can be traced through the establishment of the enclosure commission of 1548–9. The proclamation which heralded the commission refers to the influence of 'divers supplications and pitiful complaints of his majesty's poor subjects', and vigorously argues that the poor must be protected from 'the insatiable covetousness' of enclosers.[70] It claims:

> all that land which heretofore was tilled and occupied with so many men, and did bring forth not only divers families in work and labor, but also capons, hens, chickens, pigs, and other such furniture of the markets, is now gotten, by insatiable greediness of mind, into one or two men's hands and scarcely dwelled upon with one poor shepherd, so that the realm thereby is brought to a marvelous desolation . . . and Christian people, by the greedy covetousness of some men, eaten up and devoured of brute beasts and driven from their houses by sheep and bullocks.

The government's acceptance of the charges of 'insatiable covetousness' accords significant power to the 'complaints' of the 'poor subjects'. The document raises the language of complaint to a status of cultural authority, as it endorses the identification of 'insatiable greediness', through which 'Christian people [are] eaten up and devoured of brute beasts'.

After the collapse of the commission, John Hales, one of its principal protagonists, defended its operations by arguing the corrosive nature of self-interest in the commonwealth.

> It maye not be liefull for every man to use his owne as hym lysteth, but everye man must use that he hathe to the most benefyte of his Countreie. Ther must be some thynge devysed to quenche this insatiable thurst of gredynes of men, Covetousnes must be weded out by the rootes, for it is the distruccion of all good thinges.[71]

Hales focuses on a man's rights over 'his owne'. Indeed his assertion of the overriding interest of 'the most benefyte of [one's] Countreie' has

70 *Tudor Royal Proclamations*, ed. Paul L. Hughes and James F. Larkin (3 vols., New Haven and London, 1964–9), vol. 1, pp. 427–8.
71 'The Defence of John Hales agenst certeyn sclaundres and false reportes made of hym', printed in *A Discourse of the Common Weal of England*, ed. Elizabeth Lamond (Cambridge, 1893), pp. lxiii–lxiv.

been used by more than one historian to summarize the 'common program or theory' which united the 'commonwealths men'.[72] Further, his definition of socio-economic order is grounded within the language of complaint, with its stress on covetousness expressed in conventionally emotive terms. By a strategy similar to that of the enclosure proclamation, Hales expresses a significant political agenda through the tone and perspective of complaint.

Such defences of the gospellers' vision for the commonwealth, however, had little impact within the atmosphere of conservative reaction that prevailed in the wake of the rebellions. Seymour was deposed; and, while the leading preachers and pamphleteers remained active, their subsequent works evidence a distinct anxiety in the face of political change. In terms of the Tudor state's future relation to strategies of complaint, perhaps the most significant text from these later Edwardian years is Sir John Cheke's response to the 1549 rebels, *The hurt of sedicion howe grevous it is to a Commune welth*.[73] Cheke's decision to adopt the term 'commonwealth' underlines its undeniable contemporary currency. Yet his careful attention to the definition of the term throughout his treatise indicates a determined attempt to erase its radical potential. Thus a nation without gentlemen (a goal which he ascribes to Kett) would be 'a mervelous tanned common welth' (sig. A6b); addressing himself to the rebels, he declares, 'If ritches offend you, bycause ye would have the lyke, then thyncke that to be no commen welth, but envie to the commen welth' (sig. A8a). Throughout, he constructs a discourse of socio-political exclusion which stands in direct contrast to Crowley's attempt – albeit impractical – to incorporate even the beggar into the body politic. To Cheke, the rebels are 'nastye vagabundes', 'idell loyterers', 'robbers', 'ungodly rablementes', and 'loitring beggers' (sigs. B4b, B8a, D3b, E4a). With deceptive ease Cheke underlines the threat to property and order by depicting the rebels in terms of their supposed lowly socio-economic degree. In the rhetoric of authoritarian backlash, the powerless 'poorest plowman' of the complaint tracts translates into the threatening 'nasty vagabond' of popular revolt.

Although the mid-Tudor discourse of agrarian complaint was fundamentally conservative, it is apparent that it was never quite

---

[72] Chester, *Hugh Latimer*, p. 172; see also A. F. Pollard, *England under Protector Somerset* (London, 1900), p. 216.
[73] Four edns (1549–76); references are to the first edition.

dissociated from traces of communism and rebellion. Cheke's challenge thus presages a gathering reaction within government and Church alike. His imperious reply to the rebels' populism, moreover, throws further light upon the construction of a discourse of Protestant nationhood out of the turmoil of the mid-Tudor period. Richard Helgerson, in his recent study of Elizabethan forms of national identity, delineates an apocalyptic discourse of 'social levelling' in John Foxe's *Actes and Monumentes*, and links this to the formative years of the man and his Church in mid-Tudor England.[74] During the reign of Elizabeth, however, Helgerson claims that Foxe's version of nationhood was gradually overwhelmed by a conservative discourse of Christian apology. Like Foxe's book, the Edwardian discourse of complaint was widely influential throughout the following century, but never regained the central and authoritative place that it claimed in the mid-Tudor years. Rather, its later significance is principally that of an established, but no longer indisputable, orthodoxy: a once vital vision for the fields of the nation which was steadily refashioned or rejected. The following chapters will trace these revisionary processes in detail. The impetus toward a reassessment of the complaint tradition, however, is also apparent in the reign of Edward; an examination in the present context of the contemporary *Discourse of the Commonweal* will reveal a remarkably prescient critique of the Edwardian milieu of the Protestant gospellers.

THE LIMITATIONS OF COMPLAINT: SIR THOMAS SMITH'S *DISCOURSE OF THE COMMONWEAL*

Sir Thomas Smith, who served as secretary to Seymour, wrote his *Discourse of the Commonweal of This Realm of England* at the height of the cultural movement with which this chapter has been concerned.[75] Smith's preface gestures toward this context, as he states his desire to consider 'the manifold complaints of men touching the decay of this Commonweal that we be in' (p. 11). Yet Smith was clearly never comfortable with the political climate of the early Edwardian years. In 1550, for example, he remarked that Seymour 'had surrounded

---

[74] *Forms of Nationhood*, ch. 6.

[75] I will follow Mary Dewar's attribution of the *Discourse* to Smith (and also her argument that it was written in 1549), although the identity of the author does not materially affect my arguments. References are to Dewar's edition of the text (Charlottesville, 1969).

himself with "hotlings" who "devise commonwealths as they list".[76] Consequently, the *Discourse* adopts a significantly distanced and critical stance toward the 'manifold complaints' of the time. In contrast to the morally weighted diatribes of the preachers and pamphleteers, Smith uses a dialogue structure in order to consider a variety of views on the contemporary social and economic problems. He declares his intention to include 'such persons as were members of every estate that find themselves grieved nowadays' (p. 13), and presents a series of discussions between a Knight, Merchant, Husbandman, Capper and Doctor. He also shuns the public distribution assumed by the complaint texts, and implies instead a tightly controlled relationship of counsel, as he writes to the anonymous recipient of his manuscript that 'this is between us two to be weighed only and considered and not to be published abroad' (pp. 12–13).[77] Within this framework Smith develops a thorough analysis of the nation's social and economic problems; and in the process the *Discourse* presents a valuable reflection and commentary upon the discourse of agrarian complaint. It at once highlights and criticizes the conventions of complaint, while working toward a newly rationalistic form of analysis.

In the first of three dialogues, after the Knight, Merchant, Husbandman and Capper have each introduced their principal grievances, Smith focuses on the last of the five speakers: the Doctor. He writes, 'Then, the Doctor, that had leant on his elbow all this while musing, sat up and said, I perceive by you all there is none of you but have just cause of complaint' (p. 22). Smith aims to establish the Doctor as the voice of analytical authority, distinguished by his learning and individual integrity. As he sits 'musing' over the complaints of the other speakers, he is introduced as a critical observer, capable of recognizing the problems facing each 'estate', yet also able to read through their rhetoric in an overriding attempt to analyse the operation of the economy. Concurrently, in contrast to texts associated with the Piers Plowman tradition, Smith carefully restrains the authority of the agrarian worker. Indeed, Smith's farmer is not a ploughman, but a 'Husbandman':

[76] BL Harleian MS 6989, f. 146; quoted in M. L. Bush, *The Government Policy of Protector Somerset* (London, 1975), p. 67.
[77] The *Discourse* was not published until 1581, four years after Smith's death. A similar strategy of counsel was adopted by the anonymous author of 'Policies to reduce this realme of Englande unto a prosperus wealthe and estate', prepared in manuscript form and addressed to Seymour; printed in *Tudor Economic Documents*, ed. R. H. Tawney and Eileen Power (3 vols., London, 1924), vol. 3, pp. 311–45.

a socio-economic category regularly used to describe smallholders of lower than yeoman status. Moreover, while the ploughman is conventionally depicted as being at the mercy of the 'possessioners', Smith emphasizes the small farmer's independence and responsibility for decisions affecting his land, to the extent that he has the Doctor refer the Husbandman to husbandry manuals, and recommends study in geometry 'for true measuring of lands' (pp. 28–9).[78] Such an approach effectively replaces the complaint tradition's binary conception of economic power, with an assumption of autonomy which anticipates the competitive environment of possessive individualism. Whereas the ploughman of the complaint tradition is fixed within the corporate identity of both manor and nation, Smith's Husbandman is urged to forge his own path, unperturbed by the actions of his landlord.

The dialogues are set on an evening after a hearing of the enclosure commission. But while Smith is acutely aware of the potential dangers of enclosure, he wants to consider the phenomenon as a symptom of change, rather than the evil denounced by the gospellers. Therefore the Husbandman's 'complaint of enclosures' (as the passage is introduced by a subheading in the manuscript) is short and conventional; it is an argument to be considered, then subsumed beneath the text's economic analysis. He says,

> Marry, for these enclosures do undo us all; for they make us to pay dearer for our land that we occupy and causes that we can have no land in manner for our money to put in tillage. All is taken up for pasture, either for sheep or for grazing of cattle. So that I have known of late a dozen plows within less compass than six miles about me laid down within these seven years; and where forty persons had their livings, now one man and his shepherd has all. (p. 17)

The entire statement is carefully constructed according to the conventions of contemporary agrarian complaint. Even the empirical evidence of displacement is infused with a polemical purpose, as the plough becomes a morally weighted index of tillage, and the activity of the 'one man and his shepherd' is represented as wasting the very 'livings' of forty. Smith clearly has much sympathy with this position; however, it is his purpose in the *Discourse* to demonstrate its inadequacy. As Ferguson

---

[78] On the significance of contemporary husbandry manuals, see below, chapter 5; on geometry and land measurement, see pp. 180–9.

writes, Smith uses his speakers to illustrate how 'investigation in such circumstances tends to take the way of least resistance'.[79]

Smith's dialogue structure thus emphasizes the impersonal and dynamic operations of a market economy. The juxtaposed complaints of the landlord, craftsman and merchant simply belie the Husbandman's attempts to explain his own problems as the result of covetousness and oppression. In contrast to the conventional image of the body politic, Smith develops an analogy which more suitably represents this newly rationalistic conception of economic process. 'To make this more plain unto you', the Doctor says, 'as in a clock there be many wheels yet the first wheel being stirred it drives the next, and that the third, and so forth until the last that moves the instrument that strikes the clock' (p. 96).[80] The most important 'wheel', or motivating force, that Smith admits into this model is self-interest. When he is pressed to name the 'necessary and efficient cause' of the problems facing all the speakers, the Doctor says:

> To tell you plainly, it is avarice that I take for the principal cause thereof. But can we devise that all covetousness may be taken from men? No, no more than we can make men to be without ire, without gladness, without fear, and without all affections . . . For every man, as Plato says, is naturally covetous of lucre and that wherein they see most lucre they will most gladly exercise. (p. 118)

Smith's use of Plato undoubtedly distorts the political philosophy of the *Republic* which, it might be said, deplores self-interest as much as the Book of Isaiah.[81] Nevertheless, his objective acceptance of covetousness effectively undermines the very rationale of contemporary complaint tracts. While the gospellers see covetousness as a sin, Smith is prepared to accept it as a fundamentally 'natural' motivation.

This premise leads to a reworking of the classic doctrine of the complaints regarding property:

> KNIGHT. Who can let [i.e. prevent] men to make their most advantage of that which is their own?
> DOCTOR. Yes, marry; men may not abuse their own things to the damage of the Commonweal. (p. 53)

John Hales stated that 'every man must use that he hathe to the most benefyte of his Countreie'; Smith's position is rather that the pursuit of

[79] Ferguson, *Articulate Citizen*, p. 291.
[80] See also Ferguson, *Articulate Citizen*, p. 293.
[81] I am grateful to Brendan Bradshaw for this observation.

personal gain is both acceptable and potentially beneficial to the nation, and must only be restrained when the interests of the 'commonweal' are threatened. The terminology of 'covetousness' is examined and rejected, as Smith works toward a more empirical appreciation of economic individualism. In this respect he anticipates a language of economic 'interest', which would underpin the movement toward capitalism of England's emergent market society.[82] In an agrarian context, Smith's radically new representation of economic practice prompts a rejection of many of the basic tenets of the complaints. In particular, Smith supports a controlled process of enclosure by agreement: 'For if land were severally enclosed to the intent to continue husbandry thereon and every man that had right to common had for his portion a piece of the same to himself enclosed, I think no harm but rather good should come thereof' (p. 50). The maintenance of tillage, meanwhile, must be upheld through an adroit manipulation of the desire for 'lucre', to be achieved through a system of taxes and controls over international trade.

With the infusion of self-interest, Smith's vision of the agrarian economy also becomes unusually dynamic. While he continues to endorse 'plenty of corn' as the primary index of national prosperity (p. 61), he is also prepared to accept regional specialization and strategies of production oriented toward the market. Considering the growth in France of labour-intensive crops such as 'vines, olives, [and] fruits', the Doctor pronounces his wish that 'as much ground as be here apt for those things would be turned, as much as may be, to such uses as may find most persons' (p. 91). Such arguments mark a distinct break from the ideal of the self-sufficient manorial estate, and move the text toward an appreciation of an expanding market economy. Indeed the *Discourse* has been described as, 'in part at least, a programme for the setting-up of new industries and introducing new crops'.[83] Significantly, as this vision emerges out of the statements of complaint in the first dialogue, it is the rational voice of the Doctor that dominates the *Discourse*. In the third dialogue, of 'remedies for the said griefs', the Husbandman makes no contribution whatsoever.

Smith's text demonstrates both the cultural significance of complaint and

---

82 See Albert O. Hirschman, *The Passions and the Interests: Political Arguments for Capitalism Before Its Triumph* (Princeton, 1977), part 1.

83 Joan Thirsk, *Economic Policy and Projects: The Development of a Consumer Society in Early Modern England* (Oxford, 1978), p. 24. On agrarian 'projects', see also below pp. 151–6.

its equally significant practical limitations. The statements of complaint in the *Discourse* highlight the extent to which certain conventions in the representation of the economy and social order had consolidated through a stream of statements from press and pulpit during the preceding years. Simultaneously, Smith's containment of the complaints and deft movement toward a new form of economic analysis prefigures the gradual collapse of this discourse as a cultural force, a process which will be the central concern of the following chapters. Smith's tentative endorsement of economic individualism in the countryside, moreover, introduces distinctive ideals and perspectives which would propel and shape the images of agrarian order presented in writing on husbandry and surveying. As he draws together the representations of complaint and moves beyond these statements toward a conception of economic process grounded on an acceptance of self-interest, Smith places his *Discourse* at the very centre of the ideological confrontation which would shape rival representations of agrarian England well into the seventeenth century.

2. Moral economics and the Tudor–Stuart Church

'My Lord I am endited by a wrong name, my name . . . is Thrift, and not
Covetousnesse'
(Richard Bernard, *The Isle of Man: or, The Legall Proceeding in
Man-Shire against Sinne*, 1626)

The death of Edward VI and the accession of the Catholic Queen Mary
in 1553 fractured the mid-Tudor cultural milieu, in which Protestant
reform had been combined with vigorous attempts (in the words of Sir
Thomas Smith) to 'devise commonwealths'.[1] That a similar context was
not established after the Elizabethan Settlement of 1559, in fact, was
partly due to the government influence of men such as Smith. In accord
with the tone and argument of his *Discourse of the Commonweal*, the
Elizabethan state consistently distanced itself from moral complaint, in
favour of an increasingly empirical and rationalistic approach to social
and economic problems.[2] This shift was reinforced by a marked absence,
for the first three decades of Elizabeth's rule, of any rural crises
comparable to those of the 1540s. From London at least, the countryside
appeared stable and prosperous; in 1585 Lord Burghley expressed to
parliament a deep satisfaction that England had enjoyed peace, and

---

[1] On Smith, see above, pp. 52–7.
[2] Smith's *De Republica Anglorum*, written in 1565 and published in 1583, further reflects
this change in political culture. In this text Smith outlines and analyses English
processes of government and administration, the social and economic orders and the
operation of the legal system. At the end of the book he contrasts his approach to that
of several other works, including *Utopia*, stating that while they define 'feigned
common wealths such as never was nor never shall be, vaine imaginations, phantasies
of Philosophers to occupie the time and to exercise their wittes', he has described
England as it 'standeth and is governed at this day the xxviii of March *Anno* 1565'
(p. 118).

plenty of corn, for twenty-seven years.[3] Hindsight reveals that the appearance of stability actually masked fundamental processes of long-term change. The population was growing rapidly (from around three million in 1559 to just over four million in 1603); inflation was a constant problem, with varying local effects but most frequently placing new burdens on the lower orders; hunger for land fuelled an expansion of agriculture into the forests, wastes and moors; the property market remained active, still affected by the sale of former church lands; and localized revolts over enclosure and other processes of agrarian change continued apace.[4] But apart from fairly constant anxiety about the poor, the view from London appeared to support an approach to socio-economic discourse which eschewed the apocalyptic fervour of the 'commonwealths men'.[5]

Within this context the sense of a common goal linking poets and preachers faded. Hence an examination of transformations of agrarian complaint, and associated revisions of mid-Tudor moral economics, may be approached most valuably in two parallel chapters, devoted respectively to texts operating primarily within a religious context, and others informed by Renaissance literary values. Any consideration of the development of religious writing must admit from the outset the vast range of material and issues involved. The hundred years following the accession of Elizabeth were marked by intense theological debate, which reshaped the structure and outlook of the early Protestant Church. The consolidation of state Protestantism in the wake of the Elizabethan Settlement also led to major shifts in the social and economic status of the Church throughout the country. The Church as an institution – with its growing network of clergymen, its administrative and financial structures and its ecclesiastical courts to control a range of religious and social activity – developed in ways which the early reformers could hardly have foreseen. Indeed the changing status of the state Church

---

[3] Joyce Youings, *Sixteenth-Century England* (London, 1984), p. 148.
[4] E. A. Wrigley and R. S. Schofield, *The Population History of England 1541–1871: A Reconstruction* (London, 1981), pp. 208–9; C. G. A. Clay, *Economic Expansion and Social Change: England 1500–1700* (2 vols., Cambridge, 1984), vol. 1, pp. 40–2, 49–51; Joan Thirsk, 'The Farming Regions of England', *AHEW IV*, p. 2; Youings, *Sixteenth-Century England*, ch. 7 ('The Land Market'); Roger Manning, *Village Revolts: Social Protest and Popular Disturbances in England, 1509–1640* (Oxford, 1988), ch. 3.
[5] On the poor, see A. L. Beier, *The Problem of the Poor in Tudor and Early Stuart England* (London and New York, 1983); Clay, *Economic Expansion and Social Change*, vol. 1, ch. 7; and Youings, *Sixteenth-Century England*, ch. 11.

underpinned a 'profound cultural change' in the religion of Protestants.[6]
The sense of revolutionary upheaval that propelled the early stages of
the Reformation gradually gave way to a widespread appreciation of the
Protestant Church as an orthodox and widely powerful institution.
Despite this complexity, a focus on the treatment of agrarian issues
within religious texts (including sermons and a range of moral and
theological manuals and treatises) will reveal certain significant trends in
the representation of rural society and economic practice. Most striking
initially is the rarity with which the attitude of complaint is adopted in
relation to social and economic issues. Furthermore, this rhetorical shift
is accompanied by a marked change of emphasis. The gospellers'
diatribe against the preeminent social sin of covetousness gives way to a
focus on the conscience and motivations of the godly man, while the
Edwardian tendency to idealize the poor and dispossessed is
overwhelmed by a gathering attack on the morality of those on the
margins of parish life. Indeed, it is ultimately the industrious husbandman
or yeoman who is drawn to the moral centre of Protestant representations
of rural life, his productivity claimed as tangible evidence of moral
rectitude. In the broader context of agrarian representation to be traced
in later chapters, this transformation of complaint assumes a crucial
significance, as it at once parallels and facilitates widespread movements
toward the endorsement of individual and national 'improvement' within
a dynamic market society.

These are broad patterns traced in the uncertain sands of late Tudor
and early Stuart religious writing. I hope here to substantiate these
arguments, yet also to convey a sense of the diversity, debate and discord
apparent in representations of agrarian England produced by members of
the clergy. In the interests of coherence and clarity, the chapter will be
structured into two parts, concerned respectively with the reigns of
Elizabeth and the early Stuart kings. The bulk of the chapter will be
devoted to the Elizabethan period because it is in these years that the
discursive conventions fostered by the mid-Tudor Protestants can be
seen gradually to give way to significantly new visions of the land and
new versions of moral economics. Following from this, the final section
will concentrate on the consolidation and refinement of the emergent
vision, within a context of impending economic, religious and political
crisis.

---

[6] Patrick Collinson, *The Religion of Protestants: The Church in English Society
1559–1625* (Oxford, 1982), p. 238.

PLOUGHMEN, PREACHERS AND PURITANS IN THE REIGN
OF ELIZABETH I

Given the significance of the mid-Tudor years in this study, it will
be useful to consider initially the transmission of relevant authors, texts
and ideas into the reign of Elizabeth. Indeed, the changing face of
radical Protestantism is immediately apparent in the unfolding careers
of the surviving mid-Tudor gospellers. For example the prolific
publisher and pamphleteer Robert Crowley, after spending most of
Mary's reign in exile, resumed an active public role on issues of religious
and social policy; however, his attitudes and interests were substantially
reformulated within the new environment of the Elizabethan Church.[7] In
one of his few extant texts from this period, the 'Gylde halle Sermon' of
1574, Crowley revises his earlier position.[8] Considering the relationship
between covetousness and wealth, he states that, 'The common sort of
men have none other note to know a covetous man by, but rytches ... But
ritches is not a note to know a covetous man by. Ritches is the gyft of God
. . . God geveth ritches to whom he lusteth.'[9] The statement subtly
distances Crowley from both his regular Edwardian identification with
the 'common sort of men', and his consistent emphasis on the social
duties of the rich. Instead he adopts a more judicious voice, as he presents
an implicit justification for the accumulation of wealth. But while
Crowley appears not to have maintained his rage in relation to social
issues, his activities in the vestiarian debate which wracked the mid-
Elizabethan Church assumed similar characteristics to his Edwardian
agitation. In particular the anti-vestiarian faction, which in many respects
presaged the emergent Puritan challenge to the religious establishment,
seized from the outset upon the polemical use of printed pamphlets. In
contrast to the coherent social vision of the works of the middle of the
century, however, the vestiarian debate focused the Protestants' attention
inward, on the very definition of their Church. Therefore, despite the

---

[7] See J. W. Martin's essay on 'Robert Crowley in Two Protestant Churches', in *Religious
Radicals in Tudor England* (London, 1989), pp. 147–69.
[8] Crowley gained regular access to the pulpit after being preferred early in the reign
of Elizabeth to the London living of St Giles Cripplegate. He was ordained by Bishop
Ridley in September 1551, but apparently received no ecclesiastical preferment under
Edward VI (Martin, *Religious Radicals*, p. 159; Martin, 'The Publishing Career of
Robert Crowley: A Sidelight on the Tudor Book Trade', *Publishing History*, 14 (1983),
p. 86).
[9] *A Sermon made in the Chappel at the Gylde halle in London, the .xxix. day of
September, 1574* (1575), sig. C4b.

continuities in Crowley's radicalism, his interests and perspectives shifted decisively away from those which had propelled the preaching and publishing of the reign of Edward VI.[10]

Evidence from publishing history reinforces an impression of substantial changes in attitudes toward the expression of social grievances. The Marian regime had an immediate impact on the publishing trade, as it rigorously suppressed the sale of Protestant material. The *Prymmer or boke of private prayer* (which contained the forceful prayer 'For Landlordes', quoted in chapter 1) made a mischievous Protestant irruption into the reign when it was published in the same form, but with the prayers for Edward simply rewritten for the new queen.[11] The remainder of the text – like almost all of the works considered in chapter 1 – could hardly have been acceptable to the Marian regime, and its next appearance was delayed until 1560.[12] Moreover, this vacuum of social and economic criticism was not filled to any extent by Catholic writers. It appears that, by 1553, the textual strategies of complaint were bound, in the popular imagination, to the movement of Protestant reform.[13] And whilst a Protestant presence was maintained throughout the Marian years by texts printed on the Continent and smuggled into England, these publications invariably focus on religious issues.[14] The associated socio-economic agenda of the Edwardian years, by comparison, slips from prominence.[15]

Although the accession of Elizabeth reasserted a firm Protestant control over the publishing trade, there was no significant attempt to revive the mid-Tudor tradition of complaint. Indeed the catalogue of Edwardian works reprinted during the reign suggests an intention to establish a Protestant history and literary heritage, in which the socio-economic conditions and controversies of Edward's reign play

---

[10] Martin draws an interesting parallel with the changing interests of Thomas Lever (*Religious Radicals*, p. 169).

[11] (1553; STC 20374); see above, pp. 39–40.

[12] (STC 20375).

[13] On the Marian regime's failure to exploit the power of print, see Martin, *Religious Radicals*, ch. 6. See also his discussion of Miles Hogarde, one Catholic author who does engage in social complaint (ch. 5).

[14] David Loades claims that 'some seventy works of a polemical or pastoral nature' were printed abroad and smuggled into England in the five years of Mary's reign (*Politics, Censorship and the English Reformation* (London and New York, 1991), p. 132).

[15] See, for example, Bartholomew Traheron's *A Warning to England to Repente* (1558), probably printed in Wesel. Despite occasional references to covetousness, and similarities to the Edwardians' tone and presentation, Traheron concentrates his attention almost entirely on anti-Catholic polemic.

only a peripheral part.[16] Hence emphasis is placed on poetry and sermons, rather than prose pamphlets.[17] For example, Crowley's only Edwardian publication to be reissued under Elizabeth was his *Epigrammes*, in 1573.[18] More than any of his other texts, the *Epigrammes* offer Crowley's social morality in pithy, aphoristic statements, while the poetic form and satiric mode lay some claim to an enduring literary relevance. William Langland's *Vision of Piers Plowman*, which Crowley as editor had attempted to apply to the circumstances of 1550, also reappears in an edition by Owen Rogers in 1561.[19] Although he retains Crowley's summaries of the text, Rogers attempts to shake off some of his predecessor's didacticism, as he omits most of the marginal notes which had guided the Edwardian reader through the text. But even in this form the poem did not find a wide audience; after it had run through three separate editions in 1550, Rogers's was the last until the nineteenth century.[20]

Furthermore, the republication of sermons and religious tracts was frequently marked by changes in their printed form, which subtly reinforce a sense of temporal and cultural distance separating the reader from the context of their original delivery. Most importantly, the works of several preachers were gathered together for publication in collected editions. For example, Thomas Becon's *Jewell of Joy* (which contained the enclosure complaint quoted at length in chapter 1),[21] which was first issued as a black-letter octavo pamphlet in 1550?, reappears in the ambitious three-volume folio edition of his *Worckes* published by John Day in 1564. This publication, with its multiple dedications and prefaces, full-page illustration of the author and an incongruous title-page

---

16 The arguments presented here are offered as a modification of John N. King's claims for the significance of a 'Reformation tradition' in the latter half of the sixteenth century (*English Reformation Literature: The Tudor Origins of the Protestant Tradition* (Princeton, 1982), pp. 443–56; and see also his specific arguments about Edmund Spenser's debt to the early Protestants, in *Spenser's Poetry and the Reformation Tradition* (Princeton, 1990)).

17 Of the radical prose pamphlets considered in chapter 1, Henry Brinkelow's *Complaynt of Roderyck Mors* was the single significant work to be reprinted in a similar format (1560?).

18 Crowley also published in 1567, for the first time, *The Opening of the Wordes of the Prophet Joell*, an apocalyptic catalogue of abuses written late in the reign of Henry VIII.

19 (STC 19908).

20 John N. King, 'Robert Crowley's Editions of *Piers Plowman*: A Tudor Apocalypse', *Modern Philology*, 73 (1975–6), p. 345.

21 See above, pp. 43–4.

woodcut previously used for William Cunningham's *Cosmographical Glasse*, draws the *Jewell*'s enclosure complaint into a markedly different typographical – and thus cultural – context. The radical pamphlet is incorporated into a handsome collection to adorn the study of the Protestant gentleman.

The collected edition of Latimer's sermons presents a more important case-study, both because of their greater currency under Edward VI and because the publication as *27 sermons* was reprinted at regular intervals throughout the sixty years following its first issue in 1562.[22] All editions appeared in a quarto format, and the revised 1571 edition is representative in its use of eighty-nine sheets of predominantly black-letter type – a size which would have priced the book beyond the means of some of those who bought the 1550 seven-sheet octavo 'Last Sermon before King Edward VI', but still a far more affordable item than the 790-sheet folio edition of Becon. The very presentation in a collected volume, however, transforms the sermons. The chronological ordering, which is standard from 1571, suggests a corpus of works and thought, so that individual statements of complaint are tempered by their textual proximity to the more moderate approach of other sermons. Moreover, martyrdom brought down upon Latimer a pall of posthumous orthodoxy. While his major statements of complaint had been proclaimed from the perspective of a righteous individual (to his enemies, a 'seditious fellow')[23] within a maelstrom of corruption, Augustine Bernher's preface to *27 sermons* attempts to further the preacher's growing reputation as one of the founding fathers of the national Church. The prescriptive energy of his 'Sermon of the Plough' is turned retrospectively upon Latimer himself, as Bernher writes that even under the adversity of the mid-1540s, he 'began to set fourth his plough, & to till the ground of the lord'.[24] Ultimately, these expressions became fixed in a historical context, within a narrative that suppressed the socio-economic turmoil of the Edwardian period beneath a celebration of the triumph of Protestantism. This interpretation is reinforced by a woodcut illustration of Latimer preaching before Edward VI and Edward Seymour, Protector Somerset, while at the foot of the pulpit a woman reads the Bible.[25] The image draws the preacher to the centre of

[22] Seven edns (1562–1607).
[23] 1571 edn, fol. 104[b].
[24] 1562 edn, sig. ¶1[a].
[25] See illustration 1.1.

a coherent reform movement based on the government of the Protestant king and the authority of the vernacular scriptures.[26] Latimer's Protestant ploughman survives in the vocabulary of the Elizabethan pulpit. Edward Bush, for example, cites the arguments of 'Maister Latimar' to support his argument for the extension of a preaching ministry. 'In the cuntry for want of tylling & oft plowing . . . there springeth fourth brambles, bryars and weedes', he declares.[27] Anthony Anderson exploits more fully the agrarian significance of the figure in an attack on 'carnall Gospellers', who 'suck the bloud of their Tenants and inferiors'. 'These men', he writes, 'can and doe fyrst pull downe Tyllage, and . . . drive the poore plowman to feast with pease breade on Christmas daye.'[28] From the outset of the Elizabethan era, however, the ploughman seems to slip from the central symbolic position he occupied in mid-Tudor representations of the Christian commonwealth. Crucially, the preachers no longer align themselves with the suffering of the rural labourer; and consequently the social model of agrarian complaint is redrawn. Even Anderson opens a critical distance from his ploughman in an argument about faith and righteousness. 'Our wants in this profession in these oure dayes', he states, 'bewray from top to toe, in the Courte and thence throwe the Countrie, from the Nobilitie, to the Plowman and his mate' (sig. B3[b]). The objective tone of the criticism exposes the ploughman to moral judgement alongside his landlord. The covetousness of the rich becomes just another symptom of moral decay, rather than the definitive index of corruption it had been to the gospellers.

This change in the rhetorical structure of moral and social criticism can be aligned with a widely consistent shift of focus in preaching, from social justice to social order. The roots of this change perhaps lie in the reaction to the 1549 revolts;[29] however, the consolidation of a national Church under Elizabeth clearly compounded the trend. While the early Reformation seized upon the Bible as a socially and culturally liberating force, it was transformed through time into a symbol 'of order,

---

[26] The printer of Latimer's *sermons*, John Day, also used the woodcut in John Foxe's *Actes and Monumentes*, from the first edition of 1563. (See further John N. King, *Tudor Royal Iconography: Literature and Art in an Age of Religious Crisis* (Princeton, 1989), pp. 95–7.)

[27] *A sermon preached at Paules crosse on Trinity sunday, 1571* (1576), sigs. F2[b]–F3[a].

[28] *The Shield of our Safetie* (1581), sigs. C2[b]–C3[a].

[29] Brendan Bradshaw argued this case in a paper delivered to the Tudor Seminar, University of Cambridge, June 1991.

discretion, age, and dominance in the local community'.[30] While the gospellers' conception of their Church and nation had been informed by a sense of apocalyptic struggle, the later Elizabethan Church was characterized rather by a discourse of orthodox apology.[31] Interestingly, the Martin Marprelate pamphlets invoked texts of the Piers Plowman tradition as authorities for their newly radical voice of reform.[32] This appeal to tradition to bolster a challenge to the Elizabethan establishment, however, merely serves to highlight the distance the Church had moved from its origins in the mid-Tudor Reformation.

Agrarian complaints survive nonetheless, but they must be retrieved from a variety of disparate contexts. The Elizabethan Puritan Philip Stubbes, for example, devotes two pages of his *Anatomie of Abuses* to a conventional attack on covetous landlords, which focuses especially on enclosure. 'For these inclosures be the causes, why rich men, eat up poore men, as beasts doo eat grasse. These I say are the Caterpillers, and devouring locustes that massacre the poore, & eat up the whole realme to the destruction of the same.'[33] Similarly, the extraordinarily successful *A Plaine and familiar Exposition of the Ten Commaundements*, published at the tail-end of the Elizabethan era by John Dod and Robert Cleaver, draws into its framework of religious and moral instruction several attacks on covetousness which include examples from an agrarian context. Under an analysis of the Eighth Commandment they focus on the encloser, conventionally introducing the complaint with the biblical authority of Isaiah 5.8. They continue:

> These caterpillers what do they? what say they? Goodly words & faire pretences you shall have. O this will be for the good of the common-weale, and of the inhabitants, this will prevent much strife and contention, when things be parted, and every man knowes his owne, & they lye not in common thus; and besides it will nourish wood, and such like. And thus under pretence of a common good, they bring to passe a common evill by getting all to themselves, & sweeping men from the earth. These commonly be great theeves.[34]

Interestingly, Dod and Cleaver update the traditional image of

30 Collinson, *Religion of Protestants*, p. 238.
31 Richard Helgerson, *Forms of Nationhood: The Elizabethan Writing of England* (Chicago and London, 1992), ch. 6.
32 David Norbrook, *Poetry and Politics in the English Renaissance* (London, 1984), p. 63.
33 Four edns (1583–95); 1st edn, sigs. I8ᵇ–K1ᵃ.
34 Eighteen edns (1603–35); 1605 edn, p. 309.

'caterpillers' of the commonwealth by incorporating a rebuttal of contemporary justifications of enclosure. This level of sophistication in argument, and attention to changing economic language, comes to characterize Stuart texts, as will be seen below. Concerned to expose hypocrisy, Dod and Cleaver ultimately dismiss the aims to prevent 'strife and contention', to 'nourish wood', and to ensure that 'every man' should know 'his owne', with stark biblical imperatives against covetousness and theft.

Despite their moments of fervour, in texts such as those of Stubbes and Dod and Cleaver, informed by the changing interests and attitudes of the Elizabethan Church, statements of agrarian complaint are markedly detached from Edwardian traditions of preaching and publication. Both these books are lengthy, and carry complimentary dedications to a member of the gentry or nobility, while neither work makes any attempt to identify with the economically oppressed, or to concentrate at length on their interests and grievances. Stubbes's identification of 'abuses', which is best known for its attack on the theatre, principally focuses on contemporary practices and popular customs which offend his nascent Puritan sense of morality. His universally caustic vision of society is underlined in an earlier claim that covetousness affects all social degrees, not just landowners (sig. I7ᵃ). Dod and Cleaver are similarly detached from the gospelling tradition, as they include their brief considerations of agrarian issues within a didactic primer intended to improve the religious and moral conduct of the individual reader. Hence both works illustrate an important consequence of the growing tendency of religious texts to focus on the mind and motivation of the individual. By comparison with the Edwardians' interest in 'social' sins, religious writers in subsequent decades increasingly turn their attention to offences against codes of personal morality. Moreover, the new moral focus highlights practices associated with the town and city rather than the country. Popular targets include drunkenness, whoredom, Sabbath violation and swearing, while the escalating debate on usury and mercantile practice dominates the sphere of economic relations.[35] Consequently, instances of agrarian abuses and oppression tend to be raised merely as particular illustrations of moral decay, rather than as fundamental causes of corruption in the

---

[35] Patrick Collinson, *The Birthpangs of Protestant England: Religious and Cultural Change in the Sixteenth and Seventeenth Centuries* (London, 1988), pp. 18–19. On usury, see Norman Jones, *God and the Moneylenders: Usury and the Law in Early Modern England* (Oxford, 1989), ch. 6.

body politic. The extent of this trend is emphasized by a study of Paul's Cross sermons, which finds 'little sustained invective on the question of enclosures' at this crucial forum after the reign of Edward VI.[36] This change of emphasis undermines traditional representations of the commonwealth as an organic unit. Indeed, one of the most important consequences of the theological arguments associated with Puritanism, as several contentious but valuable studies have argued, was the 'rise of a spirit of individualism'.[37] The effects of this shift upon perceptions of national social and economic order become apparent in *A Treatise of the Vocations*, published in 1602 by the prominent Puritan divine William Perkins.[38] Perkins defines a vocation – or 'calling' – as 'a certaine kind of life, ordained and imposed on man by God, for the common good' (p. 727). Each person, he writes, must choose a vocation which is 'honest and lawfull', and for which he is 'fit'; ultimately, 'Every man must so enter [a vocation], that he may truely in conscience say; God hath placed me in this calling, be it never so base a calling' (p. 737). While these statements uphold the early Protestant emphasis on a 'common good' which transcends individual interests, the bulk of the text specifically focuses on the individual's choice of and commitment to a vocation. In contrast to Crowley's Edwardian *Voyce of the laste trumpet*, which structures a static vision of social order indebted to the medieval doctrine of estates, Perkins offers no coherent vision of society.[39] The godly individual is placed within a more flexible socio-economic order, less regulated by the biblical standards of morality propounded by the gospellers.

A vital corollary of this attitude is the responsibility it places upon the individual for his or her own maintenance. As Norman Jones has argued in relation to contemporary perceptions of usury, the combined influences of a theology of faith alone and Puritan demands for freedom of conscience promoted a more liberal attitude toward individual aspirations. 'By removing the centre of moral judgement from the

36 Millar Maclure, *The Paul's Cross Sermons 1534–1642* (Toronto, 1958), pp. 127–8.
37 Christopher Hill, *Society and Puritanism in Pre-Revolutionary England* (London, 1964), ch. 14. See also Max Weber, *The Protestant Ethic and the Spirit of Capitalism*, translated from the German by Talcott Parsons (London, 1930); and R. H. Tawney, *Religion and the Rise of Capitalism* (London, 1922).
38 References are to *Works* (3 vols., 1608–9 edn), vol. 1. See Christopher Hill's important arguments about this text in his essay 'William Perkins and the Poor', in *Puritanism and Revolution: Studies in Interpretation of the English Revolution of the Seventeenth Century* (London, 1965 edn), pp. 215–38.
39 See above, pp. 47–9.

community to the individual conscience', the new theologians 'admitted that what each person intended by one's actions could only be judged by intention. This had the practical effect of freeing individual action.'[40] Perkins, then, faces the question of whether one person may lawfully have two farms, and dismissively replies,

> it may as wel be demaunded whether it be lawfull to have two coates at once or no: for in a common-wealth all must not be equall: but some above, some under others in regard of wealth. And therefore such as have sundry farmes, whether it be by inheritance or by honest purchase, may lawfully injoy them. (p. 740)

In accepting the dynamics of 'honest purchase' and 'inheritance' Perkins tentatively moves toward an outright endorsement of the prosperous and acquisitive Christian worker. Ultimately it is not necessary within the present context to argue that Protestantism or Puritanism promoted a spirit of capitalism. More fundamentally, by focusing so sharply on the role and morality of the individual, the bulk of religious writing published under Elizabeth subverted the predominantly social vision of the Edwardian Protestants, and thus established a more accommodating cultural context for the emerging proponents of 'improvement', 'thrift' and 'property'.

To this point all the evidence has been drawn from texts written with a national perspective, consistent with the generalizing vision of the mid-Tudor gospellers. Yet at a time when the Church was rapidly expanding its preaching ministry, to bring Protestantism to the 'dark corners of the land', the views of agrarian England produced from local pulpits also demand consideration.[41] Importantly, the expansion of the pastoral and institutional networks of the Church placed individual members of the clergy within webs of local circumstances which would almost inevitably influence their statements.[42] The Elizabethan vicar who kept his cattle and their fodder in the churchyard and church porch

---

[40] Jones, *God and the Moneylenders*, p. 174.
[41] On the spread of preaching, see Christopher Hill, 'Puritans and "the Dark Corners of the Land"', in *Change and Continuity in Seventeenth-Century England* (London, 1974), pp. 3–47. More recent arguments about the dissemination of Protestant teaching are surveyed by Christopher Haigh, in 'The Recent Historiography of the English Reformation', in *The English Reformation Revised*, ed. Haigh (Cambridge, 1987), pp. 19–33.
[42] See Collinson, *Religion of Protestants*, chs. 2–3.

was undoubtedly an extreme example of a farming clergyman.[43] His case, however, highlights the situation of a ministry drawn into activities which might well erode any motivation to apply to agrarian practices the gospellers' moral fundamentalism. Furthermore, the widening influence of Calvinist theology, with its focus on the godly individual, challenged preexistent models for perceiving the parish community.[44] If religious commitment is seen as voluntary, then the religious community becomes one articulated in terms of exclusion. The individual – minister or parishioner – is encouraged to think less of a geographical parish than of a community of the godly; and the shadowy category of 'ungodly' might well be linked in popular perceptions with the poor, the itinerant and other marginal social types. The moral sins attacked from the contemporary pulpit – such as drunkenness and swearing – were frequently those associated with the lower orders.

Such notions of the godly community were often reflected in the relations between preachers and their patrons.[45] Indeed the very distribution of the preaching ministry was frequently dependent upon the economic strength of a region, so that parishes with the greatest social 'need' – from a traditionalist's point of view – may rarely have seen a preacher. By contrast, the most active preachers were to be found in more affluent areas, where the 'lay-controlled cleric' often owed his employment to the wealthier members of the community.[46] Richard Bancroft, writing around the early 1580s, seizes upon this relationship for the purposes of an attack on Elizabethan Puritans. He describes the procedure of a Puritan (or 'precisian') sermon, which begins with a 'longe prayer without premeditacion':

> then followeth the Text, which must conteyne some severe reprehension and judgement: whereof some paraphrasticall discourse beinge made, then followe certen notes: which they terme, the makinge an use of the generall doctryne.
>
> This application must not touche in anye case the grosse synnes of their good Maisters, either oppression of the poore, enhauncing of Rentes, enclosinge of common groundes, sacriledge, symonye, pride, contempt of

[43] Collinson, *Religion of Protestants*, p. 106.
[44] See Hill, *Society and Puritanism*, ch. 14; and Collinson, *Religion of Protestants*, ch. 6.
[45] See Collinson's important discussion of 'magistracy and ministry', in *Religion of Protestants*, ch. 4.
[46] Collinson, 'The Godly: Aspects of Popular Protestantism', in *Godly People: Essays on English Protestantism and Puritanism* (London, 1983), p. 4; J. J. Scarisbrick, *The Reformation and the English People* (Oxford, 1984), pp. 169–70.

magistrates, of lawes, of ceremonyes and orders ecclesiasticall, nor anye suche like horrible synnes wherewith all the most of our precise gentlemen are infected.

At the end of the sermon, 'the cheif gentleman in the place begynnynge with a gronynge, but yet with a lowde voyce crieth most religiously, *Amen*. And then the whole companye of that sect followe. *Amen*. *Amen*.'[47] Although Bancroft writes with a clear polemical purpose, in an attack by one faction within the Elizabethan Church on another, his argument bears consideration. Simply, he claims that the economic power of religious patrons causes the preachers to abandon the established social mission of the Protestant Church. Issues such as the 'oppression of the poore' and the 'enclosinge of common groundes' are overlooked by a preaching ministry increasingly concerned with the maintenance of social stability.[48]

Nevertheless the very contents of Bancroft's list of abuses allegedly neglected by the Puritans indicates a continuing motivation among at least some of the clergy to tackle the social sins identified so forcefully in the middle of the century. In spite of overwhelming changes in the doctrine and cultural status of the national Church, persistent strands of complaint continue to surface in various local contexts. The work of Francis Trigge, rector of Welbourn, Lincolnshire, from 1589 to the early years of the seventeenth century provides a particularly striking example. Trigge responded to the rural crises of the 1590s by reviving the rhetoric of the 1540s. In *A Godly and Fruitfull Sermon Preached at Grantham . . . 1592*, he draws upon the apocalyptic imagery of Isaiah 24 to predict the wrath of God to be visited on the world for its sins.[49] Twelve years later he turned specifically to agrarian issues, in a pamphlet entitled *To the Kings most excellent Majestie. The Humble Petition of Two Sisters; the Church and Common-wealth: For the restoring of their ancient Commons and liberties, which late Inclosure and depopulation,*

---

[47] *Tracts Ascribed to Richard Bancroft*, ed. Albert Peel (Cambridge, 1953), p. 72.

[48] Shifting attitudes toward the poor among economically independent Puritans are evident in the minutes of the Dedham *classis* (a conference of preachers which met during the latter sixteenth century in the clothing towns around the Essex–Suffolk border). The only specific reference to poverty adopts a judgemental position, as it describes the existence of some '"froward poor men" of the village of Wenham, who were "every way disordered"' (Collinson, 'The Godly', p. 4).

[49] Two edns (Oxford, 1594, 1595); 'Behold, the Lord maketh the earth empty, and maketh it waste, and turneth it upside down, and scattereth abroad the inhabitants thereof' (Isaiah 24.1–2).

uncharitably hath taken away.[50] Here the Lincolnshire clergyman presents a bold national vision, founded upon a perception that James I has been ordained as 'a second *Salomon* in this our Israel' (sig. A6ᵃ). His moral judgements set uncompromising biblical standards against attitudes of economic individualism. Indeed he rounds upon divergent strands of biblical interpretation:

> these Inclosers alledge that saying of the gospell, *Is it not lawfull for me to doe with mine owne as I list?*[51] They must remember, that parable represents unto us that great Landlord of all Landlords, the King of heaven; he may say so only, and none else. (sig. C8ᵃ)

With his strident assertion of the doctrine of stewardship, Trigge reaffirms the appreciation of agrarian change propounded by the early Protestants. He subsequently grafts secular arguments and indigenous verbal traditions onto this model as, for example, he recites,

> an olde prophesie, that Horne and thorne shall make England forlorne. Inclosers verifie this by their sheepe and hedges at this day. They kill poore mens hearts, by taking from them their auncient commons, to make sheep pasture of; and by imposing upon them great rents, and by decaying tillage; so that now they are forlorne having no joy to live in the world.
> (sig. D5ᵃ)

Finally, after a consideration of the history and present condition of various types of land tenure, he concludes with the warning that depopulating enclosure is simply a sin, 'whereof God shall make speciall inquirie at the day of judgement' (sig. G1ᵇ). His work thus demonstrates with striking clarity the continuing importance of traditional values of moral economy. While it is safe to conclude that the Elizabethan Church increasingly distanced itself from such moral fundamentalism, and gradually embraced radically new ideas of economic practice and social order, it is equally apparent that the moral codes endorsed by Trigge exerted a significant residual influence throughout the early modern period.

THE CHARACTER OF THE GODLY FARMER

Hugh Latimer's text for his powerful 'Last Sermon Before King Edward VI' (Luke 12.15) was taken up seventy years later for a Paul's Cross

50 Two edns (both 1604); references are to the first edition.
51 The source, Matthew 20.15, is cited in a marginal note.

sermon by Jeremiah Dyke.[52] Paul's Cross remained, in the seventeenth century, a national forum; and the Paul's Cross sermon was maintained as a distinct type, 'an exhortation addressed to all estates of the realm, entreating of God's judgement and His mercy' for the sins of the nation.[53] But Dyke adopts a significantly modified tone of exhortation compared with his predecessors of the middle of the sixteenth century. Identified on the title-page of his sermon as a 'Minister of Gods word at Epping in Essex', Dyke was a moderate in thought and expression, in keeping with the consensual face of the Jacobean Church.[54] His sermon eschews the urgent voice of national prophecy adopted by the mid-Tudor gospellers in favour of a regional minister's measured tone of moral instruction. The preacher analyses various definitions of covetousness, then describes the 'symptoms' of the sin as manifested in the individual sinner. Typical of his approach is an early consideration of the image from 1 Thessalonians 2.5 of 'a cloke of covetousness':

> It is a colouring, and a cloking sinne. It is a sinne that weares the cloke and livery of thrift, providence, good husbandrie, honest care for a mans owne, without which a man is worse then an infidell. It is fit therefore that this false colour and complexion be washed off, and that this monster be uncloked and uncased. (p. 13)

As he strips off the layers of hypocrisy to reveal the essential evil of covetousness, Dyke identifies insidious attempts to redefine the sin. Interestingly, he concentrates his attack on terms such as 'thrift', 'good husbandrie' and 'honest care for a mans owne', all of which will be shown in later chapters to be involved in a discourse of agrarian improvement. Dyke clearly perceives a growing challenge to his ideals; however, he directs his 'counterpoison' not with the Edwardians' vivid images of corruption, but with an analytical concentration on the mind of the covetous man and his self-serving manipulation of language. The

---

[52] *A Counterpoison against Covetousnes* (1619); on Latimer's sermon, see above, pp. 45–6.

[53] Collinson, *Birthpangs*, p. 20; Maclure, *Paul's Cross Sermons*, p. 118.

[54] In this respect Jeremiah Dyke, whose religious writings enjoyed considerable currency throughout the seventeenth century, must be distinguished from his father, William, a popular Puritan clergyman silenced by the Elizabethan authorities. See Patrick Collinson, *The Elizabethan Puritan Movement* (London, 1967), pp. 373–4, 405; DNB, sub. Dyke; and Gwen Dyke, 'Puritan Preachers: The Dykes of Norfolk and Essex', in *Religious Dissent in East Anglia*, ed. E. S. Leedham-Green (Cambridge, 1991), pp. 87–90. On the 'Calvinist consensus' within the Jacobean Church, see Collinson, *Religion of Protestants*, pp. 81–2.

oppressed ploughman as social critic is succeeded by the scathing analyst of the human conscience.

Dyke's analysis of the corrupt mind is informed at once by Calvinist theology and the shift of interest from 'social' to 'moral' sins noted above. His strategy thus typifies a trend in seventeenth-century religious texts toward a focus on the individual 'character'. Indeed the conjunction of Calvinism and the Jacobean vogue for the satiric subgenre of Theophrastian 'character' writing clearly informs and enriches both literature and religious discourse in the early decades of the seventeenth century.[55] There is a Jonsonian relish, for instance, in a contemporary preacher's focus on 'covetous Land-Lords, that stretch their Rents on the Tenter-hookes of an evill conscience'.[56] And Joseph Hall, whose 1590s satires will be considered in chapter 3, overtly aligns himself with this literary strain in his 1634 sermon, *The Character of Man*. This sermon hones in on the sin of pride:

> There are but two things . . . that the naturall man is most proud of, Knowledge and Power; surely if he had one of these to purpose, he could be proud of neither: Know thy self, O man, and be proud if thou canst. Why then doth the rich Landlord grate upon his poor scraping Tenant? Why doth the silken Courtier brow-beat his russet Countryman? Why doe potent Lords . . . trample upon that peasantly mold which nature hath not in kind differenced from their own . . . Why doe we, how dare we insult on each other since we are all under one common doom of miserable mortality?[57]

Hall's sporadic references in his works to agrarian exploitation have prompted one recent critic to speak of moral outrage directed at wealthy landowners.[58] A closer attention to the language and context of such passages, however, prompts a significant modification of this judgement. Here Hall is principally concerned with the consciences of the 'potent Lords'; his expression consistently avoids the complaint tradition's sympathetic identification with those of a 'peasantly mold'. Hall's moral

---

55 See Patrick Collinson's remarks on this relationship, in *The Puritan Character: Polemics and Polarities in Early Seventeenth-Century English Culture* (Los Angeles, 1989), p. 13.

56 Thomas Adams, *Workes* (1629), p. 53; from his 1612 Paul's Cross sermon, *The White Devil or The Hypocrite Uncased*.

57 *Diverse Treatises* (1662), p. 112.

58 Richard McCabe, *Joseph Hall: A Study in Satire and Meditation* (Oxford, 1982), pp. 53–72. McCabe here links Hall's 'social concerns' in his verse satires and sermons. I will return to his criticism of the former on pp. 89–90.

focus is not the social sin of covetousness but the moral sin of pride; his outrage is directed less at economic exploitation than at the troubled mind of a hypocrite.

The prevalent seventeenth-century interest in the individual mind is developed at length in Richard Bernard's allegory, *The Isle of Man: or, The Legall Proceeding in Man-Shire against Sinne.*[59] Bernard, a popular religious author influenced by Jacobean satire, defines his aims in terms of forensic inquiry. His book will 'discover to us our miserable and wretched estate through corruption of nature. For the laying open hereof, there is a lively description of sin, with the power, nature, fruits, & effects thereof' (sig. N6ᵃ⁻ᵇ). In a lengthy scene depicting the legal trial of Covetousness, Bernard rigorously pursues the contemporary 'cloaking' of covetousness in new economic language, and depicts the malignant influence of the sin within an apparently godly community. There are recurrent quibbles in the proceedings about the name of Covetousness, who variously claims that he is properly called 'Good-husbandry' and 'Thrift' (pp. 23, 204). This issue is finally resolved by Master Proof, who describes how the ideals of thrift in the countryside have 'turned basely covetous' (p. 214). At the heart of this line of argument stands the evidence of depopulation given by Poverty, a former freeholder in the parish of Wealth, who charges that Covetousness has evicted 'many honest Inhabitants and good house-keepers', and set in their place 'a Shepheard and his Curre to feed his flockes' (p. 183). Covetousness's defence of his actions highlights Bernard's satiric attack on the language of individualism and improvement:

> Touching their *Landlords* depopulating of the *Towne of Wealth*, they their own selves were the very cause thereof, for that worthy Knight and my kinsman, Sir *Worldly Wise*, when hee saw how some by suits of Law, others by Drunkennesse and Ryot, others by Pride and Idlenesse did waste their estates, so as they were neither able to till their land, nor stocke their grounds, he bought their estates one after another, and so left them to buy or hire for themselves elsewhere. (pp. 190–1)

Sir Worldly Wise (an apparent model for John Bunyan's Mr Worldly Wise, in *The Pilgrim's Progress*) is described by Covetousness as a 'good Common-wealths man' (p. 191), a term which is a site of ideological dispute throughout the period covered by this study. Bernard uses him to barb his argument that the traditional language of the

---

[59] Eleven edns (1626–40); references are to the first edition.

'commonwealth' has been appropriated and craftily moulded into a language of competition, exclusion and oppression. In the discourse of the agrarian improver, Bernard's satire suggests, the 'drunkenness' and 'idleness' of the lower orders offer a convenient moralistic justification for exploitation. The godly individualist is exposed as a hypocrite, who blithely dismisses the moral economist's values of charity and community.

Bernard's combination of moral allegory with an analysis of contemporary economic discourse further typifies an increased sophistication in much of the Church's social criticism in the seventeenth century. A similar impetus prompted the Suffolk preacher Thomas Carew to anatomize exploitative practices in his local clothing industry, with a particular attention to working conditions and rates of pay,[60] while Charles Fitz-Geffrie applied a traditional social morality to the operation of rural markets in three sermons entitled *The Curse of Corne-horders* (1631). But whereas such men recognized a need to update and elaborate the moral imperatives of complaint, other religious writers were clearly being swayed by arguments of 'improvement'. When a series of poor harvests at the end of the 1620s again raised the national priority of agrarian issues, the most striking aspect of the debate is a widespread uncertainty about the morality of enclosure. Archbishop Laud, who headed a series of commissions of inquiry into enclosure in the 1630s, apparently shared the mid-Tudor gospellers' moral indignation toward the act.[61] (The authority which such attitudes continued to exert at the grass-roots of English society was repeatedly emphasized in the numerous local revolts which flared from the late 1620s into the 1640s. In years which 'were probably among the most terrible . . . through which the country has ever passed', this form of popular political action was perhaps the most effective method through which the commons proclaimed their pressing needs and expectations.)[62] Yet in both Church

---

60 'A Caveat for craftsmen and Clothiers', in *Certaine godly and necessarie Sermons* (1603).
61 Joan Thirsk, 'Agrarian Problems and the English Revolution', in *Town and Country-side in the English Revolution*, ed. R. C. Richardson (Manchester, 1992), p. 170.
62 On the rural hardship of the period, see Peter Bowden, 'Agricultural Prices, Farm Profits, and Rents', in *AHEW IV*, p. 621. Several historians, however, have discerned a rising element of class hatred in the rural riots and revolts of this particularly volatile period. While opinions are divided about the extent, significance and origins of such feeling, its existence would appear to indicate at once the intensity of the rural crises in these years, and dissatisfaction with traditional strategies of complaint and the ideology upon which they were based. In other words, the belief in a society structured around

and state circles the debates over rural change increasingly embraced considerations of economic diversity and agrarian improvement. Supporters of enclosure typically prefaced their arguments with sincere denunciations of *depopulating* enclosure, but claimed that this was an infrequent and preventable aberration rather than a necessary consequence of the controversial act. Successive governments generally appear to have agreed. A flurry of anti-enclosure rhetoric and prosecutions in the 1630s had some important local effects but appears in retrospect as a late attempt by the Crown to reassert its commitment to moral economy in the face of social and political upheavals. The long-term movement away from the moral absolutism of complaint, by comparison, can be traced throughout the decades of political upheaval and into the Restoration.[63] On the eve of the Revolution, Joan Thirsk has argued, the pursuit of depopulators was 'treated primarily as a revenue-raising device, rather than as a remedy for social evils'.[64]

The extent to which the clergy was by this time split on the morality of such issues is illustrated in a pamphlet debate between two ministers in the 1650s. John Moore's *The Crying Sin of England, Of not Caring for the Poor* (1653) insists upon the morality of the doctrine of stewardship, in a sermon focused throughout upon the exploitation of the lower social orders.[65] The response of Joseph Lee, however, confronts Moore's social morality with a moralized justification for improvement.[66]

'vertical' bonds of local community, may have been seriously challenged for the first time by perceptions of 'horizontal' ties of socio-economic class. Given the extent to which the national Church had identified itself with the prevailing discourses of hierarchical order, its position of moral authority would inevitably be undermined by class identity and hostility. (As I will argue in chapter 4, such a challenge to the Church's authority helps to explain the extraordinary outpouring of radical thought associated with the English Revolution.) Brian Manning presents a summary of recent arguments and studies in this field in the new introduction to *The English People and the English Revolution*, 2nd edn (London, 1991).

[63] The significance of the 1630s actions against depopulating enclosure remains a point of conjecture. Kevin Sharpe and Joan Thirsk both document a reinvigorated assault on the practice, motivated in part by Archbishop Laud's 'almost fanatical prejudice against enclosers'; however, Thirsk also places this movement alongside concurrent government attempts to improve yields from Crown lands, and argues that throughout the revolutionary years there was little concerted momentum toward agrarian reform (Sharpe, *The Personal Rule of Charles I* (New Haven and London, 1992), pp. 471–3; Thirsk, 'Agrarian Problems', p. 170 and *passim*).

[64] Joan Thirsk, 'Changing Attitudes to Enclosure in the Seventeenth Century', in *The Festschrift for Professor Ju-Hwan Oh* (Taegu, Korea, 1991), p. 530. See also Thirsk, 'Agricultural Policy: Public Debate and Legislation', *AHEW Vii*, pp. 298–388.

[65] See also his *A scripture-word against inclosure* (1656).

[66] *Considerations Concerning Common Fields and Inclosures* (1654).

Interestingly, Lee begins by attempting to prize apart rhetoric from reason in Moore's sermon:

> It is true, that in the pathetick part of his discourse he appeareth very zealous in behalfe of the poor, and bitter enough against those that oppresse them . . . but the rationall part of his discourse . . . is not indifferently extended unto all Inclosures, but expresly limited and restrained unto such as unpeople towns and uncorne Fields. (p. 2)

The very strategy of complaint is challenged, in a text that rationally focuses on 'the greatest advantage to the common-wealth, that can be raised out of land' (p. 3). More significant still is Lee's willingness to counter Moore's biblical interpretation and moral judgement. Even Isaiah 5.8, which had underpinned enclosure complaints since the Middle Ages, is open to reinterpretation. Lee claims that:

> it is a wonder unto me, how Mr *Moore* . . . can imagine, that the holy Ghost, who knoweth very well . . . how to expresse himself, by laying field to field, till there be no place, should mean the inclosing of common fields, rather then the throwing open of inclosures: whereas indeed to throw open inclosures . . . that so there may be no place for any man to enjoy his own with peace and quietnesse, must needs be laying field to field. (p. 16)

The desire to 'enjoy one's own' – a central cry of the discourse of agrarian improvement – is moralized with the astonishing support of the central text of Lee's opponents. Subsequently, his attitude toward the problem of poverty is articulated in accordance with an ethos of godly individualism. On enclosed land, he argues, the farmer, 'by raysing greater profit to himselfe, shall be better able, both to pay weekly contribution for the relief of the impotent poor, and to bear his part in the raysing of a stock to set the able poor on work' (p. 8). In a twist of argument which effectively inverts Moore's language of complaint, Lee colours the economic aim of 'raysing greater profit' with a brilliant hue of moral rectitude. Not only is 'the moral economy in retreat', it is confronted by a cogent rival version of moral economics.[67]

For all the audacity of Lee's arguments, his Christian morality is impeccably orthodox within the changing English Protestant context

---

[67] See Joyce Oldham Appleby's excellent analysis of the debate between Moore and Lee in a chapter entitled 'The Moral Economy in Retreat', in *Economic Thought and Ideology in Seventeenth-Century England* (Princeton, 1978). I will develop the analysis of a rival version of moral economics in part II, and particularly in chapter 7.

traced throughout this chapter. By contrast with the Tudor gospellers' sympathetic identification with the rural poor and representation of socio-economic power in binary terms, the clergyman of the middle of the seventeenth century was just as likely to celebrate the godly improver of the land operating within a dynamic market economy. Indeed, it is firmly from the latter standpoint that Thomas Fuller's *The Holy State* defines the various duties and responsibilities of those involved in the agrarian economy.[68] His essay on 'The Good Landlord' – which offers a striking contrast to the Edwardian prayer 'For Landlordes' quoted in chapter 1 – teaches a lesson of industry and economic stimulus:[69]

> *His rent doth quicken his Tenant but not gall him.* Indeed 'tis observed, that where Landlords are very easy, the Tenants (but this is *per Accidens*, out of their own laziness) seldome thrive, contenting themselves to make up the just measure of their rent, and not labouring for any surplusage of estate. (p. 99)

'The good Yeoman', meanwhile, eagerly embraces the quest for 'surplusage of estate' and subsequent social mobility. He is 'a Gentleman in Ore', who '*improveth his land to a double value by his good husbandry* . . . By marle and limestones burnt he bettereth his ground, and his industry worketh miracles, by turning stones into bread' (pp. 116–18). Fuller's emphasis on the labour and productivity of the rural gentry and yeomanry represents a powerful form of Christian georgic; and as such, it directs our attention away from Latimer's version of georgic, which celebrated the labour of the ploughman within a stable manorial structure, and toward the texts which will occupy our attention in chapters 5 to 7.

[68] Four edns (1642–63); references are to the first edition.
[69] See above, pp. 39–40.

3. The rural vision of Renaissance satire

> Oh happy daies of olde *Deucalion*,
> When one was Land-lord of the world alone!
>
> (Joseph Hall, *Virgidemiarum*, 1598)

When Sir Philip Sidney looked back upon his country's literary history, in his *Apology for Poetry*, he recognized little of value written in the first half of the sixteenth century. Of the poetry, prose and drama published during the mid-Tudor years – which provided the basis for my analysis of agrarian complaint in chapter 1 – Sidney saw no more than the products of 'base men with servile wits'.[1] The only writer from the period he singles out for praise is the Earl of Surrey, in whose *Lyrics* are 'many things tasting of a noble birth, and worthy of a noble mind' (p. 133). George Puttenham, in his *Arte of English Poesie*, couples Sir Thomas Wyatt with Surrey.[2] Both men stand as 'lanternes of light' to later ages because of their 'loftie' conceits and 'stately' styles (p. 62). Neither of these two poets, however, can be linked in any significant way to the vigorous tradition of 'English Reformation literature' which drew together strands of religious, social and economic criticism in the middle of the sixteenth century.[3] That the Elizabethan poetic theorists should praise Surrey and ignore a writer such as Robert Crowley thus highlights a disagreement about the nature and purpose of poetry, which effectively distinguishes Renaissance literary ideals from the practices which underpinned mid-Tudor complaint. Crowley had received a humanist education, yet he eschewed classical poetic models in favour of a style grounded in medieval and biblical polemic.[4] By contrast, the emerging

---

[1] Ed. Geoffrey Shepherd (London, 1965), p. 132.
[2] (1589); ed. Gladys Doidge Willcock and Alice Walker (Cambridge, 1936).
[3] See John N. King, *English Reformation Literature: The Tudor Origins of the Protestant Tradition* (Princeton, 1982).
[4] King, *English Reformation Literature*, pp. 340–1.

Renaissance poetics looked to the classics and to recent Continental models; Puttenham's praise of Wyatt and Surrey, for example, notes that they 'very naturally and studiously' imitated 'their Maister *Francis Petrarcha*' (p. 62).

This chapter examines the effects of Renaissance ideals of poetic practice upon preexistent conventions which had shaped both the expression of social criticism and the representation of agrarian England. Contrary to the version of literary history propounded by Sidney and Puttenham, I will argue that the influence of the Reformation 'gospellers' was far from insignificant in later decades. Yet it is equally apparent that the poets and dramatists of the latter sixteenth and early seventeenth centuries crucially revised the strategies of their native predecessors. Central to this process was satire, the preeminent genre for the expression of social criticism, according to Renaissance theory. Satire emerges, in the wake of the complaint tradition, as a sophisticated vehicle for morally grounded critique of ideological and socio-economic change. It is a genre equipped to scrutinize the complex processes of a fluid market-oriented society; at its best, its incisive attention to language highlights discourses which underpin such a society. An underlying question throughout the chapter, however, concerns the ideological status of satire. Much of the literature of concern here is bound for its very survival to the market society it excoriates, and a troubled awareness of this complicity generates an anxiety which informs the genre. While admitting from the outset the breadth and variety of Renaissance satire, I will argue that this tension produces an attitude toward rural change characterized by a deeply troubled ambivalence. By the early decades of the seventeenth century, satire reaches out toward the world of individualism and mercantilism with a shuddering embrace.

In the first section I will trace the development in the latter sixteenth century of a mode of verse satire informed by the growing influence of classical models. As will be seen, early Renaissance satire was by no means divorced from native traditions of complaint; however, by the 1590s, an intense interest in the genre shaped English satire into a mature and coherent form, significantly distanced from the attitudes and values of the Reformation gospellers. The subsequent section will pursue the satiric vision into the professional theatres of London, first considering developments in Tudor morality plays, before focusing on the sophisticated satire of Jacobean 'city comedy'. In its depiction of a grotesque world of economic flux and contest, city comedy stages the challenge to traditional rural values posed by the ethics of nascent capitalism.

THE RISE OF FORMAL VERSE SATIRE

In 1578 an obscure writer named John Wharton published a poem which combines social criticism with a turgid versification of biblical texts. The title-page reads:

> WHARTONS Dreame. Conteyninge an invective agaynst certaine abhominable Caterpillers as Userers, Extorcioners, Leasmongers and such others, confounding their divellysh sectes, by the aucthor of holy scripture, selected and gathered by John Warton Scholemaister. Seneca[:] In iuventute cogitavi bene facere, ut in senectute bene moriar. Sapiens 3[:] The soules of the righteous are in the handes of the Lorde, and the paynes of death shall not toutch them.

The statement immediately draws attention to the converging strands of influence in the text. A debt to the complaint tradition is signalled by the choice of a dream vision (the structural basis of William Langland's *Piers Plowman*) and a dependence on the Bible, to the extent that Wharton figures his own role as that of a 'selector' and 'gatherer' of relevant passages. A statement of his didactic purpose, on the verso of the title-page, also invokes one of the leading Edwardian gospellers, as he declares of his poem: 'Perused and thought well of, for the correcting of vice, and terrifyinge of the wicked: by these following. *John Fox[e]. Robert Crowley. William Wager. Thomas Buckmaister, and others'*.[5] Yet Wharton also wants to align his work with classical traditions. On the title-page, the quote from the apocryphal 'Wisdom of Solomon' is juxtaposed with the more secular wisdom of Seneca. Further, in his dedication he quotes Erasmus and discusses the value Cicero accords to 'letters', while subsequent commendatory verses attest to the poetic merit of the work at hand.

Wharton's fifteen pages of preliminary material seem more than a little extravagant preceding only twenty-three pages of text. Moreover the poem's ballad metre and traditional Christian morality (including its use of the standard biblical texts of early Protestant polemic, with a citation of Isaiah 5.8 to support his enclosure complaint (sig. D1ª)) belie his attempt to fashion a new cultural context for his work. His clumsy effort, however, serves to focus attention on a significant literary trend,

---

[5] As noted above (pp. 61–2), Crowley's own activities under Elizabeth significantly departed from his social and religious polemic of the mid-Tudor years. William Wager's moral interludes will be considered below, pp. 93–5.

gathering in momentum and sophistication throughout the reign of Elizabeth. This movement would reach its apogee in the verse satires of the 1590s, while its beginnings can be observed a generation earlier. Two years before the publication of *Whartons Dreame*, for example, George Gascoigne wrote *The Steele glas*, which revises the tradition of estates satire; and in 1579 Edward Hake reissued his ballad-metre *Newes out of Powles churchyarde . . . Wherein is reprooved excessive seeking after riches*.[6] Like Wharton, Hake combines a complaint against covetousness with an attempt to present a literary work grounded upon classical traditions, as he quotes Horace on the title-page and includes five dedicatory and commendatory verses, two in Latin.

Both Gascoigne and Hake define their work as 'English Satyrs'.[7] In John Peter's study of *Complaint and Satire in Early English Literature*, this term highlights a transitional phase during which satirists drew liberally upon the resources of complaint.[8] For in the 1570s, at least, the Elizabethans did not clearly distinguish between the two genres. Thomas Drant, the first English translator of Horace's satires, printed Jeremiah's 'wailyngs' in the same volume, on account of a common purpose in the works to attack sin and hypocrisy.[9] Puttenham looks to vernacular traditions in his history of the genre, as he describes the satirist as a 'kind of Poet, who intended to taxe the common abuses and vice of the people in rough and bitter speaches', and names as his only English example, 'he that wrote the booke called Piers plowman' (p. 26). He suggests that satire was first developed in the form of 'certaine poems in plaine meetres, more like to sermons or preachings then otherwise' (p. 30). The increasing influence of classical models, however, caused Renaissance writers to revise the traditional tone and social vision of their native predecessors.[10] For Sidney, satire accords with his central definition of poetry as 'delightful teaching' (p. 103). He states that the satirist, 'sportingly never leaveth till he make a man laugh at folly, and at length ashamed to laugh at himself, which he cannot avoid without avoiding the

---

6 Unfortunately there are no extant copies of the first edition which, Hake claims, predated this by twelve years (sig. A3ᵃ).
7 The phrase and spelling is Hake's, from his title-page. Gascoigne, similarly, proclaims his poem as 'a satyre'.
8 (Oxford, 1956), p. 109.
9 *A Medicinable Morall, that is, the two Bookes of Horace his Satyres [and] The Wailyngs of the Prophet Hieremiah*, edited and translated from the Latin by Thomas Drant (1566). I am grateful to Bradin Cormack for bringing this text to my attention.
10 On the emergence of formal satire, see Raman Selden, *English Verse Satire 1590–1765* (London, 1978), ch. 2.

folly'. (Drant had made a similar point, proclaiming that in his volume 'the plaintive Prophete *Jeremie* should wepe at synne: and the pleasant poet *Horace* shoulde laugh at synne' (sig. A3ᵃ).) Sidney supports his claim with a subtle appeal to classical precedents, by adapting Persius's comment about Horace: 'Omne vafer vitium ridenti tangit amico' (pp. 116–17).[11] A classically grounded satire is thus characterized for Sidney by a deceptively playful tone and a capacity to pry into the conscience and motivations of the individual. Such strategies were compounded by the contemporary religious movements discussed in chapter 2. As the Puritan preacher refined his pursuit of individual immorality and hypocrisy, so the satirist aimed to 'breake the Closset of mans private sin'.[12]

This conjunction of theological and literary movements effectively shattered the organic – and essentially agrarian – conception of the Christian commonwealth upon which complaint insisted. For the gospellers and 'commonwealths men' of the middle of the sixteenth century, the rural manor was considered to be the very foundation of social, economic and political order in England. Towns and markets – and even the court – could be dismissed as aberrant outgrowths on the body politic. The vision of satire, by comparison, converges with that of the Elizabethan Church upon the individual afloat in the uncertain milieu of the early modern town. It replaces the troubled idealism of complaint with a more cynical representation of the increasingly confusing, fragmented nature of life and discourse in the sprawling urban world. And just as the conscience of each person becomes a focus of attention, so the individual is accorded economic agency. As a consequence, the complainant's insistence upon a simple binary relationship of economic power between oppressor and oppressed is replaced by more complex images of competition; and the focus of attention is more frequently turned to the socially mobile 'middling sorts', such as rural yeomen and urban tradesmen.[13] Moreover, the abuses of the countryside are

---

11 The full quotation, from Persius's *Satires*, I, translates: 'Horace, sly dog, worming his way playfully into the vitals of his laughing friend, touches up his every fault.'

12 George Wither, *Abuses Stript and Whipt* (1613); facsimile edn (Spenser Society, 1871), p. 46. Recent studies of Renaissance satire have analysed the differing uses of Horace, Juvenal and Persius as models. The current approach, however, aims to focus on conventions generally employed by Renaissance satirists; variations in style will not be noted unless they significantly affect the arguments. (The best introduction to these issues is provided in Selden, *English Verse Satire*, ch. 1.)

13 On this social category, see *Middling Sort of People: Culture, Society, and Politics in England, 1550–1800*, ed. Jonathan Barry and Christopher Brooks (Basingstoke, 1994).

increasingly approached from a satiric perspective forged in the town. They are thus drawn into a broad and baffling web of corruption; the mercantile ethics identified in the town are seen to be perverting irreparably the traditional order of rural life.

In accordance with this satiric perspective, the rural labourer becomes a distinctly problematic figure. As I argued in chapter 1, the mid-Tudor discourse of agrarian complaint propels its moral invective against covetous landlords through the perspective of the downtrodden tenant or labourer. The figure of Piers the Ploughman, loosely derived from Langland's poem, stands at the centre of this tradition; and Puttenham's comments about Langland attest to the lingering reputation of his work in the latter sixteenth century. Yet Gascoigne's introduction of *'Peerce plowman'* into *The Steele glas* typifies the less certain world of Renaissance satire. He writes that Peerce shall:

> clime to heaven, before the shaven crownes.
> But how? forsooth, with true humilytie.
> Not that they hoord, their grain when it is cheape,
> Nor that they kill, the calfe to have the milke,
> Nor that they set, debate betwene their lords,
> By earing up the balks, that part their bounds:
> . . .
> Nor that they can, crie out on landelordes lowde,
> And say they racke, their rents an ace to high,
> When they themselves, do sel their landlords lambe
> For greater price, then ewe was wont be worth.
> I see you *Peerce*, my glasse was lately scowrde.   (sig. H2ᵇ)

Gascoigne's pentameter, blank-verse line marks an immediate contrast with the thumping didacticism of the mid-Tudor gospellers' favoured verse forms, and facilitates a more measured and complex treatment of the ploughman. In a heavily ironic progression, the passage moves from a conventional endorsement of Piers's 'humilytie' into a criticism which undermines the ploughman's status as an ideal figure. Indeed Gascoigne opens to question the very rationale of traditional statements of complaint, as he suggests a dubious self-interest motivating tenants who 'crie out on landelordes lowde', yet themselves sell 'their landlords lambe' at inflated prices. The complaint tradition placed Piers at the foundation of the body politic; Gascoigne anxiously defines an economic agent breaking free from corporate notions of social identity. His work – in a manner typical of Renaissance satire – isolates an early modern 'subject' being shaped by emergent literary, religious and socio-economic discourses.[14] And such recognition of subjectivity prompts the satirist to interrogate the ploughman with the same ferocity turned on his landlord: Piers, like every other member of society, is exposed to the harsh glare of the satirist and his 'steel glass'.[15]

The wave of verse satires written in the 1590s consolidated the Renaissance conception of the genre. The 1590s was a decade troubled by harvest failures, dearth and rural unrest to an extent unlike any period since the turbulent years of the middle of the sixteenth century. But the response of the satirists stands in stark contrast to that of the Edwardian commonwealths men. The latter were propelled by a genuine belief in the potential for massive social reformation, directed by the imperatives of biblical morality. The satirist's vision, by comparison, was shaped by the consolidating 'cynical and elitist' outlook of his genre.[16] Satire became a 'fashionable affair', and the authors regularly 'make every effort to disclaim any connection with native satire and to stress their classical correctness, their learning, and their unconcern for being read by the vulgar'.[17] Furthermore, the satire of the 1590s was a literature of the marketplace. Despite their conventional attacks on market practices, the satirists were themselves implicated in the web of incipient capitalism in London. Men such as Joseph Hall and John Marston were

14 Several recent studies have analysed changing constructions of subjectivity in Renaissance literature; however, the role of satire in these processes awaits further consideration. (See especially Catherine Belsey, *The Subject of Tragedy: Identity and Difference in Renaissance Drama* (London and New York, 1985); and Louis Adrian Montrose, 'The Elizabethan Subject and the Spenserian Text', in *Literary Theory/Renaissance Texts*, ed. Patricia Parker and David Quint (Baltimore, 1986), pp. 303–40.)

15 Gascoigne's treatment of Piers highlights a contemporary rejection of the ploughman as an idealized complainant. This trend is most noticeable in prose pamphlets: in *Newes from the North* (1579), attributed to Francis Thynne, Piers appears as merely one character in a rambling dialogue principally concerned with abuses in the legal system; in Thomas Nashe's *Pierce Penilesse his Supplication to the Divell* (1592) he becomes an impoverished scholar; and in Henry Chettle's *Piers Plainnes seaven yeres Prentiship* (1595) he is a shepherd in a pastoral anti-court satire. One probable exception to this pattern unfortunately has not survived. In 1580 'R. B.' published *The ploughmans complaint of sundry wicked livers in verse* (STC 1061), but there are no extant copies of the work. For an overview of representations of Piers from 1362 to 1625, see Myrta Ethel McGinnis, '"Piers the Plowman" in England, 1362–1625: A Study in Popularity and Influence' (unpublished Ph.D dissertation, Yale University, 1932), chs. 6–7.

16 Selden, *English Verse Satire*, p. 46.

17 Alvin Kernan, *The Cankered Muse: Satire of the English Renaissance* (New Haven, 1959), p. 39.

distanced, by virtue of their own middling origins, from the courtly milieu envisaged by Sidney and Puttenham as the true cradle of poetry. They were gradually turning away from the established structures of aristocratic literary patronage, toward a marketplace for poetry created by the printing presses and sprawling urban conglomerate of London.[18] Indeed, the rapid growth of London in the late sixteenth century – and the manifold social tensions this aroused – provided at once the impetus and the audience for satirists. This cultural situation is the source of much of the literary vitality of the decade, as evidenced by the periodic spats between rival authors increasingly aware of the *value* of literary reputation. It places the satirist in an ideal position to scrutinize the practices and rhetoric of a market-oriented society; yet it almost inevitably erodes any claims he lays to a position of secure moral authority.

Treatment of agrarian issues in the satire of the 1590s is typically torn between an impetus toward moral outrage and a despairing cynicism about the possibility for reform. Rural concerns continue to arise in this poetry, but the problems of the countryside are no longer represented as simple and correctable products of moral corruption. Instead the satirist's view of the land perceives agrarian problems merely as further symptoms of a social and economic system devoid of morality. This pervasive assumption reshapes even conventional attacks on depopulating enclosure, such as that launched by Thomas Bastard in his *Chrestoleros*:

> Sheepe have eate up our medows & our downes,
> Our corne, our wood, whole villages & townes,
> Yea they have eate up many wealthy men
> Besides widowes and Orphane childeren.
> Besides our statutes and our iron lawes,
> Which they have swallowed down into their maws.[19]

Bastard employs imagery characteristic of enclosure polemic since More's *Utopia*.[20] Within the new generic context, however, such statements achieve an impact significantly different from that of the

---

[18] Richard Helgerson presents an important analysis of this development in Renaissance literary culture, in *Self-Crowned Laureates: Spenser, Jonson, Milton, and the Literary System* (Berkeley, 1983), pp. 122–44. Helgerson is specifically concerned with Ben Jonson, whose satiric drama will be considered further below, pp. 104–9.

[19] *Chrestoleros. Seven bookes of epigrames* (1598), p. 90.

[20] See above, p. 23.

complaint tradition. Bastard's introductory poem, to a volume of over one hundred satiric epigrams, proclaims an indiscriminate survey

> of frauds, of policies,
> Of manners, and of vertues, and of times,
> Of unthrifts, and of frends, and enimies,
> Poets, Physitions, Lawyers, and Divines,
> Of usurers, buyers, borowers, ritch and poore,
> Of theeves, of murtherers by sea and land,
> Of pickthankes, and lyers, flatterers lesse and more,
> Of good and bad, and all that comes to hand.   (p. 1)

The view of society as an uncontrollable welter of vice and hypocrisy eschews from the outset the assertive didacticism and moral fundamentalism which underpinned the complaint tradition. With a satirist's ironic opacity, Bastard finds 'comfort' rather in the fact 'that my booke is of the fashion' (sig. A3^b).

The characteristic social perspective of satire refines the vision of agrarian life noted in Gascoigne's *Steele glas*. Richard Barnfield strips all social and economic activity down to the motivation of covetousness, or the pursuit of 'Lady Pecunia':

> For her, the Townsman leaves the Countrey Village:
> For her, the Plowman gives himselfe to Tillage.[21]

His markedly ambivalent appreciation of the role of money in a market society is epitomized in a comment that '*Pecunia*, is, as shee is used; / Good of her selfe, but bad if once abused' (sig. C3^b). In such an environment previously dominant assumptions about economic power and oppression are crucially revised. Early in the seventeenth century, when Samuel Rowlands introduces a poem with the title 'Wretched Husband-man', the farmer is in fact the target of his attack (as a corn-hoarder) rather than the victim one might have expected.[22] The satiric interrogation of a rampant market culture identifies pecuniary and competitive motivations even among the most lowly members of the commonwealth.

The most detailed consideration of agrarian conditions in the satires of

---

21 *The encomion of lady Pecunia* (1598); *The Complete Poems*, ed. George Klawitter (Selinsgrove, 1990), p. 155. Hake had provided an analogous vision twenty years earlier through his use of 'Sir Nummus' as the central character in *Newes out of Powles churchyarde*.

22 *Looke to it: For, Ile Stabbe Ye* (1604), sig. D1^b.

the 1590s is contained in Joseph Hall's *Virgidemiarum*.[23] Richard McCabe, in a recent study of Hall, attributes his interest in the countryside to his upbringing among the 'middling sorts' of the troubled county of Leicestershire.[24] (This local context suggests a parallel with the background of Hugh Latimer earlier in the century.)[25] But while Hall's adoption of a Horatian model embraces a certain commitment to positive values, his tone remains sceptical; his ethical foundation is in Stoicism rather than the gospellers' biblical fundamentalism.[26] In *Virgidemiarum* V.3 Hall focuses on the process of enclosure, and begins by looking back to the common-field system:

> And so our Grandsires were in ages past,
> That let their lands lye all so widely wast,
> That nothing was in pale or hedge ypent
> Within some province or whole shires extent:
> As Nature made the earth, so did it lie,
> Save for the furrows of their husbandrie. (p. 84)

As emphasized by the final rhyme on 'lie' and 'husbandrie', the poem argues that the ploughed furrows of the manorial fields actually reinforce the natural 'lie' of the land. This structure, however, is represented as irrecoverably lost, and the poem admits no interaction between past ideal and present reality. These assumptions inform his subsequent address to the encloser:

> Go to my thriftie Yeoman, and upreare
> A brazen walle to shend thy land from feare,
> Do so; and I shall praise thee all the while,
> So be, thou stake not up the common stile;
> So be thou hedge in nought, but what's thine owne,
> So be thou pay what tithes thy neighbours done,
> So be thou let not lye in fallowed plaine,
> That which was wont yeeld Usurie of graine. (p. 85)

23 Published in two parts (1597–8); references are to *Collected Poems*, ed. Arnold Davenport (Liverpool, 1949).
24 My interpretation of Hall's satire differs from that of McCabe, who argues that the focus on agrarian issues is motivated by a committed and straightforward moral reaction to agrarian change. See McCabe, *Joseph Hall: A Study in Satire and Meditation* (Oxford, 1982), pp. 53–72.
25 More than one-third of Leicestershire's villages were affected by enclosure in the sixteenth century (C. G. A. Clay, *Economic Expansion and Social Change: England 1500–1700* (2 vols., Cambridge, 1984), vol. 1, p. 76). Compare the more sanguine view of the county offered by the chorographer William Burton (below, p. 238).
26 See Selden, *English Verse Satire*, p. 67.

The passage is based upon a grudging acceptance of the inevitability of enclosure; yet it is laden with irony. The opening couplet links the yeoman's desire to define absolute property rights with the emergence of a socially corrosive 'feare' that these rights will be breached. After the catalogue of potential abuses which may arise from the demarcation of property, Hall's image of the 'Usurie of graine' reaped in the common-field system reiterates the perceived futility of enclosure. The reference to usury further evokes the expansive – and essentially pecuniary – ambitions of the 'thriftie Yeoman'. But it was the old system, destroyed forever by the yeoman's enclosure, which 'was wont' to yield such wholesome riches of grain for the sustenance of the community. The landscape of hedgerows and individualism offers no equivalent promise.

Subsequently, it is in a tone approaching that of pastoral nostalgia that Hall exclaims:

> Oh happy daies of olde *Deucalion*,
> When one was Land-lord of the world alone!   (p. 85)

The statement carries a definite echo of mid-century assertions of the doctrine of stewardship, which admits the absolute property rights only of God. But the particularities of Hall's reference inject a satiric complexity which reinforces his distance from traditional statements of agrarian complaint. For Deucalion and his wife Pyrrha were understood in classical mythology to have been the only survivors of the great flood; like Noah, Deucalion was the one good man preserved from the otherwise universal destruction of the species. Therefore, Hall suggests, the only world without property is a world without people. Given this scathing and cynical assessment of socio-economic practice, the ideals insisted upon in the discourse of complaint become no more than a distant standard by which to judge the essential sinfulness of humanity.

The Bishops' Ban of 1599 effectively halted the flow of formal verse satire.[27] The satiric impetus continued to produce sporadic publications of verse, yet the coherent movement of social satire based on classical models was not – within the period of this study – revived to any comparable extent. Seventeenth-century verse satire was refined, rather,

---

[27] On this attempt by the Church to suppress the publication of satire, see Richard A. McCabe, 'Elizabethan Satire and the Bishops' Ban of 1599', *Yearbook of English Studies*, 11 (1981), pp. 188–93.

as a genre for political and religious controversy.[28] It is thus appropriate
(before moving to the contemporary theatre) to conclude a consideration
of verse satire in the final years of the sixteenth century. Indeed Hall's
ideological shrug toward the 'thriftie yeoman' at once typifies the place
of satire within the flux of late sixteenth-century England, and anticipates
the stage of Jacobean city comedy. Whereas agrarian complaint
represented economic power being imposed with ruthless force by
covetous landowners upon humble tenants, satire concentrates rather on
the middling ranks of merchants, artisans and yeomen. Hall pinpoints the
language of 'thrift' and of proprietary rights over 'one's own'. A decade
later, one of the few Jacobean writers of social satire focuses similarly on
the 'reaching Yeomanry' who 'have growne wealthy through good
Husbandry'.[29] The discourses to be considered in chapters 5 to 7 have
altered the terrain of the debate over agrarian change; and the satirist
responds with a distinctly anxious uncertainty, Hall's hedging structure
of 'So be . . . So be . . . So be . . . ', paralleling Gascoigne's earlier 'Not
that . . . Nor that . . . Nor that . . . '

SATIRE AND THE STAGE

My principal concern in this section will be Jacobean satiric comedy. But
while this genre was clearly influenced by Elizabethan verse satire, it
must also be placed within the context of vigorous native dramatic
traditions; consequently, the following pages will first consider those
traditions, before concentrating on the Jacobean stage. The development
of English drama in the sixteenth century is often treated as a forgettable
period of transition between the medieval mystery play and the theatre of
Shakespeare.[30] Whatever critics may argue about their literary merit,
however, the extant morality plays from the century practically
demand consideration in a study concerned with the expression of social
and economic criticism.[31] For these plays contain a rich seam of

[28] See Selden, *English Verse Satire*, p. 3.
[29] Wither, *Abuses*, sig. G6b.
[30] See Alan C. Dessen's analysis of this critical strain, in *Jonson's Moral Comedy*
(Chicago, 1971), pp. 8–10.
[31] Discussion of these plays is often unnecessarily confused by shifting terminology,
including 'moralities', 'morality plays' and 'moral interludes'. In the interests of
clarity I will regularly use 'morality play' as an inclusive term, while I will also
occasionally draw attention to early interest in comedy as a form. (See also T. W. Craik,
The Tudor Interlude: Stage, Costume, and Acting (Leicester, 1967), p. 1; and David M.
Bevington, *From 'Mankind' to Marlowe: Growth of Structure in the Popular Drama of
Tudor England* (Cambridge, Mass., 1962), pp. 8–10.)

contemporary comment, which frequently incorporates a concern with the conditions and practices of the countryside. Moreover, the vitality and popularity of the genre is unquestionable. Early commercial troupes performed at court, in the halls of the nobility and gentry, and in open-air forums throughout the country. Printed texts, designed for use by professionals and amateurs alike, further ensured the influence of the plays. In the current context, a consideration of these texts will add an important dimension to an appreciation of the development – and distinctive vision – of early seventeenth-century satiric comedy.

The early history of the morality play indicates a certain ideological malleability as characteristic of the form. Thus David Bevington notes that the moralities had a marked 'independence from Christian doctrine, and were more flexible in doctrinal content – Catholic one day and violently anti-Papist the next, concerned with spiritual matters in one reign and with politics or social problems in another'.[32] This quality also allowed for consideration of particularly radical streams of thought. In the early sixteenth-century *Gentylnes and Nobylyte* (probably written by John Heywood), for example, some of the most extreme socio-economic ideas of the time are aired by a Ploughman who bursts in on a conversation between a Knight and a Merchant.[33] He subsequently dominates the play, as he moves from a conventional argument for the primacy of agriculture within the commonwealth, to an incisive critique of the bases of landed wealth. 'Grete possessions' gained by inheritance, he claims, 'Make no gentylmen but gentyl condycyons'; the laws of property are based on a history of 'tyranny', 'vyolence' and 'extorcyon' (lines 598, 601, 606). Bevington is probably right, however, to assess this play as an 'example of humanist drama intended solely for sophisticated tastes'.[34] The lack of action and the intellectual standard of argument – which belies the ploughman's recurrent claims to a rude, untutored wisdom – distance the text from the mainstream development of the morality play. It must serve, rather, as an indication of the radical potential of the form, and as a further reminder of the extraordinary ferment of social thought encompassed within the Piers Plowman tradition of the first half of the sixteenth century.[35]

[32] Bevington, *From 'Mankind' to Marlowe*, p. 114.
[33] Printed c. 1525 and probably first performed several years earlier. Richard Axton surveys evidence regarding authorship and date in his edition, *Three Rastell Plays* (Cambridge, 1979); references are to this edition.
[34] Bevington, *From 'Mankind' to Marlowe*, p. 42.
[35] See above, pp. 28–9.

The flexibility of the form also made it a troublesome tool for the mid-Tudor Protestants. John Bale wrote plays of religious and social polemic similar in temper to a Latimer sermon; but despite his efforts, the morality play was never bound to the movement of Protestant reform.[36] Indeed soon after the death of Edward VI, the early Marian *Respublica* effectively turned the morality play form against the Protestant gospellers, by allegorizing the previous reign as a government of Avarice, Insolence, Oppression and Adulation – vices which deceive Respublica by disguising themselves respectively as Policy, Authority, Reformation and Honesty.[37] The Edwardian project to refashion the Christian commonwealth is thereby rebuffed as one hypocritically steeped in the very corruption it claimed to be attacking. Yet after the religious and political upheavals of the mid-Tudor years, the morality plays of Elizabeth's reign follow a more consistent pattern of development.[38] Critics notice in these texts a transitional or hybrid quality. In their form, the plays became markedly more self-contained and distanced from the audience, a movement reinforced by a growing awareness of classical dramatic structure.[39] In content, the traditionally predominant spiritual orientation increasingly admitted secular elements, as the dramatists embraced more complex representations of social interaction.[40]

The mid-Elizabethan plays of William Wager in many respects typify this development. As noted above, the verse pamphlet *Whartons Dreame* claimed Wager – alongside Robert Crowley and John Foxe – as one who had 'perused and thought well of' the text, 'for the correcting of vice, and terrifyinge of the wicked'. Like Wharton's early essay in satire, Wager's plays combine an outlook rooted in the Reformation tradition with a sense of the widening literary potential of his genre. *Enough Is as Good as a Feast* (1570?) stages a battle for the soul of Worldly Man.[41] The

---

[36] See, especially, *A Comedy Concerning Three Laws of Nature, Moses and Christ*, c. 1548 (Tudor Facsimile Texts, London, 1908); and *King Johan*, ed. Barry B. Adams (San Marino, 1969).

[37] *Respublica: An interlude for Christmas 1553*, attributed to Nicholas Udall, ed. W. W. Greg (Early English Text Society, Oxford, 1952).

[38] On the popularity of the genre, see Dessen, *Jonson's Moral Comedy*, p. 10.

[39] Anne Righter, *Shakespeare and the Idea of the Play* (London, 1962), ch. 1.

[40] See Dessen, ch. 1; Bernard Spivack, *Shakespeare and the Allegory of Evil* (New York, 1958), chs. 7–8; Bevington, *From 'Mankind' to Marlowe*, p. 141.

[41] *'The Longer Thou Livest' and 'Enough Is as Good as a Feast'*, ed. R. Mark Benbow (London, 1967). Paul Whitfield White places this play within a tradition of Protestant social polemic, in *Theatre and Reformation: Protestantism, Patronage, and Playing in Tudor England* (Cambridge, 1993), pp. 94–9.

forces of evil are led by Covetous, who assumes the central role of
the Vice and declares his preeminence among the sins. 'Covetous is the
root of all evil; / Therefore, Covetous is the chiefest that cometh from the
devil' (lines 433–4). Medieval dramatic conventions here converge with
the gospelling tradition of the middle of the century: a debt reinforced by
the prophet Jeremiah, who enters to proclaim the strict morality of the
doctrine of stewardship and to remind Worldly Man of the 'weeping and
gnashing of teeth' that awaits him in hell (lines 1185–8, 1195–1208). For
his part, Worldly Man is figured as a rural landowner, and his oppressive
practices are highlighted by the complaint of a Tenant. The mid-Tudor
discourse of complaint is briefly embodied on the Elizabethan stage, as
the Tenant turns to the audience and asks:

> O masters, is not this even a lamentable thing,
> To zee how landlords their poor tenants do wring?
>
> (lines 981–2)

Yet Wager combines traditional statements of complaint with more
innovative literary strategies. Most notably, he introduces a satiric
concern with contemporary practice and discourse. While the disguise of
Covetous as Policy is conventional, his adoption of the role of estate
steward to Worldly Man fixes attention on a social type increasingly
associated with commercial practices of landowning (line 1055).[42]
Moreover, the renaming of Inconsideration as Reason and Precipitation
as Ready Wit focuses on an emergent language of economic rationalism,
evident in contemporary husbandry manuals.[43] Wager's critique of this
language is pursued at length in a debate over the definition of 'enough',
in which Worldly Man speaks as a zealous agrarian improver:

> Policy and Ready Wit: now the truth is so,
> There is no man living that can spare you two.
>
>   .   .   .
>
> For without a ready wit, who can answer make?
> Without a policy all commodities will slake
> A ready wit will soon gather and conceive
> What he shall forsake and what he shall receive.
>
> (lines 761–8)

---

[42] See D. R. Hainsworth, *Stewards, Lords and People: The Estate Steward and His World
in Later Stuart England* (Cambridge, 1992), ch. 1.
[43] Wager, in fact, highlights here the remarkable prescience which is so characteristic of
Renaissance social satire. In chapter 5, I will trace the emergence of 'reason' as a
central tenet of agrarian improvement; however, my analysis will show that this ideal
is given only shadowy definition before the consolidation of the agricultural reform
movement in the seventeenth century.

Wager presents here a social type over which ideological battles would be fought throughout the early modern period: the man who places market interests of 'commodities' before moral considerations of 'commonwealth'. Moreover, Worldly Man directly confronts traditional idealizations of the poor, as he claims that one may well 'be more heavenly . . . having riches / Than if you had nothing' (lines 823–4). In a manner which anticipates the arguments of the Puritan divine William Perkins, complaint is confronted with an ideology of godly individualism.[44]

In this respect *Enough Is as Good as a Feast* also highlights a gathering secularism in the Elizabethan theatre. The figures of the morality play during these years 'changed from simple personifications of vice and virtue into more complex and composite social types'. Covetousness fractured into a host of 'worldly men'. Consequently, 'relationships among the characters, long assumed to be static properties of the characters themselves, were now allowed to develop in a more or less linear sequence of scenes'.[45] This development was propelled at once by the literary movements with which I am concerned here, and by the religious changes considered in chapter 2. In Jean-Christophe Agnew's enlightening explication of the theatre and contemporary religious discourse, 'Elizabethan drama shared in the movement from moral abstraction to social type that had marked the late medieval sermon and that was beginning to influence the literature of characters.'[46] Combined, these converging cultural influences propelled the Elizabethan theatre toward a secular – and characteristically satiric – vision.

This shift gradually affected the representation of countrymen and women. In the Henrician *Gentylnes and Nobylyte*, the Ploughman asserts his role at the foundation of the socio-economic order; he tells the Knight and Merchant that 'every thyng whereby ye do lyf / I noryssh it and to you both do gyf' (lines 307–8). He is also satisfied with his position, and states that he would not change his 'lyffyng / For to be made a grete lorde or a kyng' (lines 425–6). Despite his occasionally remarkable social criticism, then, he affirms his affinities with the typical ploughman of the complaint tradition: harshly articulate, outspoken about the moral decay

44 On Perkins, see above, pp. 68–9.
45 Jean-Christophe Agnew, *Worlds Apart: The Market and the Theater in Anglo-American Thought, 1550–1750* (Cambridge, 1986), pp. 108–9. See also Bevington, *From 'Mankind' to Marlowe*, pp. 116–19.
46 Agnew, *Worlds Apart*, p. 116.

around him, yet committed to an ideal of a strictly ordered body politic. Not surprisingly, this convention in characterization had a lasting influence on Elizabethan drama. T. W. Craik notes the conventional dress, on the contemporary stage, of figures of Simplicity, Honesty and Plain Dealing as countrymen. Further, in the late Elizabethan *A Knacke to knowe a Knave*, Honesty introduces Piers Ploughman, who complains directly to the king about the competitive and rapacious practices of 'Walter the husbandman'.[47] The confrontation between the two rural figures sets the values of the complaint tradition against the man devoted to 'rais[ing] the markets' and 'increas[ing] his store' (sig. B2a). Piers complains that all the problems of the countryside have arisen

> by this unknown Farmer:
> For there cannot be an aker of ground to be sold,
> But he will find money to buy it: nay my Lord, he hath money
> to buy whole Lordships, and yet but a Farmer.   (sig. E3a)

The king endorses Piers as 'one of the best members in a common wealth' (sig. E3b), before Honesty dispenses appropriate punishments and rewards. The resolution stamps the strident moralism of the complaint tradition upon the form of the drama.

Yet the *Knacke*, performed in the age of Marlowe and Shakespeare, has an anachronistic ring (enhanced by its historical setting, which invites the audience to see Piers as a figure from the literary past as much as a farmer from the present). The mainstream developments in Elizabethan drama, by comparison, were converging upon a contemporary urban setting. As I argued above in relation to the parallel trend in verse satire, this shift prompts a radical reassessment of the moral ideals to which the ploughmen of both *Gentylnes and Nobylyte* and *A Knacke to knowe a Knave* appeal. The new plays increasingly question whether any group or individual is worthy of idealization. In Thomas Lupton's *All for Money*, for example, Money gloats of his hold over all levels of society:

> The Doctor, the draper, the plowman, the carter
> In me they have their joye and pleasure.[48]

Here the typically urban obsession with money is represented as also

47 Anonymous (1594); facsimile edn, ed. G. R. Proudfoot (Malone Society, Oxford, 1963).
48 (1578); Tudor Facsimile Texts (London, 1910), sig. A4a.

permeating the countryside, to infect even the once honest ploughman. The country can offer no positive values to counter the predominant ethic of self-interest. Furthermore, the stage was increasingly crowded by images of moral sins associated with the town. Just as contemporary preachers were turning their attention from the social sin of covetousness to individual depravities such as drinking, gambling and swearing, so the claims to preeminence of Wager's Covetous were being matched on the stage by a host of rival Vices. This development underpins satiric attacks on the lower social orders: a comic strategy itself interrelated with the gathering interest among Puritan preachers in the immorality of the poor.[49] The figure of the honest labourer is challenged on the Elizabethan stage by that of the idle waster; the oppressed ploughman is jostled by the shady vagrant. Ulpian Fulwell's *Like Will to Like*, for example, follows the road to damnation taken by Tom Tospot, Ralfe Roister, Cutbert Cutpurs and Pierce Pickpurs; as the prologue declares, the play is concerned to show 'To what ruin ruffians and roisters are brought'.[50] Similarly, *Common Conditions* creates the three tinkers Shifte, Drifte and Unthrifte.[51] Such plays also exploit the stereotyped figure of the lowly countryman as a figure of fun for an urban audience. The heavy accent (or 'Cotswold speech') of Wager's Tenant in *Enough Is as Good as a Feast* has the capacity to provoke a laughter of cultural superiority, while even the simple figure People in *Respublica*, despite occupying the moral centre of the play, elicits humour in his garbled references to the title character as 'Rice-Puddingcake'. Developments in dramatic comedy reinforced this tendency. The university play *Gammer Gurton's Needle* is accurately described as a 'college-man's laugh at unlearned country folk', who stumble and curse their way across the stage.[52] Morality play and comedy alike thus presage Jacobean satiric comedy, in which 'the countryside ceased to be the locus of enduring values and was ridiculed as the home of the peasant and the boor'.[53]

---

49 On the shift in religious discourse, from an idealization of to an interrogation of the poor, see above, pp. 67–9.

50 (1568); facsimile edn, *Two Moral Interludes* (Malone Society, Oxford, 1991), sig. A2ᵃ. Fulwell's creation was prefigured in *Respublica*, where Avarice complains that he is 'besieged nowe of everye cutpurse'; wherever he goes, 'piers piekpurse, plaieth att organes under my gowne' (lines 1244–6).

51 Ed. C. F. Tucker Brooke (New Haven, 1915).

52 (Performed 1566); Bevington, *From 'Mankind' to Marlowe*, pp. 33–4.

53 Kate McLuskie, '"Tis but a Woman's Jar": Family and Kinship in Elizabethan Domestic Drama', *Literature and History*, 9 (1983), p. 230. See also Jonathan Haynes, *The Social Relations of Jonson's Theater* (Cambridge, 1992), pp. 62–3.

These developments direct our attention to the professional theatre of early seventeenth-century London. One might see the journey toward that milieu, meanwhile, as curiously prefigured in a 1604 pamphlet by Thomas Middleton; a brief consideration of this text may help to elucidate the transition ahead. Middleton was a leading playwright of Jacobean city comedy. His early prose text *Father Hubburds Tales*, however, combines a satiric mode indebted to the poets and pamphleteers of the preceding decade with a renascent strain of agrarian complaint.[54] The central story scours the conspicuous consumption and moral depravity of merchants, lawyers and minor gentry in London; yet it is narrated by a 'brow-melting husbandman' – an honest worker drawn in the manner of the oppressed ploughman of complaint – who travels to the city in pursuit of his young landlord (p. 65). The latter is a prototype for the spendthrift gull of city comedy. On the death of his father he has left the patrimonial land for London, and has immediately fallen prey to a host of the city's economic predators. In an extended description of the landlord's opulent city dress, the Husbandman comments that his 'glorious rapier and hangers . . . drunk up the price of all my plough-land in very pearl, which stuck thick upon those hangers as the white measles upon hog's flesh . . . Thus was our young landlord accoutred in such a strange and prodigal shape, that it amounted to above two years' rent in apparel'. The mercer and tradesmen 'had fitted my young master in clothes, whilst they had clothed themselves in his acres, and measured him out velvet by the thumb, whilst they received his revenues by handfuls' (pp. 70–1).

Middleton's narrator is remarkable for his combination of traditional rural values with an urbane tone of satire. This point is not lost on the city wits when he confronts them; 'they little dreamed', he remarks, 'that we ploughmen could have so much satire in us as to bite our young landlord by the elbow' (p. 75). By contrast, the emerging milieu of city comedy allows young landlords to consume their wealth without reminders of its source.[55] The drama is loosed from the framework of social morality

54   *The Ant and the Nightingale: or Father Hubburds Tales* (1604); references to *Works*, ed. A. H. Bullen (8 vols., London, 1886), vol. 8. Compare the analysis of a didactic style of satire in Middleton's early dramatic efforts, in George E. Rowe, Jr., *Thomas Middleton and the New Comedy Tradition* (Lincoln and London, 1979), ch. 2.
55   My treatment of city comedy will focus particularly on the drama of Ben Jonson, Thomas Middleton and – to a lesser extent – Philip Massinger. The form, or subgenre, is documented in: L. C. Knights, *Drama and Society in the Age of Jonson* (London,

which Middleton's Husbandman brings with him from the country; and the ideal of an organic rural community gives way to a society in which the characters 'have ties not to each other, but only a direct tie of self-interest and survival to the city itself'.[56] The result, as Jonathan Haynes argues in relation to Ben Jonson's city comedy, is a vital form of 'satirical realism'. 'These plays, individually and collectively, are set in an extended, secular, social dimension . . . The moral and imaginative inheritance of the moralities is still very much alive . . . but they have been reformulated in the new secular environment.'[57]

Therefore, while the dramatists retained an abhorrence for the acquisitiveness and moral corruption they perceived around them (as L. C. Knights has demonstrated),[58] the defining attitude of their plays is more problematic, closer to the anxious resignation of Joseph Hall than the moral fundamentalism of Robert Crowley. This new complexity is largely due to the rising influence in the playhouses of the satiric mode, which drew the comedies away from the moral certitude inherent in the structure and purpose of the morality play. The medium thus has a capacity to resist, or subvert any authorial moralizing, as I will argue below in an analysis of Jonson's *The Devil is an Ass*.[59] Moreover, this formal characteristic in the drama is compounded by the cultural status of the professional theatre in Jacobean London.[60] Even more so than the verse satire of the 1590s, satiric drama was crucially implicated in the contemporary market society by virtue of its institutional basis in the new theatre companies. Don Wayne pursues the ramifications of this position by analysing the relationship between audience and author satirically defined in the Induction to Jonson's *Bartholomew Fair*, in which the Stage-Keeper announces 'Articles of Agreement, indented, between the *Spectators* or *Hearers* . . . on the one party; And the *Author of*

1937); Brian Gibbons, *Jacobean City Comedy* (London, 1968). See also, *Four Jacobean City Comedies*, ed. Gamini Salgado (Harmondsworth, 1975).
[56] Gail Kern Paster, *The Idea of the City in the Age of Shakespeare* (Athens, Ga., 1985), p. 152.
[57] Haynes, *Social Relations of Jonson's Theater*, pp. 6–9.
[58] *Drama and Society in the Age of Jonson.*
[59] See also Agnew, *Worlds Apart*, p. 110.
[60] The most important recent contribution is Douglas Bruster's *Drama and the Market in the Age of Shakespeare* (Cambridge, 1992). See also Haynes, *Social Relations of Jonson's Theater*; Agnew, *Worlds Apart*, ch. 3; Walter Cohen, *Drama of a Nation: Public Theater in Renaissance England and Spain* (Ithaca and London, 1985); and Don E. Wayne, who directly confronts Knights's *Drama and Society* in 'Drama and Society in the Age of Jonson: An Alternative View', *Renaissance Drama*, new series, 13 (1982), pp. 103–29.

Bartholmew Fayre . . . on the other party'. The contract binds the author to provide a play 'made to delight all, and to offend none', and cedes to the audience the right to 'like or dislike' according to the price they have paid. Hence 'it shall bee lawfull for any man to judge his six pen'orth, his twelve pen'orth, so to his eighteene pence, 2. shillings, halfe a crowne . . . Provided alwaies his place get not above his wit'.[61] This dramatic device, writes Wayne, 'is a cranky bit of satire; but it also constitutes an acknowledgement, however grudgingly, of the growing power of audiences in the public theatres'; and as such it 'reflects the weakening in the early seventeenth century of a reliable order of shared assumptions'. Consequently, the agreement supports Wayne's important argument that 'after his early theatrical triumphs, culminating in *Volpone* (1606), Jonson begins to show signs of a disturbed awareness that his own identity as poet and playwright . . . depended on the same emerging structure of social relationships that he satirized in his plays'.[62]

The quintessential landscape of city comedy is the marketplace.[63] The grotesque machinery of self-interest which the plays depict is typically set in motion by the arrival in town of a frivolous young gentleman. From the outset, therefore, the fundamental relationship between city and country is defined by exploitation: London is a world of competitive consumers, who greedily seize upon the 'autumnian blessing' drawn 'by sweat from the rough earth'.[64] As one conman states:

> we poor gentleman that want acres
> Must for our needs turn fools up, and plough ladies
> Sometimes.[65]

This process of representation turns the gaze of the market upon rural society and agrarian process, as the power of the city is seen to sprawl uncontrollably outward into the countryside. As a result, attempts to

---

[61] *Ben Jonson*, ed. C. H. Herford, Percy Simpson and Evelyn Simpson, 1st edn (11 vols., Oxford, 1925–52), vol. 6, p. 15.

[62] Wayne, 'Drama and Society in the Age of Jonson', pp. 15–16.

[63] Douglas Bruster, in fact, argues that the traditional critical attention to plays with a London setting has caused an artificially restricted categorization of 'city comedy' (*Drama and the Market*, ch. 3); and he rejects a generic approach in favour of an analysis of a far more widespread 'materialist vision' in Renaissance drama. While I would endorse the weight of his argument, it will be less contentious within the terms of the current study to concentrate here on plays which combine Bruster's 'materialist vision' with consistent reference to an English context.

[64] Middleton, *Michaelmas Term* (performed 1606); ed. Richard Levin (London, 1967), Inductio lines 6, 9.

[65] Meercraft, in Ben Jonson's *The Devil is an Ass* (performed 1616); III.i.367–9.

associate the land with values of stability and order – values which would affix a positive morality to the satire – are regularly frustrated. Most importantly, landowners are immediately reduced, on entering the arena of the city, to the level of economic competitors in possession of valuable commodities.

Philip Massinger appears to have been particularly unsettled by the social implications of this perception, and he attempts to counter the impetus toward economic anarchy by including virtuous members of the aristocracy in his plays. *A New Way to Pay Old Debts*, for example, sets the rise and fall of Sir Giles Overreach against the stable patrician ideal embodied in Lord Lovell. Although the play is generally considered a city comedy, the action does not actually require Lovell to move far from his hereditary seat in Nottinghamshire.[66] Middleton's plays, by comparison, embrace with characteristic satiric relish the social instability of London. His errant landlords tend to be of the lower gentry or upper yeomanry, the strata of society on which Renaissance verse satire increasingly focuses its attention. They are, moreover, frequently in financial trouble before their arrival in London, and this reduces them to competition on the citizens' terms. *A Trick to Catch the Old One* begins in 'a Leicestershire town', where Witgood admits to having squandered his property; his movement to London is impelled by an attempt to regain his lands through trickery.[67] The journey – like that of the old husbandman in *Father Hubburds Tales* – asserts the economic power of the citizens of London. The subsequent resolution apparently thwarts that power, as Witgood regains his property and returns to the country; however, his success is achieved only by matching deceit with deceit. The apparent assertion of traditional structures of landholding in the face of city usurers is thus laced with a destabilizing irony. As George Rowe recognizes, while Middleton's plays are 'filled with conventional ideas of order . . . these codes bear little relation to the events the plays depict'.[68]

In such a world, landowning is reduced to a relationship of rapacious desire. Quomodo, the draper and usurer of *Michaelmas Term*, fantasizes: 'Oh, that sweet, neat, comely, proper, delicate parcel of land, like a

---

66 Date of composition and staging unknown; first published 1633 (Massinger, *Plays and Poems*, ed. Philip Edwards and Colin Gibson (5 vols., Oxford, 1976), vol. 2).

67 First performed c. 1604–6; ed. G. J. Watson (London, 1968).

68 *Thomas Middleton*, p. 10. See, further, Margot Heinemann's comparison of Massinger and Middleton, in *Puritanism and Theatre: Thomas Middleton and Opposition Drama under the Early Stuarts* (Cambridge, 1980), pp. 101–4.

fair gentlewoman i'th'waist, not so great as pretty, pretty; the trees in summer whistling, the silver water by the banks harmoniously gliding' (II.iii.82–6). The land – like the virtuous countrywomen in a number of city comedies, agency in the marketplace typically being constructed as masculine – is laid bare in the citizen's imagination for his projected act of appropriation. Indeed his dreams of 'golden days' suggest a mercantile restatement of the pastoral tradition: rather than using the pastoral mode to celebrate the place of the gentry within an organic rural community (a central strategy of Ben Jonson's poem 'To Penshurst', as I will argue in chapter 9), Quomodo filters pastoral through a mind cankered by his commitment to self-advancement. The satiric intent is unmistakable, and unmistakably conservative. Yet it is a troubled conservatism. Strikingly, attempts to contrast the seething corruption of the city with an environment of morality, stability and fertility are relentlessly broken down by the material vision of the plays. In the Induction to *Michaelmas Term*, the allegorical figure representing the Term lays aside a white robe symbolizing conscience – 'That weed is for the country' – and adopts instead a 'civil black'. The driving logic of the play asserts the power of the city, and all that it represents, over the country; acquisition of land becomes the most important measure of success in the competitive flux of the market.[69] In an extension of Joseph Hall's despairing vision of the countryside, the institution of property is seen to be bereft of moral underpinning. The satire represents a world in which natural produce and rural virtues are inexorably transformed into commodities, in which the power to impose a pastoral fantasy upon the countryside is ceded to individuals most successful in the national marketplace concentrated in the city.

The most notable strategy employed in the plays to assert this pervasive appropriation of country by market-oriented city is the use on stage of legal documents.[70] Jonson's Induction to *Bartholomew Fair* heralds the consistent satiric attack of city comedy upon the law. A structure that once enforced moral values is seen to have been emptied of morality by the forces of individualism; it has replaced an ethics of social conservatism with the amoral power of market forces. It is perfectly

69 Rowe makes a similar point in his discussion of *Michaelmas Term*, but does not pursue the implications of the economic power of the city over the country to this extent (*Thomas Middleton*, p. 63).
70 As Raymond Williams observes, in the economic contests dramatized in city comedy 'it is titles to property ... which are passed and schemed for' (*The Country and the City* (London, 1985 edn), p. 51).

appropriate, therefore, that the desires of the citizens should be pinned to the variety of legal deeds, mortgages and land titles that appear in the plays. Luke Frugal, in Massinger's *The City-Madam*, dreams of,

> A mannor bound fast in a skin of parchment,
> The wax continuing hard, the acres melting.[71]

Quomodo watches his gull sign a bond, and delights: 'Now I begin to set one foot upon the land. Methinks I am felling of trees already' (*Michaelmas Term*, II.iii.338–9). And Witgood addresses his redeemed mortgage in the verse of a lover:

> Thou soul of my estate I kiss thee,
> I miss life's comfort when I miss thee.
> Oh, never will we part again,
> Until I leave the sight of men.
> We'll ne'er trust conscience of our kin,
> Since cozenage brings that title in.
>
> (*A Trick*, IV.ii.87–92)

The plays focus on the attitudes and rhetoric of early capitalism: a structure of discourse epitomized by the incessant 'What do you lack?', asked of visitors to Bartholomew Fair.[72] The exaggerated concern with documents of land-title pursues the levelling acquisitive logic of this discourse to the very foundation of social and economic order in the countryside. Whereas traditional representations of rural England focus on the role of the landlord as a godly steward within the manorial community, satiric comedy follows the implications of a world in which the market strips away all moral imperatives from social and economic relations. Land, like the fruit and toys of Bartholomew Fair, is claimed by the market as a commodity.[73]

---

[71] Performed 1632; *Plays and Poems*; vol. 4, III.iii.36–7.
[72] Cf. Bruster's analysis of a 'fetishization of commodities' in Renaissance drama (*Drama and the Market*, p. 42).
[73] This strategy of dramatic satire acutely highlights perceptions – and fears – that the very concept of landownership was being refashioned under the influence of market forces. In C. B. Macpherson's analysis, 'the spread of a capitalist market economy . . . brought the replacement of the old limited rights in land by virtually unlimited rights'. In consequence, 'As property became increasingly salable absolute rights to things, the distinction between the right and the thing was easily blurred . . . The thing itself became, in common parlance, the property' ('Capitalism and the Changing Concept of Property', in *Feudalism, Capitalism and Beyond*, ed. Eugene Kamenka and R. S. Neale (London, 1975), pp. 110–11). I will return to these issues relating to the representation of the land as property in my discussion of a discourse of estate surveying, in chapter 6.

The significance of the satiric perspective is best considered, at this point, by concentrating briefly on one particular text. Ben Jonson's *The Devil is an Ass*, first performed in 1616, is founded on a playful gesture toward the Tudor morality play.[74] Satan grants the inept devil Pug twenty-four hours to wreak havoc on London, but Pug's efforts are consistently thwarted by the more sophisticated corruption of the city.[75] In London, the devil is an ass. The play revolves around the Norfolk gentleman Fitzdottrel, whose wealth and wife become the objects of desire in two intertwined plots. Fitzdottrel is himself committed from the outset to the pursuit of money and social status, and his preparedness to participate in a particularly dubious marketplace inevitably precipitates his downfall. The values of that marketplace are embodied most notably in Meercraft, who is announced to Fitzdottrel by the broker Ingine as a 'great projector':

> FITZDOTTREL.   But what is a projector?
> I would conceive.
> INGINE.   Why, one Sir, that projects
> Wayes to enrich men, or to make 'hem great,
> By suites, by marriages, by undertakings:
> According as he sees they humour it.
> FITZDOTTREL. Can hee not conjure at all?
> INGINE.   I thinke he can, sir,
> (To tell you true).   (I.vii.9–15)

Joan Thirsk has provided a somewhat more reliable answer to Fitzdottrel's question; and in chapter 5, I will pursue some of the contemporary debates surrounding agrarian 'projects'.[76] Jonson, however, fixes upon the promoter of entrepreneurial business ventures as a figure symbolic of the 'conjuring' involved in a mercantile system. Meercraft claims:

> Sir, money's a whore, a bawd, a drudge;
> Fit to runne out on errands: Let her goe.
> *Via pecunia!* when she's runne and gone,

[74] References are to *Ben Jonson*, vol. 6.
[75] Robert N. Watson discusses the complex issues of genre in the play, in *Ben Jonson's Parodic Strategy: Literary Imperialism in the Comedies* (Cambridge, Mass., 1987), ch. 7.
[76] Thirsk, *Economic Policy and Projects: The Development of a Consumer Society in Early Modern England* (Oxford, 1978); see also below, pp. 151–6.

And fled and dead; then will I fetch her, againe,
With *Aqua-vitae*, out of an old Hogs-head!   (II.i.1–5)

Significantly, in all of Meercraft's schemes nothing is actually produced;
he merely manipulates money in order to make money, his mercantile
machismo reinforced by his derogatory feminization of the coinage. In
this respect he stands in direct contrast to the stable and naturally
productive order traditionally associated with the country. He underlines
this satiric point in his declaration that changes in landholdings are
merely the 'vicissitudes' of 'nature'. The husbandman's assumption of
regular seasonal change is translated into the merchant's perception
of economic flux. Meercraft's Nature 'makes / No man a state of
perpetuity, Sir' (II.iv.38–9).[77]

In order to cheat Fitzdottrel out of his inherited lands, Meercraft
proposes a project which plays on his gull's desire for still more property.
It involves the recovery of 'drowned land', or fenland, an issue of
enormous concern throughout the seventeenth century.[78] The drainage
of the fens was projecting on a vast scale, involving considerable
financial risks for the entrepreneur, and enormous social upheaval for
the existing inhabitants of the land.[79] In Jonson's play, Meercraft's
fraudulent project to make Fitzdottrel the 'Duke of Drown'd-land'
epitomizes the exploitation of a preexistent rural order by the acquisitive
ethos of the city. Significantly, the negotiations all take place in London,
where Meercraft illustrates his plan through the use of bogus surveyors'
maps. He declares, 'I have computed all, and made my survay / Unto an
acre' (II.i.52–3). Fitzdottrel later tells his wife:

This man defies the *Divell*, and all his works!
He dos't by *Ingine*, and devises, hee!
He has his winged ploughes that goe with sailes,
Will plough you forty acres, at once! and mills,

[77] See also Katharine Eisaman Maus, who valuably compares 'Satiric and Ideal
Economies in the Jonsonian Imagination', *English Literary Renaissance*, 19 (1989),
pp. 42–64.
[78] The controversy surrounding the draining of fenland presumably lay behind James I's
attempts to have Jonson's play 'concealed' (see Haynes, *Social Relations of Jonson's
Theater*, p. 32).
[79] Joan Thirsk presents a fine analysis of traditional fenland society and economy in the
county of Fitzdottrel's fantasies, in *English Peasant Farming: The Agrarian History of
Lincolnshire* (London, 1957), ch. 1. The upheavals caused by the drainage projects are
documented in K. J. Lindley, *Fenland Riots and the English Revolution* (London,
1982).

> Will spout you water, ten miles off! All *Crowland*
> Is ours, wife; and the fens, from us, in *Norfolke*,
> To the utmost bound of *Lincoln-shire*! we have view'd it,
> And measur'd it within all; by the scale!
> The richest tract of land, Love, i' the kingdome!
>
> (II.iii.45–53)

Jonson's humour is derived from a grotesque exaggeration of the language of economic individualism and agrarian improvement. Measurement 'by the scale' accords the estate maps a similar status to that conventionally given in city comedy to legal documents; the satiric effect, in each case, depends on the reduction of a site of community to a type of portable property.[80] Consequently, Fitzdottrel simply claims the land as 'ours', freed from any competing claims and pliable to the desires of the agrarian improver. In the mind of the gull, the superlative in the phrase 'richest tract of land' inevitably reflects upon his own expansive desires.

As the play progresses, Jonson clearly attempts to impose a resolution based on conservative standards of morality; and in this respect, *The Devil* presents a valuable study in the characteristic vision of city comedy. A sense of underlying moral ideals is regularly asserted by Eustace Manly, whose very name proclaims an association with sound, English, patriarchal virtues. Manly periodically comments on the action, convinces his friend Wittipol to abandon his sexual pursuit of Frances Fitzdottrel, and engineers a conclusion which thwarts Meercraft and protects the Fitzdottrel land. Anne Barton interprets this progression as morally satisfying, and draws attention in particular to the thematic development around the word 'trust'. She writes:

> Jonson seems to have been determined to activate the whole spectrum of its possible meanings, from the narrowly legalistic to the emotional and abstract. At the end of the comedy, these two extremes come together in the feoffment, the deed of trust by which Fitzdottrel surrenders possession of his land. This document, devised by the scoundrels Meercraft and Everill to ruin Fitzdottrel, who has trusted their stratagems in his usual gullible way, becomes the focus for trust of another and superior kind: the loyalty and 'fruitfull service' which ultimately unite Wittipol, Manly and Mistress Fitzdottrel in a league of honourable and disinterested affection.[81]

But this interpretation of 'trust' as a stable source of ethical value,

[80] I will consider the representational strategies of estate maps on pp. 189–94, below.
[81] *Ben Jonson, Dramatist* (London, 1984), p. 229.

upon which comic ideals of community may be founded, becomes increasingly problematic once one attends to the significance attached to the word in the world of the play. Manly himself acknowledges that trust can be a decidedly slippery concept. He says, for example, that while it was Everill's 'crime, so to betray mee: / I'am sure, 'twas more mine owne at all to trust him'; 'Deceiving trust', he says of the predator, 'is all he has to trust to' (IV.i.46–7, 54). In the light of these comments, I would argue that Jonson's play on 'trust' in fact typifies the markedly frustrated moralism of *The Devil is an Ass*. The moral forces triumph only when they accept the inherent dangers of trusting; and their ultimate assertion of control over the threatened deed of trust is only effected by adopting themselves the strategies of 'deceiving trust'. Like the law, trust becomes morally malleable. While certain values remain, these are continually compromised by the city; the movement toward a resolution is grounded as much on competitive tactics as it is on moral absolutes.

A crucial element of ambivalence also remains in the treatment of Frances Fitzdottrel. In contrast to her husband, Frances is associated throughout with the traditional values of the country, whereas the mechanisms of the market constantly operate to redefine her as merely another valuable commodity. In the opening act, her husband forms a 'contract' with Wittipol whereby the latter 'purchases' fifteen minutes of conversation with her (I.vi.63, 75). Fitzdottrel's assumption of a proprietorial power is epitomized in his subsequent request of a supposed London lady of fashion, to 'Melt, cast, and forme her as you shall thinke good! / Set any stamp on!' (IV.i.444–5). Manly's speech that concludes the play proclaims a resolution which apparently protects Fitzdottrel's 'modest, and too worthy wife' (V.viii.160); however, it is surely more than a modern attention to the representation of women which prompts a certain distaste in a conclusion that celebrates Frances's virtues as a subservient spouse. Her husband, moreover, is unredeemed: his second-to-last line dismisses Frances as 'a whore' (V.v.150). Suitably, the insult aligns with a rhetoric of exploitation which runs throughout the play, and thus reasserts at the last the amoral imperative of the market-place. While Manly may have been able to manipulate the law for moral ends in his handling of the deed of trust, the contract of marriage imposes a lasting order of abuse. The final scene thus frustrates the comic impetus toward a celebration of love and community.[82] As Kathleen

[82] See also Mary Beth Rose's analysis of love and sexuality in city comedy. She argues that the momentum toward comic conclusions consistent with romantic comedy is

McLuskie argues of Jonson, his typical refusal to celebrate unequivocally love and social harmony is largely motivated by an overriding commitment to a sharp satiric vision.[83] The 'city', one might say, overwhelms the 'comedy'.

Early in *The Devil is an Ass*, Fitzdottrel is preoccupied by a desire to get to the theatre, where he intends his opulent appearance to 'publish' himself as 'a handsome man' (I.vi.34). Similarly to the *Bartholomew Fair* Induction, these references to the cultural place of the London playhouses serve to remind the audience of their own complicity in the world of fashion and individualism satirized in the plays. The fact that the 'new play' Fitzdottrel is so keen to see is actually called *The Devil is an Ass*, moreover, curiously reflects upon the role of Jonson's own drama within Fitzdottrel's society (I.iv.21–3). For while playwrights 'could write plays against fashion', they themselves 'had to be fashionable';[84] and while they could write plays satirizing the market, the texts ultimately assumed their own positions within a competitive literary marketplace. The troubled ambivalence that pervades the stage of Jacobean city comedy is that of a satirist all too well aware of the breadth and complexity of the corruption he scours.

Throughout the latter sixteenth and early seventeenth centuries, the development of satire facilitated a sophistication in social criticism which far outstrips anything related to the complaint tradition. Renaissance satire, in both verse and drama, frequently achieves remarkable insight into the practices, motivations and discourses of a developing market society. Rural England becomes a landscape of competition and exploitation, within which no individual or social group can remain wholly innocent or virtuous. Ploughmen, yeomen and landlords alike devote themselves to paths of individualism, cloaking their motives with conveniently moralized rhetoric. Despite the continuing motivation toward complaint, the once solid ideals of moral economy appear tarnished and ineffectual. In the face of the emergent discourse of 'improvement' – the discourse to be analysed in chapters 5

---

typically 'qualified' or 'deflected': 'sexuality in city comedy is equated primarily with social disjunction and with sin' (*The Expense of Spirit: Love and Sexuality in English Renaissance Drama* (Ithaca and London, 1988), p. 50).

[83] *Renaissance Dramatists* (Atlantic Highlands, N. J., 1989), p. 159.

[84] Haynes, *Social Relations of Jonson's Theater*, p. 64.

to 7 – the satirist presents an incisive but strangely impotent criticism. Just as Jonson opens the door of his theatre to Fitzdottrel, so satire turns awkwardly out to accept its place within the society it wishes to condemn.

4. *Agrarian communism*

> When Adam delved and Eve span
> Who was then the gentleman?

During the reign of Edward VI, as the Protestant 'gospellers' sought to refashion their commonwealth, Hugh Latimer declared that 'The poorest plowman is in Christ equall with the greatest Prince that is.'[1] With its cautious distinction between an abstract 'Christian' equality within the new Church and any notion of social or economic equality, such a statement highlights the curious amalgam of moral outrage and political conservatism which characterized the complaint tradition analysed in the preceding chapters. From Bishop Latimer in the middle of the sixteenth century to Bishop Joseph Hall in the early seventeenth century, the discourse of agrarian complaint yoked appeals for social justice to demands for social stability. The consequences, as I have shown, were often troubling. The Edwardian pamphleteer Robert Crowley advises the destitute rather to 'lye in the streates & dye' than to take more forthright action.[2] The rewards for the poor and oppressed – as John Bunyan would agree at the end of our period – were principally those of the afterlife. Latimer's ploughman, Crowley's beggar and Bunyan's poor and itinerant pilgrim can all look forward – in Crowley's words – to being 'crowned at Gods hand' (sig. A3ᵇ). By contrast, any suggestions that one might link orthodox statements of complaint with a programme of social levelling were rigorously rejected.

As typified by Latimer's aphorism, however, the discourse of complaint naggingly suggests the potential for moral lamentation to sprawl outward into a radical critique of the social and economic fabric of the nation. As noted in chapter 1, Sir Thomas Elyot feared that the

---

[1] *27 sermons*, 2nd edn (1571), fol. 108ᵇ. See also above, pp. 30–2.
[2] *The Voyce of the laste trumpet* (1550), sig. A3ᵃ.

word 'commonwealth' might be taken to imply communal property;[3] and even the most careful of the 'commonwealths men' could slip on occasion into a tenor which would have confirmed his fears. Crowley writes in his *informacion and Peticion agaynst the oppressours of the pore Commons of this Realme*:

> we are all one mans chyldren, and have (by nature) lyke ryght to the richesse and treasures of thys worlde whereof oure natural father Adame was made Lord and Kinge. Which of you can laye for hym selfe any naturall cause whye he shoulde possesse the treasure of this wor[l]de, but that the same cause may be founde in hym also whome you make your slave? By nature (therefore) you can claime no thynge but that whiche you shall gette with the swet of your faces.[4]

It would be futile to speculate whether Crowley would have written more consistently in this vein had the political pressures of his age been different. The more important point, in the present context, is the unsettling spectre of communist thought to which both Elyot and Crowley, in different ways, draw our attention.[5] For most of the early modern era, strict censorship ensured that any expression of theories of common property and social revolution would be either totally suppressed or significantly distorted. In a study of representations of agrarian England in the early modern period, however, it is crucial to acknowledge the constant presence of such arguments. It is equally important, furthermore, to pursue those strains into the turbulent years of the middle of the seventeenth century, when proponents of communism were liberated from the constraints of monarchy and censorship.

The two sections of the chapter will divide at the collapse of censorship in 1640. In the first section I will trace some of the disparate strands of communist discourse from the later Middle Ages up to the early seventeenth century. The subsequent section will focus on the revolutionary milieu, and the writings of Gerrard Winstanley, the radical pamphleteer and leader of the 'true levellers', or 'Diggers'. For despite the failure of the Digger movement, which dwindled into a desperate

---

[3] See David Norbrook, *Poetry and Politics in the English Renaissance* (London, 1984), pp. 49–50.

[4] Second edn (1548), sigs. A7ᵇ–A8ᵃ. See further Norbrook, *Poetry and Politics*, p. 53.

[5] The word 'communism' was not coined until the nineteenth century. In the broad sense of 'a theory which advocates a state of society in which there should be no private ownership' (OED 1a), however, it is almost unquestionable that a range of early modern social critics and theorists were familiar with the concept. I will use the word and its derivatives in this inclusive manner.

struggle for the survival of a few dozen people on a meagre patch of ground outside London, Winstanley emerges from the page as an adept manipulator of language, with an extraordinary ear for rival discourses of rural order. On the one hand, he seizes upon the radical potential within the discourse of complaint, and proclaims from this basis a coherent vision of the earth as a 'common treasury' for all. On the other hand, he plays upon a discourse of agrarian improvement, in an arch attempt to justify his own extraordinary model for national renewal.

TRACES OF COMMUNISM BEFORE 1640

The peasant rebels of 1381 gathered behind their cause a radical tradition of folk wisdom when they confronted their betters with the question,

> When Adam delved and Eve span
> Who was then the gentleman?

The couplet appears to have originated in England in the early Middle Ages, and was subsequently disseminated across Europe through the fourteenth and fifteenth centuries.[6] Its impact could be modified considerably according to context; however, to a certain extent the lines attained a life of their own, directing a sly attack upon both accepted structures of property and ideological supports such as the doctrine of stewardship. It surfaces, for example, in both Henrician and Elizabethan drama; it is confronted in a sixteenth-century conduct manual for the gentry, and its currency after 1640 suggests an unabated popular vitality within aural and local cultures.[7] Yet it is almost impossible to gauge the extent to which such a scrap of provocative proverbial wit might indicate a coherent and continuing communist vision for the fields of the nation. While many of the radical ideas voiced in the middle of the seventeenth century can be traced to the Middle Ages, the nature of their transmission and influence throughout the rule of the Tudors and early Stuarts

---

[6] Albert B. Friedman, '"When Adam Delved . . .": Contexts of an Historic Proverb', in *The Learned and the Lewed: Studies in Chaucer and Medieval Literature*, ed. Larry D. Benson (Cambridge, Mass., 1974), pp. 213–30.

[7] See, for example, *Gentylnes and Nobylyte*, in *Three Rastell Plays*, ed. Richard Axton (Cambridge, 1979), lines 485–6; *Life and Death of Jacke Straw* (1593), quoted in Annabel Patterson, *Shakespeare and the Popular Voice* (London, 1989), p. 46; *The Institucion of a Gentleman* (1568 edn), sig. *7ᵇ; and Christopher Hill's discussion and examples, in 'From Lollards to Levellers', in *The Collected Essays of Christopher Hill, Volume Two* (Brighton, 1986), p. 100.

remains highly uncertain.[8] A sixteenth-century predecessor of Gerrard Winstanley may have lived, thought and died within the confines of a local rural community or religious sect, but the realities of censorship mean that we can hear of such individuals and their ideas 'only through the distorting medium of their enemies' attacks'.[9] Within this context, it will be appropriate here to consider various sources which may have informed communist thinking, while concurrently drawing together some surviving traces of such thought.

'Theories of lost rights, of a primitive happy state', writes Christopher Hill, 'have existed in nearly all communities.'[10] In Renaissance England, the most important sources for such theories were the Christian narrative of the Fall and the classical myth of a golden age. In Eden, Adam and Eve are instructed to 'dress and keep' a boundless garden ideally structured around their needs (Genesis 1–2). Classical authors trace a similar pattern of paradise lost, pivoting on the rise of Jupiter. Even in Virgil's *Georgics*, the predominant celebration of agricultural labour is placed in a framework of irreparable loss. As translated for a seventeenth-century audience, Virgil states:

> For *Jove* himselfe, loath that our lives should prove
> Too easie, first caused men the ground to move,
> Fill's mortall hearts with cares, nor sufferd he
> The world to fall into a Lethargy.
> Before *Joves* reign no Plow-man till'd the ground:
> Nor was it lawfull then their lands to bound:
> They liv'd in common all: and every thing
> Did without labour from earths bosome spring.[11]

The description conflates universal myth with local particularity; references to property markers and the symbolic ploughman (stretching the Latin plural *coloni*), in particular, invite English analogies. Despite the literary context and its inevitably elite audience, the contrast of

---

[8] Christopher Hill speculates about modes of transmission for radical thought in 'From Lollards to Levellers'.

[9] Christopher Hill, *The Religion of Gerrard Winstanley, Past and Present* Supplement 5 (1978), p. 11.

[10] 'The Norman Yoke', in *Puritanism and Revolution: Studies in the Interpretation of the English Revolution and the Seventeenth Century* (London, 1958), p. 50.

[11] *Georgics*, I.121–8; trans. Thomas May (1628), p. 7 ('pater ipse colendi / haud facilem esse viam voluit, primusque per artem / movit agros, curis acuens mortalia corda, / nec torpore gravi passus sua regna veterno. / ante Jovem nulli subigebant arva coloni; / ne signore quidem aut partiri limite campum / fas erat: in medium quaerebant, ipsaque tellus / omnia liberius, nullo poscente, ferebat').

present reality with a lost ideal serves to consolidate a vital cultural myth. And while both biblical and classical versions of the myth stress the permanent exile of humanity from paradise, the notion of a golden age beyond the bounds of property proved remarkably malleable when removed from the strictures of cultural orthodoxy. Indeed, throughout early modern Europe, evidence of popular and radical streams of thought demonstrates an ongoing plundering of existing cultural stores.[12]

Within scholarly circles, the awareness of classical and patristic debates over private and common property prompted a further appreciation of potential alternatives to the existing system. In a condensed summary of the complex issues passed down to the Renaissance, C. B. Macpherson notes that private property

> was attacked by Plato as incompatible with the good life for the ruling class; defended by Aristotle as essential for the full use of human faculties and as making for a more efficient use of resources; denigrated by earliest Christianity; defended by St. Augustine as a punishment and partial remedy for original sin; attacked by some heretical groups in mediaeval . . . Europe; [and] justified by St. Thomas Aquinas as in accordance with natural law.[13]

It was within this scholarly context that Sir Thomas More depicted a communist state in *Utopia*: a land by no means free of labour, but devoid of private property and socio-economic distinctions. As observed in chapter 1, More had no intention that *Utopia* should be read beyond the Continental humanist circles for which it was written, and in 1533 he declared that he would rather burn his book than see it translated into the vernacular.[14] Yet Ralphe Robynson's translation of 1551 – the preface to which suggests the possible application of the text to contemporary discussions of 'the common wealthes affaires' – marked the first and most significant attempt to pull the text in the opposite direction (sig. +3ᵃ). Over the following century, the idea of Utopia was added

12 As Carlo Ginzburg has shown in his classic study of an Italian miller early in the print era, the myths and rhetoric of an elite culture can undergo a vital sea-change when filtered through to a popular context (*The Cheese and the Worms: The Cosmos of a Sixteenth-Century Miller*, trans. John Tedeschi and Anne Tedeschi (London, 1980)). Harry Levin explores the significance of the golden-age myth, principally at the level of an elite culture, in *The Myth of the Golden Age in the Renaissance* (Bloomington and London, 1969).

13 'The Meaning of Property', in *Property: Mainstream and Critical Positions*, ed. C. B. Macpherson (Toronto, 1978), p. 9.

14 Norbrook, *Poetry and Politics*, pp. 30–1, 32.

to the cultural stock of myths of a communist state, as successive generations debated the relation of the Utopian model to More's native land. Thus the author is claimed by subsequent social critics as 'a great common-wealths man'; and the project of uprooting covetousness is heralded as a means of returning England 'to its first simplicity or . . . to a Christian utopia'.[15] Tellingly, the radical potential of the image is also a recurrent source of anxiety in the rhetoric of socio-political conservatism. Sir Thomas Smith declared to his Elizabethan audience that Utopia was merely one of a number of 'feigned commonwealths such as never was nor shall be, vaine imaginations, phantasies of Philosophers to occupie the time and exercise their wittes'.[16] By the revolutionary decades of the middle of the seventeenth century, the need to insist upon such an interpretation became increasingly pressing. Those who 'drive at a parity to have all men alike', insisted one writer, are followers of 'a Utopian fiction'.[17]

The ideals which underpin the communism of Utopia found further resonance through the prevalent but amorphous concept of natural law, which posited certain fundamental individual rights. Edmund Spenser, for example, links the subversive Fox in *Mother Hubbard's Tale* to this tradition, in a comment on the history of social inequality:

> There is no right in this partition,
> Ne was it so by institution
> Ordained first, ne by the law of Nature
> But that she gave like blessing to each creture,
> As well of worldly livelode as of life,
> That there might be no difference nor strife,
> Nor ought cald mine or thine.[18]

Although the Fox speaks as the lazy villain of Spenser's fable, his neat juxtaposition of a 'law of Nature' against a contrived order of property and competition – with its divisive language of 'mine or thine' – bears consideration. Indeed such arguments troubled both clergymen and

---

[15] Francis Trigge, *To the Kings most excellent Majestie* (1604), sig. F8ᵇ; Peter Chamberlen, *A Voice in Rhama* (1547), quoted in Christopher Hill, *The World Turned Upside Down: Radical Ideas During the English Revolution* (New York, 1972), p. 92.

[16] *De Republica Anglorum* (1583), p. 118.

[17] John Cooke, *Unum Necessarium: or, The Poore Mans Case* (1648), p. 36. Cooke also glances toward a classical philosophy of communism, as he dismisses 'that erroneous opinion of Plato' (p. 12).

[18] (1591); *Poetical Works*, ed. J. C. Smith and E. De Selincourt (Oxford, 1970), lines 143–9. (See also Hill, 'Norman Yoke', p. 52.)

lawyers throughout the sixteenth and seventeenth centuries, prompting a range of responses in justification of property. Many conceded that the law of nature embraced community of property, but claimed the necessity of private ownership in the cause of security and civilization. 'It was thought meet by generall good liking of all nations to bound out the dominions of everie man in severall proprietie: which course all the civill nations in the world doo inviolablie and lawfullie practise, notwithstanding the first law of nature was to the contrarie', Richard Cosin wrote in 1584. John Donne agreed that 'all mankind is naturally one flock feeding upon one Common', but private property was 'reasonably induc'd' for the sake of 'society and peace'.[19] In an important offshoot from this supposition, proponents of New World colonization supported their territorial claims with the argument that nature gives rights of property to whomever labours on vacant soil, a position not unrelated to Winstanley's assertions of the rights of the Diggers to the commons and wastes of England.[20]

More importantly, observations from the New World were used to support arguments that the natural state of human society precluded private property. Peter Martyr, the chronicler of the Columbian expeditions, remarked on the lack of any signs of property-holding in Cuba: 'these natives enjoy a golden age, for they know neither *meum* nor *tuum*'.[21] Later, Michel de Montaigne's famous essay 'On Cannibals' (available in English translation from 1603) celebrated a society of primitive communism which highlights, by contrast, the imperfect institutions of civilization. The savages are commanded only by the 'laws of nature'. Indeed, the land without riches, poverty, contracts, falsehood and covetousness offers a model which, on earth, 'exceed[s] all the pictures wherewith licentious Poesie hath proudly imbellished the golden age . . . to faine a happy condition of man'.[22] Shipwrecked on a desert island in Shakespeare's *The Tempest*, the honest courtier Gonzalo recalls Montaigne, in a speech motivated by a simple longing for social harmony.[23] A similar longing was clearly alive amidst the turbulence of the middle of the seventeenth century, and thus helped to shape

---

[19] Quoted in J. P. Sommerville, *Politics and Ideology in England, 1603–1640* (London, 1986), p. 147.
[20] Sommerville, *Politics and Ideology*, p. 146.
[21] Quoted in Levin, *Myth of the Golden Age*, p. 60.
[22] *Essayes*, translated from the French by John Florio, ed. J. I. M. Stewart (New York, n.d.), p. 164.
[23] *The Tempest*, II.i.141–66.

Winstanley's conception that the fundamentally natural laws of the universe reflect values of cooperation and Christian community. Ironically, the representation of the 'state of nature' in the contemporary writings of Thomas Hobbes would be immensely more influential than Winstanley's idealism, as revolution lurched toward the restoration of both monarchy and the order of property. Hobbes's man in the state of nature is in effect the antithesis of Winstanley's: a competitive individualist afloat in a world of profit and loss.[24]

The work of Winstanley will highlight the extent to which the various myths, philosophies and fictions of common property established a vital cultural context within which a radical reformer might formulate a model for social revolution. Before 1640, by comparison, the history of attempts to give coherent shape and purpose to communist theories remains unclear; however, persistent traces of evidence suggest at least a vague and fragmentary heritage within popular political movements and radical religious sects. On the Renaissance stage, Shakespeare asserted a link between the 'many-headed monster' of popular uprisings and garbled arguments of social levelling.[25] In *II Henry VI*, for instance, the mob masses for a clumsy revolution:

FIRST REBEL. I tell thee, jack Cade the clothier means to dress the commonwealth, and turn it, and set a new nap upon it.
SECOND REBEL. So he had need, for 'tis threadbare. Well, I say, it was never merry world in England since gentlemen came up. (IV.ii.5–10)

While Shakespeare appears to have been concerned to discredit contemporary forms of popular protest, it is possible that arguments such as those ascribed to Cade and his followers were troublingly resilient to authoritarian disdain.[26] In Shakespeare's native county early in the seventeenth century, for example, 'The Diggers of Warwickshire' asserted their intention to arise and 'manfully dye' rather than 'be pined to death' by the effects of enclosure and encroachment.[27] Similarly, in

---

[24] See Hill's comments on 'Hobbes and Winstanley: Reason and Politics', in *The World Turned Upside Down*, pp. 313–19.
[25] See also Christopher Hill's enlightening study of representations of rioters and rebels in the century before 1640, in 'The Many-Headed Monster', in *Change and Continuity in Seventeenth-Century England* (London, 1974), pp. 181–204.
[26] Richard Helgerson considers Shakespeare's representations of commoners and rebels – and reviews recent arguments surrounding this issue – in *Forms of Nationhood: The Elizabethan Writing of England* (Chicago and London, 1992), ch. 5.
[27] BL Harleian MS 787, no. 9; printed in *The Marriage of Wit and Wisdom*, ed. J. O. Halliwell (London, 1846), pp. 140–1.

the Oxfordshire Rising of 1596, one of the leaders was said to have 'intended to kill the gentleman [sic] of that countrie, and to take the spoile of them', as the first step toward a national revolution. It was, he claimed, 'but a monethes work to overrunne England'.[28]

Such quotations must be placed in the context of broad agreement among historians regarding the conservative nature of rural riots in early modern England. As noted in chapter 1, agrarian uprisings were typically motivated by a desire to protect preexistent rights and social relations.[29] But while it appears that no riot or rebellion in the period was raised on an overtly communist platform, such beliefs frequently surfaced at the fringes of popular movements. During the Pilgrimage of Grace in Henrician Norfolk, one rebel proclaimed that 'yt were a good turn yf ther were as many jantylman in Norff [sic] as ther be whyt bulls', while Peter Clark finds 'sporadic . . . outbursts of seditious language and primitive levellerism' in the otherwise conservative history of popular protest in Kent.[30] Moreover, as Christopher Hill argues, the rhetoric of the rural riot could easily be pushed by radical elements toward suggestions of social levelling. In 1549, 'men were saying "there are too many gentlemen in England by 500"; "gentlemen have ruled aforetime, and they [i.e. the commons] will rule now"'.[31] By the seventeenth century, one historian has discerned an 'approaching class hatred' in the widespread local upheavals of the pre-revolutionary years.[32] As the inexorable forces of socio-economic change polarized the propertied and unpropertied, the lower orders were increasingly prompted to question traditional rural ideals of community and morality. 'England was still very far from being a class society, but the lines were beginning to sharpen, the horizontal ties linking the "respectable" and dividing them from the poor to cut across the vertical ones of local identity.'[33] The massing forces of

28 Edwin F. Gay, 'The Midland Revolt and the Inquisitions of Depopulation of 1607', *Transactions of the Royal Historical Society*, new series, 18 (1904), p. 238.
29 This central argument underpins both Roger B. Manning, *Village Revolts: Social Protest and Popular Disturbances in England, 1509–1640* (Oxford, 1988); and David Underdown, *Revel, Riot and Rebellion: Popular Politics and Culture in England, 1603–1660* (Oxford, 1985).
30 C. E. Moreton, *The Townshends and Their World: Gentry, Law, and Land in Norfolk c. 1450–1551* (Oxford, 1992), p. 71; 'Popular Protest and Disturbance in Kent, 1558–1640', *Economic History Review*, 2nd series, 29 (1976), p. 380.
31 'Many-Headed Monster', p. 182.
32 Buchanan Sharp, *In Contempt of All Authority: Rural Artisans and Riot in the West of England, 1586–1660* (Berkeley, 1980), p. 8.
33 Underdown, *Revel, Riot and Rebellion*, p. 20.

revolution, meanwhile, could only have encouraged marginal cries for a class-based assault on the power of the gentry.[34]

The gathering ideological ferment of the seventeenth century also highlights the significance of radical religious sects as fertile plots for the propagation of communist thought. Indeed, throughout the early modern era the potential conjunction of the power of the mob with subversive religious doctrine presented the most threatening scenario of social upheaval to the state and landowners alike. By definition, sects challenge theological orthodoxy; and in Tudor and Stuart England, their attacks frequently focused upon the bonds linking the Church with structures of economic and political power. Hill notes that 'William Tyndale in 1528 had alleged that the hierarchy of his day said to the King and lords "these heretics would have us down first, and then you, to make of all common." The argument was repeated by the Elizabethan bishop Bancroft, and became a commonplace.'[35] The apparent social threat of sectarianism was further supported by the recent history of the Lollards, who were associated from the outset with notions of common ownership. Anne Hudson traces this link to John Wycliffe's 'views on dominion, that only the just have true possession; since the just are by definition in perfect charity, they would wish to share their goods, whether spiritual or temporal'.[36] As Hudson argues, this is not a particularly strident position, nor was it ever central to Wycliffe's thought. Yet the popular association of the Lollards with the 1381 revolt, and the debt which the peasants' leader John Ball declared to the preaching of Wycliffe, inevitably influenced the future of Lollardy; and it is likely that communism was considered a significant commitment by many of those of the lower socio-economic orders attracted to the movement through the fifteenth and early sixteenth centuries.[37] Certainly one text linked to Lollardy, *The Praier and Complaynte of the Ploweman unto Christ*, outstrips almost any other contemporary work of religious and social complaint with its 'very radical theory of the nature of property'.[38] 'Who that beth in charite possesseth thy goodes in comune, and nat in propre', it states. 'And than

---

[34] See Brian Manning's arguments regarding the significance of the gulf between gentry and commons, in *The English People and the English Revolution*, 2nd edn (London, 1991).

[35] *The World Turned Upside Down*, p. 26.

[36] *The Premature Reformation: Wycliffite Texts and Lollard History* (Oxford, 1988), p. 374.

[37] Hudson, *Premature Reformation*, pp. 66–7, 128–33.

[38] The anonymous text could, according to Hudson, *Premature Revolution* (p. 11), date from any time between 1384 and 1530; it was published around 1531, probably at

schall there none of hem seggen "thys ys myne", but it is goodes that God graunteth to us spenden it to hys worschupe' (sig. E6ᵇ).

The publication of *The Praier and Complaynte of the Ploweman* on the eve of the Reformation in England suggests at least an informal connection between Lollardy and radical movements such as Anabaptism. By the 1530s, Anabaptists were coming to the attention of the English authorities; and, throughout the history of Catholic and Protestant attacks on the sect, the issue of common property was of particular concern. Thus a Henrician pardon granted to heretics in 1540 specifically excluded the Anabaptists, noting 'their insistence that "all things be common"'.[39] And as the Protestant Church was increasingly enmeshed with institutions of state power, the potential of religious threats to the order of property remained a constant source of anxiety. The Edwardian 'Exhortation concerning Good Order' expresses a fear that without an observance of existing social and political structures, 'all thynges shal be common, and there must nedes folow all mischief and utter destruction, both of soules, bodies, goodes and common wealthes', while the Martin Marprelate controversy, in the reign of Elizabeth, prompted further authoritarian justifications of 'the good gifts of God', such as 'Lordshippe, dominion, lands, riches, money & such like'.[40] Nonconformist groups, by rejecting the governance of the state Church, inevitably courted accusations of social heterodoxy. Even the relatively affluent members of the Family of Love, a sect established in England by followers of the Dutch mystic Hendrick Niclaes, were attacked as 'seekers for a paritie and commixion of all states'.[41] After the collapse of censorship in the 1640s, English translations of a number of Niclaes's works were published by the notorious sectarian printer Giles Calvert, around the same time as he was working on Winstanley's early pamphlets.[42]

Antwerp (STC 20036): Helen C. White, *Social Criticism in Popular Religious Literature of the Sixteenth Century* (New York, 1944), p. 27.

[39] George Huntson Williams, *The Radical Reformation* (London, 1962), p. 403.

[40] *Certayne Sermons, or Homelies* (1547), sig. R1ᵇ; Thomas Cooper, *An Admonition to the People of England*, 3rd edn (1589), p. 204. See also Hill, *The World Turned Upside Down*, p. 92; and Paul Elman, 'The Theological Basis of Digger Communism', *Church History*, 23 (1954), p. 214.

[41] *A supplication of the Family of Love* (Cambridge, 1606), p. 20; quoted in Christopher W. Marsh, *The Family of Love in English Society, 1550–1630* (Cambridge, 1994), p. 203. Ironically, Marsh's research into the group's practices of mutual economic support reveals a predominant tough-minded mercantilism, rather than any inclinations towards social levelling (pp. 157–61).

[42] George H. Sabine, introduction to Winstanley's *Works* (Ithaca, 1941), p. 28.

Turning toward the radical outpouring of the middle of the seventeenth century, it is important to note at once a resilient undercurrent of dissatisfaction with the conservatism of orthodox complaint, and a certain cultural preparedness for the sustained arguments of writers such as Gerrard Winstanley. The disparate traces of communist thought apparent throughout the centuries preceding 1640 suggest no great coherence or consistency; they do, however, indicate a subversive vitality throughout a broad range of contexts. On the surface, there can be little relation between an elite culture discussing the respective merits of Plato and Aristotle, and a popular culture in which an enclosure rioter echoes the rebels of 1381. Yet the heterogeneity of the traces should not be allowed to outweigh evidence that many people were able to envisage an alternative structure of social and economic relations for rural England. Latent similarities – highlighted in the syncretic vision of Winstanley's works – are perhaps more important than any coherent processes of intellectual or political development.

GERRARD WINSTANLEY AND THE REVOLUTIONARY MILIEU

Freedom of the press between 1641 and 1660 permitted, for the first time since the introduction of print, the coherent expression of a wide range of radical ideas. Moreover, while many such ideas had a considerable heritage, the discourse of the revolutionary period was impelled by a sense of almost infinite potential for refashioning the social and political substance of the country. The very possibility of a nation without a monarch removed, at a stroke, the keystone of hierarchical notions of the body politic and social order, and a host of writers and reformers focused upon the potential ramifications of this one revolutionary act. Some challenged the system of law and justice, which was perceived as an imposition of the 'Norman yoke' symbolized by the Stuart king.[43] Religious sectarians saw the abolition of monarchy as also encompassing a rejection of the state Church and its structure of episcopal rule. And Winstanley was not alone in linking 'kingly power' to property, economic competition and warfare; covetousness, he proclaims, is 'the great Law-giver of . . . Kingly Government' (pp. 529–30).[44] Never before had the commonwealth and its structures of ideology seemed so

---

[43] See Hill, 'Norman Yoke', pp. 67–82.
[44] All Winstanley references are to *Works*, ed. Sabine.

malleable. One writer typified the prevailing mood when he told parliament, 'God hath put the Nation like wax into your hands, that you may mould and cast it into what Form your Honours please.'[45]

In the countryside, there were early indications that the revolutionary parliaments would fulfil many expectations of national reformation. Agrarian issues had attained fresh prominence in the wake of poor harvests in the 1620s and 1630s, which in many areas had exacerbated problems of rural poverty to the point of mortality crisis.[46] The old sore of depopulating enclosure, concomitantly, was returned to 'the forefront of public debate on the eve of the Civil War'.[47] With the benefit of hindsight, the urgent political action of these years had little lasting impact upon the unfolding processes of social and discursive change.[48] But it is understandable that at the time reformers would link the political upheaval in the capital to the gathering pressure for rural action on behalf of the lower orders. Thus the demise of 'kingly power' appeared to many to provide opportunities – not unlike those perceived by religious reformers at the dissolution of the monasteries a century earlier – for a redistribution of resources. Ironically, as historians have documented, those who did manage to purchase land during the Interregnum generally 'wanted to improve the cultivation . . . along capitalist lines, so as to maximize the national wealth, and with it their own'.[49] Moreover parliament typically placed agrarian problems 'low in the list of priorities', and it appears that its interest in agrarian reform waned considerably from the late 1640s.[50] Yet for a person with radical leanings, such trends merely reinforced the sense of urgency propelling

---

45 William Sprigge, *A Modest Plea for an Equal Common-wealth Against Monarchy* (1659), sig. A2ª.
46 See Andrew B. Appleby's analysis of the mortality crisis of 1623, in *Famine in Tudor and Stuart England* (Liverpool, 1978), pp. 121–32.
47 Joan Thirsk, 'Agrarian Problems and the English Revolution', in *Town and Country-side in the English Revolution*, ed. R. C. Richardson (Manchester, 1992), p. 170.
48 As I argued in chapter 2, the spate of enclosure debate in the 1630s – for all its vehemence – indicates that the ideological certainties that had underpinned the discourse of agrarian complaint throughout the preceding century were gradually being replaced by scepticism and outright opposition.
49 Hill, 'The Agrarian Legislation of the Revolution', in *Puritanism and Revolution*, p. 156. See also Thirsk, 'Agrarian Problems and the English Revolution', p. 173, though she also gives local examples of 'idealist aspirations' being put into place (pp. 188–9).
50 Thirsk, 'Agrarian Problems and the English Revolution', p. 174; Hill, *The World Turned Upside Down*, p. 44.

reformist proposals. The opportunity was alive as long as the monarchy was expunged and the press was free.

The one proposal for agrarian reform which attracted considerable interest among both parliamentarians and radical pamphleteers, and which therefore established something of a context for Winstanley's communism, was the idea of an 'agrarian law' which would restrict the size of land holdings. The agrarian law was adapted from Roman practices of dividing conquered territory, though its most famous proponent, James Harrington, traces its origin to the ethics of 'God himself, who divided the land of Canaan unto his people by lots'.[51] On the surface, this concept promised to level inordinate socio-economic distinctions, which in turn unbalanced the structures of political power. Harrington's 'Commonwealth of Oceana' (a thinly veiled image of the author's land) is thus

> founded upon an equal agrarian; and if the earth be given unto the sons of men, this balance is the balance of justice, such an one as, in having due regard unto the different industry of different men, yet *faithfully judgeth the poor. And the king that faithfully judgeth the poor, his throne shall be established forever.*[52] Much more the commonwealth; seeing that equality, which is the necessary dissolution of monarchy, is the generation, the very life and soul of a commonwealth. (p. 220)

The definition engages a deep-rooted desire, inherited from previous generations of reformers and radicals, for a greater 'equality' or 'balance' in property relations. In agreement with Winstanley's notion of the demise of 'kingly power', that equality is represented as surging forth as the 'necessary' consequence of the 'dissolution of monarchy'.

It must be emphasized, however, that the conception of an agrarian law is firmly grounded in an acceptance of private property. Even in the clean-slate environment of Oceana, Harrington defined the agrarian as a 'fundamental law', which states 'what it is a man may call his own, that is to say property, and what the means be whereby a man may enjoy his own' (p. 100). Harrington's goal was not to overthrow the legal and economic structures of private ownership, but rather 'to establish a balance of property which would prevent excessive competition and excessive accumulation'.[53] The most practical proposals of the time to

[51] *The Commonwealth of Oceana* (1656); *'The Commonwealth of Oceana' and 'A System of Politics'*, ed. J. G. A. Pocock (Cambridge, 1992), p. 13.
[52] Proverbs 29.14.
[53] Christopher Hill, Introduction to Winstanley, *The Law of Freedom and Other Writings*, ed. Hill (Cambridge, 1983), p. 50. Harrington's Utopia of freeholders roughly

bring such ideals to bear upon the complex structures of land tenure in England were designed principally to reduce the property of the wealthiest, and thus to provide more opportunities for industrious individuals from the middling sorts to become landowners. In this respect the reformers linked the agrarian law to the flood of contemporary interest in rural improvement. As I will argue in the following chapters, the discourse of agrarian improvement consistently shifted the focus of concern in the countryside away from the downtrodden ploughman of the complaint tradition, toward the yeoman, who was eulogized as independent, innovative and concerned in his labour with the profit of both himself and his country. This influence is also apparent in the democratic Calvinism of the Levellers, the political group to which Winstanley reacted by coining for his own followers the title 'True Levellers'. In a movement at least partly caused by a political desire to distance themselves from Winstanley's Digger experiment, the Levellers in the late 1640s publicly repudiated ideas of common property. A manifesto of 1649 declared that they 'never had it in our thoughts to level men's estates, it being the utmost of our aim that . . . every man with as much security as may be enjoy his property'.[54]

A late proponent of the agrarian law assured his readers that 'an Agrarian . . . may be introduc'd, without breaking down the hedge of any mans propriety'.[55] By contrast, for Winstanley the hedges were the very problem that he wanted to uproot. In fact Winstanley seized upon the hedge, which had long been identified in the popular imagination with enclosure, as a central symbol of property, the law, political and religious exclusion, and 'kingly power'. In a highly metaphorized attack on the kingly power and 'his son Propriety', Winstanley describes the law as 'but the strength, life and marrow of the Kingly power, upholding the conquest still, hedging some into the Earth, hedging out others; giving the Earth to some, and denying the Earth to others' (p. 388).[56] As he weaves together allusions to enclosure, the Norman yoke, the last Stuart king and the laws of property, Winstanley reinforces his fundamental

---

corresponds with the social vision presented a decade earlier by Gabriel Plattes in *Macaria* (1641).

[54] Quoted in David W. Petegorsky, *Left-Wing Democracy in the English Civil War: A Study of the Social Philosophy of Gerrard Winstanley* (London, 1940), pp. 161–2; see also Hill, *The World Turned Upside Down*, pp. 95–6.

[55] Sprigge, *A Modest Plea*, p. 85.

[56] Christopher Hill also draws attention to Winstanley's description of religious sects, which 'are like the inclosures of land which hedges in some to be heirs of life, and hedges out others' (pp. 445–6): (*Religion of Gerrard Winstanley*, pp. 52–3).

contention that the 'bondage of Civil Propriety' lies at the very heart of the web of problems facing his contemporary reformers (p. 257). It is from this point that I wish to approach Winstanley's communist vision for rural England. In doing so, one should not expect to find perfect clarity or coherence: his pamphlets were written for various different purposes and audiences, and suggest a mind actively grappling toward a cogent theory. The aim here, rather, will be to focus on Winstanley's striking representations of existing practice within, and revolutionary potential for, the English countryside.

Winstanley was profoundly dissatisfied with the social criticism propounded by the established Church. Its emphasis upon the punishments and rewards of the afterlife, he believed, abandoned principles of social justice to the defence of an order grounded upon oppression. This doctrine is 'a cheat; for while men are gazing up to Heaven, imagining after a happiness, or fearing a Hell after they are dead, their eyes are put out, that they see not what is their birthrights' (p. 569).[57] By contrast, Winstanley placed himself from the outset of his publishing career within radical traditions of religious mysticism.[58] In one of his first tracts he explains why 'I use the word Reason, instead of the word God, in my writings', by drawing a distinction between 'mans reason' and 'the Spirit Reason'. He asks:

> But is mans reason that which you cal God? I answer, mans reasoning is a creature which flows from that Spirit to this end, to draw up a man into himselfe: it is but a candle lighted by that soul, and this light shining through flesh, is darkened by the imagination of flesh; so that many times men act contrary to reason, though they thinke they act according to reason.
>
> . . . but now the Spirit Reason, which I call God . . . is that spirituall power, that guides all mens reasoning in right order, and to a right end: for the Spirit Reason, doth not preserve one creature and destroy another . . .

---

57 See further, Petegorsky, *Left-Wing Democracy*, pp. 190–1.
58 The extent of the debt remains a point of contention among historians. At the extremes of the debate, he is seen either as a millenarian whose religious beliefs determined his social doctrine, or as a man who broke with his roots in mysticism to develop a fundamentally secular theory of oppression and revolution. See, for example, Winthrop S. Hudson, 'Economic and Social Thought of Gerrard Winstanley: Was He a Seventeenth-Century Marxist', *Journal of Modern History*, 18 (1946), pp. 1–21; and compare George Juretic, 'Digger No Millenarian: The Revolutionizing of Gerrard Winstanley', *Journal of the History of Ideas*, 36 (1975), pp. 263–80. Hill reviews the debate in *Religion of Gerrard Winstanley*, pp. 1–2.

but it hath a regard to the whole creation; and knits every creature together
into a onenesse; making every creature to be an upholder of his fellow.

(pp. 104–5)

This manipulation of conventional terminology establishes his
determined opposition to contemporary notions of 'reason', which were
widely employed to promote agrarian improvement and economic
development. Such uses of 'mans reasoning', he counters, are motivated
rather by 'imaginative' forces of covetousness and division. By contrast,
he represents the 'Spirit Reason' as a force which sweeps aside
seventeenth-century individualism to establish a genuine religious
community.[59]

From this basis in mystical thought Winstanley developed his belief
that property is essentially an artificial structure of exclusion and
oppression. In *The True Levellers Standard Advanced*, the first manifesto
of the ill-fated Digger community, he moves toward a mythic
explanation of the Fall as an uprising of 'selfish imagination' against the
'Spirit Reason':[60]

> And hereupon, The Earth (which was made to be a Common Treasury
> of relief for all, both Beasts and Men) was hedged in to In-closures by the
> teachers and rulers, and the others were made Servants and Slaves: And
> that Earth that is within this Creation, made a Common Store-house for all,
> is bought and sold, and kept in the hands of a few, whereby the great
> Creator is mightily dishonored, as if he were a respector of persons,
> delighting in the comfortable Livelihood of some, and rejoycing in the
> miserable povertie and straits of others. From the beginning it was not so.
>
> (p. 252)

The biblical echoes evoke the narrative of Genesis. But, as Hill argues,
Winstanley inverts the traditional belief that labour and property are
inescapable consequences of the Fall; instead he presents the very
process of hedging the land 'in to In-closures' as the act which causes, or
defines, the Fall. Consequently, the legal and economic institution of
property must be seen as an unnecessary social construction, 'whereby

---

[59] These arguments were not entirely original. T. Wilson Hayes discusses similar
positions adopted by Winstanley's predecessors and contemporaries, in *Winstanley the
Digger: A Literary Analysis of Radical Ideas in the English Revolution* (Cambridge,
Mass., 1979), pp. 93–102.

[60] Petegorsky traces the rise and fall of the Digger movement in *Left-Wing Democracy*,
ch. 4.

the great Creator is mightily dishonored'. 'Exploitation, not labour, is the curse.'[61] Winstanley strips away idealizing discourses surrounding land-ownership, and places the very concept of property at the core of the competitive market society he perceived in England. He defines 'the buying and selling of the Earth, with the fruits of the Earth' as a basic denial of the laws of nature and creation: it is 'an Imaginary Art . . . and breeds discontent, and divides the creation, and makes mankinde to imprison, enslave, and destroy one another' (pp. 463–4). Therefore abuses of the market – a common theme throughout the tradition of agrarian complaint literature – are seen not as the results of individual corruption, but as the natural consequences of a cankered system. In *The Law of Freedom*, he asks:

> Is not buying and selling a righteous Law? No, It is the Law of the Conqueror, but not the righteous Law of Creation: how can that be righteous which is a cheat? . . .
>
> When Mankinde began to buy and sell, then did he fall from his Innocency; for then they began to oppress and cozen one another of their Creation Birth-right. (p. 511)

From this perspective, a landlord is by definition no more than an 'earthmonger',[62] and thus in the same category as one who fraudulently sells a 'bad Horse or Cow, or any bad commodity' at a market (p. 511). What binds the hereditary landlord, the corrupt rural merchant and also the labourer working for hire is their daily affirmation of the 'imaginary' and 'kingly' power of economic competition.

Winstanley's vision for the revolutionary overthrow of the system of property was first conceived in a mystical experience, to which he repeatedly returns in his writings:

> As I was in a trance not long since . . . I heard these words, *Worke together. Eat bread together*; declare this all abroad. Likewise I heard these words. *Whosoever it is that labours in the earth, for any person or persons, that lifts up themselves as Lords & Rulers over others, and that doth not look upon themselves equal to others in the Creation, The hand of the Lord shall be upon that labourer: I the Lord have spoke it and I will do it*; Declare this all abroad. (p. 190)

---

61 Hill, *The World Turned Upside Down*, p. 131.
62 This coinage is from an anonymous Digger tract (Keith Thomas, ed., 'Another Digger Broadside', *Past and Present*, 42 (1969), p. 61).

The practical method by which this change is to be effected varies in the course of Winstanley's works. In this early passage, the author is merely a medium for a millenarian message; subsequently, the vision is used in justification of the Digger communities; and finally, the more secular argument of *The Law of Freedom* proposes that parliament should construct a modified version of the envisaged state of Christian community. Yet the contention that 'True Commonwealths Freedom lies in the free Enjoyment of the Earth' was at once the logical corollary to his theory of oppression and the foundation for all his representations of a reformed nation (p. 519). Once this principle is observed, he claims, the Norman yoke will finally be shed and 'kingly power' eradicated. The resultant state of 'commonwealths freedom' is thereby raised to a mythic plane: principally, through biblical myths of a promised land. 'Let Israel go free', he cries. Through an audacious mythic logic, 'the Babylonish yoke laid upon Israel of old', gives way to 'the last enslaving Conquest which the Enemy got over Israel, [which] was the *Norman* over *England*' (pp. 264, 259). Winstanley's solution binds the biblical narrative to a characteristic form of pantheism:

> And hereby thou wilt *Honour thy Father, and thy Mother*: Thy Father, which is the Spirit of Community . . . Thy Mother, which is the Earth, that brought us all forth . . . Therefore do not thou hinder the Mother Earth, from giving all her children suck, by the Inclosing it into particular hands.
>
> (p. 265)

The gendered language is a commonplace of rural description; however, Winstanley's construction of the 'Spirit of Community' is more telling. As indicated by the lists of men's names appended to their manifestoes, the Diggers were concerned to level the economic disparities between households, but not to challenge gender hierarchies within those households. Winstanley may have been aware of contemporary arguments of sexual radicalism. His own revolutionary vision, however, was erected upon a moral economy which remained consistent with that of conservative godly instruction.[63]

While the searing idealism of the belief that covetousness can be 'killed' informs his work throughout (p. 159), Winstanley also developed a more subtle line in practical political reform. This process was bound to the aims of the Digger experiment at St George's Hill, and culminated

---

63 Christopher Hill documents more radical reconceptions of gender roles in *The World Turned Upside Down*, ch. 15.

in the extensive utopian model proposed in his final tract, *The Law of Freedom*. In particular, he increasingly refines his vision of the earth as a common treasury, to concentrate immediately on the land which might be defined more widely as 'common'. Indeed the most striking aspect of the various strands of these arguments running through his later pamphlets is his exploitation of the etymological links between 'commonwealth', 'common land' and 'common people'. In a defence of the Diggers, he confronts the opposition of local freeholders:

> we are Englishmen equall with them, and rather our freedome then theirs, because they are the elder brothers and . . . call the Inclosures their own land, and we are the younger brothers, and the poore oppressed, *and the Common lands are called ours*, by their owne confession.
>
> (p. 282; my italic)

It is hard to believe that Winstanley was unaware of the legal status of common lands within the manorial system, which lends little support to his assertion-by-homonym.[64] His play on an accepted language of representation, however, deftly exploits a potential latent throughout the long tradition of anti-enclosure complaint. In a linguistic ploy that would have justified the worst fears of Sir Thomas Elyot, Winstanley asserts that the 'common land' – and also the 'commonwealth's land' stripped from the Crown and Church – belongs by right to the 'poor commons' who had fought to overthrow the kingly power.[65] In accordance with the ideals of the Digger commune, the worker 'takes the *Common-earth* to plant upon for [his] free livelyhood, endeavouring to live as a free *Commoner*, in a free *Common-wealth*, in righteousness and peace' (p. 575).

Winstanley also sought to bind this principle of social justice for the commoners to contemporary arguments for agrarian improvement. The emphasis on 'righteous labour, and the sweat of our browes' was fundamental to the Digger commune (p. 260), yet Winstanley's version of georgic vitally translated that of his forebears among the sixteenth-century 'commonwealths men'. For while Latimer celebrated the labours

---

[64] The contemporary agrarian improver Walter Blith neatly contrasts his aims with Winstanley on this point. He states: 'Although I indeavour so mainely to worke my Improvements out of the Belly of the Earth, yet am I neither of the Diggers minde, nor shall I imitate their practice, for though the poore are or ought to have advantage upon the Commons, yet I question whether they as a society gathered together from all parts of the Nation could claime a right to any particular Common' (*The English Improver Improved* (1652), sig. c2ᵇ).

[65] Winstanley defines 'commonwealth's land' on pp. 557–8.

of the ploughman within the ideally self-sufficient social and economic unit of the manorial estate, Winstanley's Digger proposed to expand the breadth and quality of cultivation in the commonwealth in order to raise the commoner from both subservience and the struggle for subsistence.[66] 'Manure' thus becomes a crucial word in Winstanley's vision, linked to the quiet improvement of both land and poverty.[67] 'The common Land', he declares, 'hath lain unmanured all the dayes of . . . *Kingly* and *Lordly* power'; the Diggers promise to make that land 'fruitfull with Corne' as part of the national renewal (p. 408). To parliament, he employs 'the very words . . . as had been used by the gentry in their tracts and treatises' on improvement:[68]

> But truly it will not be to your loss, to let your fellow Creatures, your equals in the Creation . . . quietly improve the Waste and Common Land, that they may live in peace, freed from the heavie burdens of Povertie; for hereby your own Land will be increased with all sorts of Commodities, and the People will be knit together in love, to keep out a forreign Enemy that endeavours . . . to destroy our inheritance. (p. 356)

Here the anxiously restricted 'equality' claimed by Latimer for his ploughman is transformed into an opportunity for the seventeenth-century 'equals in the Creation' to act as independent agents within an expanding commonwealth. He dismisses at a stroke the prevalent seventeenth-century economic concern for finding work for the poor: 'By this means within a short time', he claims, 'there will be no begger nor idle person in *England*' (p. 414).

Winstanley's ambitious attempt to marry traditional strategies of agrarian complaint with the powerful imperatives of improvement highlights his extraordinary appreciation of the power of language in his

---

[66] Anthony Low's discussion of 'Georgic and Christian Reform' similarly notes a distinction between Winstanley and his medieval and Reformation forebears. In *Piers Plowman*, he writes, labour is seen as the solution to the problem of oppression and greed, whereas Winstanley believed – along with contemporary 'improvers' such as Samuel Hartlib – that labour could avert poverty and help to initiate a new golden age (*The Georgic Revolution* (Princeton, 1985), ch. 5, p. 218). I will return to this issue in chapter 7.

[67] See Hill, *The World Turned Upside Down*, p. 104.

[68] Thirsk, 'Agrarian Problems and the English Revolution', p. 183. I believe, however, that Thirsk exaggerates the significance of this strand of argument when she subsequently claims that 'The Digger movement . . . was the offspring of the programme for improving commons, one of the prominent items in the Stuarts' reform of Crown lands' (ibid.).

society.[69] He recognized that language was intertwined with structures of exclusion and oppression, and he tried to assert, on behalf of the commoners, a repossession of the power of representation. If the earth was to become a 'common treasury' in practice, a revolution was also required to replace the existing discourses of property and exploitation. Yet such a goal, set against the momentum of social and cultural change, was almost inevitably unattainable. Indeed, as I will argue in the following chapters, the predominant discourse of agrarian improvement was inexorably bound to an appreciation of the land as property. Therefore, despite the undeniable endurance of an undercurrent of radical social thought throughout the early modern period, the ultimate cultural impact of communism upon the representation of agrarian England was negligible. While a writer with the perception of Winstanley throws valuable light upon discourse and power in rural England, his communist programme could never overturn the orthodox structures of language and practice.

[69] David Lowenstein develops a similar interpretation of Winstanley's works, but focused principally on his religious writing, in 'The Powers of the Beast: Gerrard Winstanley and Visionary Prose of the English Revolution', in *Renaissance English Prose: New Essays in Criticism*, ed. Neil Rhodes (forthcoming, Binghamton, 1996). (I am grateful to Professor Lowenstein for providing me with a copy of this piece before its publication.)

Part II

Imperatives of improvement

5. Husbandry manuals and agrarian improvement

> 'I am confident all men are thirsty enough after profit and increase, yet few studiously industrious in this designe'
>
> (Walter Blith, *The English Improver Improved*, 1652)

In the wake of the vigorous tradition of agrarian complaint traced in the preceding chapters, the publication in 1611 of *The Commons Complaint*, by Arthur Standish, signals a significant cultural watershed.[1] Standish was troubled by the rural uprisings in the Midlands around 1607; however, his response eschews the traditional morality of the discourse of complaint. As he writes in his preface, he had seen that from dearth,

> too oft ariseth discontentments, and mutinies among the common sort, as appeared of late by a grievance taken onely for the dearth of Corne in Warwick-shire, Northampton-shire, and other places, about which time the mindes of many were molested: wherupon I tooke the first occasion to imploy my studie and travell in this busines, hoping by Gods helpe to prevent such inconveniencies, as too oft doe spring out of the desperate tree of want. (sigs. B2ᵇ–B3ᵃ)

While Standish clearly sympathizes with those of 'the common sort' affected by dearth, he nonetheless distances himself from the 'molested mindes' of rioters. In contrast to the moral absolutism which characterizes agrarian complaint, Standish raises the authority of empirical research into the causes and possible prevention of dearth. As the title-page proclaims, his method is to state 'speciall grievances', then to explain 'remedies for the same'.

Standish's interest in a progressive reform of agrarian practice places him in the midst of a gathering wave of English husbandry writing. This

---

[1] This text went through four editions in two years (1611–12); references are to the third edition (1611; STC 23201.5). Standish's second publication, *New Directions of Experience*, was equally successful, running through five editions in three years after its first publication in 1613.

tradition was initially dependent upon the revival of classical texts early in the age of print. From 1470 works by writers such as Columella, Cato, Varro and Palladius were regularly published on the Continent,[2] while Xenophon's *Oeconomicus* or *Treatise of Housholde* appeared in six English editions between 1532 and 1573.[3] The emergence of English works can be dated from the publication of John Fitzherbert's *Boke of Husbandrye*, which went through twelve editions in thirty years after its initial printing in 1523?, and a further six before the turn of the century.[4] The Elizabethan publication of Thomas Tusser's widely read *Five Hundred Points of Good Husbandry* added further impetus to the movement, consolidating a populist dimension to husbandry writing. Subsequently, Standish's publications mark an important shift toward empiricism and innovation – powerfully clarified in the contemporary works of Francis Bacon – which impelled discourse on agriculture throughout the seventeenth century.

The central ideals of the manuals are to a large extent epitomized by the shifting signification of the term 'improvement'. Etymologically, there is an important distinction between the verbs (both of Old French derivation) 'improve' and 'approve'. The latter, which can be traced back to the thirteenth-century Statute of Merton,[5] has a literal meaning, 'To make profit to oneself of (e.g. land), by increasing the value of rent. esp. Said of the lord of a manor enclosing or appropriating to his own advantage common land' (OED). Yet throughout the sixteenth and seventeenth centuries this specifically legal term was increasingly collapsed into 'improve', which in one of its earliest recorded uses meant 'To turn *land* to profit; to inclose and cultivate (waste land); hence to make land more valuable or better by such means' (OED 2b). In a movement propelled by a 'sense of moral duty to exploit more efficiently the riches of the natural world', the cry of agrarian improvement

---

[2] G. E. Fussell, *The Classical Tradition in West European Farming* (Newton Abbot, 1972), pp. 87, 99.

[3] References are to the 1537 edition.

[4] Unless stated otherwise, references are to the second edition (1530?). There is a continuing debate over whether the book was written by John Fitzherbert or his brother Sir Anthony, the prominent legal writer. As this issue has only peripheral significance in the current study, I will accept the more traditional attribution to the former. Fitzherbert also wrote the first printed surveying manual, the *Boke of Surveying* (1523), which provided the basis for the textual tradition to be considered in the following chapter.

[5] Although the Statute of Merton exists only in Latin, its phrase 'faciant commodum suum' translates the Old French *aproent* (OED).

could be used to justify anything from an expanded use of manure to large-scale commercial development.[6] Significantly, this meaning also took on a more explicitly pecuniary sense, as it merged into OED 3: 'To enhance in monetary value; to raise the price or amount of . . . As said of lands and rents . . . land that was "emprowed" or inclosed and cultivated being enhanced in value or in rent'. As the writers on husbandry engaged this range of significations, 'agrarian improvement' was consolidated as a concept which conflated qualitative changes in agricultural productivity with increases in financial returns. In this form, it became the catchcry of a new age of agrarian change.

The following sections will trace the development of an early modern discourse of agrarian improvement through four distinct, yet overlapping, groups of texts. The first section will consider early works aimed toward manorial lords, which argue that measures of 'improvement' will merely reinforce the preexistent order of their estates. In the second, I will identify a radically new language of 'thrift' and 'profit' in English publications from the late sixteenth and early seventeenth centuries. The third section will examine arguments surrounding the commercial initiatives associated with agrarian 'projects'. And in the final section, I will argue that developments in seventeenth-century publications at once consolidate and vitally extend preexistent native traditions. In these texts the discourse of agrarian improvement is given a shape and force which underpinned the impending 'revolution' in both agricultural practice and socio-economic thought.[7]

THE ORDER OF THE COUNTRY FARM

Fitzherbert's *Boke of Husbandrye* contains a chapter entitled 'a shorte informacyon for a yonge gentylman that entendeth to thryve'. Beginning with the self-serving exhortation, 'I advyse hym to get a copy of this present booke and to rede it frome the begynnynge to the endynge', the chapter immediately focuses on Fitzherbert's assumed reader. Significantly, this reader is a gentleman in charge of a sizeable estate, and

6 Joan Thirsk, 'Plough and Pen: Agricultural Writers in the Seventeenth Century', in *Social Relations and Ideas: Essays in Honour of R. H. Hilton*, ed. T. H. Aston et al. (Cambridge, 1983), p. 300; Joan Thirsk, 'Agricultural Policy: Public Debate and Legislation', in *AHEW Vii*, p. 312.
7 See Eric Kerridge's arguments about seventeenth-century agrarian advances, in *The Agricultural Revolution* (London, 1967).

his recommended routine is one of supervision rather than manual labour. Fitzherbert writes that he should:

> go aboute his closes, pastures, feeldes, and specyally by the hedges, and to have in his purse a payre of tables, and whan he seeth anythynge that wolde be amended, to wryte it in his tables . . . And whan he cometh home . . . at nyghte, than let hym call his bayly . . . and to shewe hym the defautes, that they may be shortly amended . . . and thus let hym use dayly, and in shorte space he shall sette moche thynge in good ordre.
>
> (fol. 47ᵃ⁻ᵇ)

This vision of a productive and stable order on a manorial estate lies at the heart of Fitzherbert's work. In an extensive treatment of agricultural practice, he attempts to cover all aspects of husbandry necessary for a self-sufficient estate, from the construction of the plough to the gelding of calves. But while he presents some innovative advice (Eric Kerridge describes him as the leading expert in Midland agriculture in the sixteenth century[8]), he neither questions nor challenges the traditional socio-economic structure of the manor. Rather, his appreciation of agrarian 'improvement' is bound to an essentially conservative model of 'good ordre', directed by the manorial lord.

Fitzherbert's insistence on the order of a large estate aligns with classical traditions of husbandry writing. In his *Treatise of Housholde*, Xenophon argues that there is 'a certaine science of gyding and ordring of an house' (fol. 7ᵇ); and the Latin texts similarly assume that the reader will be an established landlord. In sixteenth-century Europe, these approaches were applied to contemporary manorial structures governed by a landlord from the upper gentry or nobility. The dominant assumption of an ordered patriarchal structure is aptly incorporated into the German title of 'house father literature' (*Hausväterliteratur*), which was given to husbandry writing of the period.[9] This tradition was entrenched in England in the later sixteenth century, when the classical texts and Fitzherbert's explication of an ordered manor were joined on the bookstalls by two major publications from the Continent: Conrad Heresbach's *Foure Bookes of Husbandry*, translated from the original 1570 Latin edition by Barnabe Googe in 1577; and *Maison Rustique, or The Countrie Farme*, translated from the French by Richard Surflet in

8 *Agricultural Revolution*, p. 102.
9 Joan Thirsk, 'Making a Fresh Start: Sixteenth-Century Agriculture and the Classical Inspiration', in *Culture and Cultivation in Early Modern England: Writing and the Land*, ed. Michael Leslie and Timothy Raylor (Leicester, 1992), p. 20.

1600.[10] These texts, each of which enjoyed multiple editions in England,[11] are even more explicit than Fitzherbert's in their fashioning of assumed publics fixed within the ranks of the landed gentry. Googe's book has a woodcut of his family arms on the verso of the title-page, and in his dedication to Sir William Fitzwilliam he adopts the idiom of the settled rural landowner, describing the work as 'a rude draught of the order and maner of the . . . Countrey lyfe' (sig. A2b). An introductory statement in *The Countrie Farme* simply states that the book deals not with 'ordinarie husbandmen, the fonde and ignorant sort . . . but of renowmed men which have loved and caused to florish the life and exercises of the countrie house' (sig. b5b).

Given these statements, it is fair to assume that the texts aligned with this 'country farm' tradition were almost exclusively read by manorial lords. Indeed the Latin works are necessarily directed toward an educated elite, while the size of the contemporary texts (editions of the *Boke of Husbandrye* range from twelve to seventeen sheets, *Foure Bookes of Husbandry* covers fifty-four sheets and *The Countrie Farme* 140) would have made them unaffordable to most farmers of lower than gentry status. Typical of the 'gentleman farmers' reading the texts – though perhaps more enthusiastic than most – was Sir John Newdigate (1571–1610) of Warwickshire, who included husbandry in a rigorous programme of studies. 'The most precise and ambitious scheme', his biographer writes, 'is that of March 1601. Rising at 3 a.m., he would spend an hour "serving God", six hours about household affairs, ten hours studying justice, husbandry, and history, and, after a final hour "serving God", retire to bed at 9 p.m.' Among the texts he used for his lessons in agriculture were Heresbach's *Husbandry* (in English) and Pliny's *Of Husbandry*.[12] Although none of Newdigate's books and notes on husbandry have survived, marginal annotations left in extant copies of the manuals by other contemporary readers provide further evidence of the texts in use. A heavily annotated copy of Heresbach's *Husbandry* in the Folger Shakespeare Library, for example, assumes the status of a

---

10 *Maison Rustique* was first published in France in a 1554 Latin edition by Charles Estienne, and was expanded by Jean Liebault for a 1570 French edition. For convenience, the STC's principal attribution to Estienne will be adopted here.

11 *Foure Bookes of Husbandry* went through seven editions (1577–1631); *The Countrie Farme* ran into three (1600, 1606, 1616).

12 V. M. Larminie, *The Godly Magistrate: The Private Philosophy and Public Life of Sir John Newdigate 1571–1610*, Dugdale Society Occasional Papers, no. 28 (Oxford, 1982), pp. 7, 28, 31.

commonplace book on agricultural thought and practice. Nicholas Wanton (1554?–1618) crammed the margins of his Heresbach with notes ranging from pithy, moralistic verse about the diligence of the good husbandman, to specific details about his own farm yields and local prices of agricultural commodities.[13] The title-page of Wanton's book, bearing his name, arms and miscellaneous notes, is reproduced as illustration 5.1.

These husbandry manuals celebrate the position of the 'house father', whose anticipated desires are encapsulated in the catchphrase 'profit and pleasure'. The conflation of *utilitas*[14] and *voluptas*, derived from classical usage, reinforces the conservative ideal of an estate in which the landlord's aim is the achievement of no more than a modest surplus. It is assumed, therefore, that any impetus toward 'improvement' will be organized around a necessarily stable and conservative framework. As Estienne writes at the beginning of *The Countrie Farme*, his book will describe everything necessary 'concerning the pleasure or profit of a countrie farme, especially such a one as a man ought to desire, which would live carefully and within the compasse of reason, upon the labouring of his land' (p. 3). With a subtle emphasis falling on the verb 'ought', Estienne's statement attempts to shape the attitudes of his assumed public. The 'desires' of the proper and established landlord on his country farm, he suggests, will necessarily be restrained within the conservative bounds of 'reason'.[15]

By focusing so intently on a preexistent socio-economic unit, the manuals can represent new empirical standards not as a means toward personal improvement, but rather as steps toward the imposition of a truly natural order on an estate. This helps to explain their insistence on the landlord's supervisory role in the fields. Heresbach equates supervision and fertilization, in his use of the classical axiom that 'the best doung for the feelde is the maisters foote' (fol. 3ᵃ).[16] The manorial order is also regularly linked to the will of God. As Heresbach writes in one of his most sustained panegyric excursions,

13 Folger STC 13197, copy 1.
14 The gradual shifts of meaning which the English word 'profit' undergoes in the course of the sixteenth and early seventeenth centuries will be considered on p. 149, below. At this stage it will avoid confusion to invoke the signification intended in the Latin, which means usefulness, utility, serviceableness, expediency, benefit or advantage.
15 On pp. 161–2, below, I will argue that in the seventeenth century 'reason' is refashioned as a markedly more dynamic concept.
16 Joan Thirsk traces the classical origins of this saying in 'Plough and Pen', p. 298.

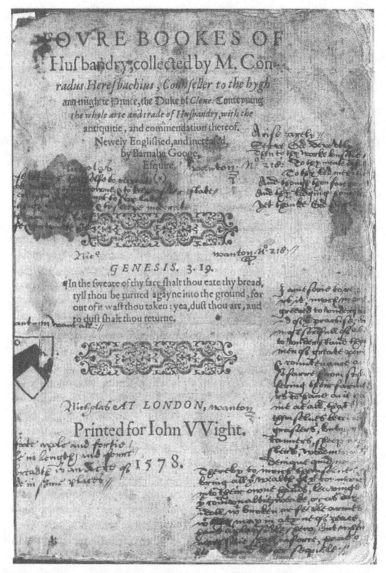

5.1 Annotated title-page of Nicholas Wanton's copy of Conrad
Heresbach, *Foure Bookes of Husbandry*, second English edn, 1578.

Cicero calleth it the mistresse of justice, diligens, and thriftinesse: some others call it the Mother and Nurs of al other artes. For wheras we may live without the other, without this we are not able to sustayne our life: besides, the gayne that hereof aryseth, is most godly, and least subject to envie, for it hath to deale with the Earth, that restoreth with gayne such things as is committed unto her, specially yf it be furthered with the blessing of GOD. The only gentelmanly way of encreasing the house, is the trade of husbandry. (fol. 6ª)

Husbandry is both 'gentelmanly' and 'godly'; and the 'gayne' and 'encrease' it brings are sanctioned by a combination of classical and biblical authority. Consequently, the active landlord is drawn into the centre of a vital and essentially natural order of life and productivity.

Yet the very attention to the profits and pleasures of the landowner brings concerns of personal advancement into uneasy juxtaposition with the controlling model of a static order, in a manner which presages subsequent developments in English husbandry writing. Nowhere is this tension more apparent than in Heresbach's treatment of Genesis 3.19: 'In the sweat of thy face shalt thou eat bread . . .' (which Googe uses as the title-page epigraph for the English edition). Whereas the traditional Christian interpretation accepts these words as evidence of the essential subjection of lord and labourer alike before God, Heresbach uses the text to support his contention that 'this profession and this gayne, is most acceptable to GOD'. Moreover, he subsequently reflects upon the 'gayne' which husbandry can bring to the individual husbandman, as he claims that, 'By husbandry were made riche the godly Fathers, *Abram, Loth, Jacob,* and *Joab*' (fol. 6ᵇ). Heresbach's shift from a natural order (endorsed by God) to the riches of godly individuals thus opens a field of economic activity in which manorial 'order' lists unsteadily toward personal 'improvement'. In *The Countrie Farme,* Jean Liebault unwittingly pinpoints this underlying tension when he defines the aim of husbandry as being 'to increase that which is ours' (sig. A8ª), a statement which verges on tautology, as it attempts to draw an anticipated 'increase' into the existing bounds of property. The consequences become apparent in a later discussion of the sale of surplus corn, which Estienne claims will bring to the landlord 'an incredible summe of money' (p. 704). For, he continues,

it is my intent and purpose that this our countrey house should be an other *Pandora,* furnished and flowing with store of all manner of good thinges and commodities, in such sort, as that the neighbour townes might have

recourse and seeke unto it in cases of their necessities and wants, but
without taking or receiving any thing at their hands but money, as the price
and sale of the wares shall amount and come unto. (p. 704)

Here the ideal of manorial self-sufficiency is transformed, through an
engagement with the market, into an unending process of accumulation.
While the restraints of 'reason' prevent the landlord from expanding his
estate in a form of capitalist competition, the success of the 'ordered'
estate leads unavoidably to a mounting stockpile of wealth.

Discussion of tenants and servants in the texts raises similar tensions.
Agrarian complaint focuses on the interests of the lower orders, and
asserts the need for traditional moral values to protect them from the
dangers of covetousness and oppression. By comparison, one of the more
striking aspects of the manuals is their distinct lack of people: Fitzherbert
and Estienne, for instance, give no consideration to the treatment of
tenants.[17] This ellipsis was perhaps encouraged by the example of the
classical texts, which are often more concerned with the purchase of
slave-labourers than the rights of tenant farmers.[18] But in the sixteenth
century, when increasing numbers of landlords were deciding to farm
their own demesnes, such an omission was more significant.[19] The
manuals depict the country farm as a field open to the innovative
intentions of the lord, and subtly suggest that demesne farming in fact
mirrors a truly 'natural' agrarian order. The best dung for the field is the
master's foot. In consequence, the 'people' of the manor tend to be
depicted as specialist employees rather than independent tenant farmers.
Heresbach, in fact, fashions his entire book around dialogues involving
specialists, who contribute their knowledge to the landlord's definitive
model of order.

THE THRIFT-COVETING FARMER

The final edition of Fitzherbert's *Boke of Husbandrye* during the period
of this study appeared in 1598, exactly thirty years after its previous

---

[17] Admittedly Fitzherbert's *Boke of Surveying*, which he clearly intended as a companion
volume to the *Husbandrye*, fills many of these gaps. The textual treatment of tenants
and property rights in the surveying manuals will be a major concern of the following
chapter.

[18] See, for example, Varro, *On Agriculture*, edited and translated from the Latin by
William Davis Hooper (Loeb Classical Library, London, 1934), pp. 406–7.

[19] See Thirsk, 'Making a Fresh Start', pp. 15–18.

144   *Imperatives of improvement*

publication.[20] By this time the printer, James Roberts (who probably also edited the text), decided that the book required updating; he writes that he has 'labored to purge [the text] from the barbarisme of the former times' (sig. A3ᵃ). This 'purge' actually touches very little of Fitzherbert's practical information and advice; however, its effects suggest an attempt to refashion the controlling rhetorical and representational strategies of the ageing text, in accordance with more recent developments in writing on husbandry. In a dedication to Henry Jackman – whose opposition to the conservative tillage bills of 1597 was considered in the Introduction – Roberts praises the 'commodity and benefit' of the book, 'arising not to one estate alone, nor to any private person, but to all in generall' (sig. A3ᵃ).[21] This egalitarian tone is furthered in his amendments to the 'shorte informacyon for a yonge gentylman that entendeth to thryve', which becomes 'Fitzherbarts generall instruction to *all men* how to thrive' (p. 144; my italic). Like Jackman in the parliamentary debates of the previous year, Roberts is concerned to move from Fitzherbert's original focus on the role of the landlord within a manorial structure toward a vision of a commonwealth in which 'all men' have a social responsibility to work for a general agrarian improvement. He reinforces this position in the course of the chapter by instilling a newly dynamic quality into the verb 'to thrive'. The reader becomes one 'that hath a zealous opinion to thrive'; Roberts also introduces the noun derived from the verb, to define 'the thrift-expecting man', 'him that is enamoured of thrift' and 'the thrift-coveting person' (pp. 144–5).

The use of 'thrift', a word which does not appear in the original, goes a long way toward defining Roberts's attempt to reshape the significance of the text. As documented by the OED, 'thrift' develops during the sixteenth century from an identification with 'thriving or prospering; prosperity, success, good-luck' (OED 1a), toward meanings which take more account of the individual's efforts. Two uses of the word which the OED dates from the second half of the century are: 'means of thriving; industry, labour; profitable occupation' (OED 1b); and 'economical management, economy; sparing use or careful expenditure of means; frugality, saving' (OED 3a). In these senses 'thrift' emerges as an ideal which legitimizes and celebrates the economic aspirations and achievements of individuals. Roberts's introduction of the word indicates an attempt to realign Fitzherbert's text behind this ideal, in the

---

20 (STC 11004).
21 On Jackman, see above, p. 11.

manner of a newer – and distinctly English – style of husbandry manual which emerged from the latter half of the sixteenth century. These texts reformulate the discourse of agrarian improvement observed in the more conservative manuals of the country farm. They appeal directly to 'thrift-coveting' farmers throughout the social order, and depict an economic structure sufficiently malleable to accommodate the expansive desires and aspirations associated with individual 'improvement'.

The presentation of these books was increasingly designed to encourage the diffusion of their information, either directly or indirectly, through to the middle and lower orders. Indeed their size and language differ markedly from the exhaustive, classically influenced works of 'house father literature'. In his *Perfite platforme of a Hoppe Garden* (1574), for example, Reynolde Scot dismisses the 'Arte of Rhetoricke' and declares rather his intention to 'write plainly to playne men of the Countrie', men 'placed in the frontiers of povertie'. The book's detailed woodcut illustrations are stated to be for the education of 'him that cannot reade at all'.[22] Leonard Mascall, who wrote *The first booke of Cattell* (1587) and *The Husbandlye ordring and Governmente of Poultrie* (1581), claims in his preface to the former that the information is 'Plainely and perfectly set forth, as well to bee understood of the unlearned husbandman, as of the learned gentle man' (sig. A4ᵃ).[23] And in the voluminous works of Gervase Markham in the early seventeenth century, the desire to reach 'the honest plaine English Husbandman' becomes almost an article of faith.[24] This project is best evidenced by the six-sheet octavo publication of *Markhams methode, or epitome* (1616?), an abridgement of his earlier works on the treatment of disease in animals.[25] In the preface to this text, Markham claims that friends had criticized *Markhams maister-peece* (1610) because 'the greatnesse of the booke and the great price thereof, deprived poore men of the benefit'. In response he has prepared a shorter and simpler book in which he undertakes to demonstrate how, 'with twelve medicines, not of twele [sic] pence cost, and to bee got commonly every where, I will cure all the diseases that are in Horses' (sig. A7ᵇ).

---

[22] Sigs. B2ᵇ, B3ᵇ. The text went through three subsequent editions (1576, 1578, 1653).
[23] The *booke of Cattell* ran through thirteen editions (1587–1662), while the *Governmente of Poultrie* was only published once.
[24] For a bibliographical description of Markham's various works on husbandry, see F. N. L. Poynter, *A Bibliography of Gervase Markham 1568?–1637* (Oxford, 1962), ch. 4. The quotation is from *The English husbandman. The first part* (1613), sig. ¶2ᵇ.
[25] Six edns (1616?–33).

The work which best illustrates both the populist intentions of this emergent native tradition, and its promotion of a discourse of the 'thrift-coveting farmer', is Thomas Tusser's *Five Hundred Points of Good Husbandry* (first published in 1557 as *A hundreth good pointes of husbandrie*). Tusser's collection of doggerel, which led the market for over half a century, combines miscellaneous practical and moral advice with a calendar of lessons for the husbandman and 'huswife'.[26] But despite the text's unquestionable currency within Elizabethan and Jacobean England, both literary and cultural historians have been notably hesitant to deal with it. On the one hand, scholars working within the traditional literary canon claim that the work is simply not their preserve. C. S. Lewis, for instance, admits that he is 'doubtful whether [it] is to be treated as literature'.[27] On the other hand, those more concerned with the popular culture of the period disagree, and attempt to push the *Points* into the realm of literature. Louis B. Wright, in his 660-page *Middle-Class Culture in Elizabethan England*, accords Tusser no more than a couple of footnotes;[28] and Laura Stevenson, in a study of merchants and craftsmen in 'popular literature', claims that the *Five Hundred Points* is, after all, georgic literature intended for the gentry, and that the impression of simplicity is no more than a 'pose'.[29] Agrarian historians, meanwhile, accord Tusser a grudging though slightly embarrassed recognition. Joan Thirsk's studies of husbandry manuals regularly mention him but concentrate on more innovative – though less popular – writers in prose.

The cultural significance of the *Points* may be clarified by a consideration of changes in the presentation and structure of the book throughout its publishing history. While there are minor differences between any of the editions, the principal developments were made in 1573, when it was first published as *Five hundreth points*.[30] The expansion at this stage was hardly the five-fold increase the change of title suggests; however, it involved some significant additions. Tusser included a number of poems to precede the calendar. With titles such as 'A Preface to the Buyer', 'The

---

26 Twenty-three edns (1557–1638); references are to the modern edition by Geoffrey Grigson (Oxford, 1984).
27 *English Literature in the Sixteenth Century Excluding Drama* (Oxford, 1954), p. 262.
28 (Chapel Hill, 1935), pp. 198n, 565n.
29 Laura Caroline Stevenson, *Praise and Paradox: Merchants and Craftsmen in Elizabethan Popular Literature* (Cambridge, 1984), pp. 140–1.
30 This also initiated the book's greatest period of influence, as it went through three editions in 1573 and a further eleven before the turn of the century.

Commodities of Husbandrie' and 'The Ladder to Thrift', these poems help to establish an ideological context for the following agricultural information. The calendar is also accompanied for the first time by 'abstracts', which compress each month's lessons from the four-line tetrameter stanzas to pithy dimeter summaries, usually in couplets. While Tusser's only description of this strategy says nothing about its purpose, it is surely consistent with an attempt to fix information in the minds of the illiterate or semi-literate.[31] It further supports an impression that the book was intended for the use of small farmers unaccustomed to books, rather than for the entertainment of the gentry.

Perhaps the most significant change of 1573 is in the order of the calendar, shifting the start of the agricultural year from August (where *A hundreth good pointes* begins) to September. While this maintains an association with the harvest as the end of a natural cycle, the rewritten opening of 'Septembers Husbandrie' in *Five Hundred Points* focuses rather on the changes of tenure which would occur at Michaelmas. Tusser writes,

> At Mihelmas lightly new fermer comes in,
> new husbandrie forceth him new to begin;

and he warns his reader to

> Provide against Mihelmas, bargaine to make,
> for ferme to give over, to keepe or to take.   (p. 30)

In contrast to the texts of the 'country farm' tradition, Tusser assumes a readership of tenant farmers operating within a dynamic economic system. This emphasis is furthered in his unfolding self-representation as a battling tenant, in pieces such as his dedicatory poem to Lord Thomas Paget and the autobiographical 'Authors Life'. Although he continues to claim the status of 'gentleman' on title-pages, he increasingly writes of an experience of husbandry in which,

> Great fines so neere did pare me,
> great rent so much did skare me,
> great charge so long did dare me,
> that made me at length crie creake.   (p. 4)

The smallholder's ethics are further inscribed in the points of

---

[31] See 'A lesson how to conferre every abstract with his month', usually printed on the verso of the title-page from 1573 (but not reprinted in Grigson's edition).

'huswifery', which incorporate women into the labours of farm management. While the country farm tradition takes only passing notice of women, Tusser appreciates the interdependence of the gendered labours of husbandman and 'huswife':

> Though husbandrie seemeth to bring in the gaines,
> But huswiferie labours seeme equall in paines.[32]   (p. 157)

Tusser's central achievement is to apply the ideals of improvement to the interests of the smallholder, and thereby to lend a freshly radical edge to the language of 'thrift'. Tusser begins his poem 'The Ladder to Thrift' with the advice:

> To take thy calling thankfully,
> and shun the path to beggery.
> To grudge in youth no drudgery,
> to come by knowledge perfectly.
> To count no travell slaverie,
> that brings in penie saverlie.
> To folow profit earnestlie
> but medle not with pilferie.
> To get by honest practisie,
> and keepe thy gettings covertlie.   (p. 13)

The poem deftly moves from a conservative language of rural order toward a new suggestion of the opportunities for individual improvement through 'thrift'. The exhortation to 'take thy calling thankfully' echoes traditional Christian doctrine which assumes a fixed social structure; yet here the socio-economic basis of husbandry as a 'calling' is significantly more flexible.[33] Through an application of 'perfect knowledge', Tusser's husbandman is able gradually to accumulate his pennies, in a manner analogous to Estienne's landlord who is a seller and not a buyer. But whereas the more conservative Estienne would presumably perceive the 'saving' tenant as a threat to the very basis of agrarian society, Tusser

---

[32] Markham's *The English House-Wife* maintained Tusser's model of female labour. This book gained wide currency as part of *A Way to get Wealth*, 9 edns (1623–60); and *Countrey Contentments*, 7 edns (1615–60). It was published separately in 7 edns (1623–60).

[33] Tusser's poem was nonetheless considered sufficiently godly to be borrowed, a few years after its first publication, by the anonymous author of a manual of religious instruction (*A Booke of Christian Questions and Answers* (1579), sigs. D3ᵇ–D4ᵇ). Sixty years later, it was equally congenial to the more secular economic wisdom of Henry Peacham, who quotes a couplet at the conclusion of *The Worth of a Peny* (1641), p. 34.

depicts a socio-economic structure which will accommodate such aspirations. His counsel to 'keepe thy gettings covertlie' reinforces his ideal of a steady, slightly secretive, rise through the social order.[34] Similarly, Tusser's injunction to 'folow profit earnestlie' carries an etymological flexibility crucial to the development of an individualist discourse. In traditional usage the word 'profit' meant a general advantage or benefit (OED 1a, 2a); in a specifically agrarian sense it might be equated with the gross yield from a harvest. This explains the principal significance of the phrase 'profit and pleasure', in which 'profit' is a direct translation of the Latin *utilitas*, a word which bears almost no financial connotations. Tusser, however, concurs with a widespread shift in the concept of profit toward a more explicitly pecuniary basis. In his riddle poem on husbandry, he writes:

> I seeme but a drudge, yet I passe any King
> To such as can use me, great wealth I do bring.
>
> . . .
>
> So many as loove me, and use me aright,
> With treasure and pleasure, I richly acquite.
>
> (pp. 11–12)

The classical 'profit and pleasure' neatly translates into 'treasure and pleasure'. By the time of Markham's writing there was still less hesitancy about the profit-motive: a 1623 collected edition of his works bore the title *A Way to get Wealth*.

These developments were intertwined with a heightened appreciation of personal property. The growing insistence on the demarcation of land and property rights will be considered at greater length in the following

---

[34] To be 'thriftless' would have a contrary effect. This term also shifted in meaning during the later sixteenth century, as the more passive sense of 'not thriving or prosperous; unsuccessful; unfortunate' (OED 1) gave way to a judgemental usage, as 'devoid of thrift; without frugality or economy; wasteful, improvident, spendthrift' (OED 3). Tusser's contemporary William Harrison clearly intends the latter sense, as he recommends the 'whip of justice' for the 'thriftlesse poore, as the riotour that hath consumed all, the vagabond that will abide no wheres, but runneth up and downe from place to place (as it were seeking woorke and finding none)': ('An Historicall description of the Iland of Britaine', printed with Raphael Holinshed's *Chronicles*, 2nd edn (3 vols., 1586), vol. 1, fol. 106ᵇ). Quentin Skinner's analysis of uses of 'spendthrift' from the late sixteenth century suggests a further development, as the language of thrift was moulded 'in order to describe and express a new disapproval of the aristocratic ideal of conspicuous consumption' ('Analysis of Political Thought and Action', in *Meaning and Context: Quentin Skinner and His Critics*, ed. James Tully (Cambridge, 1988), p. 115).

chapter; here we can note the tentative emergence of an ethos which rejects the traditional model of local communities bound by a network of social duties and responsibilities. Tusser's individualism is epitomized in an exhortation 'never to crave, but to live of thine owne' (p. 19), a statement taken from a consideration of lending, in his poem 'Good Husbandlie Lessons'. While he admits that lending to a neighbour will win 'love' and 'credit', his clear implication is that the practice is best discouraged.[35] In 'Septembers Abstract' he is more forthright:

> Who goeth a borrowing,
> goeth a sorrowing.
> Few lends (but fooles)
> their working tooles. (p. 27)

At a time when Tusser's instructions were being read throughout the country, William Shakespeare echoed his ethics of individualism in the words of the fussy Polonius, who advises his son,

> Neither a borrower, nor a lender be,
> For loan oft loses both itself and friend,
> And borrowing dulls the edge of husbandry.[36]

For the agrarian reformer, the inevitable corollary of such arguments is a rejection of the common-field system. Indeed one of the longest poems in Tusser's *Five Hundred Points* is 'A Comparison Betweene Champion Countrie and Severall', which repeatedly emphasizes the greater 'wealth' and 'profit' of enclosed land. In the course of his argument Tusser manages to invert the language of anti-enclosure polemic, as he describes the dangers to unenclosed cornfields posed,

> By custome and covetous pates,
> by gaps, and by opening of gates. (p. 135)

---

[35] By contrast, John Walter uses Tusser's claim that 'lending to neighbour, in time of his neede, / winnes love of thy neighbour, and credit doth breede' (p. 19), to support his argument that local credit relationships, driven as much by concerns of community as by those of the market, frequently helped to alleviate potential crises of subsistence in early modern England. Thus Tusser's note of ambivalence here perhaps evidences the residual influence of notions of moral economy, which appear to have exerted particular sway within rural communities in times of dearth (Walter, 'The Social Economy of Dearth in Early Modern England', in *Famine, Disease and the Social Order in Early Modern Society*, ed. John Walter and Roger Schofield (Cambridge, 1989), p. 106).

[36] *Hamlet*, I.iii.75–7.

The association of 'custom' with 'covetousness' takes his individualism to an extreme at which any of the traditional claims that impinge upon the farmer's sovereignty are depicted as a form of theft. He subsequently presents a ringing endorsement of the order of enclosure:

> More profit is quieter found
> (where pastures in severall bee:)
> Of one seelie aker of ground,
> than champion maketh of three.
> Againe what a joie is it knowne,
> when men may be bold of their owne!   (p. 138)

Such cries for economic liberty would propel the enclosure movement throughout the following centuries. Enclosure could be promoted as a means through which landlords and tenants alike are made 'bold of their owne'.[37] Its imposition of a newly rigorous order and definition in the apportionment of property rights is depicted as leading to a universal improvement, which furthers the interests of the commonwealth.

While Tusser's *Five Hundred Points* lacks the innovative empiricism which shapes agricultural writing in the seventeenth century, its punchy didacticism proclaims month by month the newly radical potential of a language of 'improvement'. From Tusser to Markham, English writers insisted upon the interests of small farmers and the particularities of native conditions; and their works thus laid a vital foundation for the later texts of 'agricultural revolution'. Before focusing on the achievement of the seventeenth-century writers, though, it will be useful to consider briefly the particularly stark challenge to traditional ideals of rural order presented by economic projects.

FROM MANOR TO MARKET: AGRARIAN PROJECTS

Reynolde Scot, whose *Perfite platforme of a Hoppe Garden* (1574) was the first published manual in English on the production of a single crop, was clearly unsettled by the potential uses of his work. In his preface he lashes the 'covetous man', who 'placeth his private profite before common humanitie, to erect unto himselfe and his posteritie, a kingdome of vanitie and ydlenesse'. He requests that his reader

---

[37] Compare Robert Crowley's prescient attack on the rent-raiser, who justifies his actions with the argument 'That wyth hys owne he myghte / alwayes do as he lyste' (*One and thyrtye Epigrammes* (1550), sig. E1ᵇ). See above, pp. 40–2.

blame not this poore trade for that it maketh men riche in yeelding double profite, neyther reproove me bicause by these presents I give notice therof, in publishing this order, but comdemne the man, or rather the mynde, that wresteth it to serve his miserable affection, or covetous humour.

(sig. B1ᵇ)

Scot's fear that his book might fall into the wrong hands serves to highlight, at an early date, the particular tensions which arise in the representation of commercial production within a developing market economy. In contemporary language, the producer vilified by Scot would generally be known as a 'projector'; and his 'project' would be seen as analogous to a wide range of plans for economic development.[38] Joan Thirsk traces economic arguments in favour of projects to Sir Thomas Smith's mid-Tudor *Discourse of the Commonweal.*[39] In the decades that followed, discourse surrounding projects honed the ideals of improvement to a new edge. Thirsk has demonstrated how the popular reputation of projectors was besmirched in the early decades of the seventeenth century due to widespread problems of fraud and corruption.[40] But despite the often dubious practice, the language engaged in the promotion of projects ultimately survived from its origins in the sixteenth century to influence a reorientation of rural production toward an international market economy.

A typical and particularly prominent agrarian project, the production of woad, will provide a focus for my investigation. The production of the blue dye from woad promised high financial rewards to entrepreneurs capable of assembling the necessary capital expenditure and large unskilled workforce. Woad had generally been imported from France; however, in the 1580s there was a huge expansion in production throughout England.[41] The government's reaction to this phenomenon struck a familiar late Tudor combination of conservative rhetoric and rational inquiry. In 1585 'A proclamation against the sowing of woade' stated that,

---

[38] While small 'hop gardens' were often cultivated for the private use of a family, the prevalence of commercial producers is also apparent, as illustrated, for example, in Robert Reyce's *Breviary of Suffolk, 1618*, which notes the rise of 'hoppe masters' (ed. Lord Francis Harvey (London, 1902), p. 31). (See also below, p. 249.)

[39] *Economic Policy and Projects: The Development of a Consumer Society in Early Modern England* (Oxford, 1978), pp. 13–16; see also pp. 52–7, above.

[40] *Economic Policy and Projects* identifies a 'constructive phase of projects' from 1540–80, followed by a 'scandalous phase' which ran through the reign of James I.

[41] Thirsk, 'Farming Techniques', p. 174; *Economic Policy and Projects*, pp. 3–4.

a late attempt of breaking up and tilling of very fertile grounds to sow woad is upon a late private and inordinate gain practiced, to the manifest grief of [Elizabeth's] people in divers places where the same is used; and that the excessive gain found thereby, without regard to the public weal, is like both to continue and increase this attempt, to the great damage of the commonweal.[42]

The document immediately assumes a damaging conflict between the desire of certain individuals for 'private and inordinate gain', and the interests of the 'commonweal'. Yet at the same time the government signalled its willingness to move beyond this conservative reaction, as it established an inquiry to examine more thoroughly arguments for and against the crop.[43] In the absence of printed texts on individual projects (largely due to their specialist and occasionally secretive nature), the records of this inquiry provide a valuable archive through which to document the projector's influence upon the representation of the countryside.[44]

The inquiry drew responses that range from direct appeals by individual woad producers to longer tracts which consider each side of the debate. The main points of the case against the crop are outlined in 'A Breif Report of the Commodeties and discommodeties said to growe by the greate use of oade within the Realme', dated 1586.[45] It states that,

By tourning up both pastuer areable and medowe groundes to oad, the husbandman shall neither be able to maintain his plowe rather in good state to till withall, nor sheepe to maintain his areable groundes, neither kyne to make his provision for his household, which is his cheefest stave.

(fol. 124b)

The argument assumes an ideal model of agrarian order structured around the interests of the small tenant farmer producing for the subsistence of his family. From this perspective, the production of woad is depicted as an innovation propelled by the corrosive agent of covetousness. In a closing consideration of the effects of woad 'Generallie to the common Wealth', the writer reinforces this position by juxtaposing two divergent senses of the word 'profit'. He concedes that

---

[42] *Tudor Royal Proclamations*, ed. Paul L. Hughes and James F. Larkin (3 vols., New Haven and London, 1964–9), vol. 2, p. 516.

[43] Thirsk, *Economic Policy and Projects*, p. 29.

[44] A considerable number of documents relating to this inquiry are collected in the Burghley Papers, BL Lansdowne MS 49.

[45] BL Lansdowne MS 49, fols. 124b–125b.

woad will 'bring soch exceding profitt and gain to them that can tell howe to order and use it'; yet in a broader consideration of the wellbeing of the community, he writes, 'it is said by some to maintain a vanitie, we lose the victualls, to kepe a colour we lose the clothe, and to practise a newe experience we spoile our selves therby of assured profitt' (fol. 125ᵃ⁻ᵇ).

The most detailed defence of woad brought forward in response to the inquiry was also written by a man directly involved in several distinctly commercial schemes of agrarian improvement. In fact the figure of Robert Payne – projector, surveyor, estate steward in England and Ireland, and publicist of agrarian improvements – offers a particularly apt illustration of the Elizabethan rural entrepreneur.[46] Whilst Payne's life of questionable financial management and deception of patrons, and his death when in prison for debt, was not typical of the projector, his forthright justification of the pursuit of profit through commercial development carried the logic of agrarian improvement to a new extreme. In 1585 Payne was involved in a woad project at Wollaton, Nottinghamshire, principally funded by Sir Francis Willoughby. The proclamation against woad drew him to London, where he campaigned for the relaxation of restrictions. In a 1586 petition to Burghley, he pleads the benefits of woad to the commonwealth, and offers to 'publish in print the trewe use of woade, and the grounde apt for it in a pamflet of a penny price, which should throughly teach the meanest to worke the same, and drawe a great nomber into it for profytt sake'.[47] The stated desire to appeal to the profit-motive of even the 'meanest' is of dubious sincerity, given the financial circles within which Payne moved himself; however, his belief that such a strategy might sway the government cannot be dismissed so lightly. In a sense, the suggestion marks a logical extension of Scot's attempt to direct his *Perfite platforme of a Hoppe Garden* toward the poor; but whereas Scot hedges his text with traditional arguments against covetousness, Payne's concept of 'profytt sake' floats freely within a market economy.

The text Payne had in mind was probably the unpublished tract he presented to the Privy Council in the same month.[48] Titled 'A breefe

---

[46] Biographical information is derived from R. S. Smith, 'A Woad Growing Project at Wollaton in the 1580s', *Transactions of the Thoroton Society of Nottinghamshire*, 65 (1961), pp. 26–46.

[47] BL Lansdowne MS 49, fol. 88ᵃ.

[48] BL Lansdowne MS 121/21; printed in Smith, 'A Woad Growing Project', pp. 40–6. References are to Smith.

discription of the true and perfitt makinge of woade', the piece combines detailed practical instructions for woad production with a strenuous defence of the crop. He begins by conceding a little ground to his opponents, claiming that 'the trade hathe heretofore receaved a generall sclander raysed throughe a number of greedie persons who have not used but for there owne lucre abused the same' (p. 40). In line with contemporary discussions of soil types and regional differentiations, however, he claims that the interests of the nation will best be served by the cultivation of woad in some areas. He writes:

> I hartelie praie . . . that the saied trade maie be utterlie exempt from those places where it maie do any generall harme to the Common wealth. But this know (gentle reader) Englande is no grange, and that there be manie convenient places in this lande most fitt for that purposse. (pp. 40–1)

The statement that 'Englande is no grange' subtly undermines the arguments of his opponents. A grange, in this period, could be 'a repository for grain' (OED 1); a farm or country house (OED 2a, 3); or 'an outlying farmhouse belonging to . . . a feudal lord' (OED 2b). In all these senses the term is linked to a manorial model of arable production. Payne's use of it, alongside evidence of regional conditions unsuited to tillage, suggests that the traditional rural ideal is inapplicable as a model for the general management of the country. Hence he can raise the cry for agrarian improvement, as he links the cultivation of woad to the more general movement toward the improvement of infertile land, a position he underlines later in the tract with lengthy instructions about the 'mucke or soyle most apte to manure grounde for woade'.

Payne's principal justification for the project is that it provides employment; it is here that he exhibits an unmistakably capitalist strain. He claims that,

> The quantitie of fortie acres will kepe in worke one hundered and sixtie persons, the moste parte weomen and children, one theerde parte of the yere: there wages beinge soe smale as withe any good consyence maie be geven, viz. to the greatest number but fowre pence a daie. Yet see what greate good it dothe the poor laboringe man that before this tyme kept his wiffe and familie with his owne bare wages whiche did not exceede 3s. 4d. a weeke; now his wiffe and two children by this meanes bringe in more for a good space together by 5 or 6s. a weeke. (p. 41)

The call of 'work for the poor', which is consistently raised in arguments in support of projects, coalesces with traditional paternal ideals. In

Payne's construction of the agrarian economy, however, the poor are newly figured as a socio-economic group defined by their availability for labour. His determination of daily wages by the criterion that they should be 'soe smale as withe any good consyence maie be geven', evidences the entrepreneur's attempt to keep a stable workforce while maximizing his own returns. The representation of an agrarian economy in which whole families become wage labourers, furthermore, subverts the conservative image of a household supported by the earnings of the man. Payne simply rejects such a model, in favour of an objective appreciation of the value of unskilled manual labour in a commercial enterprise. It is totally in accord with the perspective of the tract that he should draw to a close with 'A note of the greatest charge, and an indifferent gaine, of a good acre of grounde converted to woade', concluding that the entrepreneur can make 'de claro' (i.e. 'clear profit') £8 16s. Over the following hundred years, hosts of commercial producers, rural industrialists, fen-drainers and other enthusiasts of rural enterprise, would promise far more.

AGRARIAN IMPROVEMENT AND AGRICULTURAL REVOLUTION

By the middle of the seventeenth century a new generation of agricultural reformers fully appreciated both the achievements and shortcomings of their predecessors. Thus Walter Blith admits the prevalent mood of 'scandall & prejudice . . . against new projections', but expresses his confidence that the cause of industry and improvement can be impelled nonetheless by the fact that 'all men are thirsty . . . after profit and increase' (sig. e2b).[49] Blith's approach, in the most comprehensive agricultural text of the period, typifies the agenda of agrarian improvement in the seventeenth century. Writers were aware of the origins of English husbandry writing, yet were also conscious of a need to reexamine the established arguments of reform. The likes of Tusser and Scot are thus acknowledged, but are seen to fall short of a newly rigorous set of standards.[50] In the course of the seventeenth century, the

[49] Blith's important work was first published as *The English Improver*, 2 edns (both 1649); and subsequently expanded for publication as *The English Improver Improved*, 2 edns (1652, 1653). All references are to the first edition of *The English Improver Improved*.

[50] See, for example, Samuel Hartlib, *Samuel Hartlib His Legacy of Husbandry*, 3 edns (1651, 1652, 1655), 3rd edn, p. 89.

discourse of agrarian improvement is consolidated in a form which would underpin representations of the land well into the eighteenth century. Most importantly, the texts demonstrate a widespread appreciation of the agricultural and commercial implications of regional differences; the rise of a language of 'reason' in application to both farming practice and tenurial relationships; and the consolidation of social and economic 'freedom' as a dominant ideal.

The method adopted by Arthur Standish early in the seventeenth century – to pursue 'remedies' for 'grievances' in the countryside – appears boldly objective and scientific in comparison with the representations of agrarian practice considered in the preceding sections of this chapter. But while Standish in many respects anticipates a new empiricism, his approach was not totally without precedent. The classical agricultural texts frequently stress the need for empirical investigation: 'there should be no neglect anywhere of experimentation in many forms', Columella asserts.[51] Although the potential economic significance of this dictum was perhaps overlooked by early readers, widespread interest in botany, herbs and gardens among the gentry and nobility laid a foundation for subsequent developments in agrarian thought and practice. Plants from the Continent and the New World became the currency of informal social and intellectual networks among the higher social orders.[52] Artichokes, for instance, enjoyed a surge of popularity in the middle of the sixteenth century, fuelled in part by a belief that they aided the conception of male children.[53] In accordance with these patterns of interest, the majority of writing on botany catered principally to an educated elite, as evident in lavish and ambitious works such as John Gerard's *Herball or generall historie of plants* (1597) and John Parkinson's *Paradisi in Sole* (1629). Such texts may have offered little for the 'thrift-coveting' husbandman; however, in the longer term, their scientific approach and presentation of botany as a subject worthy of a gentleman's attention significantly furthered the development of English agriculture.

---

[51] *On Agriculture*, ed. and trans. from Latin by Harrison Boyd Ash (Loeb Classical Library, 3 vols., Cambridge, Mass., 1941), vol. 1, p. 55; quoted in Thirsk, 'Making a Fresh Start', p. 23.
[52] Joan Thirsk, 'Agricultural Innovations and Their Diffusion', in *AHEW Vii*, pp. 536–7; Charles Webster, *The Great Instauration: Science, Medicine and Reform 1626–1660* (London, 1975), p. 467.
[53] Joan Thirsk, 'The Fashioning of the Tudor–Stuart Gentry', *Bulletin of the John Rylands University Library of Manchester*, 72 (1990), p. 70.

A growing sense of the national possibilities for agricultural change is concurrently apparent in both the publications and government policy of the early seventeenth century. In the Houses of parliament, enthusiasts of gardening and proponents of economic development contributed to a series of debates on rural issues (such as those of 1597 and 1601 considered in the Introduction). Landlords and lawmakers increasingly challenged assumptions about the nationwide primacy of a manorial economy based on the production of grain. Regional specialization was driven at once by falling grain prices and the strengthening tentacles of a market economy, while an assault upon forests, fens and wastes gathered pace, with private landlords deriving encouragement from the example set by the Crown throughout the reigns of James and Charles.[54] Agricultural writing also embraced a more dynamic appreciation of agrarian practice. The estate surveyor John Norden, for example, brought 'local knowledge of remarkable range and precision' to a lengthy section in his *Surveiors Dialogue*, 'shewing the different natures of Grounds, how they may be imployed, how they may be bettered, reformed, and amended'.[55] 'I am of opinion', he declared, 'that there is no kinde of soile, be it never so wilde, boggy, clay, or sandy, but will yeeld one kind of beneficiall fruit or other' (p. 167). The gentleman enthusiast Sir Hugh Plat applied a slightly more arcane mind to the practice and theory of manure (among other interests) through a series of publications around the turn of the century. Further, an appreciation of readers for local detail is demonstrated by the remarkable and enduring popularity of Gervase Markham's *The Inrichment of the Weald of Kent*.[56]

Within this context, the importance of Francis Bacon lies not so much in his originality as in his capacity to elevate 'to a coherent intellectual system what had hitherto been the only partially spoken assumptions of practical men'.[57] The improvement of agriculture took its place within a comprehensive Baconian programme which asserted the value of empirical learning as 'a fruitful womb for the use and benefit of man's

[54] See Joan Thirsk, 'Seventeenth-Century Agriculture and Social Change', in *The Rural Economy of England: Collected Essays* (London, 1984), p. 205.
[55] Thirsk, 'Agricultural Innovations and Their Diffusion', p. 534; 3 edns (1607, 1610, 1618), 2nd edn, p. 145. On Norden, see also below, chapter 6.
[56] According to Joan Thirsk, *The Inrichment* was published by Markham from an anonymous manuscript, which bears the hallmarks of 'precise observation and ripe experience' ('Plough and Pen', pp. 303–4). It ran through eleven editions, 1625–95.
[57] Christopher Hill, *Intellectual Origins of the English Revolution* (Oxford, 1980 edn), p. 87.

life'.[58] For the agrarian improver, Bacon defined as a moral duty the goal of expanding the range of human knowledge over the natural world:

> For as the Psalms and other scriptures do often invite us to consider and magnify the great and wonderful works of God, so if we should rest only in the contemplation of the exterior of them as they first offer themselves to our senses, we should do a like injury unto the majesty of God as if we should judge or construe of the store of some excellent jeweller, by that only which is set out toward the street in his shop.[59]

Man was to be 'the helper and interpreter of nature'; and this expansive vision was in fact consistent with the prevailing Calvinist teaching of the first half of the seventeenth century.[60] As I argued in chapter 2, the development of Protestant theology from the latter sixteenth century effectively fractured the previously dominant corporate representation of the nation by focusing on the faith and conscience of the individual. Bacon offered justification for specifically scientific endeavour by arguing that an individual's pursuit of knowledge for the good of humanity is consistent with religious virtue.[61] Such beliefs, which also informed georgic writing, propelled a crucial Protestant drive to untangle the cause of improvement from webs of religious resistance.[62]

Bacon's agenda for the advancement of learning provided the foundation for a movement toward scientific research and economic development, which eventually took root in England in the decades after 1640. The impending political and religious upheaval of this time generated unprecedented enthusiasm for a wide range of reformist programmes, and while Gerrard Winstanley saw this as an opportunity to mould a state in which the land would be 'a common treasury for all', agricultural improvers were no less zealous in their conception of a land transformed through human labour and ingenuity.[63] Like Bacon, they were attracted to a radical 'protestant belief that the fall of man was not irreversible; spiritual salvation would be accompanied by a renewal of his dominion over nature'.[64] At the centre of this movement stood

---

[58] Bacon, *Works*, ed. J. Spedding et al. (14 vols., London, 1857–74), vol. 3, p. 286.
[59] *Works*, vol. 3, p. 300.
[60] Webster, *Great Instauration*, p. 329.
[61] Hill, *Intellectual Origins*, p. 92.
[62] I will further explore the Protestant ethics of labour and improvement in the works of Bacon and his successors in chapter 7. (See especially pp. 212–17.)
[63] On Winstanley, see above, pp. 124–31.
[64] Webster, *Great Instauration*, p. 329.

Samuel Hartlib.[65] While Hartlib's own practical achievements had little lasting effect, his crucial role was as a mentor, publisher and informal coordinator of the new generation of 'commonwealths men'.[66] As one admirer wrote, he was 'like the rich flanders soile, in its most improved cultivation . . . that for one . . . barly corne voyd of charge doe render me 2000 fold'.[67]

The works of the 'Hartlib circle' of reformers revised and consolidated the discourse of agrarian improvement. Most importantly, a vital combination of preexistent assumptions and modern directions informed their conception of the place of agriculture within a market economy. Bacon had been relatively unconcerned with the economic aspects of 'improvement'; indeed, he scornfully dismissed the 'vulgar and degenerate' ambition of those who seek knowledge only for purposes of individual advancement.[68] Yet his emphasis on the identity of truth and utility also offered ample justification for the improver.[69] His essay 'Of Riches', in fact, boldly states that 'The improvement of the ground is the most natural obtaining of riches; for it is our great mother's blessing, the earth's.'[70] The agricultural reformers of the Hartlib circle needed little more encouragement. Husbandry was for them enmeshed with economic assumptions derived at once from the history of agrarian discourse and the influence of their quotidian circumstances. The Elizabethan Reynolde Scot, as observed above, had been troubled by the possible appropriation of his teachings by a 'covetous man', while at the turn of the century, an early work on commercial gardening represents primary producers as 'the Lords Stewards', who should 'sell with consciences' to the poor.[71] But by the middle of the seventeenth century, a language of individualism and pecuniary gain suffuses the discourse of improvement. All men, writes Blith, are naturally 'greedy in searching out all opportunities of Improvement . . . the Land is capable of' (*English Improver*

65 On the Hartlib circle, see Charles Webster's introduction to *Samuel Hartlib and the Advancement of Learning* (Cambridge, 1970).
66 Ralph Austen, for example, expresses his admiration for 'good Common-wealths-men, who have written of the *Improvement of lands*' (*A Treatise of Fruit-Trees*, 3 edns (1653, 1657, 1665), 3rd edn, p. 1).
67 Letter from William Spenser to Hartlib, 21 October 1650; Hartlib Papers 46/7.
68 Quoted in Hill, *Intellectual Origins*, p. 94.
69 Webster discusses the apparent inconsistencies in Bacon's attitudes toward utilitarian values and individual gain, in *Great Instauration*, pp. 336–8.
70 *Works*, vol. 6, p. 461.
71 On Scot, see above, pp. 151–2; Richard Gardiner, *Instructions for the Manuring, Sowing and Planting of Kitchin Gardens* (1603); facsimile edn (Amsterdam, 1973), sig. A2b.

Improved, p. 86); husbandry, in the words of Ralph Austen, becomes an 'art' of 'lawfull usury' (*Treatise of Fruit-Trees*, p. 14).

The true 'commonwealths man' in the countryside was refashioned as a godly individualist. 'What else makes a Common-wealth, but the private-wealth?' asked Edward Misselden in 1623.[72] For the following generation of agricultural reformers the logic was unquestionable, and Tusser's ideals of thrift and profit were duly transformed into principles of national renewal. 'I know none can drive on publique ends without private aims', Blith declared; his goal, which he carefully distinguished from those of the Levellers and Diggers, was 'to make the poor rich, and the rich richer, and all to live of the labour of their owne hands' (p. 235, sigs. c2b–c3a). The key word in the air was 'ingenuity', a concept which focuses attention on the individual whose energy and powers of discovery would lead to previously inconceivable changes in agrarian practice. It is also a word which highlights the metamorphosis of the Elizabethan ideal of 'good husbandry'. In the works of Fitzherbert and Heresbach, 'good husbandry' had signified order, economic stability and social hierarchy. Writers concerned with the smallholder had also acknowledged the contributions of women, albeit labouring within a gendered domestic economy. The writers of the Interregnum, informed by Baconianism and Puritanism, imagined rather a landscape revitalized by restless ingenuity and specifically masculinized endeavour.[73]

On the title-page of *The English Improver Improved*, Blith couples the ideal of 'ingenuity' with 'Principles of Reason'. As Christopher Hill has demonstrated, 'reason' is a particularly malleable concept in the field of seventeenth-century political, religious and economic debate.[74] For Winstanley, 'Reason' was synonymous with 'God', and signified transcendent bonds of love, community and equality.[75] In the works of the agrarian improvers, by comparison, it is possible to identify the emergence of a modern signification which sets the logic of the market against practices grounded in custom.[76] Whereas the 'country farm'

---

[72] *The circle of commerce* (1623); quoted in Joyce Oldham Appleby, *Economic Thought and Ideology in Seventeenth-Century England* (Princeton, 1978), pp. 45–6.

[73] This aspect of the improvers' discourse accords with nascent bourgeois gender roles, whereby middle-class women were increasingly dissociated even from the restricted forms of labour and economic agency defined by Tusser, and directed rather by polite society's ideals of domesticity and feminine refinement.

[74] '"Reason" and "Reasonableness"', in *Change and Continuity in Seventeenth-Century England* (London, 1974), pp. 103–23.

[75] See above, pp. 125–6.

[76] Compare Hill's comments about Thomas Hobbes, in '"Reason" and "Reasonableness"', p. 108.

manuals of the sixteenth century had linked reason to the maintenance of a traditional order, subsequent writers increasingly stress the dynamic potential of the concept. At the beginning of the new century, Norden laments farmers who,

> because they are not generally travellers to see other places, neither hath their breeding beene judicious, but plaine according to a slubberd patterne of ancient *ignorance*, by which they only shape all their courses, as their Fathers did, never putting in practise any new devise, by the rule of more reason. (*Surveiors Dialogue*, p. 171)

The 'rule of more reason' unhinges the authority of traditional agricultural practices throughout the nation. (As we have seen, this was anticipated – with some trepidation – by the Elizabethan playwright William Wager, who depicted the vice of Inconsideration being renamed as Reason to serve the ends of economic expansion and exploitation in the countryside.)[77] Consequently the countryside becomes envisaged as a site of experimentation and diversity shaped within the framework of a market economy. The promise of 'great gain' in agrarian improvements, writes Sir Richard Weston, will necessarily be such 'that not any thing can restrain a rational man from trial thereof'.[78] Dissenters to such a creed are likely to be dismissed as poor commonwealths men: 'mouldy old leavened husbandmen', in the words of Blith (sig. e3^b). Such logic was inevitably applied to the enclosure debate, in a stream of rhetoric which branded wastes and commons as disorderly and irrational. The 'wild vacant waste lands, scattered up and down this nation . . . (like a deformed chaos) to our discredit and disprofit', put to shame 'an ingenious and industrious people', claims an Interregnum pamphleteer.[79] Through enclosure, the land will be 'cleansed and purged of [its] former deformities'.[80]

In this form, 'reason' converges upon a rhetoric of economic 'freedom'. The keynote was struck by Sir Walter Raleigh in the 1601 parliament (as quoted in the Introduction), who supported a call for the repeal of anti-enclosure legislation with the declaration that to be 'free'

---

[77] *Enough Is as Good as a Feast* (1570?); '*The Longer Thou Livest' and 'Enough Is as Good as a Feast*', ed. R. Mark Benbow (London, 1967). See above, pp. 93–5.

[78] *A Discourse of Husbandrie used in Brabant and Flanders* (1652), p. 1.

[79] 'Proposals for the Improvement of Waste Ground', 1653; printed in *Seventeenth-Century Economic Documents*, ed. Joan Thirsk and J. P. Cooper (Oxford, 1972), p. 135.

[80] Adam Moore, *Bread for the Poor. And Advancement of the English Nation. Promised by Enclosure of the Wastes and Common Grounds of England* (1653), p. 13.

is 'the desire of a true *English* man'.[81] For the improver both restrictive legislation and customary farming methods become clogs on ingenuity and industry. In the 1620s Sir Edward Coke echoed Raleigh in a description of agrarian laws as 'snares that might have lien heavy upon the subject', while, in the fields, Markham wished that 'no man' should 'binde himselfe more strictly to custome, then the discourse of reason shall bee his warrant'.[82] Moreover, 'customary and lesser profitable'[83] agricultural practices were inevitably yoked to manorial 'customs' of land tenure, as the goal of 'freedom' propelled an attack on the network of reciprocal rights and responsibilities which had previously been seen to define rural property. As parliament moved toward the abolition of the legal remnants of feudalism, thus strengthening 'the conviction that property was a private rather than a public resource', agrarian improvers challenged remaining manorial customs.[84] Preexistent structures might have promoted order and stability, but the individualistic logic of improvement demanded proportional returns for investment, ingenuity and industry. Gabriel Plattes suggested 'a Contract betweene Landlord and Tenant; whereby a just share may redound to both parties answerable to their merit', whereas Blith favoured legislation to enshrine the principle of reward for improving initiative.[85] In either case, the driving imperative was to 'free' individuals from traditional responsibilities: the new order insists that '*Regina Pecunia, Monie* is the *Queen* that commands all.'[86]

These ideals of economic freedom and strict legal definition of individual rights combined further to inform an appreciation of the central importance of 'freehold' property. As I demonstrate in the following chapter, the contemporary estate surveyor consistently proclaimed the need for every person to 'know one's own', and this assumption of title strictly definable in legal and spatial terms eroded the

---

[81] Sir Simonds D'Ewes, ed., *The Journals of All the Parliaments during the Reign of Queen Elizabeth* (London, 1682), p. 674.

[82] Quoted in Maurice Beresford, 'Habitation Versus Improvement: The Debate on Enclosure by Agreement', in *Essays in the Economic and Social History of Tudor and Stuart England, in Honour of R. H. Tawney*, ed. F. J. Fisher (Cambridge, 1961), p. 49; *Markhams farewell to Husbandry*, 5 edns (1620–49), 2nd edn, p. 152.

[83] Cressy Dymock, *An Essay for Advancement of Husbandry-Learning* (1651), p. 6.

[84] Appleby, *Economic Thought and Ideology*, p. 101.

[85] Plattes, *A Discovery of Infinite Treasure Hidden Since the Worlds Beginning* (1639; facsimile edn, Amsterdam, 1974), p. 16; Blith, *English Improver Improved*, sig. A3ᵃ⁻ᵇ.

[86] Weston, *Discourse of Husbandrie*, p. 13.

perception of landownership as a 'bundle of rights' rooted in custom.[87] The movement was reinforced by changing religious and legal attitudes toward the land. While the Church moved away from the doctrine of stewardship, the government and courts increasingly embraced a new doctrine of property. In particular, a series of struggles between parliament and Crown prompted authoritative claims from the former about the power and status of the enfranchised freeholders. 'The ancient and undoubted right of every free man', a committee of the Commons declared in 1628, 'is that he hath a full and absolute property in his goods and estate.'[88] The improvers agreed. Indeed they regularly accept the logic of the surveyor's representational practice, and inject the imperatives that landholders should employ and improve their own. As noted above, Thomas Tusser proclaimed to his Elizabethan audience that enclosure enables landholders to 'be bold of their owne' (*Five Hundred Points*, p. 138). Blith deemed Tusser's poem fit for republication in his *English Improver Improved* (pp. 87–92); however, by this time, the once innovative doctrine was thoroughly embedded in representations of the land. 'It is natural', asserted one writer, 'for all men to love propriety . . . and men do delight rather to say *this is mine*, then *this is ours*.'[89]

The rhetoric, of course, glazes over significant complexities. A tenant farmer forced after the enclosure of common fields to accept a patch of ground inadequate to support a family might well have felt that the love of property was a form of self-interest grounded in exclusion. This was Winstanley's point. But the questions begged only reinforce an impression of the impact of the discourse of agrarian improvement on the representation of rural society. The commonwealths men of the middle of the sixteenth century focused their sympathies upon the ploughman, whose labours upheld an order in which economic considerations were subject to the imperatives of a strict Christian morality. By contrast, the commonwealths men of the following century structure their representations of the country around the interests of the industrious freeholder.[90]

[87] F. M. L. Thompson, *Chartered Surveyors: The Growth of a Profession* (London, 1968), p. 3.

[88] *Proceedings in Parliament 1628*, ed. R. C. Johnson et al. (6 vols., London, 1977–83), vol. 2, p. 276; quoted in J. P. Sommerville, *Politics and Ideology in England, 1603–1640* (London, 1986), p. 157.

[89] S[ilas] T[aylor], *Common-Good: or, The Improvement of Commons, Forrests, and Chases, by Inclosure* (1652), p. 5.

[90] This trend was at once echoed and reinforced by the arguments in the Putney Debates of Henry Ireton (endorsed by Oliver Cromwell), that only freeholders have 'a permanent fixed interest' in the national constitution (*The Clarke Papers: Selections from the Papers of William Clarke*, ed. C. H. Firth (London, 1992 edn), pp. 306–7, 302).

Like the elusive 'ploughmen' of the sixteenth century, improving freeholders were unquestionably a minority interest in the country. Yet the important point here is the power of a socio-economic ideal shaped within the predominant discourse. Typically, the freeholder was figured as a man of the yeomanry or lower gentry; while the discourse might also suit the expansive aims of greater landowners, the improvers shared Bacon's preference for a land in which the wealth is well 'dispersed in many hands'.[91] Throughout the latter sixteenth and early seventeenth centuries, I have argued, these middling strata of society had been the subject of attacks by preachers and satirists, who perceived their expansive aims and commercial orientation as the greatest threat to traditional ideals of social and economic order.[92] The discourse of agrarian improvement steadily overwhelmed such anxieties. After its awkward irruption in Tusser's *Five Hundred Points*, improvement was consolidated as a discourse for the middling sorts.

This social orientation further helps to explain a lingering anxiety in the Interregnum texts about agrarian projects. Freeholding was an ideal because it allowed the ingenious farmer the opportunity to make the most of his own. Large-scale commercial developments, however, introduced broader and more questionable economic variables. Projects were widely associated with courtiers and conmen; the improvers identified with the honest and thrifty yeomanry.[93] Hence Joan Thirsk notes Blith's initial hostility toward fen-drainers: "'who under pretence of drawing water, floating land, and doing wonders" persuaded many gentlemen to pay well for their skill, but then "at last when all hath failed, a fair pair of heels hath been the greatest advantage"'.[94] By the time he published the 'improved' edition of his book, Blith had been convinced of the value of fen-draining; however, the initial suspicions of such an informed and intelligent figure within the Hartlib circle are as telling as his subsequent enthusiasm.

Therefore, while the foundations for a discourse of capitalist development had been laid in the late sixteenth century, it was not widely embraced until after the Restoration. In the meantime, Hartlib himself was utterly consistent with the ideals of the age in his commitment to a

---

[91] *Of the True Greatness of the Kingdom of Britain*; *Works*, vol. 7, p. 61. This ideal translated into political power; a 40s freehold entitled a man to vote in parliamentary elections.
[92] See above, chapters 2 and 3.
[93] See, for example, Plattes, *Discovery of Infinite Treasure*, p. 42.
[94] 'Plough and Pen', p. 309, quoting the first edition of *The English Improver* (1649).

national boom in bee-keeping. This was hardly a new proposal. From the sixteenth century, bees had been accepted as a cheap and simple means toward improvement, available to lord and tenant alike. While courtiers were discovering the lure of large-scale projects such as Robert Payne's woad production, those of more humble origins could read of a 'lawfull and honest' way to turn ten pence into ten shillings through investment in bee hives.[95] For Hartlib, the vision of small producers operating throughout the nation underpinned a sincere belief that the production of honey could 'help to turn around the domestic economy'. Appropriately, in his representation of the scheme, the 'pious industry and good husbandry' of the bees is paralleled by the conscientious labours of the nation's potential beekeepers.[96] In the words of a fellow apiarist, 'whosoever will have profit and commodity of bees' must first accept that 'they require much more diligence, paines and industrie, then either expences or cost'.[97] The freeholder-cum-bee-keeper was an eminently suitable agrarian hero for the age.

In a world of freedom, freeholders and individual industry, traditionally dominant representations of the body politic are subverted by an antithetical impetus toward the 'atomization' of the social order.[98] Consequently, attempts to represent the nation as a unit underwent a sea-change. Webster notes that in the middle of the seventeenth century, 'The well-regulated state was compared with either a watch or the human body.'[99] (The former analogy was observed a century earlier in Sir Thomas Smith's prescient *Discourse of the Commonweal*.)[100] The body, meanwhile, becomes an index of economic activity rather than social harmony. 'Money was compared with blood in the veins; economic vitality depended on the efficient circulation of money; hence the rate of flow of money provided an index of the health of the state.'[101] Such

95 Edmund Southerne, *A Treatise concerning the right use and ordering of Bees* (1593), sig. A4ᵃ⁻ᵇ. Information about bees was also available in: Thomas Hill, *The proffitable Arte of Gardening*, from the 1568 edn; Googe's translation of Heresbach, *Foure Bookes of Husbandry*; and Charles Butler, *The Feminine Monarchie* (Oxford, 1606).
96 Timothy Raylor, 'Samuel Hartlib and the Commonwealth of Bees', in *Culture and Cultivation in Early Modern England: Writing and the Land*, ed. Michael Leslie and Timothy Raylor (Leicester, 1992), pp. 105, 108. Raylor bases his study on Hartlib's *The Reformed Common-wealth of Bees* (1655). I will return to the seventeenth-century interest in bees on pp. 220–2, below.
97 John Levett, *The ordering of Bees* (1634), p. 12.
98 The concept of 'atomization' is presented in a number of Christopher Hill's studies of religious, social and economic change in the seventeenth century.
99 *Great Instauration*, p. 455.
100 See above, pp. 52–7.   101 Webster, *Great Instauration*, p. 455.

strategies reinforced the gathering emphasis on activity, growth and competition. 'Money', writes Joyce Appleby, 'acted throughout the century as the solvent of traditional social arrangements.'[102]

The most striking consequence of this shift is in the representation of the poor. For the commonwealths men of the middle of the sixteenth century, the ploughman's honest labours at the base of the post-feudal hierarchy underpinned the dominant social ideology of the time. Subsequent religious and literary developments, however, eroded this model; and the husbandry manuals reiterated such trends, with their interest in the independent energies of the improver. Their representations of the lower orders – and particularly of those dependent upon the old manorial economy of the common lands – increasingly questioned the endeavour of the poor; and the commons are dismissed as nurseries of idleness, in a stock condemnation tinged with a Calvinist sense of the moral and religious inferiority of those whom God has not seen fit to reward on earth as a sign of their status among the elect.

This is not to say that a wave of indignation toward the poor overwhelmed the improvers. A continuing high level of concern for the problem of poverty, however, was by the seventeenth century redirected toward a desire that the lower orders should be given the opportunity to improve their lot by adopting the same ideals that were raising the fortunes of their betters. The title of Adam Moore's 1653 pro-enclosure tract is indicative of the new mood: *Bread for the Poor. And Advancement of the English Nation. Promised by Enclosure of the Wastes and Common Grounds of England.* In effect, such visions of national improvement depicted the poor sharing in the fruits of economic growth by virtue of the employment created by ingenious freeholders. They would be diverted from *'Begging, Filching, Robbing, Roguing, Murthering,* and whatsoever other Villainies their unexercised brains and hands undertake', to *'Diking, Hedging, Fencing, Setting, Sowing, Reaping, Gleaning, Mowing, Making hay,* and what not? which is all *Bread for the Poor'.*[103] No doubt this is an infinitely more practical proposition than Robert Crowley's lesson of godly starvation offered to the beggars of the sixteenth century;[104] however, the reorientation of socio-economic discourse which accompanies it is crucial. John Smyth of Nibley referred to landless cottagers as 'slaves in nature though not

---

[102] *Economic Thought and Ideology,* p. 201.
[103] Moore, *Bread for the Poor,* p. 30.
[104] See above, pp. 48–9.

in lawe'.[105] Similarly, Gervase Markham appropriates a word from traditional categorizations of land, suggesting as unskilled employees for his farmer, 'some Boyes and Girles, or other waste persons'.[106] This relatively new use of 'waste', to mean 'offscourings, dregs, worthless people' (dated by the OED from 1592),[107] transforms the poor from a problem of charity into an unexploited 'productive resource' within an expanding commonwealth.[108]

The discourse of agrarian improvement had by the middle of the seventeenth century revolutionized the ways in which the English might envisage their land. For the improver, ideals of manorial order had given way to the desire for 'profit'; the honest ploughman had been displaced by the thrifty freeholder; and cries for economic freedom and rationalism were driving an assault upon the authority of custom. The predominant influence was an emergent orientation toward the standards and imperatives of a market culture. And the principal interest group behind the movement was the rural 'middling sorts': the small freeholders and rising yeomen who were prepared to embrace the new world of commerce and to dismiss the constricting morality of the complaint tradition. In chapters 8 and 9 I will consider the response of the established gentry and nobility to the changes in the countryside; and I will argue that the discourses of the elite, after initially endorsing the traditional ethics of stewardship and stability, increasingly appropriated the imperatives of improvement. The following chapters, meanwhile, will pursue developments which at once paralleled and reinforced the discourse of improvement: firstly, the estate surveyor's radical new strategies for the representation of the land; and secondly, the georgic mode, which arose in celebration of the godly individualist.

[105] Quoted in David Rollison, *The Local Origins of Modern Society: Gloucestershire 1500–1800* (London and New York, 1993), p. 247.
[106] *The English husbandman. The first part*, sig. D4ᵇ.
[107] OED 11b.
[108] See Appleby, *Economic Thought and Ideology*, ch. 6.

6. 'To know one's own': the discourse of the estate surveyor

'Heere have you also every parcel ready measured, to all purposes . . . which is a thing much helping and conducing to a partition, or devision of such manner, or Lordship.'

(Radulph Agas, *A Preparative to Plattinge of Landes and Tenements in Surveigh*, 1596)

The House of Commons debates of 1597 and 1601 over restrictive tillage legislation, considered in the Introduction, raised ideological conflicts central to the argument of this book.[1] Those supporting the acts appealed to a model within which economic relations were governed by moral or religious values, while those against called for economic freedom. Within this context Robert Johnson, representing Monmouth boroughs in 1601, raised an apparently innocuous inquiry about the geographical restrictions placed on the application of the laws. Yet his contribution drew a sharp personal rebuke from the stridently conservative voice of Edward Glascock. For Johnson was a surveyor, and Glascock seized on this fact as he announced to the House: 'I think the Gentleman that last spake hath better Skill in Measuring of Land, than Mens Consciences. I think it is a good Law, and fit still to stand on Foot: For if we lose Religion, Let us lose Land too.'[2]

Glascock distinguishes between the moral 'conscience' which he claims parliament should reinforce within the agrarian economy, and the logic of the land-measurer. From his perspective the estate surveyor is seen as an agent of those people whose covetousness threatens the existing order: most particularly, of landlords enclosing common lands

---

[1] See above, pp. 7–12.

[2] Hayward Townshend, *Historical Collections: or, An exact Account of the Proceedings of the Four last Parliaments of Q. Elizabeth* (London, 1680), p. 291. Johnson became a leading figure in the Jacobean drive toward a thorough survey of Crown lands. His work is well documented in *The Estates of the English Crown, 1558–1640*, ed. R. W. Hoyle (Cambridge, 1992).

and causing the depopulation of rural villages. Indeed the surveyor appears in this light throughout early modern statements of agrarian complaint. Writing in 1548, the Protestant gospeller Robert Crowley predicts for surveyors 'a plage, of al plages most horryble'. He warns, 'God hath not sette you to surveye hys landes, but to playe the stuardes in his householde of this world, and to se that your pore below tenantes lacke not theye necessaries.'[3] The work of the surveyor plots the downfall of rural stewardship; in the words of an early seventeenth-century writer, the surveyor is the 'Quartermaster' of enclosing landlords, who 'goes like a Beare with a Chaine at his side'.[4]

Crowley's mid-Tudor attacks focus on a relatively new figure in rural England. The medieval estate survey was typically performed by a manorial official, and involved a review of the customary 'bundle of rights which made up a manor, based on the testimony of "true and sworn men" of the district'.[5] The century between the 1520s and the 1620s, by comparison, has been identified as that of 'the birth of the modern surveyor'.[6] During this period the surveyor was increasingly seen as an independent specialist, who brought to an estate a newly legalistic appreciation of tenurial relationships and newly rationalistic standards of land measurement and estate planning. Contemporary awareness of this development is reflected in uses of the word 'surveyor' itself, which suggest the emergence of more specialized concepts of the profession from around the middle of the sixteenth century. While the word had been in use since the Middle Ages, it had generally been applied to government officials, such as the Surveyor of the King's Works.[7] Indeed the 'surveyors' employed in every county by Elizabeth I are best understood in this light, while Jacobean arguments about the role of surveyors on Crown lands focused instead on the very definition of this office.[8] The new 'surveyors', who would propel a vigorous debate about Crown lands, had gradually risen to prominence over the preceding

---

[3] *An informacion and Peticion agaynst the oppressours of the pore Commons of this Realme* (1548), sig. A7ᵃ⁻ᵇ.

[4] Donald Lupton, *London and the Countrey Carbonadoed* (1632), p. 106.

[5] F. M. L. Thompson, *Chartered Surveyors: The Growth of a Profession* (London, 1968), p. 3.

[6] Thompson, *Chartered Surveyors*, p. 7.

[7] Thompson, *Chartered Surveyors*, p. 3.

[8] On the Elizabethan 'surveyors' of Crown land, see David Thomas, 'The Elizabethan Crown Lands: Their Purposes and Problems', in *Estates of the English Crown*, p. 66. In the same volume, Richard Hoyle traces the Jacobean debate over surveying ('"Shearing the Hog": The Reform of the Estates, c. 1598–1640', pp. 212–19).

decades. The *Oxford English Dictionary* dates at 1551 the first use of the word to mean 'One whose business it is to survey land ... one who makes surveys, or practises surveying'.[9] Similarly, the first recorded use of the transitive verb with the meaning, 'To determine the form, extent, and situation of the parts of (a tract of ground, or any portion of the earth's surface) by linear and angular measurements, so as to construct a map, plan, or detailed description of it', dates from 1550. The OED's source here is another attack on surveyors by Crowley.[10]

Within this developing yet contentious field of activity, a number of practising surveyors published manuals, to explain and justify their work. These texts undoubtedly present an overdrawn image of a disorganized field, littered with poorly trained and part-time workers; however, their descriptions and arguments, intended both to educate fellow practitioners and to reshape the public perception of surveying, document the gradual definition of a set of professional ideals and objectives. Several of the manuals employ a dialogue structure in which a surveyor convinces sceptical tenants and farmers of the value of his craft. Edward Worsop's *A Discoverie of sundrie errours and faults daily committed by Landemeaters* (1582) admits from the outset the unreliability of contemporary standards, but aims to 'manifest these enormities popularly' and to defend true surveying from the suspicions of the 'common sorte' (sig. A2b). Worsop's didactic use of a dialogue form was followed, in the early seventeenth century, in both John Norden's *Surveiors Dialogue*[11] and Rooke Churche's *An olde thrift newly revived* (1612). Other texts which demand consideration range from theoretical works on geometry, including Robert Recorde's *The Pathway to Knowledge*[12] and Leonard Digges's highly successful *A Boke Named Tectonicon*,[13] to more practical manuals for the practising surveyor, such as Valentine Leigh's *The Moste Profitable and commendable science, of Surveying*,[14] and Aaron Rathborne's *The Surveyor in Foure bookes* (1616).

This chapter traces the emergence in these works of distinctly new representations of agrarian order. 'To know one's own' becomes the

---

[9] OED 3a; the word is used thus in Robert Recorde, *The Pathway to Knowledge*.
[10] OED 2; from Crowley's *One and thyrtye Epigrammes*.
[11] Three edns (1607, 1610, 1618); references are to the 1610 edition, the last to contain substantive emendations.
[12] Three edns (1551, 1574, 1602); references are to the first edition.
[13] Seventeen edns (1556–1699); references are to the 1562 edition.
[14] Five edns (1577–96); references are to the first edition.

surveyors' central imperative, as they promote a rational definition of social and economic relationships, in preference to the network of duties and responsibilities which constitutes the conservative ideal. As demonstrated by the attack on Johnson in the Commons at the turn of the century, however, surveyors faced personal and ideological criticism throughout the period. In the following section I will consider the surveyor within this context, as a discourse develops gradually, laced with defensive concessions to traditional values. The following section will consider the rise of the surveyor within this social, economic and intellectual context. The subsequent section will concentrate more specifically on technical advances in land measurement and estate mapping, the surveyors' promotion of which stimulate the most coherent and forthright representations of a world in which every landholder may truly 'know one's own'.

'PERFECT KNOWLEDGE' AND 'PRUDENT IMPROVEMENT': THE EMERGING IDEALS OF THE SURVEYOR

The earliest printed English surveying manual is John Fitzherbert's *The Boke of Surveying and Improvements.*[15] First published in 1523, this work presents a view of surveying on the threshold of the profession's modern phase. Like its companion volume, *The Boke of Husbandrye*, considered in chapter 5, the *Surveying* is based upon a traditional conception of manorial order. Fitzherbert's representation of the surveyor is in alignment with the established role of an estate steward; he explains, 'The name of a surveyour is a frenche name and is as moche to say in Englysshe as an overseer' (fol. 34ª). The description of a surveyor's duties revolves around administration of the court of survey, at which he was expected to examine records of tenure and receive tenants for their performance of homage and fealty. As prescribed by Fitzherbert, in the ceremony of homage the tenant

> shalbe ungirde and his heed uncovered and the lorde shall syt & the tenaunt shall knele before hym on bothe his knees and shall holde his handes stretched out togyder bytwene the lordes handes and shall saye thus. I become your man from this day forwarde of lyfe and or membre and of worldely honour. And to you shall be faythfull and lowly and shall

---

beare faythe to you for the landes and tenementes the which I holde of you.[16] (fol. 31[b])

Whatever the economic basis of the relationship between landlord and tenant, this ritualized representation stresses personal bonds. Fitzherbert suggests that the court of survey simply reinforces traditional assumptions of manorial community directed by the paternal figure of the lord.

From this conservative base, however, *The Boke of Surveying* documents the tentative development of a distinctly new discourse of surveying. Fitzherbert declares his desire that the landlord should have a 'parfyte knowledge' of his lands and tenants (sig. b2[a]), an ideal increasingly linked, from Fitzherbert on, with new standards of information regarding the size and legal status of landholdings. Moreover, this knowledge is clearly structured around an economic appreciation of the land; 'in myne opinyon', he writes, the 'honour and degre [of landowners] is upholden and maynteyned by reason of theyr rentes issues revenewes and profytes' (sig. b2[a]). Subsequently, as signalled in the full title of the book, this perception incorporates a concern for the 'improvement' of rents, issues, revenues and profits. In particular, the text includes probably the earliest published argument in favour of the enclosure of common lands, in a chapter headed 'Howe to make a townshippe that is worthe twentie marke a yere worthe .xx. li. a yere' (fols. 53[b]–56[a]).[17] His justification of this process strikes a further note of economic individualism, as he claims, 'tenauntes shulde exchaunge their landes with one another . . . for doute them nat but they knowe it beste, and every tenaunt for his owne advauntage wyll do it indifferently' (fol. 55[b]).

By 1567, when *The Boke of Surveying* was published for the last time, its lessons had largely been superseded by rapid changes in the practice and theory of surveying. These developments were principally propelled by economic forces, which compounded demands for improved standards in the apportionment of property rights. Inflation and a rising population placed increased pressures on the land, while the dissolution of the monasteries stimulated the private property market by releasing

---

[16] Compare the almost identical description in Sir Thomas Littleton's *Tenures*, a possible source for Fitzherbert (*Tenures in Englyshe* (1544 edn), fol. 19[b]).

[17] Also published in *Tudor Economic Documents*, ed. R. H. Tawney and Eileen Power (3 vols., London, 1924), vol. 3, pp. 22–5. (The improvement from twenty marks to twenty pounds represents an increase in value of 50 per cent.)

hundreds of estates from the hands of the Church.[18] Land, Joyce Youings writes, was increasingly perceived as 'a freely marketable commodity'. Families and individuals – and not just the men envisaged in the gendered discourse of the surveyor – were prompted to reexamine their practices of land management.[19] These developments may be illustrated by considering the actions taken by the largest single landowner, the Crown. Throughout the Tudor and Stuart reigns, attempts by the Crown to increase its revenue from the sale and management of its lands were thwarted by inaccurate and poorly kept records. The revenue commission of 1552 first suggested a comprehensive survey of all royal lands and manors to rectify the problem.[20] Fifty years later, Robert Johnson revived the proposal, as he alerted the government to the 'heaps of inconveniences that have grown through the want of authentical surveys'.[21] To adopt Fitzherbert's language of surveying, the Crown's lack of 'perfect knowledge' of the extent, nature and value of its resources was severely weakening its 'honour and degree'.

The response of the government to these problems during the reign of Elizabeth was marked by hesitancy and conservatism. The new surveyors battled to be heard within a system geared toward the maintenance of customary tenurial practices, while the doctrine of stewardship appears to have acted, at the highest levels of government, as a constant perceptual barrier to change.[22] Within this environment, the early movement toward the improvers' ideals of order and reason was headed by an assault on the relatively uncontentious problem of 'concealed' lands and lapsed feudal dues.[23] Although this move faltered under the weight of widespread corruption, the broader problems surrounding Crown land management resurfaced with fresh urgency

[18] Joyce Youings calculates that more than three-quarters of the former monastic estates had been alienated by 1558, and stresses that the dispersal was generally administered on strictly economic grounds (*The Dissolution of the Monasteries* (London, 1971), pp. 117–31).

[19] *Sixteenth-Century England* (London, 1984), p. 166; the activities of women, who are almost universally restricted to the domain of 'housewifery' in husbandry and surveying manuals, are ably documented in Amy Louise Erickson, *Women and Property in Early Modern England* (London, 1993).

[20] Thomas, 'Elizabethan Crown Lands', p. 64.

[21] 1602 letter to Sir Robert Cecil; quoted in Thomas, 'Elizabethan Crown Lands', p. 64.

[22] Hoyle, '"Shearing the Hog"', p. 214; Thomas, 'Elizabethan Crown Lands', p. 77. (Thomas quotes a contemporary biography of Burghley, which commends his maintenance of customary rents on his own lands.)

[23] C. J. Kitching, 'The Quest for Concealed Lands in the Reign of Elizabeth I', *Transactions of the Royal Historical Society*, 5th series, 24 (1974), pp. 63–78.

toward the end of the reign, creating a debate which helped to crystallize the status and discourse of the modern surveyor. Richard Hoyle writes that the history of Crown estates in the years immediately after the death of Burghley in 1598 'is one of attempts to increase revenue through the exercise of a tighter control over officers, a determination to overturn the restraint which custom placed on income and a continuing search for concealments'.[24]

Although the practical achievements of this drive never matched the motivating rhetoric, the shift in attitude was nonetheless profound. The need for revenue was henceforth yoked to a rigorous pursuit of increased knowledge, as from 1604 some 125 men were employed throughout the country on extensive (though ultimately incomplete) surveys of Crown estates and woods. The 'Great Survey', as it has become known, involved prominent surveying publicists such as Norden and Rathborne.[25] The rationale behind the programme is clearly stated by Johnson, who in the year following his brief contribution to the parliamentary tillage debates wrote to Robert Cecil claiming that the Crown rarely received a fair price in its land sales. 'The chief foundation of [these] mischiefs has been the want of authentic surveys and the preservation of Court rolls, by which there has been the loss of many rents, the confounding of tenancies, the change of tenures, perverting of customs, concealing of fines' and a host of other abuses. Interestingly, his desire for the Crown to increase its income is combined with an antagonistic attitude toward its tenants. 'Within these 60 or 80 years, and chiefly 40 or 50', he claims, 'the wit-craft of man is more and more extended, to obscure ancient customs, and pervert them to private profit.'[26] The evident suspicion in the comment – offering a stark contrast to Fitzherbert's paternalism – signals the markedly tougher attitude toward estate management that underpinned the expansion of surveying throughout England from the middle of the sixteenth century.

Structures of manorial life were also unsettled by changes in the role

---

[24] '"Shearing the Hog"', p. 204.

[25] Heather Lawrence, 'John Norden and His Colleagues: Surveyors of Crown Lands', *The Cartographic Journal*, 22 (1985), pp. 54–6. See also Sidney J. Madge, *The Domesday of Crown Lands: A Study of the Legislation, Surveys, and Sales of Royal Estates under the Commonwealth* (London, 1938), pp. 47–64.

[26] Letter dated 18 April 1602 (PRO SP 13 283A, no. 30). Johnson subsequently became a leading figure in the 'Great Survey'. Examples of his work from this period include 'Certain Notes touching Particular & exact Surveys', BL Additional MS 38444, fols. 91–2; and 'A Breviat of the Survey of his Majesty's Woods in the County of Buckingham', BL Additional MS 38444, fol. 40.

of the law in the countryside. C. W. Brooks charts a large rise in civil litigation between 1560 and 1640, and attributes the increase in part to the declining power of manorial courts over the economic and social life of an estate.[27] Property disputes were increasingly drawn beyond the manor, to be determined by the national courts in London.[28] At the same time landlords were embracing similarly legalistic standards, by replacing the steward or 'overseer' described by Fitzherbert with men such as common-law attorneys or barristers of the inns of court. The positions of amateur estate servants, Brooks writes, were 'being threatened by new ideas about estate management which stressed to landlords the advantages of using men with legal training and experience to keep their courts and handle their legal affairs'. Throughout this movement the trend was toward a solidification of 'the fluid customary claims of landlord and tenant into rights which could be maintained at common law'.[29] Concurrently, the network of use rights defined by custom within a manor was gradually eroded, frequently to be replaced with a monetary equivalent. 'Property', as E. P. Thompson claims, was being 'loosed for the market from its uses and from its social situation'.[30]

The surveying texts published from the middle of the sixteenth century increasingly present a new image of the surveyor and his craft, in line with these patterns of change. Fitzherbert's permanent manager is refashioned as a more specialized, temporary employee, who imposes new standards of knowledge and order upon preexistent structures of land management. The dialogues, in particular, promote this new image as they describe the surveyor visiting an estate and advising its various occupants. Norden's *Surveiors Dialogue* begins with a discussion between the surveyor and a tenant, in which the former convinces his initially hostile companion about the importance of his craft; following this, the surveyor discusses with the lord the constitution of a manor and

27 *Pettyfoggers and Vipers of the Commonwealth: The 'Lower Branch' of the Legal Profession in Early Modern England* (Cambridge, 1986), chs. 4–5.
28 Mervyn James argues in relation to Durham that this development promoted 'a considerable readjustment of the traditional submissive posture characteristic of most . . . tenants in the early sixteenth century', and furthered a general trend whereby landlord–tenant relationships came to be seen as contractual, rather than based on personal dependence (*Family, Lineage, and Civil Society: A Study of Society, Politics, and Mentality in the Durham Region, 1500–1640* (Oxford, 1974), pp. 79–83).
29 Brooks, *Pettyfoggers*, pp. 198, 117, 201.
30 'The Grid of Inheritance: A Comment', in *Family and Inheritance: Rural Society in Western Europe, 1200–1800*, ed. Jack Goody, Joan Thirsk and E. P. Thompson (Cambridge, 1976), p. 341.

the treatment of tenants; then he conducts a court of survey; and in books 4 and 5 he discusses land measurement and improved methods of husbandry with the tenant, now acting as a bailiff of his manor. The addition for the 1610 edition of a sixth book on the purchasing of land further binds the work to the pressing realities of a dynamic land market.

Radulph Agas, a surveyor active in the later decades of the sixteenth century, endorsed this new image through a campaign of self-promotion. In two publications and several letters sent to Burghley and other state officials, Agas consistently emphasizes the value of his specialized knowledge and experience. One of his printed texts is a single-sheet advertisement, the only survivor of perhaps dozens of such documents published by practising surveyors, which are said in one dialogue to have been found 'fixed upon posts in the streetes' of London.[31] Agas's statement focuses throughout on the definition and status of the occupation, beginning with the declaration,

> No man may arrogate to himself the name and title of a perfect and absolute Surveior . . . unlesse he be able in true forme, measure, quantitie, and proportion, to plat the same in their particulars, *ad infinitum*, and thereupon to retrive, and beat out all decaied, concealed, and hidden parcels thereof.[32]

Agas advertises the value to the landowner of the technical skills and strict empirical standards of the 'perfect and absolute Surveior'. He emphasizes the 'retrieval' and definition of information, which is figured in the rational terms of 'forme, measure, quantitie, and proportion'. The potential employee thus proclaims his ability to define the 'true' structure of an estate, a definition with social as well as economic consequences.

The ideals of 'perfect knowledge', however, required considerable justification in the face of conservative criticism. Norden, writing almost ninety years after Fitzherbert, presents in his *Surveiors Dialogue* one of the most extensive attempts to negotiate a position between the old social morality and the new standards of knowledge and reason. His figure of a discontented tenant farmer begins by attacking the surveyor. He charges: 'you looke into the values of mens Lands, whereby the Lords of Mannors

---

[31] Norden, *Surveiors Dialogue*, p. 14.
[32] *To all persons whom these presents may concerne, of what estate and degree soever* (c. 1596). See also *A Preparative to Plattinge of Landes and Tenements in Surveigh* (1596); BL Additional MS 12497, fol. 346ª; BL Additional MS 12497, fol. 342ª; BL Lansdowne MS 73, fol. 107ª; BL Lansdowne MS 84, fol. 69ª.

doe racke their Tennants to a higher rent and rate then ever before'; 'by your meanes rents are raysed, and Lands knowne to the uttermost Acre'. In his defence, the Surveyor replies,

> I perceive that the force of your strongest arguments is . . . your feare and unwillingnesse that the Lord of the Mannor, under whom, & in whose Land you dwell, should know his owne: and that you thinke it better for you, that he should continue still ignorant of what he hath, and that your estates should bee alwaies hidden. (pp. 3–4)

The argument turns on the verb 'to know'. The farmer is worried about the consequences of land being '*knowne* to the uttermost Acre', whereas the surveyor argues that the landlord has a right to '*know* his owne'. The latter phrase, used consistently throughout the surveying manuals, epitomizes contemporary justifications of the practice. It assumes a social and economic order in which rights to the land can clearly and objectively be determined, in a manner which precludes competing or loosely defined customary claims. Landownership is figured as reducible to facts and figures: a conception which inevitably undermines the matrix of duties and responsibilities which had previously been seen to define the manorial community. In the perception of the surveyor, the land is defined as property, as the landlord's 'own'.

This fundamental shift, however, was tangled in a web of anxieties and uncertainties. Indeed Norden, like almost all other contemporary publicists of surveying, maintained a commitment to traditional ideals. While the farmer's complaints suggest the emergence of an ideology that appreciates land as a commodity and tenants as free economic agents, the surveyor's typical defence clings to a representation of the moral economy of the manor, which he calls a 'little common wealth' (p. 27). In a characteristic statement, Norden says of the landlord–tenant relationship:

> And therefore ought there to be such a mutuall concurrence of love and obedience in the one, and of aide and protection in the other, as no hard measure offered by the superiour, should make a just breach of the loyaltie of the inferiour: which kind of union is no wayes better preserved . . . then by the Lords true knowledge of the particulars that every Tenant holdeth, and a favourable course in fines and rents: and by the Tenants love and thankfulnesse in all readie service and dutie towards the Lord. (sig. *2ᵇ)

The statement raises again the surveyor's ideal of 'true knowledge', yet attempts to restrain this potentially disruptive force within the bonds of 'a mutuall concurrence of love and obedience'. This is a strategy which emerges as a central convention of the surveying manuals; yet it is fraught with ideological tensions. For the methodical collection of 'true knowledge' in an estate survey overrides traditional assumptions about manorial relationships. Ideals such as 'love' and 'loyalty' are increasingly subordinated to boldly empirical standards of land quantification and valuation. Moreover, for all his insistence on a universal morality, the surveyor ultimately transmits his 'knowledge' into the hands of his employer. And Norden is orthodox in his judgement that whereas some knowledge is 'publique, as the names of grounds, the owners, their estates, buts, bounds, & such like', other information remains 'private, & to be concealed, as the quantities, and supposed yeerely values. These are for the Lord' (p. 183). Consequently the knowledge itself becomes another form of property, which serves to reinforce the landlord's economic power.

'THE WORLDE WAS MERIER, BEFORE MEASURINGS WERE USED': THE SURVEYORS' PROMOTION OF LAND MEASUREMENT AND ESTATE MAPPING

The reluctance of writers such as Norden to break with traditional conceptions of agrarian order highlights at once the continuing authority of conservative ideals and the radical potential of the surveyors' activities. In response to widespread public mistrust, the surveying publicists awkwardly attempted to link emergent values of empirical knowledge to a preexistent model of manorial community. The more immediate ramifications of the surveyors' activities, meanwhile, were rapidly becoming apparent to those involved in the agrarian economy. For example Henry Percy, Ninth Earl of Northumberland, relied heavily upon surveyors late in the sixteenth century, as he plotted a dramatic economic recovery after a period of profligacy. Indeed his modern biographer finds that Percy spent 'anything between £50 and £200 a year over many years on surveying', and that the information gathered was duly used to effect an 'improvement' of his income: from a low-point of around £3000 per year to an annual average of £6650 by the turn of the century.[33] Similarly, a defender of the questionable reputation of Thomas

---

[33] Gordon R. Batho, 'The Finances of an Elizabethan Nobleman: Henry Percy, Ninth Earl of Northumberland (1564–1632)', *Economic History Review*, 2nd series, 9 (1957), p. 441. While the inflation of the 1590s may affect the real significance of these figures, they nonetheless demonstrate a vigorous programme intended to overcome the effects of such fluctuations.

Sutton (1532–1611), a wealthy trader and coal magnate, mentions his subject's 'insight in surveys', and comments: 'seldome shall you see a great estate got by one that is not an exact accountant and a judicious Surveyor'.[34] The writer's tacit approval of an active pursuit of wealth – epitomized in his use of the verb 'to get' – underlines the almost inevitable bond within a dynamic socio-economic structure between surveying and individual aspirations. The 'judicious' survey becomes an appropriate tool for those aspiring to 'a great estate'.

Despite their regular concessions to traditional moral standards, the surveying manuals forge a set of professional ideals which would ultimately serve the interests of improvers such as Percy and Sutton. This process may be observed most notably in arguments surrounding the technological innovations of geometrical land measurement and estate mapping. These two practices, which together distinguish the 'modern' surveyor from his predecessors, prompt the writers to present distinctly new representations of the land and property relations in the countryside. Here the surveyors move toward an acceptance – and even an endorsement – of economic competition and individual improvement in a developing market economy.

The land and the 'Landemeater'

Scarcity of land and an accompanying desire for greater knowledge of existing resources prompted a reassessment of traditional methods of land quantification. In the early sixteenth century, measurement was a minor role approached in a fairly casual manner: Fitzherbert appears to envisage only a customary practice, whereby men would 'extend and tread out' the open fields.[35] This method finds a parallel in the Rogation ceremonies, or beating the bounds, a procession conceived in Catholic ritual for the purpose of blessing the fields, but subsequently embraced by the Elizabethan establishment as much for its practical function of confirming property and parish boundaries.[36] In accordance with the rationale of the medieval estate survey, these practices were intended to draw upon a collective memory of landholdings and customs. The

---

[34] 'How Mr. Sutton got his great estate', BL Lansdowne MS 825, fol. 66.

[35] See Thompson, *Chartered Surveyors*, pp. 7–8.

[36] Maurice Beresford, *History on the Ground: Six Studies in Maps and Landscapes*, revised edn (London, 1971), pp. 28–9.

local community would be reinforced by the regular affirmation of its physical bounds.

Yet the shortcomings of such a process for one seeking 'true knowledge', either for improving a manor or for land transactions, are obvious. To pursue one example, around 1572 Nathaniel Bacon wrote from Norfolk to his father, the Lord Keeper Sir Nicholas Bacon, in exasperation after his inspection of the manor of Netherall:

> I spent a hole daie & half in treadinge out the ground therof by the drag of Styfkey, & yet this notwithstandinge, I dout I have done litle good therin, for I found the drag unperfect in many places, yea so unperfect in one place as we all geassed some leafe of the boke to be lost, & than was I forced to writ as the tenantes willed me.

The Bacons, who took a meticulous interest in the management of their estates and consistently attempted to expand their fortunes through participation in the land market, would hardly be satisfied by the affirmation of an existing order. Indeed Nathaniel's concern at being 'forced to writ as the tenantes willed me' evidences a governing intention to protect an individual or family interest in the face of competing claims. Later in the letter he argues the need for further investigation and estimates that it would take a month to compile a 'perfect boke' of the property, a task for which he has already found 'two men . . . very able to direct one'.[37]

These two willing servants to the landed are unlikely to have adhered to any particularly rigorous standards in their land measurement, as traditional methods and inconsistent results remained a widespread problem throughout the early modern period.[38] Elsewhere in the Bacon correspondence, the Lord Keeper writes in frustration, 'It is very straunge to me that Boldero shoulde measure the Close called Pastur Close but for 33 acres where by Hunte's measure it is 57 acres.'[39] Within this context, the surveying manuals argue the necessity of standards that would be both accurate and nationally consistent. The earliest writer to concentrate on measurement was Sir Richard Benese, who learnt his craft as a canon of the Augustinian priory of Merton, and around 1537

[37] *The Papers of Nathaniel Bacon of Stiffkey*, ed. A. Hassell Smith, Gillian M. Baker and R. W. Kenny (2 vols., University of East Anglia, 1979, 1983), vol. 1, pp. 71–2.
[38] Alison Sarah Bendall, *Maps, Land and Society: A History, with a Carto-Bibliography of Cambridgeshire Estate Maps c. 1600–1836* (Cambridge, 1992), pp. 78–9. Bendall discusses changing methods of land measurement on pp. 129–31.
[39] *Papers of Nathaniel Bacon*, vol. 1, p. 30.

published, *This boke sheweth the maner of measurynge of all maner of lande*.[40] (Despite this link with the Church, the anti-monastic propaganda of illustration 6.1 – which suggests that monks were particularly rigorous in their surveying – does not appear to have any basis in fact.) Robert Recorde's *Pathway to Knowledge*, however, was the first text to argue for the applicability to surveying of contemporary advances in geometry, and his work thus marks a vital break with traditional methods of quantification. Recorde launches the *Pathway* with a prefatory verse, spoken by Geometry:

> Survayers have cause to make muche of me.
> And so have all Lordes, that landes do possesse:
> But Tennauntes I feare will like me the lesse.
> Yet do I not wrong but measure all truely,
> And yelde the full right to everye man justely
> Proportion Geometricall hath no man opprest,
> Yf anye bee wronged, I wishe it redrest.   (sig. $2\pi1^b$)

The juxtaposition of 'opprest' and 'redrest' in the final couplet encapsulates Recorde's central defence of geometrical measurements against the fears of conservative critics. Rather than serving the interests of the 'oppressor', geometry reinforces a preexistent order in the distribution of land, an order which actually may have been distorted through customary practice. It yields 'the full right to everye man justely', and if tenants are unenthusiastic about the new standards, it may well be because they have something to hide from the rightful 'possessors'.

Between the date of Recorde's publication and the turn of the century, interest in geometry expanded rapidly. Leonard Digges's *Boke Named Tectonicon*, 'briefly shewynge the exacte measurynge, and speady reckenynge all maner Lande, squared Tymber, Stone, Steaples, Pyllers, Globes. &c.', led the market, going through eight editions from 1556 to 1599, with further reprints stretching throughout the seventeenth century. Another important text was Euclid's *Elements of Geometrie*, which was published in an English translation of 1570. In a lengthy preface to this work, John Dee draws attention to the etymological connection between 'geometry' and 'land-measuring', and praises 'The perfect Science of Lines, Plaines, and Solides [which] (like a divine Justicier,) gave unto every man, his owne' (sig. a2^{a-b}). Even in more

---

[40] Five edns (1537?–c. 1565).

6.1 Elizabethan manuscript illustration of monks measuring land, intended to portray a link between the former monastic estates and rapacious economic practices (Huntington Library MS HM 160, fol. 35ᵃ). The supporting quote is Isaiah 57.17: 'For the iniquity of his covetousness was I wroth, and smote him.'

theoretical geometrical works, the distribution of land is frequently employed as a ready example by which to illustrate points. Arthur Hopton writes in 1611: 'as lines bound figures, so hedges bound inclosures: and angles in the field are created by the meting of hedges, as they be in figures by the section of lines'.[41] The precise, objective measurements afforded by geometry thus furthered a fundamental shift in the perception of 'one's own', at the same time that 'the concept of landed property as a bundle of assorted rights over different bits of

[41] *Speculum Topographicum: Or The Topographicall Glasse*, sig. a1ᵇ.

territory gave way to the idea that property lay in definable pieces of soil'.[42]

This development in the representation of the land is reinforced by the manuals' stress on the statute acre as a standard unit of measure. Traditionally, land was divided into units such as dayworks, ploughlands, hides and knights' fees. These measures were derived from traditional agricultural practices within a region. A hide, for instance, is defined by William Folkingham in his *Feudigraphia* as a portion 'as may be tilled with one teame . . . in a yeere and a day', and a knight's fee as 'so much Inheritance as is sufficient yearely for the maintenance of a Knight'.[43] The concept of an acre had evolved similarly. The OED notes that the original meaning of the term was '"open country, untenanted land, forest" . . . then, with advance in the agricultural state, pasture land, tilled land, an enclosed or defined piece of land, a piece of land of definite size, a land measure'. Even in the latter sense, the dimensions of the acre originally had a customary quality, derived from the quantity of land a yoke of oxen could plough in a day, while the statutory definition, which dates from the thirteenth century, was based on a standard common-field rectangular plot of four by forty perches or rods.[44] Moreover the length of the perch, though fixed by law at 16.5 feet, might in practice vary according to the land's use and value. Measures could be anywhere between twelve and twenty-four feet, and local definitions could be as idiosyncratic as that found in Buckfastleigh, Devon, during the Crown surveys of the early seventeenth century: 'sixteen foot and half one inch and one barley corn square'.[45]

The prevalence of such local customs in the quantification of land undoubtedly helped to perpetuate traditional conceptions of socio-economic order and agricultural practice. Units such as ploughlands and dayworks could reinforce existing appreciations of rates of labour and sizes of landholdings within a community, and might thereby constitute a significant perceptual obstacle to the potential improver. Rathborne,

---

[42] Thompson, *Chartered Surveyors*, p. 10.

[43] *Feudigraphia. The synopsis or epitome of surveying* (1610), p. 60. Compare Cyprian Lucar's claim that '8. hides of land make a Knights fee, which . . . is a plough till a yeare' (*A Treatise Named Lucarsolace* (1590), p. 8).

[44] OED 2a. See also Philip Grierson, *English Linear Measures: An Essay in Origins* (University of Reading, 1972), p. 24; and Ronald Edward Zupko, *A Dictionary of English Weights and Measures: From Anglo-Saxon Times to the Nineteenth Century* (Madison, 1968), pp. 3–5.

[45] Quoted by Lawrence, in 'John Norden and His Colleagues', p. 55.

in *The Surveyor in Foure bookes*, confirms the importance of such perceptions when he writes that the surveyor may often have to resort to questioning a tenant about his lands 'as he esteemeth them'. Thus 'if he know not what acres they containe (as most tenants will seeme ignorant thereof) let him expresse of his Meadow how many daies mowing, of his Arable how many daies plowing, and of his Pasture how many Beast-gates, and the like' (p. 211). By contrast, the surveying manuals' insistence on the statute acre enforces an objective national standard of quantification. Cyprian Lucar, in his 1590 *Treatise Named Lucarsolace*, is representative of the publicists in his provision of instructions for conversions to the statutory measure. He follows an astonishingly simplistic logic in his argument in favour of the latter, as he compares an acre measured by a twelve-foot perch, 'wherewith medow grounds in diverse places of England are measured to the intollerable losses of buyers', to one measured with an eighteen-, twenty-, or twenty-four-foot perch, 'which are also used in many places of this realme by measurers of wood lands to the manifold disadvantages of sellers' (p. 9). From the perspective of the land-measurer, any diversions from the statutory standard become abnormalities, which endanger the economic order of property transactions.

The manuals also promote the awareness of area measured in *square* units. Traditional representational measures, it has been demonstrated, take little consideration of square dimensions.[46] Hence the acre was conventionally defined by its standard length and breadth as a rectangular block, and the surveyor's task was perceived to be based upon linear measurement of the land. As late as 1613 Arthur Standish reminds readers of his *New Directions of Experience* that 'it is to be understood, that a statute acre doth containe in length two hundred and twenty yards, and in breadth, two and twenty'.[47] The influence of geometry prompts a perceptual leap. Edward Worsop, for example, in his *Discoverie of sundrie errours and faults daily committed by Landemeaters*, reinterprets the statutory definition of an acre when he determines that 'The words, and meaning . . . of the statute certainly is: that in what fashion soever grounds do ly, that just viii. score square perches must alwaies make the

---

[46] See Witold Kula, *Measures and Men*, translated from the Polish by R. Szreter (Princeton, 1986), p. 42.
[47] (1615 edn), p. 6.

acre' (sig. H4ᵃ).[48] Consequently, as the manuals repeatedly emphasize, an acre need not conform to the traditional conception of a rectangular block; it can also be measured over hills and through valleys, in circles and along meandering rivers. Although the practical application of these lessons may have been obvious in parts of the country for many years, the techniques and terminology of the surveyors profoundly altered appreciations of the conventional unit of land quantification. Through the imposition of a national empirical standard, acceptance of local particularity gave way to a representation of land as a commodity easily accessible and transferable within a market economy.

Not surprisingly, the new spatial rationalism in land quantification became one of the most contentious aspects of the modern surveyor's activities. Indeed cross-cultural studies have found a 'distrust of counting and measuring' to be 'typical of a great many agricultural societies'. In Poland in the eighteenth and nineteenth centuries, when new standards of measurement were being enforced, 'the peasants would often invoke the devil to lay his talons on the land surveyors'.[49] In early modern England surveyors frequently faced the threat of popular action against their attempts to measure the land: the case of tenants in Dorset who justified their obstruction of a surveyor on the grounds that they did not want 'the quantities [of their land] to be knowen by measuringe', validates the anxiety manifest in the manuals.[50]

One of the earliest of the surveying publicists to confront these traditional fears is Worsop, whose *Discoverie of sundrie errours* presents a particularly detailed argument in support of the new standards. Within the dialogue form, the sceptical clothier claims, 'The worlde was merier, before measurings were used then it hath beene since. A tenant in these daies must pay for every foote, which is an extreme matter' (sig. I2ᵇ). The statement evokes an image of a world without change, in which landlords and tenants were bound in mutually satisfying relationships within territorial boundaries acknowledged throughout the community. A surveyor's quantifications upset the very basis of these relationships, and his empirical knowledge is represented as essentially subversive within the traditional model. Worsop, speaking as the undisguised didactic

[48] Compare Digges, who clearly understands the concept of land quantification by squared units, but appears to lack the vocabulary with which to express it, as he declares that, 'an Acre by statute ought to conteine 160 pearches' (*Tectonicon*, sig. B1ᵃ).

[49] Kula, *Measures and Men*, pp. 14, 16.

[50] J. H. Bettey, 'Agriculture and Rural Society in Dorset, 1570–1670' (unpublished Ph.D dissertation, University of Bristol, 1976), p. 141.

voice in his dialogue, replies,

> Most tenants that take land after the common measurings pay for more
> then they should. Therefore if the tenant had true measure, he might live
> meryer then he doeth. Seeing most Landlords covet to let their grounds to
> the uttermost, and most tenants seeke to sell their wares at the hyest prices:
> it is verie requisite for both sides, that the land be truely measured. True
> measure is not extremitie, but good justice. (sig. I2^b)

Worsop counters his assailant's yearning for rural 'merriness' by
proclaiming an objective standard of 'justice' that will enable each
tenant to 'live meryer than he doeth'. In attempting to counter the
traditional complaint, Worsop is thus forced beyond the conservative
model, toward a socio-economic discourse based on individual
aspirations. The defender of land measurement represents the land as a
site of economic negotiation and dispute, and while his critic attacks
the assumptions of individualism, Worsop merely defends the accurate
regulation of such aspirations.

Other writers focus more directly on the importance of accurate
measurements for transactions in the land market. Benese directs his
maner of measurynge not to the manorial lord, but (as his editor writes in
the preface) 'for the commune profyte and use of every man'. He begins
his text by justifying his work: since 'in measurynge of lande many
menne, somtyme the sellers, by more measure than ryght, somtyme the
byers by lesse measure than ryght be greatly deceyved by the meters
thereof' (sigs. +4^a, A1^a). Similarly Dee, in his preface to Euclid, laments,

> God knoweth . . . how great wrong and injurie hath (in my time) bene
> committed by untrue measuring and surveying of Land or Woods, any
> way. And, this I am sure: that the Value of the difference, betwene the
> truth and such Surveyes, would have bene hable to have found (for ever)
> in eche of our two Universities, an excellent Mathematicall Reader.
>
> (sigs. a3^b–a4^a)

Dee stresses the quality of absolute 'truth' that accurate surveying brings
to the quantification of the land, and places this argument in an economic
context through his description of the 'great wrong and injurie' caused
by 'untrue measuring'. His underlying assumption that surveying is
principally of use for land transactions is reinforced in the final
suggestive link between lost revenue (presumably that sustained by the
Crown in its sales) and the corrective value of geometrical standards.[51]

---

[51] On the failure of the Elizabethan regime to take advantage of advances in surveying,
see Thomas, 'Elizabethan Crown Lands'.

The 'true' survey is thus linked to the academic programme of the 'excellent Mathematicall Reader'.

The increasing concern with the use of surveying in land sales evidences a decisive shift away from the ideals of Fitzherbert. In contrast to the medieval ideal of ordering the manor, the seventeenth-century surveyor was at least as concerned with ordering the market. Folkingham presents one of the more unapologetic justifications of this development by comparing land transactions with the grain market. Focusing on the benefits to lessees of 'true surveys', he writes:

> It is a World to see the sottish pressures urged against the admeasuring of land, yet the Use of Ponderous and Concave Measures . . . are no lesse commendable than Common in venting of Wares and Merchandize, and what greater iniquity in the using admeasurements in Grounds than in Graine? . . . Take away Number, Weight, Measure, you exile Justice, and reduce and haile-up from Hell the olde and odious Chaos of Confusion.
>
> (sig. A3ᵃ)

The market analogy liberates possessors of the land from the weight of traditional notions of moral responsibility. In contrast to Crowley's exhortation that landowners should 'playe the stuardes in [God's] householde of this world', Folkingham represents the ownership and trade in land as comparable to the 'venting of Wares and Merchandize'. In a socio-economic model which assumes that individuals will naturally seek their own advantage in competition with their neighbours, the only alternative to the order of the surveyor is 'the olde and odious Chaos of Confusion'.

This development prefigures a fundamental shift in perceptions of the land. The emergence of capitalism, it has been argued, helped 'turn place into commodities'. The market mechanism 'quantifies worth or value, and as the realm of market activity expanded, more and more things become valued in terms of their market price, rather than by their traditional value or usefulness'. In the history of economic development, increasing accuracy of measurement has meant that 'facts could be described in terms of such quantifiable units as locations, sizes, and weights, just as goods could be described in terms of prices. Experience of all kinds was thus becoming more amenable to measure.'[52] The emergence of a discourse of surveying at once justifies and furthers this

[52] Robert David Sack, *Human Territoriality: Its Theory and History* (Cambridge, 1986), pp. 48, 83.

shift. Indeed Folkingham's particularly bold statement openly rejects the traditional model of agrarian order, and insists instead upon ideals of individual economic freedom, regulated only by the order of the marketplace.

Viewing the land on 'painted paper': the influence of the estate map

The estate map was a relatively late development in the practice of the modern surveyor.[53] P. D. A. Harvey claims that 'it seems to have been only in the 1580s that it started to be generally understood that an estate survey might involve making maps'.[54] Like the changes in land measurement, the development of mapping was stimulated by advances in geometry and the production of new instruments for the surveyor. (Illustration 6.2, the title page of Rathborne's *The Surveyor*, shows one surveyor at work with a plane table, in the illustration below the title, and another with the newer theodolite, above the title.) Further, the practical application of estate maps was promoted by the courts, which increasingly ordered their preparation for use in property disputes.[55] On a wider scale, the rise of the estate map can be linked to an increasing consciousness of cartography among wealthier and better-educated members of society. By the 1580s a number of maps of Europe and the world were available in printed form from the Continent, while Christopher Saxton's *Atlas of England and Wales* (1579) was undoubtedly popular among the very landowners who were potential employers of estate surveyors.[56] As John Dee writes in his preface to Euclid, 'some, to beautifie their Halls, Parlers, Chambers, Galeries, Studies, or Libraries with . . . liketh, loveth, getteth, and useth, Mappes,

[53] On the development and significance of maps in the late sixteenth and early seventeenth centuries, see Peter Barber, 'England II: Monarchs, Ministers, and Maps, 1550–1625', in *Monarchs, Ministers and Maps: The Emergence of Cartography as a Tool of Government in Early Modern Europe*, ed. David Buisseret (Chicago, 1992), pp. 57–98; Bendall focuses on estate mapping from 1600 into the nineteenth century in *Maps, Land and Society*.

[54] 'Estate Surveyors and the Spread of the Scale-Map in England, 1550–80', publication forthcoming in *Landscape History*. (I am grateful to Professor Harvey for providing me with a copy of this paper.) See also Harvey, *Maps in Tudor England* (London, 1993).

[55] See, for example, Sarah Bendall's analysis of a series of maps associated with legal action, in 'Interpreting Maps of Rural Landscape: An Example from Late Sixteenth-Century Buckinghamshire', *Rural History*, 4 (1993), pp. 107–21.

[56] P. D. A. Harvey, 'Estate Surveyors'; and see also Richard Helgerson's discussion of cartography and chorography in *Forms of Nationhood: The Elizabethan Writing of England* (Chicago and London, 1992), ch. 3.

Chartes, & Geographicall Globes' (sig. a4ᵃ). One such devotee of cartography was William Cecil, Lord Burghley, who displayed at Theobalds a map of England showing 'the armorial bearings and domains of every esquire, lord, knight, and noble who possesses lands'.[57]

Indeed the estate map became a significant status symbol, and was especially popular among new landowners, most notably those rising from commerce and the professions, who benefited from inflation and the rapid turnover in the land market.[58] Mapping became the ultimate extra service offered by the surveyor, and the more elaborate productions could be finished with a colour-coded key to land use and decorated with the arms of the lord and illustrations of the manor house and agricultural activities. Lucar, for example, suggests the use of 'diverse good and thinne water colours, to shew a difference in your mappe betweene meadowes, pastures, arable land, wood land, hilles, valleies, and grounds belonging to sundrie tenements and severall persons'. The margins of this map should be used to record a vast range of additional information, from the quality of the soil to 'the disposition, industrie, studies, manners, trades, occupations, honestie, humanitie, hospitalitie, apparell, and other morall vertues of the inhabitants' (pp. 50–2). A slightly less ambitious – though significantly more practical – model was offered for the seventeenth-century surveyor by William Leybourn (illustration 6.3): a style which dominated the field well into the eighteenth century.[59]

A map of this kind, prominently displayed in the manor house, presents a simple and celebratory representation of a landlord's position in relation to his estate. As Thomas Randolph writes in the early seventeenth century:

> Thou severall Artists doest imploy to show
> The measure of thy lands; that thou maiest know
> How much of earth thou hast.[60]

The surveyor's controlling concern with defining property rights thus merges with a landlord's desire to celebrate his status within the land.

---

[57] Contemporary report quoted in Barber, 'England II: Monarchs, Ministers, and Maps', pp. 76–7.

[58] Alison Sarah Bendall, 'The Pride of Ownership: English Estate Maps c. 1600–1840', paper delivered at the Warburg Institute, December 1991. (I am grateful to Dr Bendall for providing me with a copy of this paper.) See also Bendall, *Maps, Land and Society*, p. 153.

[59] *The Compleat Surveyor*, 4 edns (1653–79).

[60] 'On the Inestimable Content he Injoyes in the Muses', in *Poems with the Muses Looking-Glasse: and Amyntas* (Oxford, 1638), p. 5; quoted in Bendall, p. 165.

6.2 Title-page of Aaron Rathborne, *The Surveyor in Foure bookes* (1616), with inset illustrations of a surveyor at work in the fields.

The map graphically and decoratively demonstrates 'How much of earth thou hast'. J. B. Harley argues that an estate map

> was also a seigneurial emblem, asserting the lord of the manor's legal power within the rural society. For him, the map was one badge of his local authority. Family coats of arms added within the margins were certainly for him more than mere decoration, for the right to these heraldic emblems also incorporated an individual's right, rooted in the past, to the possession of land.[61]

Simply, a map defines a manor as the lord's 'own'. The potential ramifications for the representation of manorial society are demonstrated in a map of the manor of Great Bookham, Surrey, prepared around 1614–17 by Thomas Clay, which omits the hovels of landless labourers.[62] The surveyor chooses to paint a pleasing veneer over evidence of the poorer inhabitants of the manor, who might make embarrassing requests that the lord fulfil his traditional role within the manor.

In Norden's *Surveiors Dialogue*, the farmer focuses his criticism of estate mapping on its potential for allowing the landlord to withdraw from the society of his manor. He says, 'we poore Country-men doe not think it good to have our Lands plotted out, and me thinks indeede it is to very small purpose: for is not the field it selfe a goodly Map for the Lord to looke upon, better then a painted paper?' The surveyor replies:

> I know your meaning in misliking plotting of your Land, and yet you utter not what you think: for a plot rightly drawne by true information, describeth so the lively image of a Mannor . . . as the Lord sitting in his chayre, may see what he hath, where and how it lyeth, and in whose use and occupation every particular is, upon the suddaine view. (pp. 15–16)

As considered in chapter 5, a standard adage in the conservative tradition of advice on estate management is that the best manure for the land is the lord's feet.[63] This stress on active supervision accords with representations of the manor as a community, with the lord directly involved in both the working of his land and the lives of his tenants. Norden's surveyor, by comparison, subtly reinterprets the nature of land-

[61] 'Meaning and Ambiguity in Tudor Cartography', in *English Map-Making 1500–1650*, ed. Sarah Tyacke (London, 1983), p. 37.

[62] J. H. Harvey, 'Thomas Clay's Plan of the Manor of Great Bookham, Surrey, 1614', *Proceedings of the Leatherhead and District Local History Society*, 2 (1966), p. 282.

[63] See above, p. 140.

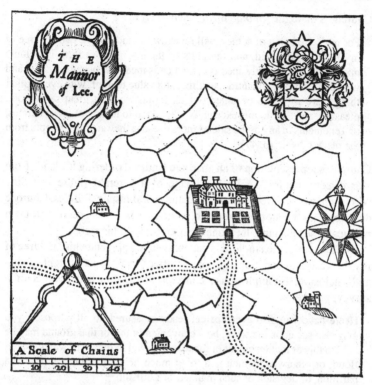

6.3 A model estate map published in William Leybourn, *The Compleat Surveyor* (1653).

ownership. He has the lord removed from the life of the estate, 'sitting in his chayre' (an image given in almost identical terms by both Lucar and Leybourn),[64] and he replaces the constant patrol of the lord's feet with 'the suddaine view' from the manor house.

The map, laid out before the landowner at a distance from the actual fields, reinforces the ultimate logic of the surveyors' representations of the land: that the 'owner' of any plot has complete control over it. As Standish writes in 1613, 'now that mens lands, as is said (not only as common Table-talk, but elsewhere) is their owne, they may do with them what they list'.[65] This attitude is further illustrated by the landowner in

---

[64] *Lucarsolace*, p. 53; *Compleat Surveyor*, p. 275.
[65] *New Directions of Experience*, sig. B1ᵇ.

Churche's dialogue *An olde thrift newly revived*:

> For my selfe being of some small revenew in land, I have two or three of
> my Manors surveyed, and the plots of them fairely set forth in colours
> upon Vellem, distinctly specifying which is meadow, pasture, arable, and
> woodland, with the quantitie, qualitie, and value thereof, with everie other
> thing there fitting to be noted, which I finde to be a great satisfaction
> pleasure, and ease to me, especially when I am to let any of those Farmes,
> or Tenements in any of the said Manors because they are farre remote from
> the place I dwell. (p. 47)

Churche's representation of an absentee landlord ordering his lands from
afar directly contrasts with the image of a paternal figure presiding
within a network of reciprocal duties and moral responsibilities. Churche
describes an economic order in which a landlord need not even
physically see his land, let alone 'manure' it with his step.

Consequently, the landlord is encouraged to appreciate his land free of
restrictive moral sanctions against practices such as sales, rent-raising
and enclosure. Radulph Agas, considering the finished product of a
survey, proclaims,

> Heere have you also every parcel ready measured, to all purposes: you
> may also see upon the same, how conveniently this or that ground may be
> layd to this or that tenement or messuage, aswel in regard of waies, water,
> floud, or otherwise: which is a thing much helping and conducing to a
> partition, or devision of such manner, or Lordship.[66]

Agas promotes the map as a learning aid for the would-be improver.
It objectifies the rational perspective insisted upon throughout the
surveying manuals, as it graphically illustrates both the concept of area
and the possibility of reorganizing landholdings. In Agas's vision, the
landlord merely sits in his study and manipulates his property, in
accordance with the criterion of 'how conveniently this or that ground
may be layd to this or that tenement or messuage'.

Agas's representation of the relation between a landowner and his land
highlights the conjunction between the practices of the early modern
surveyor and the imperatives of agrarian improvement. Indeed the
surveying texts provided a crucial impetus to the rise of a discourse of
improvement throughout the sixteenth and seventeenth centuries, a
movement which pivoted around the careers of pioneers such as Agas,

[66] *Preparative*, pp. 14–15.

Norden and Rathborne at the turn of the century. As they confronted preexistent notions of moral economy at all levels of society, the surveyors forged a vital conceptual basis for the improvers' ideals of reason, individual justice and economic freedom. Most importantly, they envisaged a structure which allowed all landholders (in the ideal expressed by Thomas Tusser) to 'be bold of their owne'.[67]

Consequently, the surveying texts helped to define a fundamentally new appreciation of the role and status of the landowner. In fact the motley assortment of dialogues, pamphlets, advertisements and textbooks published by surveyors must be situated at the forefront of significant legal, theoretical and practical developments in the perception of property. G. E. Aylmer has noted that the first attempt at a legal definition of property is made in Christopher St German's *Doctour and Student*, first published in Latin in the 1520s.[68] St German refers to 'that generall lawe or generall custome of propretye wherby goods movable and unmovable be brought in to a certayne propretye / so that every man may knowe his owne thinge'.[69] Although this statement predates by over one hundred years any identifiably modern legal appreciation of property, the echo of early surveying manuals is unmistakable.[70] In both contexts, the phrase draws attention to a desire to apportion strict rights of ownership over goods and land. Landlords and tenants alike were being encouraged to alter their appreciation of 'one's own', as a discourse dominated by moral standards and interpersonal relations gave way to one that facilitated economic individualism and competition.[71]

The manuals thereby played a vital part in the movement – stretching beyond the temporal parameters of this book – toward a capitalist appreciation of the land. In a shift of discourse which is dynamically interrelated to processes of social and economic change, the surveying publicists struggled toward a conception of property consistent with emergent capitalist ideals. In C. B. Macpherson's analysis, capitalism

---

[67] *Five Hundred Points of Good Husbandry*, ed. Geoffrey Grigson (Oxford, 1984), p. 138.

[68] 'The Meaning and Definition of "Property" in Seventeenth-Century England', *Past and Present*, 86 (1980), p. 87.

[69] *Hereafter foloweth a Dyaloge in Englysshe / betwyxt a Doctoure of Dyvynyte / and a Student in the Lawes of Englande* (1530? English edn), sig. c2ᵇ.

[70] Aylmer analyses the development of a legal conception of property in 'Meaning and Definition of "Property"'.

[71] On property in this era, see also *Early Modern Conceptions of Property*, ed. John Brewer and Susan Staves (London and New York, 1995). Due to the date of publication, I was not able to consult this book for the purpose of my analysis in this chapter.

represents property as an 'absolute right': 'a right to dispose of, or alienate, as well as to use; and . . . a right which is not conditional on the owner's performance of any social function'.[72] Consequently, as a modern theorist of human territoriality argues, the land becomes 'emptiable space', which 'makes community seem to be artificial; it makes the future appear geographically as a dynamic relationship between people on one hand and territorial molds on the other'.[73] This conception of the land was presaged on the Jacobean stage, as city conmen passed around legal deeds and titles as a form of portable property.[74] While the influence of capitalism in agrarian practice may not have been consolidated for some time, early modern social critics and reformers alike were well aware of the theoretical and conceptual issues that would underpin that shift.

Given the continuing influence of custom in the English countryside, it is hardly surprising that the greatest achievements in surveying of the middle decades of the seventeenth century were made by British practitioners working across the Irish Sea. For Ireland, where some two and a half million acres were seized in retaliation for the uprising of 1641, offered vast tracts of land which could be emptied of customary claims by the harsh logic of colonialism.[75] Surveying was embraced for its capacity to ensure that both colonial settlers and the English government would 'extract maximum value out of the available land'. 'The maps subsequently produced accorded with the most exacting standards; they embraced both forfeited and non-forfeited lands, and they included particularly elaborate detail relating to the degree of profitability of land.'[76] The work of William Petty, in particular, reasserted the bond between surveying and agrarian improvement, as his

[72] 'Capitalism and the Changing Concept of Property', in *Feudalism, Capitalism and Beyond*, ed. Eugene Kamenka and R. S. Neale (London, 1975), p. 109. See also J. P. Sommerville's analysis of the consolidation of legal concepts of absolute property in the seventeenth century, in *Politics and Ideology in England, 1603–1640* (London, 1986), pp. 151–60.

[73] Sack, *Human Territoriality*, p. 78.

[74] See above, pp. 102–3.

[75] J. H. Andrews, *Plantation Acres: An Historical Study of the Irish Land Surveyor and His Maps* (Omagh, 1985), p. 52.

[76] Charles Webster, *The Great Instauration: Science, Medicine and Reform 1626–1660* (London, 1975), pp. 435, 437. Webster also notes that the Irish surveying prompted a new wave of manuals (p. 436). Most notable were Leybourn's *Compleat Surveyor*; John Eyre, *The Exact Surveyor* (1654); Henry Osborne, *A More Exact Way to Delineate the Plot of any Spacious Parcel of Land* (Dublin, 1654); and George Atwell, *The Faithful Surveyor* (1658).

famous Down Survey established an empirical foundation for a broad view of economic expansion.[77] In the following century Jonathan Swift would revive an old debate with his satiric attacks on the exploitation of Ireland, while a new wave of British colonial expansion would proceed upon hegemonic assumptions of absolute property and economic improvement.[78] The pernicious colonial doctrine of *terra nullius*, applied in the settlement of Australia, stood for over two centuries as a legal justification for the dispossession of native communities.[79]

[77] Webster, *Great Instauration*, pp. 436–43.

[78] Swift's *Modest Proposal* (1729), which satirically proposes the exploitation of Irish children as a form of livestock, is commonly viewed as a response to the economic discourse popularized by Petty. See also his prescient attacks on colonialism in book 3 of *Gulliver's Travels* (1726).

[79] This doctrine was finally overturned by the 1992 High Court decision in the 'Mabo' case, which recognized a form of 'native title' in land. Paul Carter explores discourses of colonialism in Australia in his remarkable book, *The Road to Botany Bay: An Essay in Spatial History* (London, 1987).

7. Georgic economics

'In the sweat of thy face shalt thou eat bread, till thou return unto the ground; for out of it wast thou taken: for dust thou art, and unto dust shalt thou return.'

(Genesis 3.19)

At the tail-end of the seventeenth century, Joseph Addison proposed a definition of a literary mode that had apparently been disregarded by English authors. In his 'Essay on Georgics', published with John Dryden's English translation of Virgil, Addison stated that 'A georgic . . . is some part of the Science of Husbandry put into a pleasing Dress, and set off with all the Beauties and Embellishments of Poetry.'[1] His definition is notable, in the current context, for its subtle negotiation between form and content: between an ideal of literary decorum, bound to aesthetic values of 'majesty' and 'gracefulness'; and an acceptance of the didactic intention of georgic, as a 'Class of Poetry which consists in giving plain and direct Instructions to the Reader' (pp. 151, 145). As such, Addison glances back upon over a hundred years of English husbandry writing, and suggests that the poetic grandeur of Virgil's *Georgics* has neither been appreciated nor emulated. In true georgics, 'the Precepts of Husbandry are not to be deliver'd with the simplicity of a Plow-man, but with the Address of a Poet' (p. 145).

Addison's essay is widely seen to have heralded the great age of formal georgic poetry in England.[2] Throughout the eighteenth century, a number of writers attempted to combine descriptions of rural life with the structural and tonal features of the *Georgics*, a movement epitomized by

---

[1] (1597); references are to Dryden, *Works, Vol. 5*, ed. William Frost (Berkeley, 1987), p. 146.
[2] This interpretation provides the basis for: Dwight L. Durling, *Georgic Tradition in English Poetry* (New York, 1935); and John Chalker, *The English Georgic: A Study in the Development of a Form* (London, 1969).

James Thomson's *The Seasons* (1726–30). Yet the wealth of writing on husbandry throughout the sixteenth and seventeenth centuries, and the contemporaneous currency of classical georgic models, suggests that Addison's analysis may have served to obscure the earlier significance of the mode. This impression is supported by the work of Alastair Fowler, who argues that 'the Renaissance conception of georgic seems to have been distinctly – or indistinctly – loose'.[3] He subsequently identifies a georgic tradition running through a range of descriptive, didactic and nonfictional literature of the Renaissance.[4] Anthony Low's valuable study, *The Georgic Revolution*, adopts another approach to the period, by concentrating on 'an informing spirit' rather than a formal genre. Georgic, he writes, 'is a mode that stresses the value of intensive and persistent labour against hardships and difficulties'.[5] In accordance with this definition, he explores its influence in contexts ranging from discourses of Christian reform to the Baconian scientific movement.

One of the principal achievements of both Fowler and Low is to have redirected critical attention, from a teleological concern with the rise of formal Virgilian georgic in English, toward a contextual appreciation of contemporary perceptions of the mode. The focus is shifted from a particular generic model to the ways in which a broader range of georgic ideals and styles may have informed Renaissance writing. Hence these works create a critical context for this chapter, in which I want to consider georgic in relation to discourses of husbandry in early modern England. My main disagreement with the existing studies, however, centres on their tendency to detach literary production from economic practices and discourses. Although Low admits the economic dimension of georgic at the outset of his book, his methodology consistently discounts such concerns, in favour of ethical vision and poetic form. His attempt to distinguish a 'georgic revolution' from 'the working of sheer self-interest' is informed by a literary historian's latent desire to affirm the qualities of canonical authors and the significance of the elite culture which their works helped to shape.[6] I will adopt here a broader

---

[3] 'The Beginnings of English Georgic', in *Renaissance Genres*, ed. Barbara K. Lewalski (Cambridge, Mass., 1986), p. 109.
[4] Fowler stresses the importance of georgic's lack of fictionality in 'Georgic and Pastoral: Laws of Genre in the Seventeenth Century', in *Culture and Cultivation in Early Modern England: Writing and the Land*, ed. Michael Leslie and Timothy Raylor (Leicester, 1992), p. 86.
[5] Anthony Low, *The Georgic Revolution* (Princeton, 1985), pp. 7, 12.
[6] Low, *Georgic Revolution*, pp. 5–6, 155.

conception of culture and cultural influence, and argue that in the course of the period English writers produced a discourse which endorses the energy and diligence of the agrarian improver. By the middle of the seventeenth century 'georgic economics' consistently bound the expansive aims of the individual to a celebratory vision of national development.

THE SIXTEENTH CENTURY

While Dryden's translation of Virgil's *Georgics* may have marked a watershed in the history of formal English georgic, he was hardly working with an unrecognized text. In fact the poem enjoyed a sustained upsurge in reputation and readership across Europe from the late fifteenth century, and in England its status was reinforced by vernacular translations published in 1589, 1628 and 1649.[7] Yet it is also evident that there was no certainty among readers, before Addison, about how to respond to the poem's curious blend of well-wrought literary form and earthy didactic content. Early in the sixteenth century Sir Thomas Elyot praised the 'pleasaunt varietie' of the work: 'the divers graynes, herbes, and flowres, that be there described, that reding therin hit seemeth to a man to be in a delectable gardeine or paradise'.[8] The poem's emphasis on labour received considerably less attention, at a time when literary practice was largely determined by courtly ideals of chivalric heroism and pastoral ease. In Low's analysis, such responses demonstrate the absence of a true Virgilian georgic spirit in the period, as a result of 'a fundamental contempt for labour, especially manual and agricultural labour, on the part of England's leaders'.[9] These attitudes, he argues, were subsequently overthrown in a 'georgic revolution' of the seventeenth century.

I want to suggest that the movement toward seventeenth-century georgic was in fact more subtle than a revolutionary paradigm will admit. Indeed, once we broaden our focus from the courtly milieu of 'England's leaders' – the milieu typified for many literary historians by the man who managed in his life and poetry to amalgamate pastoral and epic modes, Elizabeth's 'shepherd knight' Sir Philip Sidney – the vital roots of

---

[7] L. P. Wilkinson, *The Georgics of Virgil: A Critical Survey* (Cambridge, 1969), p. 291. The English translations were by: Abraham Fleming (1589); Thomas May (1628); and John Ogilby (1649).

[8] *The Boke Named the Governour* (1531), fol. 32[b].

[9] Low, *Georgic Revolution*, p. 5.

English georgic will become more apparent. The argument may be introduced through the work of Edmund Spenser, whom Low represents as the single prescient 'poet of work' in a century otherwise opposed to georgic values.[10] Indeed, a number of critics have noticed the important georgic elements in *The Faerie Queene*.[11] Significantly, Spenser at several points employs Virgil's image of the poet as ploughman, thereby confronting the Italianate ideal of conduct, propounded for courtier and poet alike, of a form of artful ease (*sprezzatura*) which suppresses any evidence of struggle.[12] Furthermore, in his representation of the hero of Book I, Spenser conflates the Christian mythology surrounding England's patron saint with a markedly rural tone, by playing on the Greek word for 'farmer'. The Redcross Knight – a royal foundling – was raised on the land:

> Thence she thee brought into this Faerie lond,
> And in an heaped furrow did thee hyde,
> Where thee a Ploughman all unweeting fond,
> As he his toylsome teme that way did guyde,
> And brought thee up in ploughmans state to byde,
> Whereof *Georgos* he thee gave to name;
> Till prickt with courage, and thy forces pryde,
> To Faery court thou cam'st to seeke for fame,
> And prove thy puissant armes, as seemes thee best became.[13]

In a thematic strain crucial to the poem as a whole, Spenser infuses into the courtly ideal a sense of the value of labour as a force for individual and national honour. The activities of knight and poet symbolically collapse into the labours of the ploughman.

Within a courtly context, Spenser's invocation of such motifs appears extraordinary. Yet recent critics have demonstrated Spenser's concurrent debt to living vernacular traditions; as John N. King argues, he 'infuses the sophisticated standards of the European Renaissance, which were

10 Low, *Georgic Revolution*, ch. 2.
11 See especially William A. Sessions, 'Spenser's Georgics', *English Literary Renaissance*, 10 (1980), pp. 202–38; Andrew V. Ettin, 'The Georgics in *The Faerie Queene*', *Spenser Studies*, 3 (1982), pp. 57–71; John N. King, *Spenser's Poetry and the Reformation Tradition* (Princeton, 1990), pp. 216–20; Fowler, 'Beginnings', p. 112.
12 Daniel Javitch defines *sprezzatura* as 'the ability to disguise artful effort so that it seems natural or to make the difficult appear easy' (*Poetry and Courtliness in Renaissance England* (Princeton, 1978), p. 31).
13 Edmund Spenser, *Poetical Works*, ed. J. C. Smith and E. De Selincourt (Oxford, 1970), *Faerie Queene*, I.x.66.

based upon classical precedents, with unpretentious devices of native satire and allegory that were adopted by English protestant authors'.[14] This links Spenser's georgics to the mid-Tudor milieu of Hugh Latimer, Robert Crowley and the plethora of 'ploughman' texts of religious and social complaint.[15] In these texts the honest labour of the ploughman at the base of the social hierarchy establishes the necessary cultural authority for his harsh yet incisive critical voice. The speaker in *I playne Piers*, for instance, opens his address as though breaking from his work: 'I Piers plowman following ploughe on felde, my beastes blowing for heate, my bodye requyrynge rest, gapynge for the gayne my labours gan me yelde, upon the plowgh beame, to syt me thought it beste'.[16] Moreover the richly symbolic significance of the ploughman is regularly reinforced, throughout the early Protestant years, by inflections of biblical georgic.[17] As seen above in chapter 1, Latimer neatly merges the vernacular tradition with biblical authority in his loose translation of Luke 8.5: 'He that soweth, the husbandman, the ploughman went forth to sow his seede.'[18]

It thus becomes apparent that throughout the Tudor years a tradition of religious, social and political discourse consistently upheld the value of labour. Looking toward the later development of English georgic, however, it is important to recognize the type of labour extolled. This brings us back to Latimer's 'poorest plowman', who 'is in Christ equall with the greatest Prince that is': a statement which neatly proclaims

---

[14] King, *Spenser's Poetry*, p. 3. See also David Norbrook, *Poetry and Politics in the English Renaissance* (London, 1984), chs. 3, 5.

[15] In Low's discussion of mid-Tudor 'Christian reform', Latimer's social complaint is represented as the work of a solitary martyr ('something of a special case'), and this image supports his central argument that before the seventeenth century the georgic mode was shunned by all but a handful of remarkable individuals. My analysis above in chapter 1 – in agreement with the important work of Helen C. White, John N. King and others – suggests that Low seriously misrepresents the vital mid-Tudor reformist milieu within which Latimer produced his most powerful statements of complaint (see Low, *Georgic Revolution*, pp. 196–200; White, *Social Criticism in Popular Religious Literature of the Sixteenth Century* (New York, 1944); King, *English Reformation Literature: The Tudor Origins of the Protestant Tradition* (Princeton, 1982)).

[16] (1550?), sig. A2ᵃ.

[17] Most importantly, the mid-Tudor reformers invoke the example of Israel as the promised land, and parables of stewardship and husbandry. While Low fails to recognize the significance of these traditions in the age of Latimer, he nonetheless provides an excellent survey of the central texts and issues involved, in his discussion of 'biblical georgic' (*Georgic Revolution*, pp. 156–67).

[18] Latimer's version of the Latin 'exivit qui seminat seminare semen suum' (*27 sermons* (1571 edn), fol. 12ᵃ); see above, p. 30.

religious equality while fixing the ploughman in a socio-economic role defined by labour and deference.[19] For the labour of the ploughman was represented as a symbolic endorsement of the manorial structure, governed by the strict moral codes of the doctrine of stewardship. The godly individualist of the seventeenth century has no place within this ideology; rather, the only godly labour was perceived to be that which accorded with orthodox notions of degree. Indeed the doctrine of vocations was at this stage given an overwhelmingly restrictive force. 'Saynte Paule wrytynge to the Tessalonians, dyd put an order howe everye man should worcke in his vocation', Latimer declared. 'When I was among you (sayth he) I made this ordinaunce that who soever would not do the worke of hys vocation, should have no meate. It were a good ordinaunce in a common weale that every man should be set on worke, every man in hys vocation.'[20]

Throughout the reign of Elizabeth, however, this early Protestant tradition was gradually reoriented. In fact Spenser himself strips away many of the restrictive socio-economic connotations from his representations of rural labourers. In *The Faerie Queene*, it is important that the quintessentially English hero should have been raised at the plough, but far more important that he realizes his heritage by assuming the sword. The metaphorical weight placed on the ploughman subsumes his immediate agricultural connotations. And while critics have discerned echoes of the Protestant gospelling tradition in Spenser's earlier *Shepheardes Calender*, the satiric strains of this work consistently privilege religious over social polemic.[21] Like many gentlemen of his time, Spenser endorsed the moral significance attached to labour by the previous generation, yet saw no purpose in identifying with downtrodden labourers and reviving attacks on the covetousness of landlords. Meanwhile many of the landlords of Spenser's era were themselves becoming interested in the practice of agriculture and the notion of improvement, a movement reinforced by classical and Continental texts on husbandry, which introduced an important 'philosophical

---

[19] *27 sermons*, fol. 108ᵇ; see above, pp. 31–2.
[20] *27 sermons*, fol. 78ᵃ.
[21] Both King and Norbrook demonstrate the links between *The Shepheardes Calender* and the English Reformation tradition; however, neither notes Spenser's lack of concern with social and economic issues, which clearly distinguishes his work from that of his Protestant antecedents (King, *Spenser's Poetry*, ch. 1; Norbrook, *Poetry and Politics*, ch. 3).

justification' for the labours of the farmer.[22] Cultivation of the land, the gentleman was assured, 'was the most honourable of labours'.[23] Through a deft shift of orientation, the husbandry manuals thereby extolled the labours of the lord with the same moral force which had been applied a generation earlier to the stream of panegyric on his labourer. Landowners could be hailed as generators of national prosperity rather than idle exploiters of the labours of others.

This growing appreciation of the national significance of agriculture conditioned later sixteenth-century responses to Virgil's *Georgics*. Low notes an elitist disdain for work in the warnings of a Winchester schoolmaster in 1563, that his pupils should not despise agricultural labour, which the Romans obviously valued more highly than the English.[24] But thirty years later Sir John Harington felt no need for such a lesson of cultural difference, as he proclaimed that the poem was so well written 'that I could find it in my hart to drive the plough'.[25] Another contemporary gentleman was prepared to make a more explicit connection between the classical poet and the language of improvement: his verse miscellany 'entituled a fatherly farewell' indicates that, 'Good husbandrye ys fitt for me as Virgill doth me teache'.[26] The point was reinforced by early husbandry manuals, which treated Virgil as both a moral and a practical authority. It is thus perfectly appropriate within this context that contemporary critics should recognize as English writers of georgic the likes of 'Master Barnabe Googe, in translating and enlarging the most profitable worke of Heresbachius', and the ubiquitous Thomas Tusser, who 'hath . . . very wittily and experimentally written of [husbandry] in English'.[27]

These pioneering publications on agriculture demand recognition for their introduction of English readers to georgic ideals. Heresbach's

---

[22] Joan Thirsk, 'Making a Fresh Start: Sixteenth-Century Agriculture and the Classical Inspiration', in *Culture and Cultivation in Early Modern England: Writing and the Land*, ed. Michael Leslie and Timothy Raylor (Leicester, 1992), pp. 15–34; Thirsk, 'Plough and Pen: Agricultural Writers in the Seventeenth Century', in *Social Relations and Ideas: Essays in Honour of R. H. Hilton*, ed. T. H. Aston et al. (Cambridge, 1983), p. 297.

[23] Thirsk, 'Plough and Pen', p. 297.

[24] *Georgic Revolution*, p. 18.

[25] 'A Briefe Apologie of Poetry', in *Elizabethan Critical Essays*, ed. G. Gregory Smith (2 vols., Oxford, 1904), vol. 2, p. 207; quoted in Fowler, 'Beginnings', p. 107.

[26] John Kay, 1576; Kay Family Manuscripts, Folger MS W.b.484, p. 3.

[27] William Webbe, in *Elizabethan Critical Essays*, vol. 1, p. 265; Francis Meres, in *Elizabethan Critical Essays*, vol. 2, p. 323. See also Fowler, 'Beginnings', pp. 108–9, 116.

Foure Bookes of Husbandry, in fact, presents from the outset a remarkable lesson in georgic economics. The beginning of the first dialogue presents the courtier and government official Rigo visiting his friend Cono, who has retired from public life to concentrate on the management of his estate. Rigo approaches the estate with views preconditioned by the courtly values of the pastoral mode. Hence he idealizes Cono's life as one of 'countrey joyes and pleasures', yet concurrently deprecates this state as a mere holiday world, which must be subordinated to the honourable service of 'our common weale and state whereto we are called' (fol. 1ª). Cono's response shrewdly negotiates between pastoral assumptions and georgic initiative. As I noted in chapter 5, his argument employs the *locus classicus* of Christian georgic, Genesis 3.19 ('In the sweat of thy face shalt thou eat bread . . .') to support his contention that 'this profession and this gayne, is most acceptable to GOD' (fol. 6ᵇ). Husbandry itself is presented as a calling at least as honourable as that of the government official, a point reinforced with classical authority:

> But those that are of sounder judgement, account the husbandmen most happy, yf they knewe their owne felicitie, to whom the Earth in a farre quieter maner dooth minister a sufficient livyng.
>
>   And though with gorgeous gates the buyldynges hye,
>   With early greetinges alwayes doo not flowe,
>   Nor feelyng garnisht gaye with Imagrye,
>   Nor ritche attyre we see, nor costly showe:
>   Yet stedfast state and lyfe unskild of guyle,
>   With wealth yenough and pastures wyde at wyll,
>   And people strong traynde up to payne and toyle,
>   And youth with dyet small contented styll,
>   Where godly zeale and vertues all dyd dwell,
>   When Justice last dyd bidde the worlde farewell.   (fol. 7ª)[28]

In Cono's view of the country life, values of honesty, labour and an evocatively Elizabethan 'godly zeal' underpin a sense of both individual and national renewal. The calculated mix of georgic and pastoral highlights a crucial confluence of socio-economic, ideological and literary influences.[29]

---

[28] Googe's translation of *Georgics* II.461–74, part of the famous 'O fortunatos nimium' passage.

[29] In Alastair Fowler's analysis of generic change, 'before georgic could ascend the hierarchy, it had to undergo a phase of mixture with pastoral' ('Georgic and Pastoral', p. 87).

Admittedly, Heresbach's is a somewhat deceptive version of georgic, given the landlord's distance from the actual tilling of his ground. Yet the movement from the eulogized labour of the downtrodden ploughman in mid-Tudor complaint to the flourishing estate of the early discourse of improvement is in part effected through attention to the landlord as the supervisor and motivator of rural productivity. 'And though I have a Bailiffe as skilfull as may be', states Cono, 'yet remembring the olde sayeing, that the best doung for the feelde is the maisters foote, and the best provender for the horse the maisters eye, I playe the overseer mee selfe' (fol. 3ª). This vicarious involvement in labour permits an equation of the landlord with Virgil's 'happy husbandman'. Moreover, Googe stresses from the preface of his book that agricultural labour should be directed to serve the interests of the lord, 'for thy further profite and pleasure'. This catchcry of rural life, prominent throughout the early modern period, is suitably malleable to accommodate the emergent imperatives. As a pastoral ethos of pleasure admits a georgic pursuit of profit, so interests of order merge with initiatives toward improvement.

Tusser's *Five Hundred Points of Good Husbandry* consistently asserts the radical potential of this movement. As I argued in chapter 5, Tusser focuses on the interests of husbandmen and 'huswives' of the middling ranks, and celebrates an agrarian world in which all men may 'be bold of their owne'.[30] He gets short shrift from Low, who dismisses the 'mixture of didacticism, forehead-knuckling, and greed' in the *Points*;[31] however, this comment perhaps says more about Low's implicit desire to separate poetry from economic discourse than it does about a text which in fact marks a significant and influential stage in the development of English georgic. For Tusser binds the activity of agricultural labour to the economic interests of the husbandman with a truly disquieting intensity. His 'Introduction to the Booke of Husbandrie' states:

> GOOD husbandmen must moile & toile,
> to laie to live by laboured feeld:
> Their wives at home must keepe such coile,
> as their like actes must profit yeeld.   (p. 9)

Tusser's georgic is that of the individualist. He reshapes the mid-Tudor emphasis on labour (in accordance with concurrent movements in Elizabethan theology) and forges a direct link between the husbandman's

---

[30] *Five Hundred Points of Good Husbandry*, ed. Geoffrey Grigson (Oxford, 1984), p. 138.
[31] *Georgic Revolution*, p. 33.

'moile and toile' and his desire for an earthly reward.[32] The humble ploughman working within the conservative strictures of a corporate ideology gives way to the industrious smallholder whose pursuit of 'thrift' links the national interest to individual advancement.

Tusser subsequently proclaims the importance of husbandry in a riddle poem:

> I SEEME but a drudge, yet I passe any King
> To such as can use me, great wealth I do bring.
> Since Adam first lived, I never did die,
> When Noe was shipman, there also was I.
>
> . . .
>
> So many as loove me, and use me aright,
> With treasure and pleasure, I richly acquite.
> Great kings I doe succour, else wrong it would go,
> The King of al kings hath appointed it so.   (pp. 11–12)

The poem is concerned to elevate the status of the 'drudgery' imposed upon the descendants of Adam. Hence the sweat of the husbandman's brow is figured as a means toward an expansive vision of prosperity: the 'treasure and pleasure' is that of the worker and also of the king. Low rightly perceives a 'Virgilian theme' in the conclusion of the poem.[33] Considering the development of English georgic, however, it is equally important to recognize the progression toward that vision, through the labours and profits of the householders for whom Tusser writes.

The cultural significance of such writers is further attested by their remarkable popularity. In the reign that fostered the genius of Sidney and Spenser, Tusser's *Five Hundred Points* was the biggest selling book of poetry.[34] Moreover, this currency brought considerable influence, as the manuals boldly confronted the prevailing moral and theological anxiety about modes of labour and improvement.[35] Even the leading Jacobean enthusiast of improvement, John Norden, displays a distinct unease on such issues in his Elizabethan religious works. On one page of *A Pensive Mans Practise* he lurches from a conventional prayer of thanks to God for wealth freely bestowed and 'not gotten by mine owne industrie', to a paean on God's 'helpinge hande [given] unto the godly industrie of

---

[32] See my arguments on Elizabethan religious change above, pp. 61–9.
[33] *Georgic Revolution*, pp. 32–3.
[34] Laura Caroline Stevenson, *Praise and Paradox: Merchants and Craftsmen in Elizabethan Popular Literature* (Cambridge, 1984), p. 16.
[35] See above, pp. 146–51.

such as by their vocation and juste travaile' endeavour to attract God's providence.[36] In this context, the works of Tusser and Heresbach helped to create a basic cultural appreciation of radically new attitudes, which would be further refined and reinforced by subsequent generations.

Two manuscript miscellanies compiled by gentlemen involved in estate management provide evidence of these influences at a more practical level, as they reveal individuals sifting through the information and discourses available to those immersed in agrarian life. Thomas Fella's 'booke of diveirs devises' demonstrates a remarkably broad range of interests.[37] Much of the manuscript is devoted to detailed illustrations of plants and trees, of the kind made popular among the gentry in the gardening and botanical texts published in huge numbers in the latter half of the sixteenth century.[38] Other illustrations and captions present images of pastoral ease in the country, with courtiers and musicians relaxing in enclosed gardens (fols. 50b–51a). But these concerns are combined with a consistent attention to agrarian practice, in a manner which celebrates both the labour and productivity of the country. Most notably, Fella compiles an incomplete calendar of illustrations of rural activity, together with verse in the style of Tusser. The picture for October (illustration 7.1) is of a ploughman at work, accompanied by the caption:

> The husband man doth choose his sowing graine
> And makes it cleane before it growe to ground
> He knows at length thencrease will quit the paine
> the cleaner corne lesse darnell shalbe founde.   (fol. 53a)

Fella's ploughman is shaped by values of honest labour and aspirations for 'encrease'. The unpretentious concern with the particularities of farming, set within the author's disparate rural collection, highlights the potentially vital interaction between literary mode and agrarian practice in the English fields.

Similarly, the manuscript writings of John Kay of Woodsome – mostly in rough verse forms – combine a georgic tenor with a broad variety of information relating to his estate.[39] Indeed, the poetry reads as a particularized application of Tusser (whom Kay praises for his 'learnyd

36 (1584); facsimile edn (Amsterdam, 1971), fol. 45a.
37 Written 1585–98, 1622; Folger Shakespeare Library MS V.a.311.
38 In particular the works of Thomas Hill, as author and translator, were available in a series of editions spanning the reign of Elizabeth (STC seq. 13485–97).
39 The Kay family manuscripts, c. 1561–1642, are held in the Folger Shakespeare Library.

The plowman

7.1 'The plowman': manuscript illustration in Thomas Fella's 'booke of diveirs devises' (Folger Shakespeare Library, V.a.311, fol. 53ᵃ).

sayes') to the circumstances of one family.[40] Kay moves from traditional moralism in his 'Caveat for a Young Heyre', to a more practical tone in 'A leson for landbyers', a calendar of rural activity, and 'A Brefe note or accompte of myn owne Estate 1592'. The latter traces his father's inheritance and purchase of 'nyne oxgange in Farnley towne / that his heere myght have moore elbowe rowme', before focusing on his own husbandry:

> Besyds my brenging upp this charge
> and soms to dowghters which I payd
> Marlyng & Buyldyng Both were large
> the Costes wherof I have defrayed:
> all men Content, all men well apaid;
> My Lyving also, I have Augment
> Full fyftie poundes in peny Rent.[41]

Kay endorses the industry of the husbandman who marls and builds his way to an improved estate. Far from feeling constrained by the social morality of the mid-Tudor Protestants, he articulates a significant pride in the labours of a successful gentleman within the rural economy.

Kay turns to the enduring symbol of agrarian labour in a striking poem titled 'the Plowghe':

> The Plowghe is the Lords penne
> It write the Land to sowe our sede
> To fede the Poor that stand in nede
> Naither the Prynce no Peasants Reade
> Without this Penn, can earne their breade
> It bringeth eke to the moost & Least
> Such Foode as servith man & Beast.[42]

His celebration of agrarian production highlights the cultural distance between agrarian complaint and the post-Tusser improver. For Kay, the plough is an instrument of progressive rural development, and it is only through an energetic use of such tools that the fruits of enterprise can be passed on to the poor. The world of georgic is a world in which the opportunity for all to 'earne their breade' is elevated to a moral imperative.

But despite the varied initiatives of Elizabethan writers, from Spenser

---

[40] Folger MS X.d.445, fol. 3[b].
[41] Folger MS X.d.446, p. 66.
[42] Folger MS W.b.483, p. 1.

to Kay, georgic lacked both the literary and ideological definition it would be given by subsequent generations. The uncertain energy characteristic of the mode at this time is in many respects typified by a poem published in 1599 by Thomas Moffett, *The Silkewormes, and their Flies*.[43] Moffett is apologetic about his 'country *Muse*', for which he claims no literary authority in an age of poetics he sees as dominated by Petrarchan love, epic and historical modes (sig. π2ᵃ).[44] His poem is a long and rambling collection of classical myth, historical anecdote, moralistic digression and improving exhortation;[45] yet underlying the whole is a desire to justify the production of silk by reference to the values of the thrifty husbandman. He dismisses perceptions of silk as being only a luxury item, and stresses rather the honest labour required by both silkworm and husbandman:

> Small is the charge compared with the gaine,
> That shal surmount thy greatest cost and paine.   (p. 58)

In the closing pages, the poem's panegyric on silk draws together concerns of personal gain, providing work for the poor and raising England's status as a trading nation. A sweeping vision of national advancement is interwoven with the economic imperatives of improvement as he proclaims the profits and pleasures at hand:

> Divine we hence, or rather reckon right,
> What usury and profitt doth arise,
> By keeping well these little creatures white,
> Worthy the care of every nation wise,
> That in their owne or publique wealth delight.
> And rashly wil not things so rare despise:
>   Yea sure, in time they wil such profit bring,
>   As shall enrich both people, priest, and king.   (p. 71)

Profit 'arises' with all the reproductive powers of 'usury', to 'enrich . . . people, priest, and king'. Despite his residual hesitance about his poetic enterprise, Moffett's claims for prosperity through labour and ingenuity

---

[43] (1599); facsimile edn, ed. Victor Houliston (Medieval and Renaissance Texts and Studies, vol. 56, Binghamton, 1989).

[44] Dwight Durling's claim of 'definite Vergilian influence' in the poem is perhaps an exaggeration in the light of this generic apology (*Georgic Tradition in English Poetry*, p. 33).

[45] According to Fowler, Moffett's model for the poem was M. G. Vida's *De bombycum cura et usu* (1527) ('Beginnings', p. 117).

presage the literature of the new century, when georgic would proclaim the cause of industry and improvement with fresh assurance.[46]

THE SEVENTEENTH CENTURY

George Chapman brought a second major classical source to the attention of his Jacobean audience when he translated Hesiod's *Works and Days* (1618).[47] Alastair Fowler has noted the subsequent importance of Hesiod as an influence upon seventeenth-century georgic: a point acknowledged at the time by Virgil's translator Thomas May, who refers to the Greek poem as 'the pattern' of the *Georgics*.[48] Chapman was also keen to establish a generic link between the texts: the title-page of his translation proclaims, 'The Georgicks of Hesiod . . . Containing Doctrine of Husbandrie, Moralitie, and Pietie'. He represents the work, in his prefatory material, as digressive and philosophical, not 'dwelling on any one subject', but instructing in 'all humane affaires' (sig. A3ᵇ). Moreover, although Chapman primarily presents Hesiod's poem as an important text within a classical literary tradition, an undercurrent in his editorial commentary binds the work to contemporary issues of improvement. His dedication to Francis Bacon recognizes the latter's achievements in his *Advancement of Learning* (sig. A2ᵇ), while a number of lengthy marginal notes carefully formulate a position on the aspirations of husbandmen to 'become / Herd-full, and rich' (p. 15). In Book I, Hesiod's exhortation to his brother claims that through labour, '*Glorie* and *vertue* into consort fall / With *wealth*'; Chapman responds, 'Notwithstanding he hath no other way to perswade his unwise brother to follow his busines . . . but to propose wealth, and honour for the fruits of it: yet he prefers labor alone, joind with love of vertue and justice' (p. 15). The individualist ethos of the poem, however, continues to demand attention. Another lengthy note comments on Hesiod's claim that 'strife for riches, warmes, and fires the blood', and ultimately concedes that the poem 'showes Artizans emulation for *riches*, and approves that kinde of contention' (p. 2).

---

[46] Similarly, Thomas Churchyard praises an Elizabethan paper-making project, and traces the wealth and benefits it generates, in his poem, 'A Discription And playne discourse of paper, and the whole benefites that Paper brings, with rehersall and setting foorth in verse a Paper myll, built nere Darthford, by an high German, called Master Spilman' (printed in *A Sparke of Frendship and Warme Goodwill* (1588), sigs. C4ᵃ–E1ᵇ).

[47] Chapman's translation was published as *The Georgicks* (1618); facsimile edn (Amsterdam, 1971).

[48] 'Beginnings', pp. 117–8, 121; *Georgics* (1628), sig. A2ᵇ.

Early seventeenth-century husbandry and surveying manuals were more openly enthusiastic about the expansive potential of the georgic mode. John Norden typifies this movement in his *Surveiors Dialogue*, which sloughs off the anxiety about pecuniary gain which had marked his earlier religious writings.[49] The confident voice of the improver here proclaims the curse of labour as a challenge to the ingenuity and industry of humanity. 'As the earth . . . was given to man: and man (after divine) was enjoyned the care of earthly things . . . So is it not the least regard, that men of whatsoever title or place, should have the lawfull and just meanes of the preservation and increase of their earthly Revenues' (sig. A3ᵃ⁻ᵇ). The Elizabethan ideal of good husbandry is translated into a Christian duty:

> if men will not indevour to search for the hidden blessings of God, which he hath laid up in store in the bowels of the earth, for their use that will be painfull, they may make a kind of idle and vaine shew of good husbandry, when indeed onely plow, and sow, and charge the earth, to bring foorth fruite of it owne accord, when wee knowe it was cursed for our sakes, and commaunded to denie us increase, without labour, sweate, and charge, which also are little availeable, if we serve not him in feare and reverence, who is the Author of true labours, and of the blessings promised thereunto.
>
> (p. 197)

In this construction of a georgic economy, only the ingenious improver truly earns the 'blessings' of God. The man who merely ploughs and sows, in the traditional order recommended by the early Protestant reformers, is dismissed for his 'idle and vaine shew of good husbandry'.

Norden's concern for a new type of labour – pursued by the godly individualist working the land defined by the surveyor as his 'own' – draws strength from contemporary developments in Protestant thought. A number of important studies in this field have identified a connection between a 'Protestant ethic' and a spirit of economic individualism.[50] The early Protestant social doctrine, as already noted, was essentially restrictive; Hugh Latimer's version of the doctrine of callings, like Martin Luther's, was grounded in a commitment to established forms of

---

[49] Three edns (1607, 1610, 1618); references are to the 1610 edition.

[50] See especially Max Weber, *The Protestant Ethic and the Spirit of Capitalism*, translated from the German by Talcott Parsons (London, 1930); R. H. Tawney, *Religion and the Rise of Capitalism* (London, 1922; references are to the 1984 edition); Christopher Hill, 'Protestantism and the Rise of Capitalism', in *Change and Continuity in Seventeenth-Century England* (London, 1974), pp. 81–102.

social order and political authority.[51] In chapter 2, I argued that religious movements over the following hundred years undermined this doctrine, through an intensifying concentration on the faith and morality of the individual. The individual was increasingly liberated from the repressive authority of Church and state alike; instead, his or her own conscience was established as 'the centre of moral judgement', and only through this direct link with God could questions of social morality satisfactorily be resolved.[52] This prompted a reassessment of the concept of the vocation. As the Elizabethan Puritan William Perkins proclaimed, a vocation is not a mark of degree imposed by socio-political authority, but rather a worldly occupation chosen through an individual contract with God. 'Every man must so enter [a vocation], that he may truely in conscience say; God hath placed me in this calling, be it never so base a calling.'[53] For Norden, 'the true delight' of all men 'should be in the due prosecution of their callings: as the artificer to his trade, the husbandman to the plowe' (p. 191).

In the course of the seventeenth century, this emphasis on individuals pursuing their callings was increasingly linked to an apparently paradoxical commitment to labour in the interests of social amelioration. Despite his own rhetorical fervour, R. H. Tawney accurately identified the impact of this development:

> since conduct and action, though availing nothing to attain the free gift of salvation, are a proof that the gift has been accorded, what is rejected as a means is resumed as a consequence, and the Puritan flings himself into practical activities with the daemonic energy of one who, all doubts allayed, is conscious that he is a sealed and chosen vessel . . . Called by God to labour in his vineyard, he has within himself a principle at once of energy and of order, which makes him irresistible both in war and in the struggles of commerce.[54]

As Calvinism rose to a position of orthodoxy in Jacobean England, then, religious doctrine promoted new approaches to labour. Puritanism at once offered a powerful justification for the dignity of work, and at least an implicit endorsement of the economic aspirations of the thrifty husbandmen for whom Tusser wrote. By the 1620s these values had

---

51   See above, pp. 36–49; Weber, *Protestant Ethic*, p. 86.
52   Norman Jones, *God and the Moneylenders: Usury and Law in Early Modern England* (Oxford, 1989), p. 174.
53   *A Treatise of the Vocations* (1602); in *Works* (3 vols., 1608–9), vol. 1, p. 737.
54   Tawney, *Religion and the Rise of Capitalism*, p. 229.

become an appropriate subject for 'divine and moral meditation'; the author of *Thrifts Equipage* proclaims,

> I sing what most I wish; what's that? to thrive,
> Without least wrong to any man alive:
> A grateful Worke to all, to young and old,
> That seeke to get or to increase their gold.[55]

'Carefull *Husbandry*', '*Labour*, Care, and *Diligence*', the poem declares, will be rewarded by God's providence (p. 4).[56] Thrift is proclaimed as at once a social and a spiritual virtue, which promotes moral purity, individual wellbeing and national strength. Such perceptions of labour can be traced from the scientific empiricism of Francis Bacon, through the godly populism of George Wither, to the peripatetic energy of John Taylor.

Bacon absorbed, and adapted for his purposes, a tradition of Protestant teaching 'which equated charity with works done with intent to benefit the commonwealth or mankind'.[57] He further propelled this argument with a radical conception of the capacity of humanity to repair some of the effects of the Fall. Bacon believed that before the Fall Adam's total mastery over the natural world had been accompanied by universal knowledge of its workings.[58] Although the Fall had shattered this state of dominion, the values of labour and scientific endeavour offered the potential for a fundamental regeneration: 'For creation was not by the curse made altogether and for ever a rebel, but in virtue of that charter, "In the sweat of thy face shalt thou eat bread", it is now by various labours . . . subdued to the supplying of man with bread; that is, to the uses of human life.'[59] The curse of Genesis 3.19, as Norden suggested more tentatively, simultaneously offers the seed of a blessing. Labour in the cause of 'The Great Instauration' was a religious imperative which bound the improvement of conditions on earth to the

---

[55] Robert Aylett, *Thrifts Equipage: Viz. Five Divine and Morall Meditations* (1622), sig. A1ᵇ.
[56] Thomas Powell's contemporary pamphlet, *The Art of Thriving, Or, The Plaine pathway to Preferment* (1631), presents a similar attitude to individual endeavour, though coloured with a mildly sceptical and satiric tone.
[57] Christopher Hill, *Intellectual Origins of the English Revolution* (Oxford, 1980), p. 92.
[58] See Charles Webster, *The Great Instauration: Science, Medicine and Reform 1626–1660* (London, 1975), p. 329; Hill, *Intellectual Origins*, p. 89.
[59] *Novum Organum*, book 2, aphorism 52; in *Works*, ed. J. Spedding et al. (14 vols., London, 1857–74), vol. 1.

aim of restoring 'the sovereignty and power . . . which [man] had in his first state of creation'.[60]

This supremely idealistic conception of human labour underpinned the practical aims of the Baconian programme in its pursuit of scientific knowledge as a means to national prosperity,[61] hence the new significance accorded to the nomination of 'commonwealths man'. Early in the century, Arthur Standish notes the encouragement he has received in his agricultural research from 'many good Commonwealths men'; Ralph Austen later expresses his admiration for 'good Common-wealths-men, who have written of the *Improvement of lands'*.[62] The true commonwealths man, in the terms of this discourse, was the man of industry and ingenuity, who observed the lesson inherent in one of Bacon's favourite biblical citations, 'It is the glory of God to conceal a thing: but the honour of kings is to search out a matter' (Proverbs 25.2).[63] Indeed the achievements of Solomon provided an important authority for Bacon's argument that inquiry into nature met with God's approval, and the Proverbs are consistently quoted not only in his own works, but also in those of his successors.[64] Gabriel Plattes sets the tone for one of his tracts with Proverbs 13.11: 'Wealth gotten by vanity shall be diminished, but he that gathereth it by labour shall increase.'[65] Walter Blith, for his title-page epigraph, manipulates Proverbs 21.5: 'The thoughts of the diligent bring abundance. A diligent man shall stand before Kings.'[66]

Milton's *Of Christian Doctrine* moves from the curse of Genesis to the promise of the Proverbs:

---

[60] *Works*, vol. 3, p. 222; quoted in Hill, *Intellectual Origins*, p. 89.

[61] Webster, *Great Instauration*, p. 333.

[62] Standish, *New Directions of Experience* (1615), sig. B1b; Austen, *A Treatise of Fruit-Trees* (1665), p. 1.

[63] Webster, *Great Instauration*, p. 341.

[64] See also Graham Parry, *The Seventeenth Century: The Intellectual and Cultural Context of English Literature, 1603–1700* (London and New York, 1989), p. 138. The importance of the Proverbs to English georgic consciousness beyond the Baconian movement is evidenced by Aylett's choice of a title-page epigraph for *Thrifts Equipage*: Prov. 28.19, 'He that tilleth his land shall have plenty of bread: but he that followeth after vain persons shall have poverty enough.'

[65] Plattes quotes reasonably faithfully from the Authorized Version; *A Discovery of Infinite Treasure Hidden Since the Worlds Beginning* (1639); facsimile edn (Amsterdam, 1974), title-page.

[66] *The English Improver Improved* (1652). The Authorized Version reads, 'The thoughts of the diligent tend only to plenteousness; but of every one that is hasty only to want'; Blith's adaptation draws upon Proverbs 22.29.

INDUSTRY is that by which we honestly provide for ourselves the means of comfortable living. Gen.ii.15. 'to dress it and to keep it.' iii.19. 'in the sweat of thy face thou shalt eat bread.' Prov. x.4. 'he becometh poor that dealeth with a slack hand.' v.5. 'he that gathereth in summer is a wise son.' xii.11. 'he that tilleth his land shall be satisfied with bread.' xiv.23. 'in all labor there is profit.' xxi.5. 'the thoughts of the diligent tend only to plenteousness, but of every one that is hasty only to want.' xxii.29. 'seest thou a man diligent in his business? he shall stand before kings.'[67]

The early Protestant 'commonwealths men' of the previous century had emphasized the negative social morality of the Old Testament. By comparison, the plundering of Proverbs confirms a crucial shift of attention, from corporate interests of order and stability to individual concerns of industry and diligence.[68] Significantly, this development also replaces Tusser's controlling image of a thrifty household with a newly isolated economic agent. Just as Spenser had fused values of epic heroism and georgic endeavour in his representation of the Red Cross Knight, so seventeenth-century georgic is constructed as a mode preeminently concerned with masculine mythologies of labour. The new georgic economy effaces the labours of women, whether in the fields, in the household or in childbirth. If the curse was Adam's, so shall be the reward.

The preeminent poet within this milieu was the zealous and prolific George Wither, who yoked his absorption in contemporary polemics with a commitment to a Spenserian literary tradition. Wither's *Collection of Emblemes*, as Low has argued, contains a rich georgic strain which conflates the spiritual pursuits of the Christian with a remarkably detailed appreciation of the husbandman's labours and aspirations.[69] This vision stands out by contrast with earlier English emblem collections.[70] Geffrey Whitney's Elizabethan publication, for example, represents labour only within the traditional moral order extolled by the generation

---

[67] The passage concludes with 1 Thessalonians 4.11–12 and 2 Thessalonians 3.12 (Milton, *Works*, ed. Frank Allen Patterson et al. (18 vols., New York, 1931–40), vol. 17, pp. 231–3; quoted in Low, *Georgic Revolution*, p. 164).

[68] In the following century, Max Weber's quintessential early modern capitalist, Benjamin Franklin, seized upon Proverbs 22.29 to justify his attitudes toward business and wealth. Weber argues that the 'Old Testament rationalism' of the Puritans was 'essentially of a small bourgeois, traditionalistic type' (*Protestant Ethic*, pp. 53, 123).

[69] *A Collection of Emblemes, Ancient and Moderne* (1635); facsimile edn (Renaissance English Text Society, Columbia, S. C., 1975). See Low, *Georgic Revolution*, pp. 203–12.

[70] Cf. Low, *Georgic Revolution*, pp. 203–4.

of Latimer and Crowley.[71] He preaches against the attractions of 'worldlie wealthe' and 'immoderate gaine' (p. 23), and instructs the labourer:

> With sweate of browe, see that thou get thy meate,
> If thou be borne, with labouring hande to live:
>   And get, to eate. and eate, to live with praise:
>   Live not to eate, to live with wanton ease.   (p. 85)

Like Whitney, Wither worked with a set of plates engraved on the Continent for another author; however, the latter's representation of labour develops a freshly strident celebration of godly industry. For Wither, diligence in both spiritual and secular endeavours earns the individual significantly more than his daily bread:

> Where, *Labour*, wisely, is imploy'd,
> Deserved *Glory*, is injoy'd.   (p. 92)

Low interprets Wither's version of georgic as a revival of a 'Virgilian and Medieval attitude toward the curse of labour'.[72] By contrast, I would suggest that Wither's appreciation of labour epitomizes the converging literary, economic and religious movements of his *own* age. As he consistently grafts moral didacticism to representations of agrarian practice, Wither's poems claim a central place in the unfolding tradition of native georgic. His conflation of rural and spiritual labour is particularly apparent in a poem prompted by an illustration of a ploughman. While Wither endorses traditional celebrations of the ploughman's work, his poem revises the significance accorded the figure by his predecessors in the English Protestant tradition.

> Before the *Plowman* hopefull can be made,
> His untill'd earth good Hay or Corne will yeeld,
> He breakes the hillocks downe, with *Plough* or *Spade*;
> And, harrowes over, all the cloddie Field.
> Then, from the *leaveld-ground*, at last, he mowes
> That Cropp of grasse, which he had hope to gaine;
> Or, there, doth reape the fruit of what he sowes,
> With profit, which contents him for his paine.
>   Our *craggie Nature* must be tilled, thus,
> Before it will, for *Herbes of Grace*, be fit.

---

[71] *A Choice of Emblemes, and other Devises* (Leyden, 1586).
[72] *Georgic Revolution*, p. 211.

Our *high conceit*, must downe be broke in us;
Our heart is proud, and God must humble it.
Before good *Seed*, in us will rooting take,
Afflictions ploughes and harrowes, must prepare us:
And, that the truer *levell*, he may make,
When we are *sunck* too low, *Gods* hand must reare us.
Then, neither stormings of *Adversitie*,
Shall drowne the *Seedes of Hope*, which we have sowne;
Nor shall the *Sunne-beames* of *Prosperitie*,
Drie up their moisture, ere they ripe are growne.   (p. 144)

Wither's ploughman is fashioned as an archetypal Christian, struggling
with the problems of individual faith and salvation that dominated a
religious environment redefined by Calvinism. The principal argument
of the poem confronts the 'stormings of Adversitie' with the promise of
'Herbes of Grace' and 'Seedes of Hope'. But Wither also aligns the
language of religion with that of agricultural production. His richly
metaphorical attention to the physical labours of husbandry thereby
admits the socio-economic concerns of a farmer for a particularly earthy
'profit' and 'prosperity'. The emphasis on 'hope' – recurrent throughout
the *Emblemes* – intimates that the husbandman's desires for economic
reward may practically be inseparable from his quest for religious
salvation. Bacon had adopted a similarly evocative strategy in his
declaration that '*hope* must be the portion of all that resolve upon great
enterprises'.[73]

Hence the rewards of the Christian struggle and the quotidian
aspirations of the husbandman are collapsed into a unified goal, as is
evident in Wither's explication of the rural emblem centred on a snake
entwined in a spade (illustration 7.2):

by the *Spade*, is *Labour* here implide;
The *Snake*, a vertuous *Prudence*, doth expresse;
And, *Glorie*, by the *Wreath* is Typifide.
For, where a vertuous *Industry* is found,
She, shall with Wreaths of *Glory*, thus be crown'd.   (p. 5)

Elsewhere, he binds his religious lessons more overtly to a contemporary
discourse of improvement:

A better *Fortune* you might gaine,
If you, could take a little *paine*:

---

[73] *Works*, vol. 3, p. 310.

> If you have *Wealth*, you should have more,
> And, should be Rich, (though you are *poore*).   (p. 265)

The *Emblemes* thus merge a Calvinist attention to the faith and conscience of the individual with the parallel movement in seventeenth-century culture toward a social morality based on ideals of individual freedom.[74] As a result, Wither subtly endorses the perception that success in one's labours on earth can be 'at once the sign and the reward of ethical superiority'.[75] 'No question', argued an Interregnum pamphleteer, 'but [riches] should be the portion rather of the godly than of the wicked, were it good for them; for godliness hath the promises of this life as well as of the life to come.'[76]

The individualist logic of Wither's georgic is further embedded in a rural context in a poem which employs the analogy of a hard-working bee (p. 250). Bees were widely perceived to typify values of labour, diligence and frugality.[77] Accordingly, Wither focuses initially on the 'honest thrift' of the bees, yet ultimately shapes his poem around a predominant anxiety that others may craftily appropriate the fruits of the individual's labour. In a manner reminiscent of Tusser's backhanded remarks about the cloying customary demands placed on the husbandman by local relationships ('Few lends (but fooles) / their working tooles'),[78] Wither suggests that 'idle visitings' and 'friendly shewes of *neighbourhood*' may mask a sly attempt to prey on the productivity of others. Such are the actions of the drones:

> Sometime, their powerfull Foes doe rob them quite;
> Sometime, their *Lords*, or *Landlords*, with pretence,
> Of claiming only what is just and right,
> Oppresse them without *mercie*, or *defence*.
> Thus, by one course or other, daily, some
> (That are laborious in an honest way)
> The prey of pride, or Idlenesse become:

74 See above, pp. 162–3; and Joyce Oldham Appleby, *Economic Thought and Ideology in Seventeenth-Century England* (Princeton, 1978), p. 70.
75 Tawney, *Religion and the Rise of Capitalism*, p. 264.
76 R. Younge, *The Poores' Advocate* (1654); quoted in Tawney, *Religion and the Rise of Capitalism*, p. 264.
77 Keith Thomas, *Man and the Natural World* (Harmondsworth, 1984), p. 63; Timothy Raylor, 'Samuel Hartlib and the Commonwealth of Bees', in *Culture and Cultivation in Early Modern England: Writing and the Land*, ed. Michael Leslie and Timothy Raylor (Leicester, 1992), p. 105.
78 *Five Hundred Points*, p. 27; see above, p. 150.

7.2 'By Labour, Vertue may be gain'd; / By Vertue, Glorie is attain'd': emblem from George Wither, *A Collection of Emblemes, Ancient and Moderne* (1635).

> And, such as these, may therefore truely say,
>   That, whatsoever they to passe have brought,
>   *Not for themselves, but others, they have wrought.*   (p. 250)

While the attack on landlords revives the strategies of the complaint tradition, Wither's underlying purpose is closer to that of the seventeenth-century improver. Consequently, rather than arguing that landlords and tenants are ideally bound by ties of moral responsibility, he depicts an industrious husbandman beset by stifling claims upon his energies. The bee, like the middling farmer striving to be 'laborious in an honest way', requires above all freedom from the demands and expectations of others.

This analogical use of bees highlights a significant strand in seventeenth-century georgic. In the sixteenth century, Whitney embraced a meditation on the beehive as an opportunity to celebrate the operation of a patron's estate:

> This is the hive; your tennaunts, are the bees:
> And in the same, have places by degrees.   (p. 201)

The movement toward values of individualism, however, shifts attention away from the interests of a landlord directing the labours of others, and toward those of the industrious workers themselves. In the following century, 'bees were regarded as sound economists and good husbandmen. They were of impeccable ethical character, being clean, chaste, pious and industrious.'[79] They provided a quintessential georgic exemplar, fashioned in the interests of the age; in the words of Samuel Purchas, 'Bees are indefatigably, that I say not covetously laborious, always working, but never satisfied, always toyling, but never coming to a period of their endeavours.'[80] While writers continued to argue about the political organization adopted by bees, the seventeenth century brought widespread agreement that it was the accumulation of individual labours and energies that determined the bees' prosperity. The analogy emphasized the protection and rational organization of labour and property; those 'laborious in an honest way', as Wither proclaims, must be allowed to reap the requisite reward for their labours.

The significance attached to the labours of bees directs attention toward representations of a thriving national economy. While the basic thrust of seventeenth-century georgic focuses on the actions and motivations of the individual, a parallel development considers the potential multiplication of industrious energies on a far broader scale. Nicholas Breton's *Fantasticks* (1626) pursues such a vision in a form which marks a significant point of literary transition between Tusser's agricultural calendar of labours and James Thomson's description of rural seasons.[81] Breton writes brief prose descriptions of months and hours, which

---

[79] Raylor, 'Samuel Hartlib', p. 106.
[80] *A Theatre of Politicall Flying Insects* (1657), p. 13.
[81] References to *Works in Verse and Prose*, ed. Alexander B. Grosart (2 vols., New York, 1966), vol. 2; see Fowler, 'Georgic and Pastoral', p. 84. See also Matthew Stevenson, *The Twelve Moneths* (1661), a work in prose and verse with numerous echoes of Breton, which combines discussion of rural recreations, medical advice and lists of fairs with a richly georgic strain of rural panegyric.

combine a lightly satiric tone – indebted to the contemporary popularity of Theophrastian character literature – with a georgic vigour and breadth of interest. The descriptions cast a keen eye across the activities of the middling and lower orders in the countryside. Among a host of deftly sketched vignettes, he notices 'the Gardiner . . . sorting of his seeds', 'the Thresher in the barne [trying] the strength of his flayle', 'the Husbandman . . . scowring of his Ploughshare', 'the Mower . . . whetting of his Sythe', 'the Beaters of Hempe [giving] a hoh to every blow', 'the Dayry mayd . . . clensing of her Vessels', and 'the Chapmen [falling] to furnish the shoppes' (pp. 7, 8, 14, 15). The placement of chapmen and other 'market people' alongside rural labourers typifies Breton's appreciation of an economy founded upon agricultural industry.[82] The entire text counterpoints the labours of husbandmen with the transactions of the corn market; as the waking day sets 'the Ploughmen to their Ploughes and their Barrowes in the field', so the merchants are put 'to their accounts, the Shop-men to What lacke you? and every Trade to his business' (p. 14). Throughout the social order men and women are ordering their lives in accordance with the 'sense of time-thrift' that E. P. Thompson identifies among 'improving capitalist employers' of the period.[83]

In the calendar, Breton's progress toward the months of harvest – the 'profitable season, the Labourers gaine, and the rich mans wealth' – gathers a momentum of process and exchange:

It is now September, and the Sunne begins to fall much from his height, the medowes are left bare, by the mouthes of hungry Cattell, and the Hogges are turned into the Corne fields: the windes begin to knocke the Apples heads together on the trees, and the fallings are gathered to fill the Pyes for the Houshold . . . Waflet Oysters are the Fish wives wealth, and Pippins fine are the Costermongers rich merchandise: the flayle and the fan fall to worke in the Barne, and the Corne market is full of Bakers: the Porkets are driven to the woods, and the home-fed Pigges make porke for the market. (pp. 9–10)

The scattergun approach celebrates the diversity of economic life, in a way that simply overwhelms traditional tendencies to idealize ploughmen and reprove merchants. By moving from the husbandman to

[82] Margaret Spufford documents the activities of chapmen, and a number of chapwomen, in *The Great Reclothing of Rural England: Petty Chapmen and Their Wares in the Seventeenth Century* (London, 1984).
[83] 'Time, Work-Discipline, and Industrial Capitalism', *Past and Present*, 38 (1967), p. 78.

the consumer, Breton represents a georgic ethos of labour and productivity sprawling outward from the fields, to invigorate the entire nation.

The works of John Taylor, the water poet, espouse a similarly dynamic economic vision. Like Breton, Taylor was a prolific pamphleteer concerned more with the issues of the day than with niceties of genre; however, his very engagement with a bustling literary marketplace tends to reinforce a commitment in his writing to the values of the middling sorts. Therefore the apparent disdain for the lower orders in his pamphlets of royalist polemic needs to be set alongside the driving energy of the middling entrepreneur which shapes the majority of his work.[84] Taylor's persona as the poet of the English waterways undersets a career characterized by restless activity, local observation and economic opportunism. His typical voyage takes him through uncharted waters, on the promise of financial support settled in tavern wagers; in 1649 he writes,

> Like to the stone of *Sisiphus*, I roule
> From place to place, through weather faire and foule,
> And yet I every day must wander still
> To vent my Bookes, and gather friends good will.[85]

Significantly, this style sets Taylor apart from the descriptive mode of the chorographers, whose writings for the gentry I will consider in the following chapter. Theirs is a discourse of order and property; Taylor is a poet of process and energy. To the 'noble Thames', he declares:

> Thou in the morning when my coine is scant
> Before the evening dost supply my want.
> If like a Bee I seeke to live and thrive,
> Thou wilt yeeld hony freely to my hive.[86]

This principle of movement prompts several texts which shift the focus from the egocentric poet to the economic activities of his society.

---

[84] Cf. Low, who focuses solely on the royalist pamphlets (*Georgic Revolution*, pp. 247–9). Bernard Capp's more recent study, *The World of John Taylor the Water Poet 1578–1653* (Oxford, 1994), captures well the mercurial character of a poet unfixed between elite and popular culture.

[85] *John Taylors Wandering, to see the Wonders of the West*, p. 23; facsimile reprint in *Works... Not Included in the Folio Volume of 1630* (5 vols., Spenser Society, London, 1870–8), vol. 1.

[86] *All the Workes ... Collected in one Volume*, 1630; facsimile edn (Spenser Society, London, 1868–9), p. 559.

His *Carriers Cosmographie* provides a guide to British trade networks, to assist those wishing to transport goods to or from a market.[87] The earlier *Travels of Twelve-Pence* applies the traveller's appreciation of process to the financial transactions which propel a coin across the nation, merging a georgic imperative with a mild satire on the desire for money. In the country, the coin proclaims:

> Look on the hearbs, the flowr's, the fruits, the trees,
> Fowles of the ayre, the painefull lab'ring Bees,
> And aske their Owners why they breed and spring,
> His answere is, they must him *money* bring.
> Note but the toyling Plow-man, he is sowing,
> He's hedging, ditching, taking, reaping, mowing,
> Goes to bed late, and rises before day,
> And all to have my company, hee'll say.[88]

His later *Taylor on Thame Isis* turns to the natural and economic processes of the nation's principal waterway, with a particularity derived from the writer's own dependence upon its traffic.[89] The poem moves from a detailed description of the water cycle that nourishes both the Thames and surrounding fields, through an appreciation of the river as a trade-route, to a plea for the improvement of hazardous stretches which are hampering travel. The text closes with a prayer:

> That God his blessings will increase and spread
> On them that love this work, and on their heires,
> Their goods and chattels, and on all that's theirs:
> I wish them blest externall, and internall,
> And in the end with happinesse eternall.   (p. 27)

In the spirit of Virgil's *Georgics*, clearing the arteries of trade is praised for its potential to advance national prosperity; it becomes a task fully deserving recognition and reward.

Taylor concentrates this perspective specifically on the agrarian economy in two pamphlets concerned with different products of the land. *Taylors Pastorall* skips from a review of the literary tradition within which 'learned Poets of all times' have celebrated 'The harmlesse lives

---

[87] (1637); in *Works . . . Not Included in the Folio Volume*, vol. 2.

[88] *All the Workes*, p. 82.

[89] (1632); in *Works . . . Not Included in the Folio Volume*, vol. 1. Capp gives the background to this pamphlet, Taylor's involvement in faltering government plans to improve the Thames (*World of John Taylor*, pp. 30–1).

of rural shepheards Swaines', to an analysis of the uses and profitability of sheep.[90] In a consideration of the 'infinite numbers of people rich and poore' who have derived 'their whole dependance from the poore sheepes back', he sketches the unravelling economic process generated out of wool: 'No Ram no Lambe, no Lambe no Sheepe, no Sheepe no Wooll, no Wooll no Woolman, no Woolman no Spinner, no Spinner no Weaver, no Weaver no Cloth, no Cloth no Clothier, no Clothier no Clothworker, Fuller, Tucker, Shearman, Draper, or scarcely a rich Dyer' (p. 538). The impetus apparent here is maintained still more consistently in *The Praise of Hemp-Seed*, in which Taylor combines a celebratory description of the 'happy seed' which 'fats the earth' as it grows, with details of the 'Good industry' involved in the working of hemp.[91] Throughout the countryside it provides gainful employment:

> Besides, it liberally each where bestowes
> A living upon thousands where it growes;
> As beaters, Spinners, Weavers, and a crue
> Of haltermakers which could scarce live true,
> But for th'imployment which this little graine
> Doth use them in, and payes them for their paine.   (p. 548)

The panegyric recalls the arguments of the agrarian projectors, considered in chapter 5.[92] Taylor's achievement is to filter such claims through an appreciation of the national significance of labour; the 'beaters, Spinners, [and] Weavers' become vital cogs in the expanding rural industries involved in the working of hemp. Therefore, while Taylor perhaps owes a greater debt to Tusser than to Virgil, his celebration of labour, economic process and national development aptly demonstrates the blend of interests and influences which shaped the vision of georgic economics.

The frontispiece to Walter Blith's *English Improver Improved* strikes the keynote of seventeenth-century georgic in the midst of revolutionary upheaval (illustration 7.3). The use of Isaiah 2.4 ('and they shall beat their swords into plowshares, and their spears into pruning hooks') to encompass an illustration of a range of agricultural activities highlights the extent to which georgic ideals had been fused with values of agrarian

---

[90] *Taylors Pastorall, being both Historicall and Satyricall. or, The noble Antiquitie of Shepheards, with the profitable use of Sheepe* (1624); in *All the Workes*, p. 535.
[91] *All the Workes*, pp. 553, 547.
[92] See above, pp. 151–6.

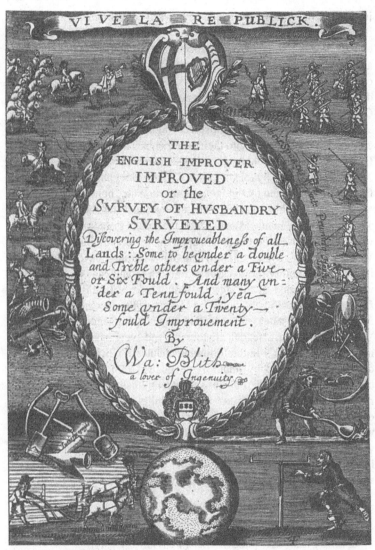

7.3 Frontispiece to Walter Blith's *English Improver Improved* (1652).

improvement. After the often awkward development of English discourse on husbandry, by the middle of the seventeenth century it was characterized by a mature confidence in the cultural status of both labour and economic development. Concurrently, out of the sixteenth-century consolidation of a georgic consciousness, one can perceive the development of a mode vitally concerned with new ideals of labour. Georgic was intertwined with the discourses of the improver and surveyor; and as Blith's frontispiece highlights, the mode injected a crucial moral imperative into their arguments. The complaint morality of Isaiah 5.8 ('Woe unto them that join house to house, that lay field to field . . .') was countered by that of Isaiah 2.4; the ploughman in the common fields was confronted by the industrious yeoman, 'bold of his own'.

Although Blith's rallying call for national regeneration through agrarian improvement was made from the side of the commonwealth, the values he espoused did not suffer upon the restoration of the monarchy. Whereas many royalist landowners may initially have shunned the improving mentality for its association with republicanism, their doubts were overwhelmed in the age of John Locke.[93] In 1704, *The Whole Duty of Man* specifically called on '*gentlemen* to recognize the *duty* of improving their estates'.[94] The landed magnates, as a recent study claims, 'had ceased to be a feudal aristocracy and were ready to embrace a market philosophy'.[95] In the following chapters I will turn to descriptive discourses fashioned by and for the gentry from the early sixteenth century to the middle of the seventeenth century. These typically represent an order of socio-economic stability and natural beauty in the countryside: the stasis of pastoral is preferred to the process of georgic. I will argue, however, that by the middle of the seventeenth century many writers incorporated georgic assumptions into their representations of the land. The discourse of Tusser, Wither and Taylor gradually came to shape the landscapes of Jonson and Herrick.

---

[93] Cf. Joyce Appleby's statement about the seventeenth century, that 'If a middle class did in fact emerge and improve its social standing, it coalesced with, rather than displaced, the existing ruling class' (*Economic Thought and Ideology*, p. 11).

[94] Christopher Hill, *The English Bible and the Seventeenth-Century Revolution* (London, 1993), p. 159.

[95] P. J. Cain and A. G. Hopkins, 'Gentlemanly Capitalism and British Expansion Overseas: I. The Old Colonial System, 1688–1850', *Economic History Review*, 2nd series, 39 (1986), p. 504.

Part III

The profits and pleasures of the land

8. Chorography: the view from the gentleman's seat

'Climate, Temperature, Plentie and Pleasures, make [Britain] to be the very *Eden of Europe* . . . for the *store of corne in the champian*, and of *Pasturage in the lower Grounds*, presseth the cart under the sheaves to the barn, and filleth the coffers of their possessors.'

(John Speed, *The Theatre of the Empire of Great Britaine*, 1611)

The surveying manuals considered in chapter 6 presented the telling image of a landlord 'sitting in his chayre' with a representation of his property laid out before him.[1] The survey, in a quite literal sense, brought the lord a greater knowledge of and sense of control over his land. In a parallel development, which produced a wave of cartographic and written descriptions of the country and its individual counties between the middle of the sixteenth and the middle of the seventeenth centuries, the English 'took effective visual and conceptual possession' of their nation.[2] This movement was propelled by similar motivations and technological advances to those apparent in early modern surveying. As Richard Helgerson has argued, 'The function of such books is precisely to make the land visible, to set it before us in such a way that we will know both its greatness and its particularity, a particularity in which its primary viewers, the landowning gentry of England and Wales, had their part.'[3] This upsurge of interest in the land among the gentry helped to formulate a coherent and authoritative celebratory image of rural England, which would subsequently influence a wealth of rural

---

[1] The quotation is from John Norden, *The Surveiors Dialogue* (1610 edn), p. 15.
[2] Richard Helgerson, *Forms of Nationhood: The Elizabethan Writing of England* (Chicago and London, 1992), p. 107; published, in an earlier version, as 'The Land Speaks: Cartography, Chorography, and Subversion in Renaissance England', in *Representing the English Renaissance*, ed. Stephen Greenblatt (Berkeley, 1988), pp. 327–61. A. L. Rowse first drew attention to this material, in 'The Elizabethan Discovery of England', in *The England of Elizabeth* (London, 1950), pp. 31–65.
[3] *Forms of Nationhood*, p. 145.

literature. In the final part of *God Speed the Plough*, I wish to consider this view of the land, drawn from the gentleman's seat: in the first place, in a discourse of discovery and description; and in the second, in the poetics of rural life and landscape.

The texts of concern in this chapter set out to survey the nation or individual counties, in accordance with a form of description known to contemporaries as 'chorography'. William Cunningham, writing in 1559, stated that chorography 'sheweth the partes of th'earth, divided in themselves. And severally describeth, the portes, Rivers, Havens, Fluddes, Hilles, Mountaynes, Cities, Villages, Buildinges, Fortresses, Walles, yea and every particuler thing, in that parte conteined.'[4] Subsequent English authors consistently overlaid historical concerns upon the geographical frame. An interest in antiquarian studies underpinned the early development of chorography, from the ambitious forays of John Leland in the reign of Henry VIII, to the crowning achievements of William Camden around the turn of the century.[5] Further, the chorographic tradition increasingly embraced the particular histories of the owners of the land, traced through studies in genealogy and heraldry. At a time of unprecedented upheaval in the land market, these investigations offered the gentry a sense of stable economic order and social hierarchy, founded upon the bedrock of the past.

Indeed, in the face of the sheer weight of antiquarian and genealogical information in English chorography of the late sixteenth and early seventeenth centuries, the topographical programme upon which the genre was based often appears to have been abandoned.[6] A governing identity with the land, however, determined both the structure and discourse of the texts. Whereas chronicle history invites the reader to identify with the monarchy, chorography implies that 'loyalty to England . . . means loyalty to the land'.[7] Moreover, the conjunction of topographical frame with genealogical detail combines patriotic celebration of the nation with an attention to the owners of the countryside. John Speed's *Theatre of the Empire of Great Britaine* claims that in England and Wales the

---

[4] *The Cosmographical Glasse* (1559), fol. 7ª. Both the concept and Cunningham's text are based upon Ptolemaic theory.

[5] See F. J. Levy, *Tudor Historical Thought* (San Marino, 1967), ch. 4.

[6] See, for example, E. G. R. Taylor, *Late Tudor and Early Stuart Geography 1583–1650* (London, 1934), p. 9.

[7] Helgerson, *Forms of Nationhood*, p. 132.

Climate, Temperature, Plentie and Pleasures, make it to be the very *Eden of Europe* (pardon me I pray if affection passe limits) for the *store of corne in the champian*, and of *Pasturage in the lower Grounds*, presseth the cart under the sheaves to the barn, and filleth the coffers of their possessors.[8]

Speed is self-consciously idealizing. After his parenthetical admission of excessive ardour, however, he deftly progresses from the 'store' of corn in the fields, transferred to the barn, which in turn 'filleth the coffers of their possessors'. While the original 'store' is stated as a given – a natural feature of the land – the progression of the sentence inexorably commutes nature into property. The passage comes to rest, in accordance with the ideological momentum of chorography, on the final assertion of the landowners' proprietorial interests.

The conventional representations of agrarian England forged in chorography are informed by the strategies of idealization proclaimed from the very beginning of Speed's *Theatre*. Faced with the uncertainty of contemporary property relations and socio-economic conditions, the chorographers typically shaped images of rural order, fertility and beauty. The definitive chorographical view of agrarian process thus posits what might be described as a natural order of productivity in the countryside. Chorography assures the owners of the land that the maintenance of traditional structures of property will produce national conditions of stability and prosperity. But while the weight of generic convention worked to suppress considerations of agricultural practice and economic process, the force of local interests and individual enthusiasms frequently stretched such constraints. Hence many of the texts admit concerns of change, improvement, process and labour; and the conjunction of idealized stability and improving initiative, pastoral ease and georgic energy, gives chorography a remarkable complexity of vision. The following sections, therefore, will firstly consider the basic descriptive conventions developed within chorography, and secondly some of the more diverse approaches toward the representation of agrarian practice accommodated within the generic framework. As this is not an issue of chronological development, each section will consider texts from across the period of concerted chorographical activity, roughly 1570 to 1635. A final section will focus on Michael Drayton's massive poetic contribution to chorography, *Poly-Olbion*. A consideration of Drayton's poem, which claims a place within the chorographical

---

[8] Four English edns and one Latin translation, 1611–27; (1611 edn), sig. ¶3ᵃ⁻ᵇ.

tradition but fashions a notably idiosyncratic view of the land, will at once highlight the strategies and imperatives of the contemporary prose texts, and prepare for the subsequent analysis of rural poetry.

THE NATURAL ORDER OF PRODUCTIVITY

The 1607 Latin edition of Camden's *Britannia* (which was followed by an English translation in 1610) stands as the central achievement of the English chorographical tradition. From the frontispiece illustration of Neptune and Ceres flanking a map of Britain (illustration 8.1), the book proclaims its combination of geographical investigation and national panegyric. Camden structures the text into two sections. A series of chapters of general introduction on historical matters and the contemporary social structure, and religious and legal administration precedes a far longer perambulation of the counties. The latter section – packed with the histories of royalty, nobility and gentry – draws together the book's concerns with topography, antiquarian history, genealogy and heraldry in a manner typical of mature English chorography. Yet the 1607 edition in fact marked the end of a process of textual evolution spanning two decades. Indeed the path from the 37-sheet octavo edition of 1586 to the handsome 281-sheet folio of 1610 reveals a massive reorientation of the text, in a process shaped by the developing cultural expectations surrounding chorography.[9] The first edition was directed toward a Continental context of historical research, and follows the model established by the European antiquary and cartographer Abraham Ortelius, by concentrating on the Roman and Anglo-Saxon heritage of British place names. The bulk of the subsequent additions, by comparison, catered to the concerns of contemporary English gentlemen. In particular, Camden greatly expanded his genealogical information, in agreement with an upsurge of interest in the heritage of landowning families.[10] Chorography, like the *Britannia*, was being remodelled as a discourse of the propertied.[11]

---

[9] See F. J. Levy, 'The Making of Camden's *Britannia*', *Bibliothèque d'Humanisme et Renaissance*, 26 (1964), pp. 70–97; and Levy, *Tudor Historical Thought*, pp. 152–9.

[10] This focus was reinforced by Camden's appointment in 1597 to the second highest position in the College of Arms (Sir Anthony Wagner, *Heralds of England: A History of the Office and College of Arms* (London, 1967), p. 221).

[11] Despite the numbers of propertied women in early modern England, Camden is also typical of the chorographers in his construction of landowning as a masculine prerogative. (See Amy Louise Erickson, *Women and Property in Early Modern England* (London, 1993).)

8.1 Frontispiece to William Camden, *Britannia* (1610 English edn).

The six Latin editions, and subsequent English translation, of the *Britannia* punctuate the years of greatest chorographical activity. Camden's reappraisal of the purpose of his text thus highlights the important generic developments of the period, as scholarly antiquarianism merged with local concerns of genealogy and heraldry. This movement was institutionalized within the Society of Antiquaries, a group of some forty men which met on a regular basis from about 1586 to 1608.[12] The initial publication of the *Britannia*, and the foundation of the Cotton Library soon afterwards, bolstered the Society in its early stages. By contrast to Camden's early orientation toward the Continent, the Society was distinctly insular in its concentration on English subjects and sources.[13] To quote T. D. Kendrick, its main focus was on

> what has been called the 'practical' past, the past that was immediately important in their own lives and thoughts, and discoverable through the study of subjects of portentous antiquarian solemnity, such as ancient law, the origin of institutions, offices, customs, privileges, and the like, and in the history of land-tenure and of the measurement of land.[14]

It is immediately striking that this agenda involves issues which in chapter 6 were shown to be central to the growth of estate surveying. In each case, the initiative to investigate the history of customary practices and rights gives way to a more immediate concern for the application of such knowledge to the present. Thus the Society's antiquarian interests converge with a contemporary concern for the land as property; the surveyor's practical attention to the definition of one's 'own' is yoked to the gentleman's desire to legitimize his social position through recourse to history.

The main wave of chorographical writing was consolidated within this cultural context. The typical structure of the texts adopts Camden's distinction between 'general' and 'particular' description; however, the former was increasingly approached as merely a brief introduction to a comprehensive survey of localities and landowning families. This 'particular view or survey', one writer declares, recognizes 'all those Places that either by reason of some Notable Accident, or on account of their Antient or Moderne Lords, deserve to be remembered'.[15]

---

12 Linda Van Norden, 'The Elizabethan College of Antiquaries' (unpublished Ph.D dissertation, University of California at Los Angeles, 1946), p. 113.
13 Van Norden, 'Elizabethan College of Antiquaries', p. 352.
14 *British Antiquity* (London, 1950), p. 114.
15 John Coker, *A Survey of Dorsetshire* (London, 1732), p. 9.

Consequently, as Helgerson observes, the texts become 'repositories of proper names': 'ancient place names; names of places too small to be mapped; names of particular properties, buildings and institutions; and most of all the names of families and of individual people'.[16] Representative of the form is William Burton's *Description of Leicester-Shire* (1622), which begins with just seven pages of 'general description', including a topographical introduction and lists of castles, religious houses, fairs, markets and parks. This is followed by 310 pages of 'particular description', in which Burton works alphabetically through the county's principal settlements, castles and churches, embellishing his text with heraldic illustrations and genealogical tables. The title-page is suitably illuminated with a full-page engraving featuring figures of Fame, Truth, Leicestershire and Antiquity, while the author is incorporated into the allegory through a plan of his family estate at Lindley (illustration 8.2).

This approach to chorographical description facilitates bold, celebratory representations of the land and the agricultural uses to which it is put. Writers conventionally emphasize from the outset of their texts the fertility and beauty of the countryside. Camden claims:

> Nature tooke a pleasure in the framing [of Britain], and seemeth to have made it as a second world, sequestred from the other, to delight mankinde withall, yea and curiously depainted it of purpose as it were a certain portraict, to represent a singular beautie, and for the ornament of the universall world: with so gallant and glittering varietie, with so pleasant a shew are the beholders eyes delighted, which way so ever they glance.
>
> (p. 4)

The *Britannia* thus represents the nation as an autonomous artefact, 'framed' by Nature for 'beauty' and 'delight'. Camden's surveys of individual counties reinforce this image, as they regularly begin with short, formulaic descriptions of the natural qualities of a region. He plots broad patterns of land-use, in a manner which ascribes a basic order to topographic and economic conditions. Oxfordshire, for example, 'is a fertile country and plentifull: wherin the plaines are garnished with Corne-fieldes and meddowes, the hilles beset with woods, stored in every place not onely with corne and fruites, but also with all kinde of game for hound or hauke; and well watered with fishfull rivers' (p. 373).

Such descriptive strategies shape an associated view of agricultural

---

[16] Helgerson, 'The Land Speaks', p. 349.

production. From the frontispiece illustration of Ceres, bedecked with corn and fruit, to the introductory sentences in the county descriptions, Camden defines a natural order of productivity, within which the land pours forth its fruits for the use of humanity. In a text which is increasingly moulded around the interests of the landed gentry, this strategy occludes considerations of the processes and labours involved in agrarian production. His images of natural abundance instead suggest an invariable movement of 'natural wealth' from the land to its owners: his readers. In the description of Oxfordshire, the succession of passive verbs establishes a sense of natural and pleasing inevitability in the productive process. The land is '*garnished with* Corne-fieldes and meddowes', '*stored . . . with*' corn, fruits and game, and '*well watered with* fishfull rivers'. (This practice is maintained throughout the *Britannia*, with a range of analogous passive constructions including 'furnished with', 'abounding in' and 'embroidered with'.)[17] Ultimately, as stated in the initial clause, Camden insists that Oxfordshire simply '*is* a fertile country and plentifull'.

These strategies were adopted by Camden's contemporary chorographers. Burton states that one region of Leicestershire 'is exceeding rich ground, yeelding great increase of Corne in abundance of all kindes, and affordeth many good & large sheepe Pastures'. That the pleasing pastures had in many cases been established through practices of depopulating enclosure, in a county wracked by painful rural upheaval throughout the 150 years before Burton wrote, scarcely affected his perception. Leicestershire, he claims, 'yeeldeth great delight and profit every way'.[18] John Speed's structure demands that he cram his written descriptions of counties onto individual pages, which precede the lavish maps around which the *Theatre* is structured.[19] (See his map of Surrey,

---

[17] Philemon Holland's English translation reinforces Camden's strategy. In fact Holland's regular use of 'stored' is an innovation; and although the other constructions are generally justified by Camden's text, Holland frequently extends and regularizes the Latin.

[18] *Description of Leicester-Shire*, p. 2. C. G. A. Clay notes the social havoc caused in the fields of Leicestershire, as one village in six in the county disappeared between 1450 and 1600, and more than one in three experienced some enclosure in the sixteenth century (*Economic Expansion and Social Change: England 1500–1700* (2 vols., Cambridge, 1984), vol. 1, pp. 75–6). Despite these statistics, I have found only one reference to enclosure in the *Description*: a brief comment that the ancient town of Stormsworth 'hath been . . . altogether decayed, and converted to sheep-pastures' (p. 273).

[19] The maps are then followed by an index of localities.

8.2 Title-page of William Burton's *Description of Leicester-Shire* (1622).

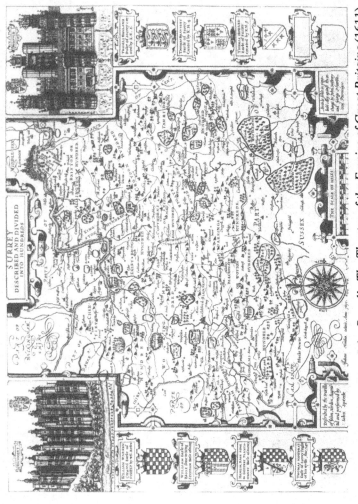

8.3 Map of Surrey, from John Speed's *The Theatre of the Empire of Great Britaine* (1611).

illustration 8.3.) He constructs condensed, paradigmatic summaries around the signifiers 'air', 'soil' and 'commodities'. Further, in a practice also characteristic of John Norden's chorographical work, the geographical précis are regularly laced with adjectives such as 'fertile', 'fruitful', 'rich', 'pleasant', 'profitable', 'plenteous', 'bounteous' and 'fat'.[20] The recurrence of such words, alone and in various combinations, invites the reader to perceive a relationship of identity between them. The *Theatre*'s description of Berkshire is typical:

> the aire is temperate, sweet, and delightfull, and prospect for pleasure inferiour to none; the Soile is plenteous of Corne, especially in the Vale of the White-horse, that yeeldeth yeerely an admirable increase. In a word, Corne, Cattle, Waters and Woods, of profit and pleasure, it gives place unto none. (p. 25)

Throughout the passage Speed elides, though never completely suppresses, considerations of the economics of agrarian productivity. After the initial praise of the air, the series of alliterative couplings moves from the aesthetic joys of the county's 'prospect for pleasure', through the annual measure of productivity in 'yeeldeth yeerely', to the commodities of 'Corne, Cattle, Waters and Woods'. The climactic phrase, 'profit and pleasure', echoes one of the catchcries of the husbandry manuals considered in chapter 5.[21] But whereas the very rationale of the manuals was the analysis of agrarian production, Speed's idealized model of rural life instead depicts the land pouring forth its fruits, for the 'profit and pleasure' of its possessors.

In a reading of Camden, Speed or Norden, the contemporary gentleman might hardly have noticed the strategies which shaped the notion of a natural order of productivity in the English countryside. Yet these basic and recurrent discursive practices, reinforced among the community of authors and readers with every new usage, increasingly informed the gentry's representations of their land. The chorographies thereby helped to establish among the landed the foundation for more complex aesthetic appreciations of productive agricultural land: a process of considerable significance for the development of rural poetry throughout the seventeenth and eighteenth centuries. Although the generic bounds of chorography do not permit its authors to pursue this

20 Stan A. E. Mendyk traces Norden's attempts to establish himself as 'the successor of Saxton in the redescription of England', in *'Speculum Britanniae': Regional Study, Antiquarianism, and Science in Britain to 1700* (Toronto, 1989), ch. 3.
21 See above, p. 140.

nascent movement toward literary fashioning, several texts demonstrate a notable awareness of the potential for such a process. Camden, for example, expands upon the *Britannia*'s prevailing tone of national celebration through frequent use of quotations from other authors, a method which allows him to urge his reader toward an aesthetic response to the land, without affecting the objective authority of his own antiquarian research. In his description of Gloucestershire he enlists William of Malmesbury. Camden quotes:

> Heere may you see the high waies and common lanes clad with apple-trees and peare-trees, not set nor graffed by the industrie of mans hand, but growing naturally of their owne accord. The ground of it selfe is enclined to beare fruits, and those both in tast and beautie farre exceeding others: whereof some will last a whole yeare and not wither at all: so that they are serviceable untill new come againe for supplie. (p. 357)

The scene is one of golden age perfection. In William's Gloucestershire labour is unnecessary, since nature provides a perennial abundance. Camden clearly does not expect his reader to accept the statement as fact; his use of such quotations, usually set in italics, regularly concedes a certain rhetorical exaggeration. The rich collection of celebratory quotations, however, consolidates the *Britannia*'s consistently aestheticized representation of the English countryside.

Camden extends this process through the use of verse. As one commentator has written, the *Britannia* is 'among other things a repository of poetry dealing with the historical landscape';[22] and as the book expanded, Camden was able to include contributions from several of his contemporaries.[23] The main purpose of verse in the book may be demonstrated in his treatment of the poem – probably his own – which appears in various fragments throughout the *Britannia*: 'The Marriage of Tame and Isis' ('De Connubio Tamae et Isis').[24] 'The Marriage' participates in the minor Renaissance tradition of river poetry, which

---

[22] Wyman H. Herendeen, 'Wanton Discourse and the Engines of Time: William Camden – Historian among Poets-Historical', in *Renaissance Rereadings: Intertext and Context*, ed. Maryanne Cline Horowitz et al. (Urbana, 1988), p. 149.

[23] Jack B. Oruch lists contributions from Michael Maschiat (first published in 1590), Sir John Stradling (1600) and Daniel Rogers (1610) ('Topography in the Prose and Poetry of the English Renaissance 1540–1640' (unpublished Ph.D dissertation, Indiana University, 1964), pp. 118–20).

[24] See the modern edition edited by George Burke Johnston, 'Poems by William Camden, With Notes and Translations from the Latin', *Studies in Philology*, 72 (1975), no. 5 (texts and studies).

developed from the middle of the sixteenth century as a form concerned to etch a national mythology onto the land.[25] In the early essays of John Leland and William Vallans, the passage of swans upon the Thames was employed as a vehicle for Tudor panegyric.[26] Camden's poem, by comparison, pays more thorough attention to the rivers and landscape, as it traces the path of the Thames, borne out of the confluence of Tame and Isis at Dorchester.[27] To reconstruct a narrative from the dispersed fragments, the poem begins in a cave in the Cotswolds, from whence Isis, the king of waters, pours forth the stream that will bear his name. The cave is richly adorned with images of the moon, the great rivers of the world and 'Britannie with riches manifold / Of goulden fleece; [and] a Coronet of wheat-ears' (p. 368). The bride makes her own stately progress to the wedding, adorned with similarly agrarian accessories:

> Up riseth *Tame* then, who know's
> Her locks with eares of corn
> Full well to knit, with kirtle green
> Her wast eke to adorn. (p. 387)

In a manner analogous to the representation of Ceres on the frontispiece, Camden conflates symbols of fertility and beauty. The abundance of grain – accepted as a standard index of rural productivity across the whole range of texts considered in this study – is placed at the head of the vision of national glorification, as symbolized at once by the groom's 'Coronet of wheat-ears' and the bride's locks knit 'with eares of corn'.

The chorographical discourse of rural abundance and beauty which Camden reiterates in 'The Marriage' almost inevitably suppresses any concern for the labours of agricultural production. As seen in Speed's panegyric on the 'Eden of Europe', the produce is transformed into a natural function of the land itself, which flows forth 'and filleth the coffers of [the land's] possessors'. A desire to conform with such conventions perhaps explains John Norden's decision to omit a

25 See Wyman H. Herendeen, *From Landscape to Literature: The River and the Myth of Geography* (Pittsburgh, 1986), especially chs. 3–5.
26 Leland, *Cygnea Cantio* (1545); Vallans, *A Tale of Two Swannes* (1590). Both poems are reprinted in *The Itinerary of John Leland The Antiquary*, ed. Thomas Hearne, 2nd edn (9 vols., Oxford, 1745), vols. 9, 5.
27 Camden was probably influenced in his approach by Edmund Spenser's marriage pageant of the Thames and the Medway in *The Faerie Queene*, IV.xi.11–53, and also by Spenser's unfulfilled plans to compose a far more comprehensive poem of English river lore and topography (see Jack B. Oruch, 'Spenser, Camden, and the Poetic Marriages of Rivers', *Studies in Philology*, 64 (1967), pp. 606–24).

manuscript passage on 'The means most usual how the people of Middlesex do live', when he brought his description of that county to the press.[28] Despite Norden's documented devotion to the cause of agrarian improvement, his chorographical achievements aptly demonstrate the gulf between the discourses of estate surveyor and county surveyor.[29] The representation of husbandmen and labourers, so crucial to the textual traditions considered in previous chapters, becomes at best a peripheral consideration for the chorographer. While not all writers are as forthright as Speed in their depiction of a land of natural abundance, the texts consistently reduce husbandmen to the status of decorative and marginal figures in the rural landscape.

The title of 'husbandman', of course, was in common usage in early modern England as a socio-economic category for legal and administrative purposes; however, in the chorographies the figure is employed as a vaguely generalized image of farmer and labourer, defined by his function rather than his rank. This process does not always disregard the labours of the farmer. In Durham, Camden notes that 'the ground being well manured . . . yeeldeth good recompense for the husbandmans toile' (p. 735). The more conventional imagery offered by chorography is apparent in Camden's description of the Isle of Wight, where the soil 'is thankfull to the husbandman, in so much as it doth affoord corne to be carried forth' (p. 273). Significantly, through Camden's tortuous syntax the husbandman emerges without agency: it is the soil that *affords* 'corne to be carried forth'. Speed also exploits this strategy. Southern Warwickshire, he writes, 'yeerely yeeldeth such plentifull harvest, that the husbandman smileth in beholding his paines' (p. 53); in Essex, the soil is 'in some place sandy and barren; yet so that it never frustrates the husband-mans hopes, or fills not the hands of her harvest Labourers' (p. 31). As in the example from the *Britannia*, Speed's labourers are syntactically rendered passive, to become mere celebrants of the natural order of productivity.

Norden further conflates economics with aesthetics in several remarkable images of the happy husbandman. The plentiful harvests of Middlesex 'maketh the husbandman to clappe his handes for joye, to see the pleasing feyledes so to laugh and singe'.[30] In Northamptonshire the

[28] Taylor, *Late Tudor and Early Stuart Geography*, p. 50; *Speculum Britanniae. The first parte. An historicall, & chorographicall discription of Middlesex* (1593).
[29] On Norden's influential *Surveiors Dialogue*, see above, chapter 7.
[30] BL Add. MS 31853, fol. 4ᵃ; cf. *discription of Middlesex*, p. 11.

physicality of labour is transmuted into a form of revelry:

> Now to call to Mynde somethinge touchinge the Husbandmans delight,
> I cannot but wonder to call to Mynde the greate heards of Cattle longinge
> to every small Parishe, Village, and Hamlett, which when in my small
> Travayle I did behold by such generall multitudes I perswaded my selfe of
> an impossibilitie, that so small Parishes and Places of so slender Accompt
> could yeeld so great a Number of kyne and other Cattle such mayne
> Fflocks of Sheepe and which made me most to marvayle were the greate
> heards of Swyne, a Beast altogether unprofittable, 'till he come to the
> Slaughter. Then his rustie Ribbs in a Frostye Morninge will please Pearce
> the Ploughman, and will so supple his Weather-beaten Lipps, that his
> Whipp and Whistle will hamer out such harmony as will make a Dogge
> daunce that delights it. But howsoever they be fed, the baser sorte of Men
> prove wealthie, and wade through the World with good countenance in
> their calling, least beholden generally to the monied Men of any Shire
> whatsoever that I knowe.[31]

Norden's use of 'Pearce the Ploughman' demonstrates the extent to which the representations of agrarian England in chorography diverge from those developed within the discourse of agrarian complaint. As shown in chapter 1, Piers is presented by the mid-Tudor reformers as the archetypal agrarian complainant: he is the honest, hard-working smallholder, oppressed by the covetousness of rural 'possessioners'. Norden, however, wrenches Piers out of this ideological context and realigns him with emergent literary conventions of pastoral celebration.[32] Neither the complaint texts nor the chorographies want to change the social order; in fact, both cling to a profoundly conservative socio-economic model. But while complaint challenges the propertied, chorography glorifies their status. In Norden's Northamptonshire, the 'wealth' of 'the baser sorte of Men' is their contentment with their lot: they are naturally without property, while riches fall, by definition, to 'the monied Men'.

A VIEW OF THE COUNTRY

The descriptive practices developed in the works of writers such as Camden, Norden and Speed attained the status of textual conventions,

---

[31] *Speculi Britanniae Pars Altera: or, a Delineation of Northamptonshire* (London, 1720), pp. 31–2.
[32] I will discuss contemporary developments in the English pastoral tradition on pp. 264–74, below.

which informed the writing of a range of chorographers and poets. The widespread awareness of these conventions is evident in Thomas Westcote's *View of Devonshire in 1630*, which circulated in manuscript among an active coterie of West Country chorographers.[33] After a discussion of agriculture in his 'general description', Westcote apologizes,

> much of this matter will seem to some overmuch, for it cannot but be thought a wide digression, if not a wandering clean out of the way, when the intent is to give you a View of the country. I read you a lecture of husbandry, supposed to be taken out of Mr. Tusser, or his like. (p. 57)

A 'View of the country', Westcote recognizes, means a view of the country's landowning families; he later defines his governing intention in the text 'to glorify and ennoble [his] country and native soil' (p. 450). The conventions of the form admit no place for 'a lecture of husbandry', in the earthy strain of Thomas Tusser.

But while Westcote overtly denigrates his own 'wide digression' from the generic norms of chorography, his discursive approach to the *View* nonetheless garners an impressive range of local agricultural information. His defensive nod toward the true direction of his 'way', therefore, should alert the reader at once to the pressures of convention and the flexibility of such standards in the hands of individual authors. Indeed, throughout the wave of chorographical writing one gains important glimpses of a bustling agrarian process underlying the slick veneer of the natural order of productivity. Even Camden commends the 'art and cunning' of the husbandmen of Romney Marsh; and among the orchards of Kent he pauses to discuss the achievements – 'to the publique good' – of Henry VIII's fruiterer, Richard Harris (pp. 350, 334). Many of the regional chorographers extend this initiative to embrace more detailed representations of agricultural practice and economic process. Such passages are typically marked by a certain hesitancy, and by hedging reassertions of the overriding imagery of natural abundance. Yet this initiative – sometimes subtle, sometimes awkward, rarely more than peripheral – injects a particularly vital note into chorography's view of the country, which would reverberate in representations of the land throughout the early modern period.

From its beginnings, chorography yoked scholarly concerns of history and topography to an eminently practical interest in the land. As noted

[33] (Exeter, 1845).

above, the agenda of the antiquarian community of Camden's era embraced issues such as the history of land tenures and measurements; and in the regional studies which flourished from the latter decades of the sixteenth century, broader issues of the national past were frequently swamped by local concerns. One of the most thorough of the county surveys (and also one of the earliest) was William Lambarde's *A Perambulation of Kent*.[34] Lambarde compiled a vast manuscript 'dictionary' of antiquarian information relating to sites throughout the nation;[35] however, he devoted his greatest attention to the county to which he moved upon inheriting a manor.[36] The *Perambulation* is structured in accordance with the interests of a gentleman seeking to comprehend his local environment. In particular, Lambarde combines his survey of the county with a lengthy discussion of local landholding customs. These issues, he asserts, determine the very 'nature' of the land; practices of inheritance are 'so inseparably knit to the land as in a manner nothing but an act of parliament can dissever them'.[37] The rhetoric of timeless order admits nonetheless an awareness of the power of knowledge, in a manner analogous to the estate surveyor's promises of rigorously empirical definitions of 'one's own'. For subsequent generations of chorographers this logic could equally suggest that the management and monetary value of estates was a matter of essential concern in any description of the land.[38]

An impetus toward social and economic analysis was furthered by the influence of related modes of description pioneered in other contemporary texts. Sir Thomas Smith's *De Republica Anglorum*, for example, sets out to describe Elizabethan processes of government and administration, the social and economic orders and the operation of the legal system.[39] Writing years before the publication of Christopher Saxton's

34 Three edns, 1576, 1596, 1640?.
35 *Dictionarium Angliae Topographicum & Historicum, An Alphabetical Description of the Chief Places in England and Wales; With an Account of the most Memorable Events which have distinguish'd them* (London, 1730).
36 Levy, *Tudor Historical Thought*, p. 140; see also Retha M. Warnicke, *William Lambarde: Elizabethan Antiquary 1536–1601* (London, 1973).
37 Lambarde is immediately concerned with the Kentish partible inheritance custom of gavelkind; quoted in Helgerson, *Forms of Nationhood*, p. 137.
38 See, for example, *The Chorography of Suffolk*, ed. Diarmaid MacCulloch (Suffolk Records Society, Ipswich, 1976); and the text which MacCulloch claims was written by the same author, although ascribed by its editor to Norden, *The Chorography of Norfolk: An Historicall and Chorographicall Description of Norffolck*, ed. Christobel M. Hood (Norwich, 1938).
39 Smith dates his text 1565, but it was not printed until 1583.

Atlas, Smith claims for his own book the status of a national survey: 'I have declared summarily as it were in a chart or mappe . . . the forme and manner of the governement of Englande, and the policie thereof' (p. 118). The work of William Harrison, meanwhile, is widely recognized as an important precursor to the chorographical tradition. His 'Historicall description of the Iland of Britaine', published as a preface to Raphael Holinshed's *Chronicles*, is proclaimed as 'a briefe rehersall of the nature and qualities of the people of England. and such commodities as are to be found in the same'.[40] The text demonstrates a catholic appreciation of social and economic process; it is, as one historian writes, 'suffused with the awareness of change'.[41] On the one hand, this perspective prompts a discussion of enclosure which harks back to the mid-Tudor social criticism, as Harrison laments the 'incroching and joining of house to house, and laieng land to land, whereby the inhabitants of manie places of our countrie are devoured and eaten up' (p. 193).[42] On the other hand, he also notes the 'amendment' of husbandry in his time: 'for that our countriemen are growne to be more painefull, skilfull, and carefull through recompense of gaine, than heretofore they have beene' (p. 109).

Harrison's analytical perception is facilitated by the structure of his text around a series of thematic chapters, rather than the perambulation embraced by his successors. Yet the pages of 'general description' in a typical chorography, and the reasonably flexible rubric afforded by the 'particular' survey, provided ample opportunity for writers to fashion subtly dynamic images of agrarian England. In particular, local agricultural practices become worthy of interest. Norden, for example, notes the practice of 'Devonshiring' (which involves burning turf and using the ashes as fertilizer) as 'a new kinde of husbandrye . . . which yeldeth favourable recompence . . . for the toyle of the husbandman'.[43] Devon's native chorographers endorse this detail in passages coloured by

---

[40] Second edn (2 vols., 1586), vol. 1, p. 1.
[41] Arthur B. Ferguson, *Clio Unbound: Perception of the Social and Cultural Past in Renaissance England* (Durham, N. C., 1979), p. 93.
[42] See also Ferguson, *Clio Unbound*, p. 94; and G. J. R. Parry's biography, which argues that Harrison's work should be placed within a tradition of 'covenant line' thought, which had found its most vocal adherents in the early years of the reign of Edward VI (*A Protestant Vision: William Harrison and the Reformation of Elizabethan England* (Cambridge, 1987), especially ch. 6).
[43] 'A Chorographicall discription of the severall Shires and Islands of Middlesex. Hamshire. Essex. Weighte. Surrey. Garnsey & Sussex. Jarsey.' (1595), BL Add. MS 31853, fol. 19ᵇ. See Joan Thirsk, 'Farming Techniques', in *AHEW IV*, p. 166.

regional pride in local ingenuity. The Elizabethan John Hooker praises 'the great industrie and travell of the husband man which spareth no chardges, forbeareth no paynes, nor leaveth any thinge undonne whereby he may enriche and make his growndes fertyle and profytable',[44] whereas Westcote claims the national preeminence of his county's husbandmen, citing the 'diversities of improvements' by which 'they have much beautified and enriched their soil' (p. 57).

Other writers pursue such concerns with a thoroughly analytical rigour. Robert Reyce's *Breviary of Suffolk, 1618* devotes a series of chapters to the county's 'commodities' (a word used in its broad contemporary sense, encompassing general qualities and conditions), from its position on trade routes to its flourishing cloth industry.[45] His description of the production of hops strikes a characteristic tone of wry detachment coupled with a meticulous appreciation of economic process, as he traces the recent boom and subsequent decline in the crop. The early 'hoppe masters', he writes, drained 'unprofitable marshes and moores', discovered that 'this kind of commodity thrived excellently well', and rapidly derived 'great profitt and abundance' from their labours. Their success attracted a wave of new projectors, 'striving thereby to extract more than an Indian quintessence'; but their efforts on poorer soil, at a time of increased national production of hops, failed to bring the desired returns (pp. 31–2). Similarly, the description of Pembrokeshire written by George Owen of Henllys compiles an almost overwhelming mass of empirical detail about agriculture and geology.[46] Owen's approach has in fact been labelled 'unchorographic', a definition which serves to focus attention on the important generic conventions of chorography, but imposes a distinction which was by no means universally apparent to his contemporaries.[47]

This notable complexity of representation might be explored further by reference to literary modes. Images of unchanging Edenic delight, and of a landscape of ease rather than of labour, fix tropes of pastoral literature onto the native fields. The underlying appreciation of agricultural and economic process, by comparison, suggests the influence of georgic. The nature of this conjunction of modes, and also its

[44] 'Hooker's Synopsis Chorographical of Devonshire', ed. William J. Blake, *Report and Transactions of the Devonshire Association*, 47 (1915), p. 343.

[45] Ed. Lord Francis Harvey (London, 1902).

[46] *Owen's Pembrokeshire*, ed. Henry Owen (4 vols., Cymmrodorian Record Series, no. 1, 1892).

[47] Mendyk, *'Speculum Britanniae'*, p. 205.

significance for studies of seventeenth-century literary history, is elucidated by Alastair Fowler's studies of the mixture of pastoral and georgic in poetry of the later Renaissance. Fowler approaches the two genres as 'alternative but overlapping domains of assumption about a similar field of interests', and argues that the rise of georgic throughout the seventeenth century was dependent upon 'a phase of mixture with pastoral'.[48] Chorography, as a form committed to a sense of order and stability rooted in history, could never be expected to embrace wholeheartedly the georgic spirit of industry and development. The marked georgic modulations in many of the chorographical texts, however, evidence a significant cultural shift, as the gentry gradually developed strategies of representation which link an overarching aesthetic view of rural order with undertones of invigorating labour and activity.[49]

Some of the later chorographies exemplify this achievement in their attention to rivers. The *Britannia*, as demonstrated above, consolidates the chorographical significance of rivers as both a structural framework for county perambulations and a vital focal point for the construction of a national mythology. Camden's successors frequently expand upon these assumptions, to endorse concurrently the economic significance of the English waterways. Norden presages the water poet John Taylor as he celebrates the 'delightfull and golden streame' of the Thames, estimating that 40,000 people are 'nourished by' the river, 'as bargemen, ferryemen fishermen and suche as they mayntaine'.[50] The Devon chorographers Tristram Risdon and Thomas Westcote deftly combine the popular anthropomorphic representations typified by Camden's 'Marriage', with particular details of agrarian process. Risdon notes, 'The Teign, near *Newton*, as it were wearied with its bounds, breaketh out and wantonly enriching these low grounds that lie open their breasts to its embraceings, made so plentiful to graziers, and no less beneficial to

[48] 'Georgic and Pastoral: Laws of Genre in the Seventeenth Century', in *Culture and Cultivation in Early Modern England: Writing and the Land*, ed. Michael Leslie and Timothy Raylor (Leicester, 1992), pp. 83, 87; see also his 'The Beginnings of English Georgic', in *Renaissance Genres*, ed. Barbara K. Lewalski (Cambridge, Mass., 1986), pp. 105–25.

[49] The significance of this pattern, at a time when economic success was especially important to maintain the social status of the propertied, will be observed further in the study of seventeenth-century rural poetry in chapter 9.

[50] 'An Exact Discription of Essex' (1594), BL Add. MS 33769, fol. 12ᵃ; on Taylor, see above, pp. 224–6.

butchers',[51] while Westcote traces the entrance into his county of the
Exe, as 'we, in hope of commodity by him, bid him welcome; and he
presently gives the spring's livery, and clothes our meadows and pastures
with a smiling verdure' (p. 95). For these writers, pastoralized panegyric
is by no means incompatible with a georgic appreciation of natural
growth and economic activity. The celebratory purpose of chorography
demands a depiction of wanton rivers and smiling meadows, yet
might also acknowledge the productive pursuits of graziers and
butchers.

Richard Carew, who wrote his *Survey of Cornwall* (1602) amidst the
cultural milieu of Camden and Speed, sustains a similarly complex view
of the land throughout his work.[52] Like William Lambarde, Carew
combined his historical interests and membership of the Society of
Antiquaries with an active involvement in the government of his county
and a lifelong commitment to the improvement and expansion of his own
landholdings.[53] His interest in the 'practical past' is evidenced by one of
the papers he delivered to the Society, 'Of the Antiquity, Variety, and
Etymology of Measuring Land in Cornwayl'.[54] In his *Survey*, Carew
adopts Camden's structural division between categories of 'general' and
'particular' description; however, his general description is slightly the
longer of the sections, and includes detailed consideration of matters
as diverse as the production of and trade in tin, and the feasts and
recreations of the lower orders. Moreover, Carew draws freely upon the
discourse of the agrarian improver, as his attention shifts from the history
of land tenures to contemporary concerns of estate management. He
praises the tenants of the county, in particular, for their willingness to
abandon the 'mingle mangle' of the common field system; enclosure
'hath directed [the husbandman] to a more thriving forme of husbandrie'
(fols. 38ᵃ, 66ᵇ).

Carew thus sets his description of the lands and histories of the county
gentry within the context of a markedly dynamic rural economy. In the
particular description he introduces a poem upon his own lineage:

51 Risdon, *The Chorographicall Description, or, Survey of the County of Devon, with the City and County of Exeter* (London, 1811), p. 142.
52 Facsimile edn (Amsterdam, 1969).
53 See F. E. Halliday's introduction to his edition of *The Survey of Cornwall* (London, 1953).
54 In *A Collection of Curious Discourses written by Eminent Antiquaries*, ed. Thomas Hearne, 2nd edn (2 vols., London, 1771), vol. 1, pp. 195–7.

> *Carew* of ancient *Carru* was
>   And *Carru* is a plowe,
> Romanes the trade, Frenchmen the word,
>   I doe the name avowe.
> The elder stock, and we a braunch,
>   At *Phoebes* governing,
> From sire to sonne, doe waxe and wane,
>   By thrift and lavishing.   (fol. 103ᵃ⁻ᵇ)

The verse at once celebrates his family's etymological link to the tilling of the soil and embraces the changing fortunes of its successive generations. The spirit of industry and improvement evident here underpins and invigorates the *Survey*'s predominantly pastoral emphasis on retirement. The attendant pleasures of property are brought more boldly to the fore in a poem eulogizing the joys of a friend's fish pond:

> The pleasure which I took at my friends pleasure herein, idlely busied me thus to expresse the same.

> I Wayt not at the Lawyers gates,
> Ne shoulder clymers downe the stayres;
> I vaunt not manhood by debates,
> I envy not the misers feares:
>   But meane in state, and calme in sprite,
>   My fishfull pond is my delight.   (fol. 106ᵃ)

The pond becomes a focus for the speaker's desire for withdrawal from the world of business. Indeed the poem pivots on the final couplet – echoed in following stanzas – which turns from the trials of the outside world to the calm 'sprite' of the landowner alone in the sanctuary provided by his own property. Set within the *Survey*, however, the poem's allure of rustic idyll is counterpointed by an insistent georgic ethos. Carew's version of chorography in this respect presages the landscape of seventeenth-century rural poetics.

Carew's juxtaposition of a rhetoric of improvement and an aesthetics of retirement suggests a view of the country fraught with ideological tensions. Yet this very uncertainty is entirely consistent with chorography's representations of the land. The georgic insurgence upon the seamless conventions of the natural order of productivity in many respects marks the limitations of the genre. Westcote's anxious recoil from his 'lecture on husbandry' denotes, above all, the pressures of generic conformity. But the convergence of interests and discourses also demonstrates the willingness of the gentry, in a period of social upheaval, to appropriate strategies from the contemporary improver. In the following chapter I will further explore the importance of this composite view of the country. The final section of the current chapter turns to a topographical poem which, on account of its vast size and idiosyncratic perception, claims a liminal status between chorography and the mainstream development of rural poetics.

CHOROGRAPHY DIGESTED IN A POEM

The title-page of Michael Drayton's 14,000-line poem claims a place within the tradition of Camden and Speed. It announces:

> Poly-Olbion. or A Chorographicall Description of Tracts, Rivers, Mountaines, Forests, and other Parts of this renowned Isle of Great Britaine, With intermixture of the most Remarquable Stories, Antiquities, Wonders, Rarityes, Pleasures, and Commodities of the same: Digested in a Poem.

The text, published in two parts in 1612 and 1622, is divided into thirty 'songs' on individual counties or groups of counties.[55] Drayton structures each song around the natural features of a region, but also introduces a wide range of historical material, including lengthy digressions on the monarchs, saints and wars of Britain. The poem's connection with contemporary historical scholarship is reinforced throughout the first book in appended prose 'illustrations' written by John Selden, the foremost antiquary of the generation after Camden. When one concentrates on Drayton's representation of agrarian conditions and practices, however, *Poly-Olbion*'s status as chorography becomes more problematic, for Drayton consistently refuses to endorse the chorographical vision of a natural order of productivity serving the interests of the landed gentry. In fact the poem signifies as much a troubled reaction as an enthusiastic contribution to the programme of Camden. Looking toward the rural poetry of the seventeenth century, *Poly-Olbion* highlights certain emergent strategies of poetic representation, yet stolidly resists their ideological implications.

Poly-Olbion takes the chorographical interest in the land to a new plane. Whereas the prose works principally employ topographical description as a structuring principle for their broader concerns, Drayton

---

[55] *Works*, ed. J. William Hebel (5 vols., Oxford, 1931–41), vol. 4.

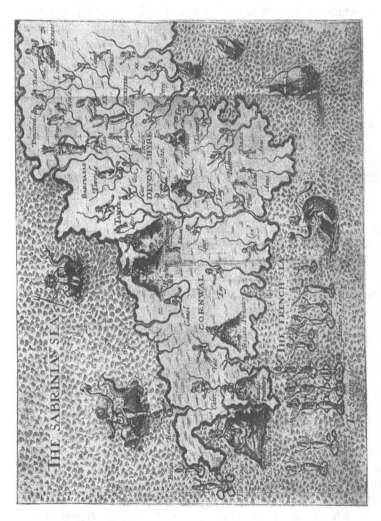

8.4 Map of Cornwall and Devon, from Michael Drayton's *Poly-Olbion* (1612).

consistently fixes attention on the land itself. The poem is devoid of genealogies, family histories, manors and castles; even towns are of secondary concern to the natural environment around them.[56] Instead, to use Richard Helgerson's formulation, the land speaks.[57] Forty-four lines into the first Song, the nymphs of the French Seas interject with a panegyric to the 'ever-happie' Channel Isles. From this point onward the poem becomes a cacophony of voices, as seas, rivers, plains and mountains proclaim their own worth, loves and rivalries. The unfolding mythology of landscape is graphically envisaged in the maps which accompany each song. Whereas the maps of Camden and Speed are intended to provide a comprehensive guide to settlements, Drayton's focus rather on the natural features of the land: rivers and mountains, in particular, are exaggerated in size and depicted as nymphs, shepherds and other anthropomorphic figures (see illustration 8.4). Drayton draws attention to this shift of emphasis when he writes that the maps will aid the reader by 'lively delineating . . . every Mountaine, Forrest, River, and Valley; expressing in their sundry postures; their loves, delights, and naturall situations' (p. vi*).[58]

The breadth and heterogeneity of *Poly-Olbion* frustrate critical attempts to define consistency and convention. Yet Drayton's contemporary and modern readers have also recognized the structural and thematic significance of the poem's variety. George Wither's commendatory verse published with the second volume praises the comprehensive nature of his 'laborious' friend's 'Topo-chrono-graphicall Poeme':

> With whatsoe're this spacious *Land* containes,
> For *Profit*, or for *Pleasure*: I o're-looke,
> (As from one *Station*) when I reade thy *Booke*.   (pp. 394–5)

More recently, Helgerson has drawn attention to the figure of the Muse, which directs the poem's movement and endows natural features of the land with the power of speech. The travels of the Muse fuse the two motivating functions of the poem – 'the perambulatory and the inspirational' – in a manner which at once echoes and revises the chorographer's survey.[59] As Drayton recurrently insists, the Muse is

---

[56] See also Bernard H. Newdigate, *Michael Drayton and His Circle* (Oxford, 1941), p. 166.

[57] See *Forms of Nationhood*, ch. 3.

[58] See also Helgerson, *Forms of Nationhood*, pp. 117–18.

[59] Helgerson, *Forms of Nationhood*, pp. 143–4.

'industrious'. Her tireless quest for detail injects a vitality and purpose into the oppressive weight of the poem's hexameter couplets.

Such features support Alastair Fowler's identification of *Poly-Olbion* as 'a massive georgic poem'. The variety, the nonfictional detail and the peripatetic energy of author and Muse, he claims, mark the poem as 'an impressive transitional work' in the development of English georgic, 'perhaps old-fashioned in its style and ambitious scale, but forward-looking in generic orientation and content'.[60] A georgic imperative is also apparent in sporadic celebrations of labour and productivity. Like the chorographers, Drayton is concerned throughout with the produce of individual regions; his rehearsal of the store of various fish and fowl in the fens of Lincolnshire, for example, musters a rich appreciation of natural abundance and human labour (XXV.31–191). The Muse also turns her eye on occasion to the industry of husbandmen:

> Now, in the finnie Heaths, then in the Champains roves;
> Now, measures out this Plaine; and then survayes those groves;
> The batfull pastures fenc't, and most with quickset mound,
> The sundry sorts of soyle, diversitie of ground;
> Where Plow-men cleanse the Earth of rubbish, weed, and filth,
> And give the fallow lands their seasons and their tylth:
> Where, best for breeding horse, where cattell fitst to keepe;
> Which goode for bearing Corne; which pasturing for sheepe:
> The leane and hungry earth, the fat and marly mold,
> Where sands be alwaies hot, and where the clayes be cold;
> With plentie where they waste, some others toucht with want:
> Heere set, and there they sowe; here proine, and there they plant.
>
> (III.347–58)

The Muse's sweep across the landscape gathers a momentum of growth and productivity. At the centre of the passage, the image of ploughmen 'cleansing' the soil combines agricultural detail with a deft celebration of labour.

But Drayton also hedges his occasional descriptions of husbandry with a telling hesitancy. A passage on Kentish orchards prompts the comment, 'But, with these tryfling things why idly doe I toy'?; a catalogue of garden produce is similarly dismissed as 'triviall' (XVIII.698; XX.61). For Drayton's appreciation of 'chorographical description' admits the activities of agriculture only as peripheral concerns, lending local life

---

60 Fowler, 'Beginnings', pp. 118–20.

and colour to the poem without significantly affecting its meaning. More commonly, in fact, he incorporates husbandmen into his controlling purpose of national panegyric. Human labourers are depicted in scenes of idealized ease, with a literary heritage in pastoral rather than georgic. The 'Sheepheards King' of the Cotswolds sits in state:

> In his gay Bauldrick sits at his lowe grassie Bord,
> With Flawns, Curds, Clowted-creame, and Country dainties stor'd:
> And, whilst the Bag-pipe playes, each lustie jocund Swaine
> Quaffes Sillibubs in Kans, to all upon the Plaine,
> And to their Country-Girles, whose Nosegayes they doe weare,
> Some Roundelayes doe sing: the rest, the burthen beare.
>
> (XIV.271–8)

This approach is furthered by Drayton's characteristic blurring of distinctions between actual labourers and mythological figures. Thus the poem's bustling array of nymphs, naiads, fawns and dryads follow similar pursuits to the shepherds of the Cotswolds: in one account, playing 'At *Hood-winke, Barley-breake,* at *Tick,* or *Prison-base*', through the 'Fountaines, Fields, and Groves' of Cumberland (XXX.134, 132).

In its representation of rural England, then, Drayton's poem attains a blend of pleasures and profits, pastoral and georgic, similar to that achieved in contemporary prose works of chorography. But there is one crucial difference. For unlike the representations of agrarian process in the mainstream chorographical tradition, *Poly-Olbion*'s natural order of productivity is rarely fixed to an order of property. With the exception of sporadic encomia upon his patrons, the poem consistently fails even to recognize the Jacobean gentry and their proprietary attachment to the land.[61] Consequently, while Drayton's antipathy for James I has widely been acknowledged as an important influence upon his work, Helgerson's argument that *Poly-Olbion* endorses instead the interests of the country gentry is more questionable.[62] Helgerson links the poem's revelation of the land to the chorographical construction of a form of patriotism no longer dependent upon the enabling figure of the monarch. Whereas chronicle history traces the acts of the nation's rulers, chorography derives its purpose from the physical form of the land

---

[61] Nor do Selden's 'illustrations' offer any sustained consideration of genealogy and heraldry; they focus rather on antiquarian research and monarchical history.

[62] *Forms of Nationhood,* especially pp. 145–6. On Drayton and James I, see also David Norbrook, *Poetry and Politics in the English Renaissance* (London, 1984), ch. 8.

and the local histories of its owners. But Drayton departs from the characteristic manner of chorography in this respect. In his prefatory statement 'To the Generall Reader', he introduces the work with the metaphor of a mythical journey into the

> Feelds of the Muses, where through most delightfull Groves the Angellique harmony of Birds shall steale thee to the top of an easie hill, where in artificiall caves, cut out of the most naturall Rock, thou shalt see the ancient people of this Ile delivered thee in their lively images: from whose height thou mai'st behold both the old and later times, as in thy prospect, lying farre under thee; then convaying thee downe by a soule-pleasing Descent through delicate embrodered Meadowes, often veined with gentle gliding Brooks; in which thou maist fully view the dainty Nymphes in their simple naked bewties, bathing them in Crystalline streames; which shall lead thee, to most pleasant Downes, where harmlesse Shepheards are, some exercising their pipes, some singing roundelaies, to their gazing flocks. (vol. IV, v*)

While the reader's journey incorporates the conventional destinations of chorography, from descriptions of 'the ancient people of this Ile' to the pastoralized 'harmlesse Shepheards' on the 'most pleasant Downes', Drayton gives a new prominence to the land itself. His metaphor recalls the structure of Camden's 'The Marriage of Tame and Isis', which also starts in a cave and then moves across a mythologized landscape. But whereas Camden's poem played a subsidiary function within the *Britannia*, Drayton's method actually inverts the chorographical hierarchy. In *Poly-Olbion* the 'embrodered Meadowes' rather than the 'ancient' (and still less the present) inhabitants, will be Drayton's central concern.

Within this perceptual framework, the fertile region does not merely provide a geographical context for chorographical description, but becomes the true subject of the poem. Drayton endorses the appreciation of fertility as an index of beauty; however, the Muse's vision subsumes 'worldly' or 'transitory' concerns beneath a mythologizing conception of the essential character of the land.[63] Hence fertility is frequently raised in boasts made by a region in an attempt to woo a paramour or overcome a rival. The Welsh valley of the River Clwyd is praised by the enamoured north wind:

---

[63] See the Muse's defence of poetry, at XXI.131–64.

With joy, my *Dyffren Cluyd*, I see thee bravely spred,
Survaying every part, from foote up to thy head;
Thy full and youthfull breasts, which in their meadowy pride,
Are brancht with rivery veines, Meander-like that glide.
I further note in thee, more excellent then these

· · ·

Thy plumpe and swelling wombe, whose mellowy gleabe doth beare
The yellow ripened sheafe, that bendeth with the eare.

(X.91–8)

The description of the valley's 'swelling wombe' of corn conventionally
asserts the beauty of the productive land. It may be aligned with
Camden's representation of Ceres on the frontispiece of *Britannia*,
or his River Tame with her 'locks [knit] with eares of corn'. The
productivity, however, is only barely connected to the interests of the
possessors of the countryside. Drayton's construction of the nation,
shaped through the voices of valleys, winds and hills, looks curiously
askance at the more overtly political struggles over the meaning of the
English landscape.

Indeed Drayton's images of natural beauty and abundance are as
often threatened as endorsed by recognition of the land's possessors.
Throughout his career, Drayton's characteristic reaction to manifestations of change was to judge the present against the idealized standards
of the past. In his early Jacobean poem *The Owle*, this approach bound
political satire to a sustained attack on 'ravenous' landlords, who enclose
common land, raise rents and entry fines, and ultimately force their
tenants from the land.[64] In *Poly-Olbion* his attention to the forests, in
particular, is underpinned by a profound disgust at the exploitative
desires of humanity. The decay of the forests was of course a significant
contemporary issue, which occupied a number of the authors considered
in chapters 5 and 6.[65] Drayton, however, pursues the problem from a new
perspective. He depicts forests not as economic resources, but rather as
coherent and vibrant geographical regions which occupy an integral
position in the natural structure of the land. Therefore his recurrent
complaints at the destruction of England's forests present the case of the
land itself against the 'base Averice' of humanity (XXIII.19). In Dorset,
the River Frome and the Muse bemoan the fate of Blackmore Forest:

---

[64] *Works*, vol. 2, lines 819–48.
[65] See, for example, Arthur Standish's *The Commons Complaint* (1611) and *New
Directions of Experience* (first published in 1613).

> Whose bigge and lordlie Oakes once bore as brave a saile
> As they themselves that thought the largest shades to spred:
> But mans devouring hand, with all the earth not fed,
> Hath hew'd her Timber downe. Which wounded, when it fell,
> By the great noise it made, the workmen seem'd to tell
> The losse that to the Land would shortlie come thereby,
> Where no man ever plants to our posteritie:
> That when sharp Winter shoots her sleet and hardned haile,
> Or suddaine gusts from Sea, the harmlesse Deere assaile,
> The shrubs are not of power to sheeld them from the wind.
>
> (II.62–71)

While the criticism that 'no man ever plants to our posteritie' echoes the calls for economic planning propounded in husbandry and surveying manuals, Drayton's appreciation of national strength is mediated through an emotive complaint at the disturbance of an ecological order. The passage evades at once the improvers' notions of renewal and expansion and the chorographers' celebrations of the fruits of the land. The English oak would be established in the eighteenth century as a symbol of the patrician values of the aristocracy; by comparison, Drayton's 'bigge and lordlie Oakes' denote a force strangely unrelated to the interests of their owners and despoilers.[66] The sense of 'losse . . . to the Land' gestures toward current political and economic arguments, but seeks refuge in a conception of nationhood beyond the reach of 'mans devouring hand'.

The only other suffering Drayton acknowledges is that of the 'harmlesse Deere', a creature which serves as a recurrent symbol of the forest environment in *Poly-Olbion*. In an ideal order, as depicted elsewhere in the poem, the deer walks free, 'a Burgesse of the Wood' (XVIII.66). With the intervention of humanity, the deer is banished; the Wyre Forest laments that,

> where the goodly Heards of high-palm'd Harts did gaze
> Upon the passer by, there now doth onely graze
> The gall'd-backe carrion Jade, and hurtfull Swine do spoile
> Once to the Sylvan Powers our consecrated soile.
>
> (VII.297–300)

The deer was not without political resonance in Jacobean culture. Deer

---

[66] On the oak in eighteenth-century culture, see Stephen Daniels, 'The Political Iconography of Woodland in Later Georgian England', in *The Iconography of Landscape: Essays on the Symbolic Representation, Design and Use of Past Environments*, ed. Denis Cosgrove and Stephen Daniels (Cambridge, 1988), pp. 48–50.

parks, royal forests and hunting, around which had developed a swathe of specialized law, were widely associated with royal prerogative and aristocratic privilege. Proponents of improvement were already representing the parks as wasted land, in a discursive strain that would reach a crescendo in the revolutionary milieu of the middle of the seventeenth century.[67] Drayton's sympathetic attention to the deer within its native environment deftly sidesteps this debate. Even the advance of agriculture is represented as a threat to the land, as introduced livestock desecrate the 'consecrated soile' of the forest. In a strategy characteristic of this sprawling chorographical epic, Drayton grapples his way toward an appreciation of nature and nation unconstrained by concerns of property and economic power.

By 1622, when Drayton published the second volume of *Poly-Olbion*, appended by a grumpy preface addressed 'to any that will read it', the chorographical tradition was on the wane. Although writers such as Westcote and Risdon continued to produce local descriptions for manuscript distribution, the sense of a vital national programme which sustained the works of Camden and his contemporaries gradually faded. Westcote wrote at a time when the values of Tusser and his successors were gaining currency throughout the social order. The next wave of regional studies, just beyond the temporal parameters of the current study, would in fact embrace the scientific concern with process and development at the heart of Baconian natural history.[68] Yet Drayton's poem also stands on the threshold of the first substantial body of landscape and topographical poetry in the history of English literature. While Drayton baulks at the convergence of an aestheticized vision of rural productivity and an identification with the interests of property, this nexus provides the foundation for the poetry of subsequent decades.

---

[67] See Raymond Grant, *The Royal Forests of England* (Stroud, 1991), ch. 13; and on forest law, John Manwood, *A Treatise and Discourse of the Lawes of the Forrest* (enlarged edn, 1620). An early critic of parks as sites of aristocratic privilege was William Harrison; in his 'Historicall description of the Iland of Britaine', he argues, 'Certes if it be not one curse of the Lord, to have our countrie converted in such sort from the furniture of mankind, into walks and shrowds of wild beasts, I know not what is anie' (p. 205).

[68] See Mendyk, *'Speculum Britanniae'*, especially pp. 24–37.

9. Rural poetics

Come Sons of Summer, by whose toile,
We are the Lords of Wine and Oile.
(Robert Herrick, 'The Hock-cart', 1648)

The 'discovery of England' delineated in Tudor and Stuart chorography was paralleled by an upsurge of interest in the poetic representation of the English countryside. Michael Drayton's *Poly-Olbion* stands alone, in this context, both for its size and its explicit identification with chorography.[1] By comparison, the overwhelming weight of rural literature assumes less cumbersome forms. From subtle evocations of the land in Elizabethan pastoral, to the particularized attention to local detail in seventeenth-century landscape poems, this literature consistently celebrates the beauty and bounty of native fields. The processes of the earth and the aspirations of its inhabitants coalesce in pageants of productivity. In the valley of the national river, Sir John Denham proclaims to his audience of the middle of the seventeenth century, the 'mowers hopes' and 'plowmans toyl' are accommodated by the reliability of a source of life which flows 'God-like' with 'unwearied Bounty'.[2]

My concern here is to analyse textual conventions which shaped representations of agrarian conditions and practices throughout a broad range of literature. The volume and significance of this material is endorsed by a correspondingly vital tradition of modern scholarship. Moreover, since Raymond Williams's pioneering materialist analysis in *The Country and the City*, critics have increasingly looked to the politics of the poetic landscape.[3] James Turner devotes a monograph to thirty

---

[1] See above, pp. 253–61.
[2] *Coopers Hill* (1642); *Expans'd Hieroglyphicks: A Critical Edition of Sir John Denham's Coopers Hill*, ed. Brendan O Hehir (Berkeley and Los Angeles, 1969), B Text, lines 176–7.
[3] (London, 1985 edn).

years (1630–60) which mark the apogee of rural verse in the seventeenth century; Don Wayne develops the most stimulating historicist analysis in the area around a discussion of a single, hundred-line poem, Ben Jonson's 'To Penshurst'.[4] Such studies will provide a context for my approach. Throughout the period, I will argue, poets were confronted by conflicting networks of influence; concerns of literary genre and tradition were jostled by moral, political and religious considerations. The resulting poetry typically suppresses considerations of social and economic process beneath predominantly celebratory images of a countryside bursting with produce and nurturing values of rural community. By the middle of the seventeenth century, poetic representations of agrarian society consistently promoted a vision of 'merry England', which provided a crucial site of confluence for interests of property, social hierarchy, political stability and economic prosperity.

The analysis must acknowledge from the outset the crucial status of pastoral conventions. Indeed, the chapter will develop the contention that pastoral was widely exploited as a mode peculiarly suited to the idealized representation of rural conditions from the perspective of the landed gentry and nobility. I will approach pastoral in a similar manner to that in which I considered georgic in chapter 7: as a mode which informs strategies of representation, rather than as a set of generic rules observed in the composition of poetry. Notoriously malleable appreciations of pastoral suffused rural poetics, in a continuum which spans from native medieval traditions, through the Elizabethan commitment to new standards of literary decorum, to the overt conflation of pastoral tropes and local detail in seventeenth-century verse. Williams decried a conspiracy: Renaissance pastoral, he claimed, fashions an 'enamelled world', freed of the 'living tensions' of agrarian process.[5] By comparison, I will aim here to move from Williams's bold identification of a disjunction between brutal rural realities and idealized literary representations, toward the agenda of newer versions of historicism. Approaching the material in the context established by the preceding chapters, I want to explore 'what pastorals *do*, and by what operations they perform their cultural work'.[6]

[4] Turner, *The Politics of Landscape: Rural Scenery and Society in English Poetry 1630–1660* (Oxford, 1979); Wayne, *Penshurst: The Semiotics of Place and the Poetics of History* (London, 1984).
[5] *The Country and the City*, p. 18.
[6] Louis Adrian Montrose, 'Of Gentlemen and Shepherds: The Politics of Elizabethan Pastoral Form', *English Literary History*, 50 (1983), p. 416.

The two sections of the chapter traverse the principal movements influencing the literature of the land throughout the years 1500–1660. The first focuses on the development of an English Renaissance pastoral tradition in the sixteenth century. Particularized native referents in this poetry tend to be oblique, and subsumed within textual forms which direct the pastoral mode away from the native fields. The subsequent section focuses on seventeenth-century verse which reverses this trend by accumulating a wealth of naturalistic detail. This movement is indebted to the pastoral mode yet stretches its bounds; in fact literary historians have discerned a 'diffusion' or 'disintegration' of pastoral in the early seventeenth century.[7] Rather than reviewing arguments concerned with the fate of pastoral, my analysis will embrace the variety of writing from the century which may loosely be categorized as rural literature. Indeed a chapter devoted to rural poetics must be drawn, by the sheer volume of relevant material, to devote greater attention to the seventeenth century.

SIXTEENTH-CENTURY PASTORAL

It is a critical commonplace that pastoral conventions proliferated and consolidated in the course of the sixteenth century. There is considerably less agreement, though, about the theoretical and formal contours of the mode. Laurence Lerner posits a mock evasion of the debate in his claim that 'the sixteenth century found no difficulty knowing what pastoral was: it was a poem about shepherds'.[8] But as Louis Adrian Montrose has argued, such a statement offers little assistance toward an appreciation of 'the culture-specific significance of [pastoral] conventions'. 'Merely to pose the question of "what pastoral really is" is to situate oneself within an idealist aesthetics that represses the historical and material determinations in any written discourse.' Rather, a historicist study should aim 'to "reproblematize" the significance of pastoral's dominant modal form – "a poem about shepherds" – and to clarify the mode's historical vicissitudes'.[9] Working within the terms of the present study, I will approach this task by initially identifying the converging, and often

---

[7] Sukanta Chaudhuri, *Renaissance Pastoral and Its English Developments* (Oxford, 1989), ch. 11; Rosemary Laing, 'The Disintegration of Pastoral: Studies in Seventeenth-Century Theory and Practice' (unpublished DPhil. dissertation, University of Oxford, 1982).

[8] *The Uses of Nostalgia: Studies in Pastoral Poetry* (London, 1972), p. 39.

[9] 'Of Gentlemen and Shepherds', pp. 416–17.

conflicting, strands of influence as writers attempt to situate themselves in relation to preexistent poetic traditions. From this basis, I want to explore the interaction between literary convention and agrarian discourse, as successive generations of poets infuse pastoral presumptions into representations of their native land.

The investigation might begin with the central pastoral figure of the shepherd. William Empson found that 'The essential trick of the old pastoral, which was felt to imply a beautiful relation between rich and poor, was to make simple people express strong feelings (felt as the most universal subject, something fundamentally true about everybody) in learned and fashionable language.' Hence the shepherd becomes the ideal vehicle for the fundamental 'pastoral process of putting the complex into the simple'.[10] If one is to situate Renaissance pastoral within the context of agrarian discourse, however, Empson's insight begs some significant questions. Is there any connection between those 'strong feelings' of the Renaissance poet and the more earthbound hopes and fears of contemporary labourers? Are we to accept the dictum of the disgruntled John Fletcher, who ascribes the failure of a Jacobean play to his audience's inability to recognize that the shepherds of page and stage are 'such, as all the ancient Poets and moderne have receaved them: that is, the owners of flockes and not hyerlings'?[11] And what is one to make of the rich allegorical potential of pastoral, which exploits the 'vaile of homely persons' in order 'to insinuate and glaunce at greater matters, and such as perchance had not been safe to have been disclosed in any other sort'?[12]

The Elizabethans' movement toward a degree of consensus on such questions involved a sweeping reassessment of late medieval antecedents. In a study of English and Continental vernacular traditions of the later Middle Ages, Helen Cooper discerns a rich field of interaction between literary and material pastoral. The contemporary French term for this kind of pastoral – *bergerie* – 'itself embraces both the realistic and artistic aspects of the shepherd world'.[13] In England, a similar conception of the pastoral world is apparent in the Towneley

---

10 *Some Versions of Pastoral* (London, 1986 edn), pp. 11, 22.

11 *The Faithful Shepherdess* (1610?); ed. Cyrus Hay, in *The Dramatic Works in the Beaumont and Fletcher Canon*, general editor, Fredson Bowers (8– vols., Cambridge, 1966–), vol. 3, p. 497.

12 George Puttenham, *The Arte of English Poesie* (1589), ed. Gladys Doidge Willcock and Alice Walker (Cambridge, 1936), p. 38.

13 *Pastoral: Mediaeval into Renaissance* (Ipswich, 1977), p. 48.

Shepherds' Plays of the late fifteenth century, which interweave a narrative of the nativity and reflections on earthly transience with the immediate concerns of peasant farmers.[14] The popularity in England of versions of *The Kalendar of Shepherdes*, adapted in the early sixteenth century from French publications, further underlines the remarkable diversity of the mode.[15] The *Kalendar*'s words and woodcuts blend moral didacticism with instructions in astronomy, physic and husbandry. Its construction as a miscellany, which embraces practical concerns of rural labour alongside Empson's 'universal subjects', typifies the vaguely defined yet culturally vital appreciation of pastoral on the eve of the Renaissance.

Alexander Barclay's *Eclogues*, also written in the early sixteenth century, fuse an appreciation for the earthy native rootedness of vernacular pastoral with a commitment to Renaissance learning and the eclogue form.[16] Indeed Barclay consistently conflates Continental literary conventions with naturalistic details of English agrarian life. In Eclogue IV, Minalcas claims that a shepherd must 'bestowe his whole labour / In tending his flockes', and rehearses the rigorous tasks involved, from the need to protect his sheep from wolves, storms and 'hurtfull pastures', to daily tasks of maintenance and care (lines 163–4, 172). He must:

> Bye strawe and litter, and hay for winter colde,
> Oft grease the scabbes aswell of yonge as olde.
> For dreade of thieves oft watche up all the night,
> Beside this labour with all his minde and might,
> For his poore housholde for to provide vitayle,
> If by adventure his wooll or lambes fayle.   (lines 173–78)

The pervasive appreciation of pastoral life as a daily struggle for subsistence admits elsewhere a sharp note of complaint. In Eclogue I, Coridon focuses on the idle lives of courtiers:

> They have no labour yet are they wel beseene,
>
> .   .   .
>
> They rest, we labour, they gayly decked be
> While we go ragged in nede and povertie.   (lines 341–6)

---

[14] *The Towneley Plays*, ed. G. England (Early English Text Society, Oxford, 1897); Chaudhuri, *Renaissance Pastoral*, p. 120.

[15] Twenty editions, in various forms, 1503–1631 (STC seq. 22407–23).

[16] *Eclogues*, ed. Beatrice White (Early English Text Society, Oxford, 1928).

Barclay's 'ragged', hard-working shepherd thus brings a tone and perspective to his social criticism which aligns with the stance of the complaining ploughman observed in the milieu of mid-Tudor reform.[17] Indeed here it may be pointless to distinguish between the modes of pastoral, georgic and complaint as understood through Renaissance conceptions of genre. In a period before the definition of a formal, classically grounded appreciation of pastoral, the rural labourer asserts his potential brusquely to shatter notions of 'a beautiful relation between rich and poor' in the English countryside.

The Elizabethan espousal of classicized ideals of pastoral decorum was as much a source of debate as a force of conformity.[18] But despite the uncertainty which surrounded the mode, developments in Renaissance poetic practice clearly helped to reinforce, and vaguely codify, the undeniable shift from Barclay to the Elizabethan lyric. Pastoral, in the Virgilian rubric for a poetic career, is the low style. Consequently the shepherd is endorsed as a figure of the aspiring poet who adopts the humble reed of the preeminent classical poet. Edmund Spenser's progression from his literary debut with *The Shepheardes Calender* (1579), to the epic fruition of *The Faerie Queene* (1590, 1596), traced the quintessential path of Renaissance literary achievement.[19] Further, since Renaissance poetics were inexorably bound to the milieu of the Elizabethan court, the outpouring of pastoral became 'dominantly aristocratic in values and style'.[20] The imperatives of an increasingly insular courtly culture combined with the emergent poetic ideals to remodel pastoral as a mode exemplary of gentility, concerned rather with the politics of the court than of the countryside. Montrose, in his perceptive article 'Of Gentlemen and Shepherds: The Politics of Elizabethan Pastoral Form', searches for traces of interplay between Elizabethan rural life and pastoral form. What he finds is that 'the suppression or marginalization of material pastoralism constitutes an essential feature of Elizabethan literary pastoralism'. He links this quality – which unquestionably distinguishes the pastoral of the latter sixteenth century from its native forebears – to the cultural demand for myths of social fixity at a time of unsettling socio-economic flux. The pastoral world, 'by reconstituting the leisured gentleman as the gentle

17 See above, pp. 30–2.
18 See Helen Cooper's exploration of this field in *Pastoral*, ch. 4.
19 Cooper, *Pastoral*, p. 127.
20 Montrose, 'Of Gentlemen and Shepherds', p. 426.

shepherd', 'obfuscates . . . a contradiction between the secular claims of aristocratic prerogative and the religious claims of common origins, shared fallenness, and spiritual equality among men'.[21]

This process effected a sharp distinction between the poetic personae of the shepherd and the ploughman. While the tenor of complaint is apparent in medieval pastoral up to the time of Barclay, the polemics of the mid-Tudor period (examined in chapter 1) preempt a bifurcation of the respective modal significance of these two rural figures. Indeed the Elizabethan pastoral myth of social fixity and natural gentility was formed in part *against* the powerful contemporary discourse of complaint. Complaint stressed the interests of the lower orders and the responsibilities of the landowners; its essentially arable ideal of manorial order, moreover, was repeatedly contrasted to the structure of pastoral farming on enclosed and depopulated land. Henry Brinkelow called the pastoral bluff as early as 1542, railing against 'lordes which are shephardes', the 'extorcyonar, grosser, incloser or gret shepard'.[22] The cultural exemplar of this tradition was rather the humble labourer whose production of grain typified the ethical values of the pre-capitalist manor. By contrast, the Elizabethans' reorientation of the shepherd consistently ignored the continuing social controversy surrounding rural labour. Renaissance pastoral manages to suggest a harmonious social structure at the same time that it fashions an 'elite community' loosed from the matrix of moral responsibility which circumscribed the landlord within the doctrine of stewardship.[23]

The characteristically idyllic vision of rural life was further sustained by a consistent occlusion of evidence of social mobility and instability. In accordance with Empson's perception, Elizabethan pastoral suggests a world of ontological differentiations and unchallengeable stasis. The rich and the poor maintain their beautiful relations by accepting, without question, the disparity in their respective positions. Pastoral interludes in romance narratives, in which courtiers adopt the guise of shepherds, reinforce this governing mythology. The noble demeanour of the disguised knights and ladies in Sir Philip Sidney's *Arcadia* is offset by the bumbling rusticity of their hosts, the comic contrasts confronting the reader at every step with the gulf between the appearance of social confusion and the pastoral premise of unassailable difference. Similarly,

---

[21] 'Of Gentlemen and Shepherds', pp. 422, 432.
[22] *The Complaynt of Roderyck Mors* (Strasburg, 1542?), sigs. D8b, B1a.
[23] Montrose, 'Of Gentlemen and Shepherds', p. 427.

Shakespeare's abandoned princess Perdita, in *The Winter's Tale*, demonstrates in her growth to maturity the predominance of regal nature over rustic nurture, and thus makes a worthy match for a prince despite having been raised from birth as a shepherdess. Such strategies also work to erase what was for the established owners of the Elizabethan countryside one of the most troubling facets of change, the dynamic individualism of the middling sorts.[24] (Yeomen, the more pragmatic William Harrison observed, 'with grazing, frequenting of markets and keeping of servants . . . doe come to great wealth, insomuch that many of them are able and doe buy landes of unthrifty gentlemen, & . . . doe make theyr . . . sonnes . . . to become gentlemen'.)[25] Any recognition of the improving initiatives and social ambitions of such farmers would have threatened to deconstruct pastoral's neat social polarities, and thereby disrupt the pastoral veneer imposed upon the English fields.

The central ethos of the pastoral world – *otium* – is also defined against the constant labour of ploughman and thrifty husbandman. Drawn from the lyrical mode of Theocritus rather than the tougher ethics and politics of Virgil, *otium* signifies 'vacation, freedom, escape from pressing business'.[26] It was on the assumption of ease – and gentility – that the shepherd could further be fashioned as both an ardent lover and a thoughtful contemplator of religion. Such assumptions in fact made the shepherd a particularly congenial figure for the Elizabethan courtier, himself committed to a mode of conduct which suppressed all traces of labour under a veneer of artful elegance.[27] This is not to say that native traditions were rejected and that the 'enamelled world' admitted no relation to the English fields. In fact much of the most vibrant pastoral of the sixteenth and seventeenth centuries self-consciously evokes the English countryside, and this tradition merges into the more explicitly English rural verse to be considered in the following section. But the process was selective. In accordance with the imperatives of *otium*, the typical landscape of Elizabethan pastoral was an arena of recreation and rejuvenation. Considerations of labour, complaint and rural business, by comparison, were left to the contemporary preacher, satirist and agrarian improver.

[24] See above, especially pp. 143–51.
[25] 'An Historicall description of the Iland of Britaine', published with Raphael Holinshed's *Chronicles*, 2nd edn (3 vols., 1586), fol. 105^b.
[26] Thomas Rosenmeyer, *The Green Cabinet: Theocritus and the European Pastoral Lyric* (Berkeley, 1969), pp. 67–8.
[27] Montrose explores some of the implications of this connection between pastoral form and courtly practice in 'Of Gentlemen and Shepherds', pp. 433–48.

This elision of rural business is apparent even in the work of the poet who did more than any other of his generation to confront contemporary political issues within the pastoral form. Spenser's *Shepheardes Calender* sets out to define a specifically English version of pastoral, which combines a classicized sense of genre, naturalistic detail, rustic linguistic strains, moral didacticism and topical polemic. Moreover, Spenser's espousal of activism and application is reinforced by the poem's cyclical structure, which offsets the static world of the eclogue with an underlying appreciation of process and mutability.[28] Yet Spenser's evocation of the pastoral age of Barclay and the *Kalendar of Shepherdes* is principally concerned to enlist native authority for a new Renaissance poetics rather than to revive the mood of the past.[29] His lack of engagement with social and economic issues, in this context, is telling. While the *Calender* demonstrates a considerable debt to a 'Reformation literary tradition', grounded in the mid-Tudor milieu of Robert Crowley and Hugh Latimer, Spenser selectively pares away strands of social complaint from the ongoing movement of religious reform.[30] His use of Piers as a speaker in the May eclogue, for example, evokes the figure's heritage in a literature of anti-Catholic polemic, yet admits no consideration of the associated tradition of social criticism. Significantly, as Ordelle G. Hill has demonstrated, Spenser is anxious to transform Piers from a ploughman into a shepherd, a process which privileges the formal interests of the Renaissance poet over the social invective of a native tradition.[31] Furthermore, while other eclogues occasionally sketch vivid images of rural life, Spenser rarely embraces any specific agrarian complaints. In the winter month of 'February', for instance, the moral allegory (with possible political applications) focuses on the aged shepherd Thenot. The vivid description of his flock, 'so weake so wan, / Clothed with cold, and hoary wyth frost' (lines 78–9), primarily reflects the fact that 'their Maister is lustlesse and old' (line 84).[32] Where Barclay

---

[28] *Poetical Works*, ed. J. C. Smith and E. De Selincourt (Oxford, 1970).

[29] See also Chaudhuri, *Renaissance Pastoral*, p. 123.

[30] I believe this strategy marks an important qualification to the otherwise persuasive arguments of John N. King in *Spenser's Poetry and the Reformation Tradition* (Princeton, 1990).

[31] Hill, *The Manor, the Plowman, and the Shepherd: Agrarian Themes and Imagery in Late Medieval and Early Renaissance English Literature* (Selinsgrove, 1993), pp. 156–69.

[32] Alan T. Bradford's study of winter landscapes in the sixteenth century confirms that interest is almost always restricted to metaphorical potential ('Mirrors of Mutability: Winter Landscapes in Tudor Poetry', *English Literary Renaissance*, 4 (1974), pp. 3–39).

might well have seized a point of social comment, the preeminent Elizabethan pastoralist evades the apparent material signification in favour of his poem's metaphorical scope.

A similar appreciation of the resources of his mode is apparent in Spenser's vision of spring, which marshals the heady idiom of pastoral lyric and particularized referents of English rural beauty in the cause of Tudor panegyric. 'Aprill' sets the 'lay' of Colin (Spenser's own poetic persona) against a backdrop of popular seasonal festivities. The political allegory invokes Virgil's 'messianic eclogue' and the pastoral of Christian nativity, while the central conceit etches a national mythology onto the English fields. Colin sings 'Of fayre *Eliza*, Queene of shepheardes all'. His lay moves toward the deftly enamelled world of rural celebration:

> Ye shepheards daughters, that dwell on the greene,
> > hye you there apace:
> Let none come there, but that Virgins bene,
> > to adorne her grace.
> And when you come, whereas shee is in place,
> See, that your rudenesse doe not you disgrace:
> > Binde your fillets faste,
> > And gird in your waste,
> For more finesse, with a tawdrie lace.
> Bring hether the Pincke and purple Cullambine,
> > With Gelliflowres:
> Bring Coronations, and Sops in wine,
> > worne of Paramoures.
> Strowe me the ground with Daffadowndillies,
> And Cowslips, and Kingcups, and loved Lillies:
> > The pretie Pawnce,
> > And the Chevisaunce,
> Shall match with the fayre flowre Delice.   (lines 127–44)

As Spenser directs the attention of his pastoral toward the cultural environment of the court, Elizabeth is translated as the apotheosis of the humble May queen. Intonations of courtly power in the catalogue of flowers reiterate the point; amidst the bundles of spring growth, 'coronations' and 'kingcups' presage 'the fayre flowre Delice'.

The audacious logic of Spenser's 'Aprill' asserts a vital, and vitalizing, identity between the land and its ruler. It thus marks an important early step toward the process Leah Marcus discerns in the pastoral of the seventeenth century, which exported 'a courtly mode to the countryside in a way that imprinted royal power on the rural landscape'.[33] Spenser offers no specific locale; however, his acute sense for evocative detail furthers a contemporary movement toward the literary articulation of an indigenous sense of landscape. Throughout the reign of Elizabeth, in fact, the figure of the monarch provided a cynosure which united pastoral lyric and national panegyric. As Helen Cooper writes, Elizabeth's

> poets found in her a symbol of a perpetual May. Extravagant as the idea may be in literal terms, it cannot be dismissed as mere flattery. The number of poets who took up the theme and the multiplicity of forms it assumed show that it fulfilled a genuine need of expression – a belief that England was a good country to live in, that the Elizabethan age was a great one, that the arts were flourishing as they had never done before, and that all these things were in some way embodied in the person of the Queen herself.[34]

In the latter years of Elizabeth's reign this pastoral of England gathered the irresistible force of cultural orthodoxy. Its vaguely defined yet overwhelming sense of national prosperity compounded Elizabethan pastoral's characteristic occlusion of the contentious fields of agrarian practice and discourse. England was elevated, through the agency of its faery queen, into a living manifestation of Arcadia.

This mythology was dramatized in the royal progresses which were a feature of Elizabeth's reign. The narrative of a temporary retreat from the world of business and government (a narrative which set *otium* against *negotium*) enacted that of pastoral romance. Like Virgilian and Spenserian pastoral, the progress entertainments frequently incorporate matters of political moment;[35] however, their consistent motivation activates the resources of the mode for the purposes of personal and national panegyric. The entertainments conflate Ovidian and folk mythologies, courtly and rural pastimes. They envisage an environment which suppresses the material under the weight of artifice accumulated

[33] *The Politics of Mirth: Jonson, Herrick, Milton, Marvell, and the Defense of Old Holiday Pastimes* (Chicago and London, 1986), p. 19. She develops this argument further in 'Politics and Pastoral: Writing the Court on the Countryside', in *Culture and Politics in Early Stuart England*, ed. Kevin Sharpe and Peter Lake (London, 1994), pp. 139–60. (I am grateful to Professor Marcus for providing me with a copy of this piece in advance of its publication.)
[34] *Pastoral*, p. 197.
[35] Louis Adrian Montrose, '"Eliza, Queene of shepheardes", and the Pastoral of Power', *English Literary Renaissance*, 10 (1980), p. 169.

by Arcadian pastoral. And in the context of a progress the weight was astonishingly physical; Elizabeth's 'roome of Estate' at Elvetham in 1591, for example, was 'all covered with boughes, and clusters of ripe hasell nuttes, the insides with Arras, the roofe of the place with works of Ivy leaves, the floore with sweete herbes and greene rushes'.[36]

Within the highly stylized world of the progress, the queen's mere presence in the countryside transforms the rural into the pastoral. An orator at Elvetham declared,

> All other creatures strive to shew their joyes.
> The crooked-winding kid trips ore the lawnes;
> The milkewhite heafer wantons with the bull;
> The trees shew pleasure with their quiv'ring leaves,
> The meddow with new grasse, the vine with grapes,
> The running brookes with sweet and silver sound.
> Thee, thee (Sweet Princes) heav'n, & earth, & fluds
> And plants, and beasts, salute with one accord.[37]

At Kenilworth Castle in 1575 a Savage Man delivered a similar eulogy:

> O Queene without compare, you must not think it strange,
> That here, amid this wildernesse, your glorie so doth raunge.
> The windes resound your worth, the rockes record your name;
> These hills, these dales, these woods, these waves, these fields
>   pronounce your fame.[38]

The rural poetry of the following century would be embedded in an ideology of property; Elizabeth's version of pastoral, by comparison, is absolutist in its representation of the monarch animating the land as she implicitly asserts her authority over it. The beauty and order of hills, dales, woods and fields manifest the power and glory of the queen.

Muted traces of agrarian concerns in the progress entertainments reveal more clearly the subtle process of pastoralization brought to bear upon the land. Montrose focuses on the figure of 'an olde Shepheard' who greets Elizabeth at Sudeley in 1591. The shepherd apologizes for the simple environment of cottages and hills, then presents a simple yet appropriate gift: 'This lock of wooll, Cotsholdes best fruite, and my poor

---

[36] Earl of Hertford, *The Honorable Entertainment gieven to the Queenes Majestie in Progresse, at Elvetham in Hampshire* (1591), sig. A2b.

[37] *Honorable Entertainment*, sig. B3b.

[38] George Gascoigne, 'The Princely Pleasures at the Courte at Kenelworth', in *The Progresses and Public Processions of Queen Elizabeth*, ed. John Nichols (3 vols., London, 1823), p. 497.

gifte, I offer to your Highnes; in which nothing is to be esteemed, but the whitenes, virginities colour; nor to be expected but duetye, shephards religion.'[39] For once, it seems, the shepherd of literature coalesces with the entertainment's specific context in a flourishing wool-producing region:

> But the economic significance of animal husbandry, farming, and wool industries disappears into encomiastic iconography: in wool, 'nothing is to be esteemed, but whitenes, virginities colour.' Here pastoral's metaphorizing process is quite explicitly a process of purification. The shepherd's assertion demonstrates that the creation of figurative pastoral discourse involves a distortion, a selective exclusion, of the material pastoral world. One of the most remarkable features of this appropriation of pastoral forms by Renaissance court culture is its transformation of what in other contexts was a vehicle of agrarian complaint, rustic celebration, and popular religion into a vehicle of social mystification.[40]

The strategy was repeated in a slightly different context the same year at Bisham, where the shepherdess Sybilla insists that it is 'By [Elizabeth] . . . that all our carttes . . . are laden with corne'; and Ceres steps forward to present her crown, 'the ornament of my plenty', to the queen.[41] Again the processes of productivity are effectively occluded. The shepherdess affirms the powerlessness of the rural community in both agricultural and political endeavours, while the classical goddess offers up her own authority over the rural world to the English monarch. 'Eliza, Queene of shepheardes all' figuratively incorporates and invigorates the English nation.

THE SEVENTEENTH CENTURY

The death of Elizabeth in 1603 fractured a literary movement which was already showing signs of wear. The pastoral mode survived into the seventeenth century and beyond; however, its Elizabethan character was lost, as the relatively stable politics and poetics of the previous era gave way in the face of crystallizing discord at court, in the Church and throughout the countryside. Yet this dispersal of pastoral was in fact accompanied by a blossoming interest among poets in the depiction of

---

[39] John Lyly, *The Complete Works*, ed. R. Warwick Bond (3 vols., Oxford, 1902), vol. 1, p. 477.

[40] Montrose, '"Eliza, Queene of shepheardes"', p. 172.

[41] *Progresses and Public Processions*, vol. 3, pp. 134, 136.

their native landscape. The latter was a diverse movement, which has received an appropriate range of critical attention. Raymond Williams perceives the pastoral mode gathering the dressing of rural detail in order to reinforce an oppressive socio-economic ideology.[42] In basic agreement with Williams is James Turner, who identifies in *The Politics of Landscape* a central impetus toward a mode of 'topographia', which asserted a new level of engagement with rural conditions while maintaining the celebratory impetus of pastoral. Alastair Fowler, by comparison, argues that the development of a descriptive, nonfictional mode overtly concerned with country life evidences a paradigm shift in Stuart literary culture from pastoral to georgic.[43] His arguments are supported, at greater length, by Anthony Low's delineation of the effects of a 'georgic revolution' upon the poetics of the land.[44]

Such divergence of opinion illustrates the dangers, yet perhaps also the necessity, of a selective critical approach to the array of material at hand. By concentrating specifically on the representation of agrarian conditions, my analysis will explore the consolidation of certain predominant movements in rural poetics. The often disparate range of literature, I will argue, is characterized by a commitment to the interests of property. In chapter 6 I traced the emergence of a modern appreciation of property through manuals of estate surveying, while chapter 8 demonstrated a concurrent movement among the gentry to realize a sense of familial value and purpose grounded in the land. Property was assuming a new significance in English culture, and the rural poetry of the century consistently dwells upon the shifting status of the landowners. In this light one can see the poetry negotiating positions between traditional ideals of stewardship and rural community on the one hand, and emergent notions of economic freedom and absolute property on the other. The poetry is rarely committed either to the ideals of a traditional moral economy or to the cause of the improvers; its interest, in the current context, lies rather in the underlying sense it provides of the propertied reassessing the ethics and aesthetics of the land.

My analysis combines considerations of both ideological and chronological development. I will begin with the anxious and unsettling pastoral of the seventeenth-century Spenserians, who self-consciously

---

[42] *The Country and the City*, especially ch. 3.
[43] Fowler, 'Georgic and Pastoral: Laws of Genre in the Seventeenth Century', in *Culture and Cultivation in Early Modern England: Writing and the Land*, ed. Michael Leslie and Timothy Raylor (Leicester, 1992), p. 86.
[44] *The Georgic Revolution* (Princeton, 1985), ch. 6.

resisted the waves of social and cultural change throughout the reign of James I. The rest of the section will trace the consolidation of an orthodox discourse of rural landscape and agrarian order, a movement which gathers momentum from such diverse influences as Jacobean social policy, classicized depictions of the 'happy man', and the politics of royalist retirement. While the immediate concerns of the Civil War predominate in rural poetry of the century's middle decades, I want to concentrate on underlying ideological shifts rather than specific political controversy. In agreement with a recent contextual study of a more restricted corpus of rural poems, I will 'assume . . . that the war was one moment within larger, revolutionary changes in England's economy and that neither the war nor that larger revolution can account for all seventeenth-century social struggle'.[45] This perspective will highlight continuity and the formation of poetic convention throughout the period, while more detailed attention to the poetry of Ben Jonson and Robert Herrick will explore some particular applications and manipulations of these conventions.

The 'English Spenserians' of the early seventeenth century saw themselves as the poetic heirs of the finest moral and prophetic traditions of the Elizabethan age.[46] In their pastoral works, however, Spenser's own impetus toward royalist panegyric gives way to a mood of embittered nostalgia, fuelled by perceptions of the weakness and corruption of the new monarch and his court. William Browne, in his baggy *Britannia's Pastorals* (1613, 1616), adopts the harsh voice of the contemporary satirist as he surveys the land:

> Here should they finde a great one paling in
> A meane mans land, which many yeeres had bin
> His charges life, and by the others heast,
> The poore must starve to feed a scurvy beast.
>
>   .   .   .
>
> The *Country Gentleman*, from's neighbours hand
> Forceth th'inheritance, joynes land to land,
> And (most insatiate) seekes under his rent
> To bring the worlds most spacious continent.[47]

---

45 Rosemary Kegl, '"Joyning my Labour to my Pain": The Politics of Labor in Marvell's Mower Poems', in *Soliciting Interpretation: Literary Theory and Seventeenth-Century English Poetry*, ed. Elizabeth D. Harvey and Katharine Eisaman Maus (Chicago and London, 1990), p. 89.

46 Joan Grundy, *The Spenserian Poets* (London, 1969); David Norbrook, *Poetry and Politics in the English Renaissance* (London, 1984), ch. 8.

47 (1613 and 1616); in *The Whole Works*, ed. W. Carew Hazlitt (2 vols. in 1, Hildesheim and New York, 1970), book 2, song 1, pp. 188–90.

Browne's approach at once challenges the idealizing momentum of rural poetics and reactivates the latent potential in English pastoral to become a mode of social criticism. In Annabel Patterson's analysis, he perceives that 'Britannia is disabled by a false pastoral premise; and it will take the analytical vision of the true pastoral, in all its generic complexity, to make the darker vision perceptible.'[48]

Despite this tendency toward moral agitation, the Spenserians' rejection of royalist panegyric, and their attention to the vicissitudes of rural life, simultaneously facilitate a new level of attention to the beauty and diversity of the land itself. Poets such as Browne and Michael Drayton, as they turned their backs on the Jacobean court, discovered a source of interest and authority in the topography and society of the countryside. The crowning achievement of this movement, of course, was Drayton's *Poly-Olbion* (1612, 1622). Drayton's strategies of national glorification signal a reorientation, however awkward or hesitant, of Renaissance rural poetics, as existing pastoral traditions are revitalized by the contemporary appetite for rural specificity. This initiative had been apparent a decade earlier in Drayton's 1606 *Pastorals*, which introduce a description of a Cotswolds shearing-feast (a passage later developed in *Poly-Olbion*).[49] In the 'Ninth Eclogue', which Drayton added when he revised his 1593 pastorals, the 'poore shepheards' are involved in a scene of natural beauty and abundance.[50] Their festivities take place 'In the fresh shaddow of their Summer Bowres / With sundrie sweets them every way to fit' (lines 50-1); and their board overflows with

> Greene Plummes, and Wildings, Cherries chiefe of Feast,
> Fresh Cheese, and Dowsets, Curds and clowted Creame,
> Spic'd Syllibubs, and Sider of the best.   (lines 46-8)

The poetic attention to rural festivities fuses the pastoral ethos of *otium* with a persuasive impression of reality. It became a popular motif with poets, finding one of its most sustained presentations in *The Winter's Tale*, and passing into the Stuart mythology of merry England. Drayton was himself concerned here with the countryside as a site of reliable

[48] Patterson, *Pastoral and Ideology: Virgil to Valéry* (Berkeley and Los Angeles, 1987), p. 144.
[49] *Poly-Olbion*, XIV.265-78. (Cf. above, p. 257.)
[50] Drayton's first pastoral poems were published as *Idea The shepheards garland* (1593); the revised version appeared as *Poems lyrick and pastorall* (1606). References are to *Works*, ed. J. William Hebel (5 vols., Oxford, 1931-41), vol. 2.

moral virtue, which could be set against the corruption of city and court. Over subsequent decades, however, rural poetics consistently invoked scenes of rural mirth to endorse symbolically an environment of property and prosperity.

Set against this movement toward an orthodox poetic vision of the country, the Spenserians are notable for their marked lack of concern with the interests of property. While Drayton and Browne are capable of describing their land and its inhabitants with remarkable sympathy and passion, their works lack the ideological certainty of so much of the rural poetry of the century. This helps to explain the lively generic disarray of both *Poly-Olbion* and *Britannia's Pastorals*. David Norbrook sees 'the very formlessness' of the latter as 'a symbol of imaginative freedom as opposed to courtly restraint'; accordingly, 'Browne associates the countryside both with political liberty and with poetic inspiration'.[51] Yet the Spenserians never managed to translate such radical notions into an established poetic code. The lacklustre reception accorded *Poly-Olbion* left Drayton disaffected; Browne left a third book of *Britannia's Pastorals* unfinished while he was still in his twenties, and turned away from pastoral. At the same time, Ben Jonson was helping to formulate a far more influential and culturally resonant approach to the poetry of the land, organized around the interests of the landed gentry.

The concept which served to galvanize the new movement was landscape. Turner finds in Drayton a 'shallow' appreciation of landscape, that insists 'on the surface', while Browne, perhaps not surprisingly, saw landscape as 'an intoxicating muddle'. For both writers, he concludes, the idea was merely 'a gimmick'.[52] The poets were responding, with understandable scepticism, to a concept recently imported from Continental developments in the visual arts. The increasing influence of this concept helped to redirect the conventions of Elizabethan pastoral toward a coherent discourse of rural and proprietorial panegyric. Turner writes,

> There is an increasing readiness to discover pleasant pictures in Nature; in the seventeenth century this impulse takes an *organized* form. Contemporary landscape began to be constructed according to clearly-defined principles, guided by a body of theory whose influence can be traced in literature as much as in art.[53]

---

[51] Norbrook, *Poetry and Politics in the English Renaissance* (London, 1984), p. 209.
[52] Turner, *Politics of Landscape*, pp. 12, 18.
[53] *Politics of Landscape*, p. 10.

The concept is clarified further in Leah Marcus's application of artistic theories of *seigneurial* landscape, in which an organizing point of perspective is provided by a country house:

> English literary pastoral makes use of a similar set of discriminations that point to differing patterns of political engagement. The Stuart genre of the country house poem . . . is a pastoral form derived from the classical epigram but also tied to a set of Jacobean and Caroline initiatives for reversing the growth of London and increasing the prosperity of the countryside. Seventeenth-century country house poems . . . present an idealised landscape dominated by a single controlling perspective: the interests of the monarch, the landowner, and the poet himself are aligned.[54]

This literary development occupies a crucial place in relation to the shifts of socio-economic discourse traced through earlier chapters. The celebration of a landscape defined as property extends the perception of the contemporary estate surveyor, whose representational practices assert the status of land as the lord's 'own'. But the poetic landscape is also a more complex environment than the estate survey. For the poets rarely embrace without question a concept of property as the 'emptiable space' of capitalism;[55] indeed, the humanist ideal that poetry should both teach and delight imposed a significant restraint upon the bold spatial theory of landscape. Much of the resonance of seventeenth-century rural verse – as Don Wayne has demonstrated with exceptional subtlety in his study of Jonson's 'To Penshurst' – can be ascribed to the poetic attempt to remould the ideals of stewardship and moral economy in accordance with the imperatives of a new age. The concept of landscape provided the poets a critical space within which to operate.

The poets' reassessment of rural ethics is nowhere more apparent than in their treatment of enclosure. Throughout the previous century, enclosure was perceived as the quintessential manifestation of the collapse, for better or worse, of a traditional social and economic order in the English countryside. While poets of the seigneurial landscape in the seventeenth century typically endorse the authority of custom against the threat of change, the driving purpose of panegyric frequently reduces their opposition to enclosure to the status of glib platitudes. The wonders of the scene in view may neatly be framed by gestures toward the crimes

[54] 'Politics and Pastoral', p. 142.
[55] Robert David Sack, *Human Territoriality: Its Theory and History* (Cambridge, 1986), p. 78; see above, chapter 6.

being committed elsewhere.[56] Meanwhile the idea of landscape promoted a very different notion of the relation between lord and land than that maintained by the sixteenth-century Protestant gospellers. It strips away the previously accepted manorial matrix of duties and responsibilities in order to celebrate the power of the propertied; it turns bonds of moral responsibility into relations of manorial charity. The very concept of landscape is therefore peculiarly attuned to the logic of enclosure, which asserts the primacy of individual rights over ties of community, and links enclosed fields to ideals of order and freedom.[57] In a poem by Richard Fanshawe, Nature asks, 'what availes my store Heapt in a common field', while for Henry More the principal beauties of the land are 'Fair Fields and rich Enclosures'.[58] Although the poets (like the chorographers) characteristically look to a stable order of landownership fixed in time by long lines of inheritance, their representations of the landscape are nonetheless enmeshed in the shift toward a radically new appreciation of property.

This complex ideology of the land was impelled, from the early years of the century, by a renewed Stuart attention to the duties of the country gentry. Felicity Heal notes that James I 'used the language of the "country" and its values with a passion that suggests conviction'.[59] But what *was* this language and what were its values? Was James reactivating the ideals of the mid-Tudor reformers, or was he rather revising malleable ideas of rural order and prosperity? Historians typically interpret the Jacobean rhetoric as a despairing complaint in the face of incipient mercantilism and individualism. James called upon

> all Noblemen, and Gentlemen whatsoever, to live in the steps and examples of their worthy Ancestors, by keeping and entertaining Hospitalitie, and charitable relieving of the poore according to their estate and meanes, not thinking themselves borne for themselves, and their families alone, but for the publique good and comfort of their Countrey.[60]

But James consistently linked arguments of stewardship to eminently

---

56 Turner, *Politics of Landscape*, p. 126. See also Wayne's comments on strategies of negative description in the country-house poem, *Penshurst*, pp. 38–44.

57 On the arguments of seventeenth-century agrarian improvers, see above, pp. 156–68.

58 Fanshawe, *Shorter Poems and Translations*, ed. N. W. Bawcutt (Liverpool, 1964), p. 21; More, *Complete Poems*, ed. Alexander B. Grosart (Hildesheim, 1878), p. 177; both quoted in Turner, *Politics of Landscape*, p. 127.

59 *Hospitality in Early Modern England* (Oxford, 1990), p. 118.

60 *Stuart Royal Proclamations*, ed. James F. Larkin and Paul L. Hughes (2 vols., Oxford, 1973–83), vol. 1, p. 357.

practical concerns of rural government and economics. In his Star
Chamber speech of 1616 he raised the spectre of 'Levellers gathering
together' (to challenge at once the order of property and the structures of
political power), and argued that the interests of 'the good government
of the countrey' would best be served by the residence of the gentry. The
mid-Tudor insistence upon social justice thus gives way to an equally
pressing focus on social order. He claimed, further, that 'the Gentlemen
lose their owne thrift for lacke of their owne presence, in seeing to their
owne busines at home': a statement which modifies the ideal of a moral
economy in an attempt to incorporate the landowners' interests of
'thrift'.[61] The traditional moralist would have decried concerns of
individual profit as antithetical to the doctrine of stewardship; James
rather endorsed the strengths, as proclaimed by Francis Bacon, of a land
in which 'the plough' is kept 'in the hands of the owners'.[62]

James reaffirmed his position in a Horatian elegy on his policy. He
told the gentry:

> The cuntrey is your Orbe and proper Spheare
> Thence your Revenues rise bestowe them there
> Convert your coatch horse to the thrifty plough
> Take knowledge of your sheepe, your corne your cowe
> And thinke it noe disparagement or taxe
> To acquaint your fingers with the wooll & flaxe.[63]

Though committed to 'Aristotelian notions of harmony and order in the ·
commonwealth',[64] the poem is also interwoven with the language of
agrarian improvement. James is concerned that existing ranks of the
gentry should reinforce their strength in the countryside by taking full
control over the business of their estates. His catalogue of rural riches in
the line, 'your sheepe, your corne your cowe', compounds with each
repetition of the personal pronoun the poem's interest in a strict order of
rural property. The idle shepherd of Elizabethan pastoral is replaced by a
georgic exemplar fully acquainted with the labours – and profits – of
husbandry. A variant manuscript text of the poem yields a telling

---

[61] *His Majesties Speach in the Starre-Chamber* (1616), sig. H2ᵇ.
[62] Francis Bacon, 'Of the True Greatness of Kingdoms and Estates'; *Works*, ed.
 J. Spedding et al. (14 vols., London, 1857–74), vol. 6, p. 447.
[63] *The Poems of James VI of Scotland*, ed. James Craigie (2 vols., Edinburgh and London,
 1955–8), vol. 2, p. 180.
[64] Heal, *Hospitality*, p. 119.

reminder of the logic of improvement: 'Take knowledge of your sheepe
...' is transfigured, 'make mony of your sheepe ...' (p. 181).
James's attempt to refashion the image of the country gentleman was
supported by a wave of interest in classical poetry of the happy rural
life.[65] At the heart of this movement stood Horace's second epode
('Beatus ille'), which reflects longingly upon the life of a man of rural
property:

> *Happie* is he, that from all Businesse cleere,
> As the old race of Mankind were,
> With his owne Oxen tills his Sire's left lands,
> And is not in the Usurers bands.[66]

Maren-Sofie Røstvig erects a questionable dichotomy between fact and
fiction when she claims that in this tradition the shepherd of Elizabethan
pastoral 'becomes metamorphosed into a farmer, and steps out of an
imaginary landscape into a real countryside'.[67] This poem, one might
counter, is as much an idyllic dream as an Elizabethan lyric of love in the
shade. (An element of urban wish-fulfilment is embedded in the poem,
framed by Horace as a speech of a city usurer fantasizing about his
future prosperity. This point was often ignored by seventeenth-century
translators, anxious to claim the poem for their own purposes.)
Moreover, the idealized representations of the country life fostered by
the widespread dissemination, translation and imitation of such poetry
depart from the pastoral of the previous century in their explicit
endorsements of rural property and productivity. Indeed any assumption
that retirement from political life also involved a withdrawal from
economic activity is clearly mistaken, contradicted also by evidence of
royalists who used their time in the country as an opportunity to take a
closer interest in the management of their estates.[68] '*Happie* is he' who
'With his owne Oxen tills his Sire's left lands'. In this period, Patterson

[65] See Maren-Sofie Røstvig, *The Happy Man: Studies in the Metamorphoses of a Classical Ideal 1600–1700* (Oslo, 1954).
[66] Ben Jonson's translation (*Ben Jonson*, ed. C. H. Herford, Percy Simpson and Evelyn Simpson, 1st edn (11 vols., Oxford, 1925–52), vol. 8, p. 289).
[67] *Happy Man*, p. 103.
[68] J. H. Bettey provides the example of Theophilus, Earl of Suffolk, who retired from the court in 1635 and devoted the last five years of his life to a vigorous programme of improvement on his Dorset estates. Like many men of the upper gentry and nobility involved in government service, Theophilus had never before had such an opportunity to take his own affairs in hand ('Agriculture and Rural Society in Dorset, 1570–1670' (unpublished Ph.D dissertation, University of Bristol, 1976), pp. 143–4).

observes, 'the cultural history of pastoral becomes truly inseparable from georgic'.[69]

The seventeenth-century landscape, in accordance with these various cultural forces, recalls the classical ethos of 'profit and pleasure'. In chapter 5, I traced the emergence in Elizabethan husbandry manuals of the figure of the landlord who combines the goals of profit and pleasure in his active supervision of a thriving estate.[70] In the following century this ethos highlights the subtle georgic energy instilled into the gentry's controlling discourse of stable rural retreat. Thus William Chamberlayne's survey of 'lovely Landskips' incorporates within a predominantly pastoralized environment of 'fresh cool shade' and piping shepherds a striking figure of rural labour:

> The painful Husbandman, whose Labour steeld
> With fruitful hopes, in a deep study how
> T'improve the Earth, follows his slow-pac'd Plow.[71]

On a broader scale, Sir John Denham surveys from Cooper's Hill a prospect of 'wealth and beauty' nourished by the Thames:[72]

> No unexpected inundations spoyl
> The mowers hopes, nor mock the plowmans toyl:
> But God-like his unwearied Bounty flows;
> First loves to do, then loves the Good he does.
> Nor are his Blessings to his banks confin'd,
> But free, and common, as the Sea or Wind;
> When he to boast, or to disperse his stores
> Full of the tributes of his grateful shores,
> Visits the world, and in his flying towers
> Brings home to us, and makes both *Indies* ours;
> Finds wealth where 'tis, bestows it where it wants
> Cities in deserts, woods in Cities plants.
> So that to us no thing, no place is strange,
> While his fair bosom is the worlds exchange. (lines 175–88)

The 'God-like' flow of 'unwearied Bounty' evokes literary fantasies of a land of Cockaigne, bursting with milk and honey. (This is, of course, a

---

[69] *Pastoral and Ideology*, p. 134.
[70] See above, pp. 137–43.
[71] *Pharonnida* (1659), I, p. 144; quoted in James Turner, *'Topographia* and Topographical Poetry in English, 1640–1660' (unpublished DPhil. dissertation, University of Oxford, 1976), pp. 48–9.
[72] *Coopers Hill*, line 226.

recurrent motif of pastoral.) But equally important to Denham's poem are the 'mowers hopes' and 'plowmans toyl'. Although the endorsement of labour is immediately undercut by the insistence on *natural* bounty, these subtle georgic modulations nonetheless contribute to the poem's mood of an expansive energy harnessed and directed.[73] This sense of an English spirit of labour and improvement underpins the poem's subsequent vision of international trade and economic expansion, which places the rural order of profits and pleasures within a developing national mythology of rural prosperity.

Denham's poem was written within an atmosphere of impending political upheaval, which lent a new urgency to dreams of economic expansion achieved within the framework of a stable social hierarchy. This context helps to explain the constraints placed upon representations of rural labour and labourers in rural poetry of the period. Denham can gesture toward commercial activity; however, the decorum of rural poetics will not admit depiction of the various chapmen, artisans and merchants crucial to the generation of a market-based prosperity. Most notably, the poetry consistently occludes the energies and aspirations of the rural middling sorts, a practice which places seventeenth-century rural poetics in the tradition of Elizabethan pastoral, and also sets it apart from the more vigorous georgic strains examined in chapter 7. The poem of the rural landscape typically polarizes rural society into the landed and the labourers: those with property in land and those with property in their own labour.[74] The otherness of the labourers serves to legitimize and stabilize the power of the landowners throughout a period actually marked by troubling conditions of uncertainty and flux.

This strategy may be illustrated by consideration of two further seventeenth-century representations of the ploughman. In Thomas Bancroft's address 'To Swarston' the ploughman provides a vital index of rural productivity:

> *Swarston*, when I behold thy pleasant sight,
> Whose River runs a progresse of Delight,
> Joy'd with the beauties of fresh flowery plaines,

---

[73] John Chalker claims the poem as georgic, in *The English Georgic: A Study in the Development of a Form* (London, 1969), pp. 67–70.

[74] Wayne notes that in the later seventeenth century John Locke 'would justify the institution of private property and its unequal distribution by deriving property in things from labor, but only after having defined labor as a thing, a form of property, a commodity equivalent to land and money' (*Penshurst*, p. 24).

And bounteous fields, that crowne the Plow-mans paines:
I sigh (that see my native home estrang'd)
For Heaven, whose Lord and tenure's never changed.[75]

Thomas Stanley's 1651 encomium on 'The Spring' observes the farmer within a conventionally feminized landscape:[76]

> Now in their new robes of green
> Are the Plowmans labours seen:
> Now the lusty teeming Earth
> Springs each hour with a new birth.[77]

Bancroft and Stanley are utterly conventional in their insistence upon the worker's 'paines' and 'labours'; the significance of the ploughman, in accordance with a rich textual tradition, depends upon his labour. Consequently the quintessential English labourer is enlisted to evoke the economic vigour of a structure of property, which is typically linked in rural poetry of the century with a system of monarchy.[78] The ploughman is also associated with a certain type of labour. His position within an arable farming system suggests a form of rural production characterized by relatively stable structures of social hierarchy. The forest and pasture regions, which tended to harbour societies at once 'more individualistic' and 'less circumscribed by ancient custom', are scarcely touched upon by landscape poets.[79] Rather, the poets are concerned to reinforce the mythology of a landscape shaped around the gentry's ideals of economic productivity and social control.

At this point I want to pursue a more detailed analysis of two of the most prominent and influential seventeenth-century poets of the land, Ben Jonson and Robert Herrick. Jonson's 'To Penshurst' initiated the form of

---

[75] *Two Bookes of Epigrammes and Epitaphs* (1639), sig. C3ᵃ.
[76] For discussions of the ways in which gender relations are commonly encoded in representations of rural landscapes, see Carolyn Merchant, *The Death of Nature: Women, Ecology and the Scientific Revolution* (London, 1980), ch. 1; and Carol Fabricant, 'Binding and Dressing Nature's Loose Tresses: The Ideology of Augustan Landscape Design', *Studies in Eighteenth-Century Culture*, 8 (1979), pp. 109–35.
[77] *Poems and Translations*, ed. Galbraith Miller Crump (Oxford, 1962), p. 91.
[78] One might note, in Bancroft's poem, the river's '*progresse* of Delight' and the fields that '*crowne* the Plow-mans paines' [my italic]. The language of royalism recalls Leah Marcus's insights about the poetic imprinting of royal power on the countryside (*Politics of Mirth*, p. 19).
[79] Thirsk, 'The Farming Regions of England', in *AHEW IV*, pp. 1–15; David Underdown, *Revel, Riot and Rebellion: Popular Politics and Culture in England 1603–1660* (Oxford, 1985), pp. 4–8.

the country house poem, which fashioned idealizations of rural estates in agreement with both Stuart social policy and classical ideals of the country life.[80] The social politics of these poems, however, have prompted critical disagreement. Country house poems have variously been read as reactionary pastoral, progressive georgic and a subtle espousal of values 'indicative of the rise of capitalism'.[81] Against this diverse backdrop of critical opinion, it will be useful to consider the place of 'To Penshurst' within the developing patterns of rural poetics which have been the subject of the current chapter. I want to focus in particular on Jonson's reappraisal of certain values of social and economic order, as he attempts to negotiate a position between traditional ideas of rural society and 'the pressures of a new age'.[82]

Jonson's poem begins with a strategy of definition by negatives, which contrasts the conditions of Sir Robert Sidney's estate with those obtaining elsewhere:[83]

> Thou art not, PENSHURST, built to envious show,
>   Of touch, or marble; nor canst boast a row
> Of polish'd pillars, or a roofe of gold:
>   Thou hast no lantherne, whereof tales are told;
> Or stayre, or courts; but stand'st an ancient pile,
>   And these grudg'd at, art reverenc'd the while.   (lines 1–6)

By isolating Penshurst as a rural ideal, the poem admits a tone of social criticism familiar from Jonson's satiric drama, aimed here at landlords who have succumbed to the moral and economic corruption which he consistently identifies in society. His specific target in the opening lines is the ostentatious 'prodigy houses', popular among the aristocracy from

---

[80] The country house poem has stimulated an extraordinary volume of critical commentary. Among the most notable contributions are: Alistair Fowler, *The Country House Poem* (Edinburgh, 1994); G. R. Hibbard, 'The Country House Poem of the Seventeenth Century', *Journal of the Warburg and Courtauld Institutes*, 19 (1956), pp. 159–74; Malcolm Kelsall, *The Great Good Place: The Country House in English Literature* (London, 1993); and Charles Molesworth, 'Property and Virtue: The Genre of the Country-House Poem in the Seventeenth Century', *Genre*, 1 (1968), pp. 141–57.

[81] See especially Williams, *The Country and the City*, p. 28; Alistair Fowler, 'The Beginnings of English Georgic', in *Renaissance Genres*, ed. Barbara K. Lewalski (Cambridge, Mass., 1986), p. 122; and Wayne, *Penshurst*.

[82] My formulation is adapted from Williams's argument that 'To Penshurst' celebrates 'an idea of rural society, as against the pressures of a new age' (*The Country and the City*, p. 28).

[83] References are to *Ben Jonson*, vol. 8.

the late sixteenth century.[84] Later in the poem he expands the range of his criticism to encompass the moral economy of the manorial estate, through an oblique reference to rural exploitation:

> And though thy walls be of the countrey stone,
>   They'are rear'd with no mans ruine, no mans grone,
> There's none, that dwell about them, wish them downe.
>
> (lines 45–7)

The comment gestures toward agrarian complaint, as it acknowledges the 'ruin' of farmers elsewhere in the country. The succession of negatives, however, reinforces the overriding panegyric purpose of the poem, drawing the reader into the confined, ideal world of Penshurst.

As the opening passage turns away from the abuses of human culture, Jonson constructs Penshurst and its owners as living manifestations of a fundamentally natural order:[85]

> Thou joy'st in better markes, of soyle, of ayre
>   Of wood, of water: therein thou art faire.   (lines 7–8)

The 'better markes' are the essential raw materials of life on a country estate, rooted in the elements of the natural world. From this basis 'To Penshurst' describes the estate's abundance of natural produce:

> The lower land, that to the river bends,
> Thy sheepe, thy bullocks, kine, and calves doe feed:
>   The middle grounds thy mares, and horses breed.
> Each banke doth yeeld thee coneyes; and the topps
>   Fertile of wood, ASHORE, and SYDNEY's copp's,
> To crowne thy open table, doth provide
>   The purpled pheasant, with the speckled side:
> The painted partrich lyes in every field,
>   And, for thy messe, is willing to be kill'd.
> And if the high-swolne *Medway* faile thy dish,
>   Thou hast thy ponds, that pay thee tribute fish,
> Fat, aged carps, that runne into thy net.
>
> . . .
>
> Then hath thy orchard fruit, thy garden flowers,
>   Fresh as the ayre, and new as are the houres.
> The earely cherry, with the later plum,

[84] Hibbard, 'Country House Poem', p. 160; William A. McClung, *The Country House in English Renaissance Poetry* (Berkeley, 1977), pp. 100–3.
[85] Wayne, *Penshurst*, pp. 41–3.

> Fig, grape, and quince, each in his time doth come:
> The blushing apricot, and woolly peach
>   Hang on thy walls, that every child may reach.   (lines 22–44)

Jonson fashions a carefully organized landscape which combines ideals of profit and pleasure. While one of the classical models for the poem, Martial's Epigram iii.58, describes a significantly more busy and confused farm, Jonson's Penshurst is a self-sufficient estate characterized by a rich and beautiful order. Not only does the land 'yield' and 'provide', but the 'painted partrich . . . is willing to be kill'd' and fish 'runne into thy net'. In the orchard the fruits observe an orderly 'time-sequence of ripening', which requires no more labour than the grasp of a child.[86]

Tenants and labourers are also incorporated into the controlling vision of natural abundance. Jonson makes no attempt to depict the physical performance of agrarian labour; instead the inhabitants of the manor are represented in procession to the country house:

> all come in, the farmer, and the clowne:
> And no one empty-handed, to salute
>   Thy lord, and lady, though they have no sute.
> Some bring a capon, some a rurall cake,
>   Some nuts, some apples; some that thinke they make
> The better cheeses, bring 'hem; or else send
>   By their ripe daughters, whom they would commend
> This way to husbands; and whose baskets beare
>   An embleme of themselves, in plum, or peare.
> But what can this (more than expresse their love)
>   Adde to thy free provisions, farre above
> The neede of such?   (lines 48–59)

On their visit, tenants and labourers 'salute' their lord and lady, yet bring no business: the only significant bond between the lord and the lower orders is that of love. But just as the poem emphasizes traditional values of manorial community, it might be seen to write over manifestations of 'an emergent system of commodity exchange in which human relationships have . . . begun to take on a commodity form'.[87] Thus the underlying economic bonds of tenure or employment are transfigured in the offerings of rural produce for the communal board. The description

---

[86] Paul M. Cubeta, 'A Jonsonian Ideal: "To Penshurst"', *Philological Quarterly*, 42 (1963), pp. 17, 21.

[87] Wayne, *Penshurst*, p. 76.

of their gifts as unnecessary additions to the 'free provisions' already on offer, and the associated suggestion of a relationship of dependence rather than reciprocity, serve to isolate the man of property through a neatly comic contrast. 'The farmer', 'the clowne', and their 'ripe daughters' signal the poem's deft evocation and containment of a georgic energy to characterize the productive estate owned and controlled by the poet's patron.

These lines further serve to define Penshurst as property. Under the doctrine of stewardship the labour of the lower orders is counterbalanced by the paternal responsibilities of the landlord. In Jonson's revision of this doctrine, the estate is eulogized as the home of the Sidney family, which the tenants and labourers approach as humble guests; the commodification of labour which accompanies this reification of property is aptly encoded in the image of women carrying 'An embleme of themselves, in plum, or peare'.[88] This reorientation of a powerful discourse of rural order is confirmed in the central scene of a feast. In the dining hall Penshurst's

> liberall boord doth flow,
> With all, that hospitalitie doth know!
> Where comes no guest, but is allow'd to eate,
> Without his feare, and of thy lords owne meat.

(lines 59–62)

The image provides a fitting climax to the preceding description of natural abundance. The community of the estate is depicted as 'not only well ordered, but powerfully integrated in the shared ritual of eating, and so in harmony with itself and its environment'.[89] Yet the scene also allows Jonson to focus briefly on the landlord and to assert his central importance within the manor. For while a concern for the land as property underpins the entire poem, Jonson consistently displaces this focus through the strategy of metonymy. Hence the repetitive use of 'thy' ostensibly refers to the land, rather than its owner; and the 'tribute fish' paid by the pond to the estate carries only a distant, pastoralized allusion to the economic power of the lord. At the meal, however, the food which has tumbled onto the table is clearly identified as 'thy lords owne', and Jonson's panegyric is clinched in the claim that tenant, labourer and poet are allowed by their patron to 'eate, / Without . . . feare'. In 'To

---

[88] On the significance of 'home' in the poem, see Wayne, *Penshurst*, especially pp. 23–8.
[89] Heal, *Hospitality*, pp. 110–11.

Penshurst', as in much subsequent topographical verse, the vision of rural order revolves around a landlord whose power is accentuated by his generous decision to observe customs of hospitality.

The cultural moment of the country house poem continued into the following generation, when Jacobean anxiety about rural order was validated by the impending collapse of the country into civil war. Marcus, however, perceives in the later poems an intensifying tendency to inscribe the arts and values of the court upon the rural estate: 'the country house itself came unmoored from surrounding landscape, from its rootedness in a larger rural topography'.[90] Her argument accords with suggestions that in the shadow of revolution pastoral became ever more bound to royalist myths of peace and prosperity, while a georgic tradition was sustained rather in discourses of scientific and political reform.[91] But perceptions of a polarization between pastoral and georgic, as the armies formed for battle, surely belies the cultural complexity of the period.[92] Although the majority of rural poetry from this period was shaped by the immediate anxieties of royalist authors, one might recognize nonetheless the continuation of a major literary trend toward a richly composite mode of rural panegyric.

Some of the most important rural verse of the time was written by the royalist Robert Herrick, who slouched into a gloomy retirement as a Devon clergyman during the Interregnum.[93] In spite of his apparent personal preference for the city, Herrick's poetry has widely been associated with the construction – in the face of social, economic and political upheaval – of an idealized 'post-feudal agrarian image of "Merry England"'.[94] His poems of rural festivities, in particular, revive 'the notion of the "emerald isle", the enclosed garden, the second Eden in which mirth will flourish as it did before the Fall'.[95] But for all the innocence and beauty of Herrick's rural world, his is also a somewhat unsettled, and unsettling, version of English pastoral. His tendency to

[90] 'Politics and Pastoral', p. 146. A similar argument has been made by Mary Ann C. McGuire, 'The Cavalier Country-House Poem: Mutations on a Jonsonian Tradition', *Studies in English Literature, 1500–1900*, 19 (1979), pp. 93–108.
[91] Patterson reviews these arguments in *Pastoral and Ideology*, p. 138.
[92] I am in agreement, here, with Low's conclusion to his long chapter on 'Georgic and Civil War' (*Georgic Revolution*, p. 294).
[93] References are to *Poetical Works*, ed. L. C. Martin (Oxford, 1956).
[94] Marcus, 'Politics and Pastoral', p. 140; see also Marcus, *Politics of Mirth*, ch. 5.
[95] Peter Stallybrass, '"Wee feaste in our Defense": Patrician Carnival in Early Modern England and Robert Herrick's "Hesperides"', *English Literary Renaissance*, 16 (1986), p. 239.

weave a strand of tough economic pragmatism into the enveloping
fabric of rural celebration is epitomized by his closing direction to the
rural labourers as they enjoy the lord's bounty in 'The Hock-cart, or
Harvest home':

> And, you must know, your Lords word's true,
> Feed him ye must, whose food fils you.
> And that this pleasure is like raine,
> Not sent ye for to drowne your paine,
> But for to make it spring againe.   (p. 102)

The crude tone of 'man-management' that Raymond Williams discerns
in these lines has consistently attracted the attention of critics concerned
with Herrick's representation of a festive landscape.[96] As Peter
Stallybrass writes, 'The lines are so radically ambivalent that they
threaten to subvert the ethic of "communal reciprocity" which is central
to the rural idyll.'[97] Yet I would suggest that, far from being exceptional,
this glance toward the socio-economic machinery which sustained
perceptions of pastoral delight is in many respects paradigmatic of
Herrick's representation of agrarian England. For as one reads through
his weighty 1648 collection *Hesperides*, a subdued but consistent strain
of earthy materialism may be seen to agitate the enamelled pastoral
veneer of his rural poems, endorsing the profits as well as the pleasures
of the land.[98]

   Hesperides announces its intentions from the frontispiece (illustration
9.1). The imagery of mythologized rural festivity which offsets the
central bust of the author establishes a mood of pastoral delight in
keeping with the evocative title, while the wreaths of poetic glory
prepared for the poet give way on the facing title-page to a large
woodcut illustration of a crown, signalling the book's commitment to the
Stuarts. The subsequent 'Argument' of the collection fixes this visual

---

[96] *The Country and the City*, p. 33.
[97] '"Wee feaste in our Defense"', p. 247; see also Marcus, *Politics of Mirth*, p. 149.
[98] Anthony Low argues, similarly, that Herrick adapted georgic for his poetry of rural
    delights. 'Herrick's georgic is significant not only because it is embodied in some of his
    finest poetry, but because it represents, at a surprisingly early period, some of the
    elements that would go into the georgic of the late Restoration and the eighteenth
    century. That georgic represents something of a compromise between Puritan
    enthusiasm for and Royalist rejection of the georgic mode – just as Whig politics
    represented something of a compromise between Puritan and Royalist ideologies'
    (*Georgic Revolution*, p. 273). The substance of my argument here is in agreement with
    that of Low; I have also been drawn, irresistibly, to several of the vibrant poems of rural
    activities that he considers.

HESPERIDES:
OR,
THE WORKS
BOTH
HUMANE & DIVINE
OF
ROBERT HERRICK *Esq.*

OVID.

Effugient avidos Carmina nostra Rogos.

LONDON,

Printed for *John Williams,* and *Francis Eglesfield,* and are to be sold at the Crown and Marygold in Saint *Pauls* Church-yard. 1 6 4 8.

9.1 Frontispiece and title-page of Robert Herrick's 1648 collection *Hesperides.*

imagery on the English countryside:

> I SING of *Brooks*, of *Blossomes, Birds*, and *Bowers*
> Of *April, May*, of *June*, and *July*-Flowers.
> I sing of *May-poles, Hock-carts, Wassails, Wakes,*
> Of *Bride-grooms, Brides*, and of their *Bridall-cakes.*   (p. 5)

The introductory statement overstates the consistency of a miscellaneous collection of poems, written throughout a career which took Herrick from the periphery of the Stuart court to the rural parish of Dean Prior.[99] Yet the verse aptly describes the volume's predominant concern to pastoralize rural England. The attention to the ephemeral beauties of native flowers heralds a chain of deftly touched descriptive epigrams interspersed throughout the book. His espousal of the festive, in the subsequent lines, extends the governing tone of pastoral into the representation of rural labour and society: a strategy Herrick pursues throughout a number of longer poems, such as 'Corinna's going a Maying', 'The Wake' and 'The Wassaile'. In their immediate cultural context these poems endorse the 'politics of mirth' promoted in the cause of political and religious order by the Jacobean *Book of Sports* and the Caroline policies of Archbishop Laud.[100] Within the course of literary history traced here, meanwhile, Herrick's poetry of rural celebration may be seen both to confirm and extend the principal achievements of seventeenth-century rural poetics. Marcus claims that Herrick's 'economics of festival' effectively '*defuses* newer ideas about how profit and labour are related by reintegrating commercial language into a larger structure in which profit is not measured primarily through money'.[101] Read in the contexts provided at once by the collection as a whole and the tradition of rural poetics, I would suggest further that Herrick's poetry cautiously espouses a dynamic georgic ethos, contained within a frame of pastoralized order. Rather than insisting upon the authority of a fading social ideal, Herrick accommodates within his rural verse the interests of seventeenth-century landowners, royalist and Puritan alike, in the improvement of their estates.

[99] The unity of the collection remains a point of critical conjecture. Ann Baynes Coiro, in the face of centuries of Herrick criticism, argues convincingly for the 'integrity' of the volume in her recent study, *Robert Herrick's 'Hesperides' and the Epigram Book Tradition* (Baltimore and London, 1988), ch. 1.

[100] James I, *The Kings Majesties Declaration to his Subjects, Concerning lawful Sports to be used* (1618; STC 9238.9); reprinted in 1633 and 1634. This context – and the literature it nurtured – is perceptively explored by Marcus in *The Politics of Mirth*.

[101] *Politics of Mirth*, p. 150; my italic.

Nestled amidst *Hesperides*'s lyrics of love and celebrations of pastoral pleasures, a number of poems offer a subdued yet insistent argument of rural endeavour.[102] 'A good Husband' depicts a figure familiar from the tradition of husbandry writing developed over the preceding hundred years:

> A Master of a house (as I have read)
> Must be the first man up, and last in bed:
> With the sun rising he must walk his grounds;
> See this, View that, and all the other bounds:
> Shut every gate; mend every hedge that's torne,
> Either with old, or plant therein new thorne:
> Tread ore his gleab, but with such care, that where
> He sets his foot, he leaves rich *compost* there.   (p. 259)

As Anthony Low observes, the poem begins with an allusion to a Horatian epigram, evoking a classicized mode of 'gentlemanly georgic'.[103] But Low fails to recognize the poem's place within a flourishing discourse of agrarian improvement. In the final line Herrick adapts the axiom introduced to English farmers in the sixteenth century by Conrad Heresbach's *Foure Bookes of Husbandry*, that 'the best doung for the feelde is the maisters foote'.[104] He thus endorses an ethos of controlled improvement under the vigilant eye of the landlord, who is vicariously involved in the labours of agricultural production through his daily rounds of supervision. The particular concerns of this 'good husband', moreover, are determined by an ideal of personal property rather than communal subsistence. His 'view' scrupulously encompasses the 'bounds' of his estate: the poem's attention to gates and hedges underscores a concern for the physical enclosure of the master's property.[105]

Several shorter epigrams extend the volume's commitment to profitably directed rural labour. Like the georgic poetry of the Puritan George Wither, considered in chapter 7, these poems often invite moral and religious applications; however, their placement within the rural

---

[102] Cf. James S. Tillman's more selective discussion of two verse epistles, in 'Herrick's Georgic Encomia', in *'Trust to Good Verses': Herrick Tercentenary Essays* (Pittsburgh, 1978), ed. Roger B. Rollin and J. Max Patrick, pp. 149–57.
[103] *Georgic Revolution*, p. 264.
[104] Translated from the Latin by Barnabe Googe (1577), fol. 3ᵃ; see above, pp. 140–1.
[105] Low similarly notes the importance of 'ownership and enclosure' in the poem (*Georgic Revolution*, p. 265).

frame of *Hesperides* fixes them immediately in the native fields.[106] The taskmaster's tone is compressed into pithy moral aphorisms:

'Nothing Free-cost'
Nothing comes Free-cost here; *Jove* will not let
His gifts go from him; if not bought with sweat.   (p. 177)

'Labour'
Labour we must, and labour hard
I' th *Forum* here, or *Vineyard*.   (p. 380)

'No Paines, no Gaines'
If little labour, little are our gaines:
Mans fortunes are according to his paines.   (p. 253)

'First work, then wages'
Prepost'rous is that order, when we run
To ask our wages, e're our work be done.   (p. 241)

The verses combine a georgic energy with traces of a patrician detachment consistent with the closing lines of 'The Hock-cart'. If the play of religious metaphor in a poem such as 'First work, then wages' points toward the labour in faith of an Anglican gentleman, the economic signification suggests rather the doctrine of a commercially oriented producer. In line with seventeenth-century discourses of rural property and agrarian improvement, Herrick explores the practical economics which underpin the prosperity of the 'good husband' in the English countryside.

Turning from these neglected epigrams to the verse epistle 'The Country life', Herrick's blend of pastoral and georgic, stasis and improvement, becomes fully apparent. As a paean to the 'Sweet Country life' of profits and pleasures the poem is in fact erected on a curious deceit, addressed to the courtier Endymion Porter rather than an established farmer. Nonetheless Herrick's depiction of the rural landlord's life accords with the doctrine of 'A good Husband':

No, thy Ambition's Master-piece
Flies no thought higher than a fleece:
Or how to pay thy Hinds, and cleere
All scores; and so to end the yeere:

---

[106] On Wither, see above, pp. 217–22.

> But walk'st about thine own dear bounds,
> Not envying others larger grounds:
> For well thou know'st, *'tis not th'extent*
> *Of Land makes life, but sweet content.*
> When now the Cock (the Plow-mans Horne)
> Calls forth the lilly-wristed Morne;
> Then to thy corn-fields thou dost goe,
> Which though well soyl'd, yet thou dost know,
> That the best compost for the Lands
> Is the wise Masters Feet, and Hands.
> There at the Plough thou find'st thy Teame,
> With a Hind whistling there to them:
> And cheer'st them up, by singing how
> The Kingdoms portion *is the Plow.*
> This done, then to th'enameld Meads
> Thou go'st; and as thy foot there treads,
> Thou seest a present God-like Power
> Imprinted in each Herbe and Flower:
> And smell'st the breath of great-ey'd Kine,
> Sweet as the blossomes of the Vine.   (pp. 229–30)

The exhortation to the courtier to suppress his ambition and draw solace
from 'th'enameld Meads' is fundamentally pastoral, and prepares the
reader for a subsequent catalogue of rural festivities which will entertain
with their 'Nut-browne mirth' (p. 231). Another version of Heresbach's
aphorism about 'the best doung for the feelde', however, highlights the
poem's persistent affirmation of agrarian productivity, while the
subsequent attention to the plough and ploughman further appropriates
for rural poetics established icons from centuries of agrarian complaint.
With the ploughman fixed in a position of employment on Porter's
estate, his activities lend a suitable vitality to the celebration of both the
English fields and the political structure they are seen to sustain. 'The
Kingdoms portion *is the Plow.*'

As 'The Country life' accumulates its catalogue of rural produce and
activities, it gathers a momentum grounded in concerns of property.
Herrick notes '*thine* own dear bounds', '*thy* corn-fields' and '*thy* Hinds'.
Rural festivities are also figured as manifestations of the lord's power
and bounty: '*Thy* Wakes', '*Thy* May-poles', '*Thy* Morris-dance', '*thy*
Whitsun-ale', '*Thy* Sheering-feast', '*Thy* Harvest home', '*thy* Wassaile
bowle' (pp. 230–1; my italic). In the wake of this coddling of the
aristocratic addressee, the final turn in the poem toward those lower in
the socio-economic hierarchy is arresting:

O happy life! if that their good
The Husbandmen but understood!
Who all the day themselves doe please,
And Younglings, with such sports as these.   (p. 231)

The lines, not unlike the troublesome conclusion to festivities in 'The Hock-cart', remind the reader of the labour-discipline which must underpin the profits and pleasures of the lord's life. Throughout 'The Country-life' the courtier is represented as himself a husbandman, whose rounds of supervision integrate him within the working life of his estate. But Herrick's final shift into a guarded authoritarian third-person signals his underlying concern with the business ethics of rural property. The true husbandmen – 'thy Hinds' – must accept not only the festivities provided by the lord, but also the need to maintain his property through the curse of labour. In a manner which foregrounds the ideology of property within which seventeenth-century rural poetics were framed, Herrick yokes the celebration of rural life to a pointed reminder of the place of the unpropertied. As James Turner demonstrates in his study of contemporary topographical poetry, 'aesthetic conceptions of the countryside' were 'sustained by a coherent ideology of Nature and Place . . . "Land" and "place" are equivalent to "propriety" – meaning in seventeenth-century English both *property* and *knowing one's place*.'[107]

There are considerable strands of continuity linking Spenser's world of spring festivities and Herrick's enamelled fields of rural property. The central cohesive force was the pastoral mode. But whereas sixteenth-century pastoral at best admitted occasional gestures toward the native countryside, by the middle of the seventeenth century pastoral assumptions enriched a far more consistent poetic attention to local detail. In the wealth of rural poetry written in the first half of the century, poets reassessed previously dominant ideals of moral economy, just as the landed gentry and nobility throughout the country struggled to define positions in response to the ideological contests traced throughout the earlier chapters of this book. The result is a lively mix of literary modes. Pastoral consistently provides a frame with its associations of beauty, bounty and natural order, while the driving imperative of rural property admits at once a concern for local particularity and a georgic spirit of labour and improvement.

[107] *Politics of Landscape*, p. 5.

The Civil War effected a certain polarization in rural poetics, as royalists retreated to the order and stasis of pastoral, while parliamentarians seized upon the reformist discourse of georgic. But although this perhaps retarded the apparent trends in poetry of the land, the writings of Herrick indicate some of the ways in which a committed royalist might still incorporate within his work a subdued tenor of improvement. In this respect his work also presages the new strains of rural poetics generated after the Restoration. For the dual victories of the interests of constitutional monarchy in 1660 and 1688 signalled a fresh affirmation of the significance of property as a political and socio-economic force. The power of the landed over the king was enshrined in the wake of the Glorious Revolution; new laws enforced the principle of primogeniture, so as to ensure the maintenance of large estates, while another series of laws proclaimed a whole catalogue of new capital offences in the cause of protecting rights of property.[108] The values and aspirations of the landowners were freshly legitimized in the arguments of John Locke, who claimed 'that the unfettered accumulation of money, goods and land was sanctioned by Nature and, implicitly, by God . . . "Government," declared Locke, "has no other end but the preservation of property."'[109]

Indicative of the development of rural poetry within this context is the work of Abraham Cowley, a royalist whose writings of the 1650s proffered an uneasy accommodation with the Protectorate. On the Restoration, Cowley helped to define the revised ethics and aesthetics of rural property. In 1661 he proposed the foundation of an agricultural college structured according to the divisions of Virgil's *Georgics*; three years later his efforts were rewarded by his election to the 'Georgical Committee' of the Royal Society. His *Essays*, published from this position of cultural orthodoxy in 1667, review the uncertain decades through which his generation had lived at the same time that they anticipate a prosperous future. The miscellaneous collection of prose and verse includes Cowley's own arguments alongside translations of the principal classical sources which had influenced ideals of rural living

---

[108] On primogeniture laws, see Tom Williamson and Liz Bellamy, *Property and Landscape: A Social History of Land Ownership and the English Countryside* (London, 1987), p. 122; on crimes against property, Douglas Hay, 'Property, Authority and the Criminal Law', in *Albion's Fatal Tree: Crime and Society in Eighteenth-Century England*, ed. Hay et al. (London, 1975), pp. 17–63.

[109] Hay, 'Property, Authority and the Criminal Law', p. 18.

throughout the seventeenth century.[110] The book blends concerns
of retirement and improvement, gardens of pleasure and fields of profit,
as it surveys 'the *employments* of a Country life' (p. 401; my italic):
its spirit captured in the axiom that the 'pleasantest work of Human
Industry [is] the Improvement of something which we call . . . Our Own'
(p. 421). At the dawn of a new era, Cowley's ingenuous conflation
of pastoral and property, classicized poetics and practical economics,
highlighted at once the complexity and underlying momentum of rural
poetics. As the propertied looked toward a period of political stability,
they were freed to revive and reinforce the subdued georgic vigour which
had characterized the overtly pastoralized literature of the previous
decades.

[110] In a cluster of passages devoted to rural concerns, Cowley moves from a prose essay
'Of Agriculture', through five verse translations from Virgil and Horace, to a poem on
'The Garden' (*Essays, Plays and Sundry Verses*, ed. A. R. Waller (Cambridge, 1906),
pp. 400–28).

Bibliography of primary sources

1. MANUSCRIPTS

Agas, Radulph, Letter to Burghley concerning mistakes in land measuring made in the fens, 1597, BL Lansdowne MS 84, fol. 69ᵃ
'Note by R. A., of what he is able to perform', 1606, BL Additional MS 12497, fol. 346ᵃ
'Note of Radulph Agas touching surveyors, and against the turning of copyholds into freeholds', 1606, BL Additional MS 12497, fol. 342ᵃ
'R. A. to Lord Burghley, showing his art of land measure', 1592, BL Lansdowne MS 73, fol. 107ᵃ
Auchar, Sir Anthony, Letter to William Cecil, 1549, PRO, State Papers Domestic, Edward VI, vol. 8, no. 56
'The Banckett of John the Reve unto pers ploughman, Larens laborer. Thomlyn Tailyor. And hobb of the hill with others', 1532, BL Harleian MS 207
Bull, Benjamin, 'A Table for measure of Lande', Bodleian Library Tanner 298
Burghley Papers, Volume on projects, BL Lansdowne MS 49
Cotton, Sir Robert, 'Topographicall Description of England', BL Sloane MS 241
Dymock, Cressy, Memorandum on the advantages of enclosure, Hartlib Papers, University of Sheffield, 64/18
'Propositions for the erectinge a Colledge of Husbandrye', Hartlib Papers, University of Sheffield, 62/42/A
Enclosure rioting depositions: Derbyshire, 1617, PRO STAC8/64/4
Fella, Thomas, 'A booke of diveirs devises and sortes of pictures', 1585–98, 1622, Folger Shakespeare Library MS V.a.311
Forrest, W., 'The Pleasaunt Poesye of Princelie Practise', BL Royal MS 17D iii
Gardner, John Thomas, Petition to Council of State on improvement of land, Hartlib Papers, University of Sheffield, 8/61A
'God spede the Plough', BL Lansdowne MS 762, fol. 5ᵃ
Hooker, John, 'Synopsis Chorographical of Devonshire', BL Harleian MS 5827
House of Commons: Anonymous speech in favour of tillage legislation, 1597, Hatfield MSS, vol. 176 (11); BL microfilm M485 (47)
'How Mr. Sutton got his great estate', BL Lansdowne MS 825, fol. 66

Jackman, Henry, Notes and Parliamentary Speech, 1597, BL Lansdowne MS 83, fol. 198ᵃ⁻ᵇ; BL Lansdowne MS 105, fols. 201ᵃ–203ᵃ

Johnson, Robert, 'A Breviat of the Survey of his Majesty's Woods in the County of Buckingham', 1608, BL Additional MS 38444, fol. 40

'Certain Notes touching Particular & exact Surveys', c. 1609, BL Additional MS 38444, fols. 91–2

Letter to Secretary Cecil, 1602, State Papers 13 283A, no. 30

Kay, Family Manuscripts, c. 1561–1642, Folger Shakespeare Library MSS W.b.482–W.b.484; X.d.445–X.d.449

Kett's Rebellion petition, 1549, BL Harleian MS 304, fol. 78

Lascelles, Thomas, Anthony Ayot and Robert Churche, 'Reasons to prove that the inclosing of Wasts and Common Forest grounds and Chases are Lawfull, Profitable, Necessarie To the King and people', c. 1604–14, BL Additional MS 38444, fols. 4–5

Le Provost, Peter, and Hugh L'Amy, proposals for the improvement of husbandry, Hartlib Papers, University of Sheffield, 53/14

Libel depositions: Dorset, 1618, PRO STAC8/42/14

Libel depositions: Ladbroke, 1608, PRO STAC8/10/18

Libel depositions: Ladbroke, 1608, PRO STAC8/105/9

Libel depositions: Ladbroke, 1608, PRO STAC8/159/6

Libel depositions: Oxfordshire, 1604, PRO STAC8/31/42

Midlands Revolt statement of complaint, 1607, BL Harleian MS 787, no. 9

Norden, John, 'A Chorographicall discription of the severall Shires and Islands of Middlesex. Hamshire. Essex. Weighte. Surrey. Garnsey & Sussex. Jarsey. performed by the traveyle and view of John Norden', 1595, BL Additional MS 31853

'An Exact Discription of Essex', 1594, BL Additional MS 33769

'Touching the Improving of Parks Forests and Chases with other like wast grounds such as his Majesty may be pleased to consent to', 1612, BL Additional MS 38444

Payne, Robert, 'A breefe discription of the true and perfitt makinge of woade', BL Lansdowne MS 121/21

Shotbolt, John, 'To the Kings most excellent Majestie: Verie necessary Considerations for the Weale Publique', c. 1611–25, BL Royal MS 18AXXV

Smith, William, 'Angliae Descriptio', 1580, BL Additional MS 10620

Spenser, William, Letter to Samuel Hartlib, 1650, Hartlib Papers, University of Sheffield, 46/7

Stansfield, James, Letter to Samuel Hartlib, 1656, Hartlib Papers, University of Sheffield, 53/10

Surveying miscellany, Bodleian Library 4° Y 75 Jur

Van Den Keere, Pieter, 'Atlas of the British Isles', Royal Geographical Society, MS 264.A.35.

Walker, Thomas, 'A Survey of Abuses in the Commons', 1609, BL Cotton MS Titus BV, fols. 256–8

Wanton, Nicholas, Annotated copy of Conrad Heresbach's *Foure Bookes of Husbandry*, Folger Shakespeare Library, STC 13197, copy 1

2. PRINTED TEXTS

Adams, Thomas, *Workes* (London, 1629)

Agas, Radulph, *A Preparative to Plattinge of Landes and Tenements in Surveigh* (London, 1596)

To all persons whom these presents may concerne, of what estate and degree soever (London, c. 1596)

Anderson, Anthony, *A Sermon preached at Paules Crosse* (London, 1581)

The Shield of our Safetie (London, 1581)

'Another Digger Broadside', ed. Keith Thomas, *Past and Present*, 42 (1969), pp. 57–68

Askham, Anthony, *A litle Herball* (London, 1561?)

Atwell, George, *The Faithful Surveyor* (London, 1658)

Austen, Ralph, *Observations upon some part of Sir Francis Bacon's Naturall History* (London, 1658)

A Treatise of Fruit-Trees, with the Spiritual Use of an Orchard (London, 1665)

Aylett, Robert, *Thrifts Equipage: Viz. Five Divine and Morall Meditations* (London, 1622)

Bacon, Francis, *Works*, ed. J. Spedding et al. (14 vols., London, 1857–74)

Bacon, Nathaniel, *The Papers of Nathaniel Bacon of Stiffkey*, ed. A. Hassell Smith, Gillian M. Baker and R. W. Kenny (2 vols., University of East Anglia, 1979, 1983)

Bale, John, *A Comedy Concerning Three Laws of Nature, Moses and Christ* (c. 1548) (Tudor Facsimile Texts, London, 1908)

King Johan, ed. Barry B. Adams (San Marino, 1969)

Ballads from Manuscripts, ed. Frederick J. Furnivall (Ballad Society, 2 vols., London and Hertford, 1868–73)

Bancroft, Richard, *Tracts Ascribed to Richard Bancroft*, ed. Albert Peel (Cambridge, 1953)

Bancroft, Thomas, *Two Bookes of Epigrammes and Epitaphs* (London, 1639)

Barclay, Alexander, *The Eclogues*, ed. Beatrice White (Early English Text Society, Oxford, 1928)

Barker, John, *A Balade declaryng how neybourhed, love, and trew dealyng is gone* (London, 1561)

Barnfield, Richard, *The Complete Poems*, ed. George Klawitter (Selinsgrove, 1990)

Bastard, Thomas, *Chrestoleros. Seven bookes of epigrames* (London, 1598)

Bateman, Stephen, *A christall glasse of christian reformation* (London, 1569)

Beale, John, *The Herefordshire Orchards, A Pattern for All England* (London, 1657)

Becon, Thomas, *The Jewell of Joy* (London, 1550?)

Worckes (3 vols., London, 1564)

Bellot, James, *The Booke of Thrift* (London, 1589)

Benese, Sir Richard, *This boke sheweth the maner of measurynge of all maner of lande* (London, 1537?)

Benlowes, Edward, *Theophila, or Loves Sacrifice. A Divine Poem* (London, 1652)

Bentham, Joseph, *The Christian Conflict* (London, 1635)

Bernard, Richard, *The Isle of Man: or, The Legall Proceeding in Man-Shire against Sinne* (London, 1626)

Best, Henry, *The Farming and Memorandum Books of Henry Best of Elmswell, 1642*, ed. Donald Woodward (London, 1984)

Blith, Walter, *The English Improver Improved* (London, 1652)

Boate, Gerard, *Irelands Naturall History* (London, 1652)

The Booke in meeter of Robin Conscience (London, 1565; STC 5633)

A Booke of Christian Questions and Answers (London, 1579; STC 3294.5)

Botero, Giovanni, *The Travellers Breviat, or An historicall description of the most famous kingdomes in the World*, translated from the Italian by Robert Johnson (?) (London, 1601)

Bourne, William, *A booke called the Treasure for traveilers* (London, 1578)

Brathwait, Richard, *Barnabe Itinerarium, or Barnabees Journall* (London, 1638)

The English Gentleman (London, 1630)

Breton, Nicholas, *Works in Verse and Prose*, ed. Alexander B. Grosart (2 vols., New York, 1966)

Brewer, Thomas, *A dialogue bewixt a Cittizen, and a poore countreyman and his wife* (London, 1636)

Brinkelow, Henry, *The Complaynt of Roderyck Mors* (Strasburg, 1542?); ed. J. Meadows Cowper (Early English Text Society, London, 1874)

Brooke, Ralph, *A Discoverie of Certaine Errours Published in Print in the Much Commended Britannia, 1594; To which are added, The Learned Mr Camden's Answer to this Book; and Mr Brooke's Reply* (London, 1724)

Brossard, D., *A booke of the art and maner, howe to plante and graffe all sortes of trees*, translated from the French by Leonard Mascall (London, 1569)

Browne, William, *The Whole Works*, ed. W. Carew Hazlitt (2 vols. in 1, Hildesheim and New York, 1970)

Browne, William, et al., *The Shepheards Pipe* (London, 1614)

Burton, William, *The Description of Leicester-Shire* (London, 1622)

Bush, Edward, *A sermon preached at Paules crosse on Trinity sunday, 1571* (London, 1576)

Butler, Charles, *The Feminine Monarchie* (Oxford, 1606)

Camden, William, *The abridgment of Camden's Britannia* (London, 1625)

Annals, or, The historie of the princesse Elizabeth, late Queen of England, translated from the Latin by R. Norton (London, 1635)

Britannia (London, 1586)

Britannia (London, 1607)

Britannia, translated from the Latin by Philemon Holland (London, 1610)

Epistolae (London, 1691)

'Poems by William Camden, With Notes and Translations from the Latin', ed. George Burke Johnston, *Studies in Philology*, 72 (1975), no. 5 (texts and studies)

Remaines concerning Britaine (London, 1614)

Campion, Thomas, *Works*, ed. Percival Vivian (Oxford, 1909)

Caradoc of Llancarfan, *A historie of Cambria, now called Wales*, translated from the Welsh by Humphrey Llwyd (London, 1584)

Carew, Richard, *The Survey of Cornwall* (London, 1602); facsimile edn (Amsterdam, 1969)

Carew, Thomas, *Certaine godly and necessarie Sermons* (London, 1603)

Carew, Thomas, *Poems*, ed. R. Dunlap (London, 1949)

Carpenter, John, *The Plaine-Man's Spirituall Plough* (London, 1607)

Carpenter, Nathanael, *Geography Delineated Forth in Two Bookes* (Oxford, 1625)

Carter, Bezaleel, *Christ his Last Will, and John his Legacy* (London, 1621)

Cato, Marcus, *On Agriculture*, edited and translated from the Latin by William Davis Hooper (Loeb Classical Library, Cambridge, Mass., 1934)

Certayne causes gathered together, wherin is shewed the decaye of England, only by the great multitude of shepe (London, 1552?; STC 9980.5)

Certayne Sermons, or Homelies, appoynted by the kynges Majestie, to be declared and redde, by all persones, Vicars, or Curates, every Sondaye (London, 1547; STC 13638.5)

Chamberlayne, William, *Pharonnida: A heroick poem* (London, 1659)

Chamberlen, Peter, *The Poore Mans Advocate* (London, 1649)

Chaucer, Geoffrey, *The Riverside Chaucer*, ed. Larry D. Benson, 3rd edn (Oxford, 1988)

Cheke, Sir John, *The hurt of sedicion howe grevous it is to a Commune welth* (London, 1549)

Chettle, Henry, *Piers Plainnes seaven yeres Prentiship* (London, 1595)

The Chorography of Suffolk, ed. Diarmaid MacCulloch (Suffolk Records Society, Ipswich, 1976)

Churche, Rooke, *An olde thrift newly revived* (London, 1612)

Churchyard, Thomas, *Churchyards Challenge* (London, 1593)

   Davy Dycars dreame (London, 1552?)

   A Myrrour for man where in he shall see the myserable state of thys worlde (London, c. 1552)

   A Sparke of Frendship and Warme Goodwill (London, 1588)

   The Worthines of Wales (London, 1587)

Churchyard, Thomas, et al., *The Contention bettwyxte Churchyeard and Camell, upon David Dycers Dreame* (London, 1560)

Clarke, William, *The Clarke Papers: Selections from the Papers of William Clarke*, ed. C. H. Firth (London, 1992)

Clay, Thomas, *Briefe and Necessary Tables for the Valuation of Leases* (London, 1622)

Cokaine, Aston, *Small Poems of Divers Sorts* (London, 1658)

Coker, John, *A Survey of Dorsetshire* (London, 1732)

A Collection of Curious Discourses written by Eminent Antiquaries, Upon several Heads in our English Antiquities, ed. Thomas Hearne, 2nd edn (London, 1771)

Collop, John, *Poems*, ed. Conrad Hilberry (Madison, 1962)

Columella, *On Agriculture*, edited and translated from the Latin by Harrison Boyd Ash (Loeb Classical Library, 3 vols., Cambridge, Mass., 1941)

Common Conditions, ed. C. F. Tucker Brooke (New Haven, 1915)
The Contention betweene Liberality and Prodigality (1602) (Malone Society, London, 1913)
The Contract of Marriage between Wit and Wisdom, ed. J. O. Halliwell (Shakespeare Society, London, 1846)
Cooke, John, *Unum Necessarium: or, The Poore Mans Case* (London, 1648)
Cooper, Thomas, *An Admonition to the People of England* (London, 1589)
Copland, Robert, *Poems*, ed. Mary Carpenter Erler (Toronto, 1993)
Corbett, Richard, *Poems*, ed. J. A. W. Bennett and H. R. Trevor-Roper (Oxford, 1955)
Cosin, Richard, *An Answer to the first and principall Treatises of a certaine factious libell* (London, 1584)
Cotton, Charles, *Poems*, ed. J. Buxton (London, 1958)
The Country House Poem: A Cabinet of Seventeenth-Century Estate Poems and Related Items, ed. Alastair Fowler (Edinburgh, 1994)
The Country-mans Recreation, or the Art of Planting, Graffing, and Gardening, in three Bookes (London, 1640)
Cowley, Abraham, *Essays, Plays and Sundry Verses*, ed. A. R. Waller (Cambridge, 1906)
Cranmer, Thomas, *The Remains of Thomas Cranmer*, ed. Henry Jenkyns (4 vols., Oxford, 1833)
Crowley, Robert, *The Fable of Philargyrie The Great Gigant* (London, 1551)
   An informacion and Peticion agaynst the oppressours of the pore Commons of this Realme (London, 1548)
   One and thyrtye Epigrammes, wherein are bryefly touched so many Abuses, that maye and ought to be put away (London, 1550)
   The Opening of the Wordes of the Prophet Joell (London, 1567)
   Pleasure and payne, heaven and hell: remembre these foure, and all shall be well (London, 1551)
   Select Works, ed. J. M. Cowper (Early English Text Society, London, 1872)
   A Sermon made in the Chappel at the Gylde halle in London, the .xxix. day of September, 1574 (London, 1575)
   The Voyce of the laste trumpet . . . callynge al the estates of menne to the right path of theyr vocation (London, 1550)
   The Way to Wealth (London, 1550)
Cunningham, William, *The Cosmographical Glasse* (London, 1559)
Curteys, Richard, *A Sermon preached before the Queenes Majestie . . . at Greenwiche* (London, 1573)
   A Sermon preached before the Queenes Majesty at Richmond (London, 1575)
   Two Sermons (London, 1576)
Cyvile and Uncyvile Life (1579); in *Inedited Tracts: Illustrating the Manners, Opinions, and Occupations of Englishmen during the Sixteenth and Seventeenth Centuries*, ed. W. C. Hazlitt (London, 1868)
Daniel, Samuel, *Complete Works*, ed. Alexander B. Grosart (5 vols., New York, 1963)
Davenant, William, *Shorter Poems*, ed. A. M. Gibbs (Oxford, 1972)

Davies, John, *The Complete Works*, ed. Alexander B. Grosart (2 vols., Hildesheim, 1968)

Davies, John, of Hereford, *Poems*, ed. Robert Krueger (Oxford, 1975)

Dawson, Thomas, *The good huswifes Jewell* (London, 1596)

De L'Isle and Dudley Manuscripts, Historical Manuscripts Commission Reports, 77

de Vere, Edward, Earl of Oxford, *Poems*, ed. J. Thomas Looney (London, 1921)

Denham, Sir John, *Expans'd Hieroglyphicks: A Critical Edition of Sir John Denham's Coopers Hill*, ed. Brendan O Hehir (Berkeley and Los Angeles, 1969)

Denton, John, of Cardew, *An Account of the Most Considerable Estates and Families in the County of Cumberland, since the Conquest till the Year 1610*, ed. R. S. Ferguson (Cumberland and Westmoreland Antiquarian and Archaeological Society, Kendal, 1887)

D'Ewes, Sir Simonds, ed., *The Journals of All the Parliaments during the Reign of Queen Elizabeth* (London, 1682)

A Dialogue betwixt a Horse of Warre, and a Mill-Horse (London, 1643)

Dickenson, John, *The Shepheardes Complaint* (London, 1596?)

Digges, Leonard, *A Boke Named Tectonicon* (London, 1562)

A geometrical practise, named Pantometria (London, 1571)

A direction to the husbandman in a new, cheape, and easie way of fertiling, and inriching areable grounds, by a mixture of certaine materialls (London, 1634)

Dod, John, and Robert Cleaver, *A Plaine and familiar exposition: Of the Eighteenth, Nineteenth, and Twentieth Chapters of the Proverbs of Salomon* (London, 1610)

A Plaine and Familiar Exposition of the Eleventh and Twelfth Chapters of the Proverbs of Solomon (London, 1607)

A Plaine and familiar Exposition of the Ten Commaundements (London, 1605)

Doddridge, John, *The History of the Ancient and moderne Estate of the Principality of Wales, Dutchy of Cornewall, and Earldome of Chester* (London, 1630)

Downame, John, *The Plea of the Poore* (London, 1616)

Drayton, Michael, *Works*, ed. J. William Hebel (5 vols., Oxford, 1931–41)

Dryden, John, *Works, Vol. 5*, ed. William Frost (Berkeley, 1987)

Dubravius, Janus, *A New Booke of good Husbandry* (London, 1599)

Dugdale, Sir William, *The Antiquities of Warwickshire* (London, 1656)

The History of Imbanking and Drayning . . . Fens and Marshes (London, 1662)

Dyke, Jeremiah, *A Counterpoison against Covetousnes: In a Sermon preached at Pauls-Crosse* (London, 1619)

Two Sermons Preached in 1622 & 1628, ed. Benjamin Winstone (London, 1896)

Dymock, Cressy, *An Essay for Advancement of Husbandry-Learning* (London, 1651)

Earle, John, *Microcosmography* (1628); ed. Alfred S. West (Cambridge, 1897)

Elderton, William, *A Ballad intituled, Prepare ye to the plowe* (London, 1570)

The Lamentation of Follie (London, 1588?)

Elizabethan Critical Essays, ed. G. Gregory Smith (2 vols., Oxford, 1904)

Elyot, Sir Thomas, *The Boke Named the Governour* (London, 1531)

Englands Helicon (1600); ed. A. H. Bullen (London, 1899)

Englands Parnassus: Or the choysest Flowers of our Moderne Poets, with their Poeticall comparisons. Descriptions of Bewties, Personages, Castles, Pallaces, Mountaines, Groves, Seas, Springs, Rivers &c, ed. Robert Allott (London, 1600)

Englands Troublers Troubled (London, 1648)

An enterlude of Wealth and Health (1554; STC 14110) (Malone Society, London, 1907)

Entertainments for Elizabeth I, ed. Jean Wilson (Woodbridge, 1980)

Erdeswicke, Sampson, *A Survey of Staffordshire* (London, 1723)

Estienne, Charles, and Jean Liebault, *Maison Rustique, or The Countrie Farme*, translated from the French by Richard Surflet (London, 1600)

Euclid, *The Elements of Geometrie*, translated from the Greek by H. Billingsley (London, 1570)

Evelyn, John, *Sylva, or a Discourse of Forest-Trees* (London, 1664)

Eyre, John, *The Exact Surveyor* (London, 1654)

F., N., *The Fruiterers Secrets* (London, 1604)

Fane, Mildmay, Second Earl of Westmorland, 'The "Fugitive Poetry" of Mildmay Fane', ed. Eleanor Withington, *Harvard Library Bulletin*, 9 (1955), pp. 61–78

Otia Sacra (1648), ed. Donald M. Friedman (Scholars' Facsimiles and Reprints, Delmar, 1975)

Fanshawe, Richard, *Shorter Poems and Translations*, ed. N. W. Bawcutt (Liverpool, 1964)

Fering, W., *A new yeres Gift, intituled, a Christal glas for all Estates to looke in, wherein they may plainly see the just rewarde, for Unsaciate and Abhominable Covetousnesse* (London, 1569)

Ferne, John, *The Blazon of Gentrie* (London, 1586)

Fish, Simon, *A Supplication for the Beggers* (London, 1529)

Fitz-Geffrie, Charles, *The Curse of Corne-horders* (London, 1631)

Fitzherbert, John, *The Boke of Husbandrye* (London, 1530?)

The Boke of Husbandrye (London, 1598)

The Boke of Surveying and Improvements (London, 1523)

Flecknoe, Richard, *The Diarium, or Journall* (London, 1656)

Fletcher, John, *The Faithful Shepherdess* (1610?); ed. Cyrus Hay, in *The Dramatic Works in the Beaumont and Fletcher Canon*, general editor, Fredson Bowers (8– vols., Cambridge, 1966–), vol. 3

Fletcher, Robert, *Poems and Translations*, ed. D. H. Woodward (Gainesville, 1970)

Floyd, Thomas, *The Picture of a perfit Common wealth* (London, 1600)

Folkingham, William, *Feudigraphia. The synopsis or epitome of surveying* (London, 1610)

Four Supplications 1529–1553 AD, ed. J. Meadows Cowper (Early English Text Society, London, 1871)

Fulbecke, William, *A Booke of christian Ethicks* (London, 1587)

Fuller, Thomas, *The Holy State* (London, 1642)

Fulwell, Ulpian, *Like Will to Like* (1568); in *Two Moral Interludes* (Malone Society, Oxford, 1991)

Gainsford, Thomas, *The Glory of England* (London, 1618)

Gammer Gurton's Needle (1575); in *Three Sixteenth-Century Comedies*, ed. Charles Walters Whitworth (London, 1984)

Gardiner, Richard, *Instructions for the Manuring, Sowing and Planting of Kitchin Gardens* (London, 1603)

Gascoigne, George (?), *The Queenes Majesty's Entertainment at Woodstock*, ed. A. W. Pollard (Oxford, 1903)

The Steele glas (London, 1576)

Gentylnes and Nobylyte (c. 1525), attributed to John Heywood; in *Three Rastell Plays*, ed. Richard Axton (Cambridge, 1979)

Gerard, John, *The Herball or generall historie of plants* (London, 1597)

Gerard, Thomas, *The Particular Description of the County of Somerset*, ed. E. H. Bates (Somerset Record Society, 15, London, 1900)

Gifford, George, *A Briefe discourse of certaine pointes of the religion, which is among the common sort of Christians* (London, 1583)

Gilpin, Bernard, *A Godly sermon preached in the Court . . . 1552* (London, 1581)

God Speede the Plough (London, 1601)

Googe, Barnabe, *Eglogs, Epytaphes, and Sonettes* (1563) (Scholars' Facsimiles, Gainesville, 1968)

Gouge, William, *Of Domesticall Duties. Eight Treatises* (London, 1622)

Greene, Robert, *The Life and Complete Works*, ed. Alexander Grosart (15 vols., London, 1881–3)

Gryndall, William, *Hawking, Hunting, Fouling, and Fishing* (London, 1596)

Guevara, Antonio de, *A Dispraise of the life of a Courtier, and a commendation of the life of the labourying man*, translated from the French by Francis Bryan (London, 1548)

Habington, William, *Poems*, ed. K. Allott (London, 1948)

Habinton, Thomas, *A Survey of Worcestershire*, ed. James Amphlett (2 vols., Oxford, 1895)

Hake, Edward, *Newes out of Powles churchyarde . . . Wherein is reprooved excessive seeking after riches* (London, 1579)

Hales, John, 'The Defence of John Hales agenst certeyn sclaundres and false reportes made of hym', in *A Discourse of the Common Weal of England*, ed. Elizabeth Lamond (Cambridge, 1893), pp. lii–lxvii

Hall, Joseph, *Collected Poems*, ed. Arnold Davenport (Liverpool, 1949)

Diverse Treatises (1662)

Works (2 vols., London, 1634)

Hannay, Patrick, *The Nightingale* (London, 1622)

Harrington, James, *'The Commonwealth of Oceana' and 'A System of Politics'*, ed. J. G. A. Pocock (Cambridge, 1992)

Harrison, William, 'An Historicall description of the Iland of Britaine', preface
to Raphael Holinshed, *Chronicles*, 2nd edn (3 vols., London, 1586)
Hartlib, Samuel, *Cornu-Copia. A Miscellanium of luciferous and most
fructiferous Experiments, Observations, and Discoveries* (London, 1652?)
A Designe for Plentie (London, 1652?)
The Reformed Common-wealth of Bees (London, 1655)
The Reformed Husband-Man (London, 1651)
Samuel Hartlib His Legacy of Husbandry (London, 1655)
Hastings, Henry, Third Earl of Huntingdon, *The crie of the poore for the death of
the Earle of Huntington* (London, 1596)
Hentzner, Paul, *Travels in England During the Reign of Queen Elizabeth*,
translated from the Latin by R. Bentley (London, 1892)
Herbert, George, *The Complete English Poems*, ed. John Tobin (London, 1991)
Heresbach, Conrad, *Foure Bookes of Husbandry*, translated from the Latin by
Barnabe Googe (London, 1577)
Herrick, Robert, *Poetical Works*, ed. L. C. Martin (Oxford, 1956)
Hertford, Earl of, *The Honorable Entertainment gieven to the Queenes Majestie
in Progresse, at Elvetham in Hampshire* (London, 1591; STC 7583)
Hesiod, *The Georgicks*, translated from the Greek by George Chapman (London,
1618)
Hill, Thomas, *The Arte of Gardening* (London, 1608)
Historical Poems of the XIVth and XVth Centuries, ed. Rossell Hope Robbins
(New York, 1959)
Hobbes, Thomas, *Leviathan*, ed. C. B. Macpherson (London, 1981)
Hogarde, Miles, *A new treatyse in maner of a dialogue, which sheweth the
excellency of mannes nature* (London, 1550?)
Hood, Thomas, *The use of two Mathematicall instruments, the crosse Staffe . . .
And the Jacobs Staffe* (London, 1596)
Hooker, John, 'Hooker's Synopsis Chorographical of Devonshire', ed. J. Blake,
Report and Transactions of the Devonshire Association, 47 (1915),
pp. 334–48
Hopton, Arthur, *Speculum Topographicum: Or The Topographicall Glasse*
(London, 1611)
Horace, *Certain Selected Odes*, translated from the Latin by John Ashmore
(London, 1621)
*A Medicinable Morall, that is, the two Bookes of Horace his Satyres [and] The
Wailyngs of the Prophet Hieremiah*, edited and translated from the Latin by
Thomas Drant (London, 1566)
The Odes and Epodes, edited and translated from the Latin by C. E. Bennett
(Loeb Classical Library, Cambridge, Mass., revised edn, 1927)
Howell, James, *Poems* (London, 1664)
*The Husbandmans Practise, or Prognostication for ever. As teacheth Alberte,
Alkin, Haly, and Ptholome* (London, 1550?)
Hutchinson, Roger, *Works*, ed. John Bruce (Cambridge, 1842)
I., C., *The Commons Petition of Long Afflicted England* (London, 1642)
I playne Piers (London, 1550?)
The Institucion of a Gentleman (London, 1568)

James VI and I, *His Majesties Speach in the Starre-Chamber* (London, 1616)
  The Kings Majestie Declaration to his Subjects, Concerning lawful Sports to be used (1618; STC 9238.9)
  The Poems of James VI of Scotland, ed. James Craigie (2 vols., Edinburgh and London, 1955–8)
James, Richard, *Iter Lancastrense; a Poem*, ed. Thomas Lorser (Chetham Society, London, 1845)
Jones, Philip, *Certaine Sermons* (London, 1588)
Jonson, Ben, *Ben Jonson*, ed. C. H. Herford, Percy Simpson and Evelyn Simpson, 1st edn (11 vols., Oxford, 1925–52)
Josselin, Ralph, *The Diary of Ralph Josselin*, ed. Alan Macfarlane (London, 1976)
The Kalendar of Shepherdes (London, 1508)
Kemp, Anne, *A contemplation on Bassets down-hill* (Oxford, 1658?)
King, Daniel, *The Vale-Royall of England* (London, 1656)
King, Henry, *Poems*, ed. Margaret Crum (Oxford, 1965)
A Knacke to knowe a Knave (1594); facsimile edn, ed. G. R. Proudfoot (Malone Society, Oxford, 1963)
The Knave in Grain (1640); ed. R. C. Bald and Arthur Brown (Malone Society, London, 1961)
La Place, Pierre de, *Politique Discourses, treating of the difference and inequalities of Vocations, as well Publique, as Private*, translated from the French by Aegremont Ratcliffe (London, 1578)
Lambarde, William, *Dictionarium Angliae Topographicum & Historicum, An Alphabetical Description of the Chief Places in England and Wales; With an Account of the most Memorable Events which have distinguish'd them* (London, 1730)
  A Perambulation of Kent (London, 1576)
Langland, William, *The vision of Pierce Plowman . . . Imprynted at London, by Owen Rogers* (London, 1561)
  The vision of Pierce Plowman, now fyrste imprynted by Robert Crowley (London, 1550)
  Piers Plowman: The B Version, ed. G. Kane and E. Talbot Donaldson (London, 1975)
Lanyer, Aemelia, *Poems*, ed. Susanne Woods (Oxford, 1993)
Latimer, Hugh, *Selected Sermons*, ed. Allan Chester (Charlottesville, 1968)
  27 sermons, ed. Augustine Bernher, 2nd edn (London, 1571)
Lawson, William, *A New Orchard and Garden* (London, 1623)
Le Choyselat, Prudent, *A Discourse of Housebandrie*, translated from the French by R. Eden (London, 1580)
Lee, Sir Henry, attr., 'The Queenes Majesties Entertainment at Woodstock', *PMLA*, 26 (1911), pp. 92–141
Lee, Joseph, *Considerations Concerning Common Fields and Inclosures* (London, 1654)
Leigh, Valentine, *The Moste Profitable and commendable science, of Surveying* (London, 1577)
Leland, John, *Cygnea Cantio* (London, 1545)

The Itinerary of John Leland The Antiquary, ed. Thomas Hearne, 2nd edn
(9 vols., Oxford, 1745)
*The Laboryouse Journey & serche of Johan Leylande, for Englandes
Antiquities*, ed. John Bale (London, 1549)
Lenton, Francis, *Characterismi: or, Lentons Leasures. Expressed in Essayes and
Characters* (London, 1631)
Lever, Thomas, *A Meditacion upon the Lordes prayer* (London, 1551)
Three fruitfull sermons, made by T. Lever 1550 (London, 1572)
Levett, John, *The ordering of Bees* (London, 1634)
Leybourn, William, *The Compleat Surveyor* (London, 1653)
Life and Death of Jacke Straw, a notable rebell (London, 1593; STC 23356)
Littleton, Sir Thomas, *Tenures in Englyshe* (London, 1544)
Llwyd, Humphrey, *The Breviary of Britayne*, translated from the Latin by
T. Twyne (London, 1573)
Loder, Robert, *Robert Loder's Farm Accounts*, ed. G. E. Fussell (Camden 3rd
series, 53, London, 1936)
Lodge, Thomas, *The Complete Works*, ed. E. W. Gosse (4 vols., London,
1875–83)
Lovelace, Richard, *Poems*, ed. C. H. Wilkinson (London, 1930)
Lucar, Cyprian, *A Treatise Named Lucarsolace* (London, 1590)
Lupton, Donald, *London and the Countrey Carbonadoed* (London, 1632)
Lupton, Thomas, *All for Money* (1578) (Tudor Facsimile Texts, London, 1910)
Lyly, John, *The Complete Works*, ed. R. Warwick Bond (3 vols., Oxford, 1902)
A Lytell Geste howe the Plowman lerned his Pater Noster (London, 1510)
Malynes, Gerard de, *A Treatise of the Canker of Englands Common Wealth*
(London, 1601)
The maner of the world now a dayes (London, 1562?)
Manwood, John, *A Treatise and Discourse of the Lawes of the Forrest* (1620)
Markham, Gervase, *Cheape and Good Husbandry* (London, 1614)
   Countrey Contentments (London, 1615)
   The English House-Wife (London, 1631)
   The English husbandman. The first part (London, 1613)
   Hungers Prevention: or, The whole Arte of Fowling (London, 1621)
   The Inrichment of the Weald of Kent (London, 1625)
   Markhams farewell to Husbandry (London, 1625)
   Markhams maister-peece (London, 1610)
   Markhams methode, or epitome (London, 1616?)
   The Second Booke of the English Husbandman (London, 1614)
   A Way to get Wealth (London, 1623)
The Marprelate Tracts [1588–1589] (Scolar Press Facsimile, Leeds, 1967)
Marston, John, *Works*, ed. A. H. Bullen (3 vols., London, 1887)
Marvell, Andrew, *Poems and Letters*, ed. H. M. Margoliouth (2nd edn, London,
1968)
Mascall, Leonard, *A Booke of fishing with Hooke & Line* (London, 1590)
   A Booke of the Arte and maner, howe to plant and graffe all sortes of trees
(London, 1572)
   The first booke of Cattell (London, 1587)

The Husbandlye ordring and Governmente of Poultrie (London, 1581)

Massinger, Philip, *Plays and Poems*, ed. Philip Edwards and Colin Gibson (5 vols., Oxford, 1976)

Maxey, Edward, *A new instuction [sic] of plowing and setting of corne* (London, 1601)

Middleton, Thomas, *Michaelmas Term* (1605); ed. Richard Levin (London, 1967)

A Trick to Catch the Old One (1604); ed. G. J. Watson (London, 1968)

Works, ed. A. H. Bullen (8 vols., London, 1886)

Milton, John, *Complete Shorter Poems*, ed. John Carey (Harlow, 1968)

Works, ed. Frank Allen Patterson et al. (18 vols., New York, 1931–40)

Moffett, Thomas, *The Silkewormes, and their Flies* (1599); facsimile edn, ed. Victor Houliston (Medieval and Renaissance Texts and Studies, vol. 56, Binghamton, 1989)

Montaigne, Michel de, *Essayes*, translated from the French by John Florio (1603); ed. J. I. M. Stewart (New York, n.d.)

Moore, Adam, *Bread for the Poor. And Advancement of the English Nation. Promised by Enclosure of the Wastes and Common Grounds of England* (London, 1653)

Moore, John, *A Target for Tillage* (London, 1612)

Moore, John, of Knaptoft, *The Crying Sin of England, Of not Caring for the Poor* (London, 1653)

A scripture-word against inclosure (London, 1656)

More, Henry, *Complete Poems*, ed. Alexander B. Grosart (Hildesheim, 1878)

More, Sir Thomas, *Utopia*, translated from the Latin by Ralphe Robynson (London, 1551)

Utopia: The Complete Works of St Thomas More, Volume Four, ed. Edward Surtz and J. H. Hexter (New Haven and London, 1965)

Moryson, Fynes, *An Itinerary . . . containing his ten yeeres travell through the twelve dominions of Germany, Sweitzerland, Netherland, Denmarke, Poland, Italy, Turkey, France, England, Scotland, and Ireland* (London, 1617)

Nashe, Thomas, *Pierce Penilesse his Supplication to the Divell* (London, 1592)

New Custome (1573) (Malone Society, London, 1908)

Niclaes, Hendrick, *A supplication of the Family of Love* (Cambridge, 1606)

Norden, John, *The Chorography of Norfolk: An Historicall and Chorographicall Description of Norffolck*, attributed to Norden by the modern editor of the unsigned text, Christobel M. Hood (Norwich, 1938)

England, An Intended Guyde for English Travaillers (London, 1625)

An Exact Description of Essex (London, 1840)

John Norden's Manuscript Maps of Cornwall and its Nine Hundreds, ed. William Ravenhill (Exeter, 1972)

Nordens Preparative to his Speculum Britanniae (London, 1596)

A Pensive Mans Practise (London, 1584)

Speculi Britania Pars: The discription of Hartfordshire (London, 1598)

Speculi Britanniae Pars: A Topographicall and Historicall Description of Cornwall (London, 1728)

Speculi Britanniae Pars Altera: or, a Delineation of Northamptonshire (London, 1720)

Speculum Britanniae. The first parte. An historicall, & chorographicall discription of Middlesex (London, 1593)

Surrey. Jo. Nordenus delineavit (London, 1594)

The Surveiors Dialogue (London, 1610)

Sussex. Johes Norden deliniavit (London, 1595)

O Marvelous tydynges both Wonders Old and New (London, c. 1570; STC 24066)

Old English Ballads, 1553–1625, ed. Hyder E. Rollins (Cambridge, 1920)

Orders devised . . . for the reliefe of the present dearth of Graine within the Realme (London, 1586; STC 9194)

Ortelius, Abraham, *The Theatre of the World*, translated from the Latin by W. Bedwell (London, 1606)

Osborne, Henry, *A More Exact Way to Delineate the Plot of any Spacious Parcel of Land* (Dublin, 1654)

Overbury, Sir Thomas, *Miscellaneous Works*, ed. Edward F. Rimbault (London, 1890)

Owen, George, *Owen's Pembrokeshire*, ed. Henry Owen (4 vols., Cymmrodorian Record Series, no. 1, 1892)

Palingenius, Marcellus, *The Zodyake of lyfe*, translated from the Latin by Barnabe Googe (London, 1560)

Palmer, Thomas, *The Emblems of Thomas Palmer: Two Hundred Poosees*, ed. John Manning (New York, 1988)

Parkinson, John, *Paradisi in Sole* (London, 1629)

Peacham, Henry (the younger), *The Compleat Gentleman* (London, 1622)

A Merry Discourse of Meum, and Tuum (London, 1639)

Minerva Britanna (London, 1612)

The Worth of a Peny (London, 1641)

The Pepys Ballads, ed. W. G. Day (5 vols., Cambridge, 1987)

Percy, Henry, Ninth Earl of Northumberland, *Advice to his Son*, ed. G. B. Harrison (London, 1930)

The Perfect Husbandman (London, 1658)

Perkins, William, *Works* (3 vols., London, 1608–9)

Philips, Katherine, *Poems* (London, 1667)

Pierce the Ploughmans Crede (London, 1553)

Plat, Sir Hugh, *A Discoverie of Certaine English wants* (London, 1595)

Floraes Paradise (London, 1608)

The Floures of Philosophie (1572); ed. Richard J. Panofsky (Scholars' Facsimiles, New York, 1982)

The Jewell House of Art and Nature (London, 1594)

The new and admirable Arte of setting of Corne (London, 1600)

Sundrie new and Artificial remedies against Famine (London, 1596)

Plattes, Gabriel, *A Description of the Famous Kingdome of Macaria* (London, 1641)

A Discovery of Infinite Treasure Hidden Since the Worlds Beginning (London, 1639)

The Profitable Intelligencer (London, 1644); facsimile edn (Amsterdam, 1974)

The Plowmans Tale (London, 1606)

Pole, William, *Collections Towards a Description of the County of Devon* (London, 1791)

Popular Music of the Olden Time, ed. William Chappell (2 vols., London, 1895)

Powell, Robert, *Depopulation Arraigned, Convicted and Condemned* (London, 1636)

Powell, Thomas, *The Art of Thriving, Or, The Plaine pathway to Preferment* (London, 1631)

The Praier and Complaynte of the Ploweman unto Christ (Antwerp, 1531?; STC 20036)

The prayse and commendacion of suche as sought commonwelthes (London, 1549?)

Proceedings in Parliament 1628, ed. R. C. Johnson et al. (6 vols., London, 1977–83)

Proceedings in the Parliaments of Elizabeth I: Volume I, 1559–1581, ed. T. E. Hartley (Leicester, 1981)

The Progresses and Public Processions of Queen Elizabeth, ed. John Nichols (3 vols., London, 1823)

The Progresses, Processions, and Magnificent Festivities, of King James the First, ed. John Nichols (4 vols., London, 1828)

A Prymmer or boke of private prayer nedeful to be used of al faythfull Christianes (London, 1553; STC 20373)

Prynne, William, *Mount-Orgueil . . . with a Poeticall Description of Mount-Orgueil Castle in the Isle of Jersey* (London, 1641)

Purchas, Samuel, *A Theatre of Politicall Flying Insects* (London, 1657)

Puttenham, George, *The Arte of English Poesie* (1589); ed. Gladys Doidge Willcock and Alice Walker (Cambridge, 1936)

Pyers plowmans exhortation unto the lordes knightes and burgoysses of the Parlyamenthouse (London, 1550?)

Quarles, Francis, *Emblemes* (London, 1635)

Randolph, Thomas, *Poems with the Muses Looking-Glasse: and Amyntas* (Oxford, 1638)

Rankins, William, *Seaven Satyres* (1598); ed. A. Davenport (London, 1945)

Rathborne, Aaron, *The Surveyor in Foure bookes* (London, 1616)

Recorde, Robert, *The Pathway to Knowledge* (London, 1551)

Respublica: An interlude for Christmas 1553, attr. to Nicholas Udall, ed. W. W. Greg (Early English Text Society, Oxford, 1952)

Reyce, Robert, *The Breviary of Suffolk, 1618*, ed. Lord Francis Harvey (London, 1902)

Rhodes, John, *The Countrie Mans Comfort* (London, 1637)

Rich, Barnaby, *Faults Faults, And nothing else but Faultes* (London, 1606)

Risdon, Tristram, *The Chorographicall Description, or, Survey of the County of Devon, with the City and County of Exeter* (London, 1811)

Rowlands, Samuel, *Looke to it: For, Ile Stabbe Ye* (London, 1604)

The Roxburghe Ballads, ed. William Chappell and J. Woodfall Ebsworth (8 vols., London, 1871–95)

A Ruful complaynt of the publyke weale to Englande (London, 1550?; STC 5611.4)

Russell, Francis, Second Earl of Bedford, *The poore peoples complaint, bewailing the death of their famous benefactor, the worthy earle of Bedford* (London, 1600?)

Rutter, Joseph, *The Shepheards Holy-Day. A Pastorall Tragi-Comaedie* (London, 1635)

S., T., *A Jewell for Gentrie. Being an exact Dictionary, or true Method, to make any Man understand all the Art, Secrets, and worthy Knowledges belonging to Hawking, Hunting, Fowling and Fishing* (London, 1614)

Saltonstall, Wye, *Picturae Loquentes, or Pictures Drawne forth in Characters* (London, 1635)

Saxton, Christopher, *An Atlas of England and Wales: The Maps of Christopher Saxton 1574–1579*, ed. Edward Lynam (London, 1936)

Scot, Reynolde, *A Perfite platforme of a Hoppe Garden* (London, 1574)

Scott, Thomas, *The Belgicke Pismire* (London, 1622)

Seventeenth-Century Economic Documents, ed. Joan Thirsk and J. P. Cooper (Oxford, 1972)

Shakespeare, William, *The Complete Works*, ed. Stanley Wells and Gary Taylor (Oxford, 1986)

Shepherd, Luke, *John Bon and Mast person* (London, 1548?)

Sheppard, Samuel, *Epigrams* (London, 1651)

The Shirburn Ballads 1586–1616, ed. Andrew Clark (Oxford, 1907)

Sidney, Sir Philip, *An Apology for Poetry*, ed. Geoffrey Shepherd (London, 1965)

   The Countess of Pembroke's Arcadia, ed. Maurice Evans (Harmondsworth, 1977)

   The Countess of Pembroke's Arcadia (The Old Arcadia), ed. Jean Robertson (Oxford, 1973)

Smith, George, *Englands Pressures: or, The Peoples Complaint* (London, 1645)

Smith, Sir Thomas, *De Republica Anglorum* (London, 1583)

   A Discourse of the Commonweal of This Realm of England (London, 1581)

   A Discourse of the Commonweal of This Realm of England, ed. Mary Dewar (Charlottesville, 1969)

Smith, William, *The Particular Description of England 1588. With Views of Some of the Chief Towns and Armorial Bearings of Nobles and Bishops*, ed. Henry B. Wheatley and Edmund W. Ashbee (London, 1879)

Smyth, John, of Nibley, *A Description of the Hundred of Berkeley in the County of Gloucester and of its Inhabitants*, vol. 3 of *The Berkeley Manuscripts*, ed. Sir John Maclean (Gloucester, 1885)

Southerne, Edmund, *A Treatise concerning the right use and ordering of Bees* (London, 1593)

Speed, Adolphus, *Adam out of Eden* (London, 1659)

Speed, John, *England, Wales, Scotland and Ireland described and abridged* (London, 1627)

   The History of Great Britaine (London, 1611)

   A Prospect of the Most Famous Parts of the World (London, 1627)

The Theatre of the Empire of Great Britaine (London, 1611)
Spelman, Sir Henry, 'Icenia: sive Norfolciae. Descriptio Topographica', in *The English Works of Sir Henry Spelman, Together with his Posthumous Works* (London, 1727)
Spenser, Edmund, *Poetical Works*, ed. J. C. Smith and E. De Selincourt (Oxford, 1970)
Sprigge, William, *A Modest Plea for an Equal Common-wealth Against Monarchy* (London, 1659)
St German, Christopher, *Hereafter foloweth a Dyaloge in Englysshe betwyxt a Doctoure of Dyvynyte and a Student in the Lawes of Englande* (London, 1530?)
Standish, Arthur, *The Commons Complaint* (London, 1611)
New Directions of Experience (London, 1615)
Stanley, Thomas, *Poems and Translations*, ed. Galbraith Miller Crump (Oxford, 1962)
Starkey, Thomas, *A Dialogue Between Reginald Pole and Thomas Lupset*, ed. Kathleen M. Burton (London, 1948)
England in the Reign of King Henry the Eighth: Part I. Starkey's Life and Letters, ed. Sidney J. Herrtage (Early English Text Society, London, 1878)
Stevenson, Matthew, *Occasions Off-spring. or Poems on Severall Occasions* (London, 1654)
The Twelve Moneths (London, 1661)
Stow, John, *A Survay of London* (London, 1603)
Strode, William, *Poetical Works*, ed. Bertram Dobell (London, 1907)
Stuart Royal Proclamations, ed. James F. Larkin and Paul L. Hughes (2 vols., Oxford, 1973–83)
Stubbes, Philip, *The Anatomie of Abuses* (London, 1583)
A supplication of the poore commons (London?, 1546)
Tasso, Torquato, *The Housholders Philosophie*, trans. T. K., *Whereunto is anexed a dairie Booke for all good huswives* (London, 1588)
Taylor, John, *All the Workes . . . Collected in one Volume*, 1630 (Spenser Society, London, 1868–9)
Works . . . Not Included in the Folio Volume of 1630 (5 vols., Spenser Society, London, 1870–8)
T[aylor], S[ilas], *Common-Good: or, The Improvement of Commons, Forrests, and Chases, by Inclosure* (London, 1652)
Thynne, Francis, *Newes from the North* (London, 1579)
Tottel's Miscellany (1557–1587), ed. Hyder Edward Rollins (2 vols., Cambridge, Mass., revised edn, 1965)
The Towneley Plays, ed. G. England (Early English Text Society, Oxford, 1897)
Townshend, Hayward, 'Hayward Townshend's Journals', ed. A. F. Pollard and Marjorie Blatcher, *Bulletin of the Institute of Historical Research*, 12 (1934–5), pp. 1–31
Historical Collections: or, An exact Account of the Proceedings of the Four last Parliaments of Q. Elizabeth (London, 1680)
Traherne, Thomas, *Poems, Centuries and Three Thanksgivings*, ed. Anne Ridler (London, 1966)

Traheron, Bartholomew, *A Warning to England to Repente, and to Turne to God from idolatrie and poperie by the terrible exemple of Calece given the 7 of March. Anno. D. 1558* (Wesel?, 1558)

Trigge, Francis, *A Godly and Fruitfull Sermon Preached at Grantham . . . 1592* (Oxford, 1595)

To the Kings most excellent Majestie. The Humble Petition of Two Sisters; the Church and Common-wealth: For the restoring of their ancient Commons and liberties, which late Inclosure and depopulation, uncharitably hath taken away (London, 1604)

Tudor Economic Documents, ed. R. H. Tawney and Eileen Power (3 vols., London, 1924)

Tudor Royal Proclamations, ed. Paul L. Hughes and James F. Larkin (3 vols., New Haven and London, 1964–9)

Turberville, George, *Epitaphes, Epigrams, Songs and Sonets* (London, 1570)

The Noble Art of Venerie or Hunting (London, 1575)

Turner, William, *The Huntyng of the Romyshe Wolfe* (Emden, 1555?)

Tusser, Thomas, *Five Hundred Points of Good Husbandry*, ed. Geoffrey Grigson (Oxford, 1984)

Five hundreth points of good husbandry (London, 1573)

A hundreth good pointes of husbandrie (London, 1557)

Two Tudor Interludes, ed. Ian Lancashire (Manchester, 1979)

Tyranipocrit Discovered (Rotterdam, 1649)

Vallans, William, *A Tale of Two Swannes* (London, 1590)

Van Den Keere, Pieter, *Atlas of the British Isles, c. 1605*, ed. Helen Wallis (Lympne Castle, Kent, 1972)

Varro, Marcus Terentius, *On Agriculture*, edited and translated from the Latin by William Davis Hooper (Loeb Classical Library, Cambridge, Mass., 1934)

Vaughan, Henry, *Works*, ed. L. C. Martin (Oxford, 1957)

Vaughan, Rowland, *Most Approved and Long Experienced Water-Workes* (London, 1610)

Vaughan, William, *The Golden Grove* (London, 1600)

Virgil, *The Bucoliks . . . Together with his Georgiks*, translated from the Latin by Abraham Fleming (London, 1589)

Eclogues, Georgics, Aeneid I–IV, edited and translated from the Latin by H. Rushton Fairclough (Loeb Classical Library, Cambridge, Mass., 1935)

Georgics, translated from the Latin by Thomas May (London, 1628)

Georgics, translated from the Latin by John Ogilby (London, 1649)

Wager, William, *'The Longer Thou Livest' and 'Enough Is as Good as a Feast'*, ed. R. Mark Benbow (London, 1967)

Waller, Edmund, *Poems* (London, 1645)

Walter of Henley, *Boke of husbandry*, translated from the French by R. Grosseteste (London, 1508?)

Walter of Henley and other Treatises on Estate Management and Accounting, ed. Dorothea Oschinsky (Oxford, 1971)

Walton, Izaac, *The Compleat Angler* (London, 1661)

Watkins, Rowland, *Flamma Sine Fuma: or, Poems without Fictions* (London, 1662)

Weaver, R., *An enterlude called Lusty Juventus* (1550?) (Malone Society, London, 1966)

Westcote, Thomas, *A View of Devonshire in 1630* (Exeter, 1845)

The Western husbandmans lamentation (London, 1645)

Weston, Sir Richard, *A Discourse of Husbandrie used in Brabant and Flanders* (London, 1652)

Wharton, John, *Whartons Dreame* (London, 1578)

Whitfield, Christopher, ed., *Robert Dover and the Cotswold Games: 'Annalia Dubrensia'* (Evesham, 1962)

Whitney, Geffrey, *A Choice of Emblemes, and other Devises* (Leyden, 1586)

Wilkinson, Edward, *His Thameseidos* (London, 1600)

Wilkinson, Robert, *A Sermon preached . . . upon occasion of the late Rebellions and Riots* (London, 1607)

Wilson, Robert, *The Coblers Prophesie* (1594) (Malone Society, London, 1914)

The Pedlars Prophecie (1595) (Malone Society, London, 1914)

The Three Ladies of London (1590) (Tudor Facsimile Texts, London, 1911)

Wilson, Thomas, *The State of England, Anno Dom. 1600*, ed. F. J. Fisher (Camden Miscellany, 16, London, 1936)

Wimbledon, Richard, *A Sermon no lesse fruteful then famous* (London, 1540?)

Winstanley, Gerrard, 'England's Spirit Unfoulded, or an Incouragement to Take the Engagement', ed. G. E. Aylmer, *Past and Present*, 40 (1968), pp. 3–15

Works, ed. George H. Sabine (Ithaca, 1941)

Wither, George, *Abuses Stript and Whipt. or Satirical Essaies, Divided into two Bookes* (London, 1613)

A Collection of Emblemes, Ancient and Moderne (1635) (Renaissance English Text Society, Columbia, South Carolina, 1975)

Haleluiah or, Britains Second Remembrancer (London, 1641)

Worsop, Edward, *A Discoverie of sundrie errours and faults daily committed by Landemeaters* (London, 1582)

Xenophon, *Treatise of Housholde*, translated from the Greek by G. Hervet (London, 1537)

Zouch, Richard, *The Dove, or Passages of Cosmography* (London, 1613)

Index

Index 323

government action against, 50–1, 76–7
in rural poetry, 279–80
popular action against, 117
progress of, 7, 32, 238
satiric representations of, 82, 87, 89–90,
259, 276–7
engrossing, 16
Essex, 244
'Exact Discription of Essex, An', *see*
Norden, John
estate surveying, *see* surveying and
surveyors
Estienne, Charles, *see Maison Rustique, or
The Countrie Farme*
Euclid, 182
Everitt, Alan, 16n, 17n
Exe (River, Devon), 251

Family of Love, 120
famine, *see* dearth
Fanshawe, Richard, 280
Fella, Thomas, 208
fens
drainage of, 105–6, 158, 165
produce of, 256
Ferguson, Arthur B., 36–7, 54–5, 248n
festivities, rural, 257, 277, 290–3, 296
feudalism, 26, 31
decline of, 163, 228
transition to capitalism, 7
Fitz-Geffrie, Charles, 76
Fitzherbert, John, 136n
Boke of Husbandrye, 1, 136, 137–8,
139, 143–4
Boke of Surveying and Improvements,
143n, 172–3, 180
Fletcher, John, 265
Folkingham, William, 184, 188–9
forests, 158, 259–61, 285
Fowler, Alastair, 199, 250, 256, 275
Foxe, John, 34, 52
'freedom', 12, 128–9, 162–3
freehold and freeholders, 163–5
Frome (River, Dorset), 259–60
fruit, production of, 13, 56, 242, 246
Fuller, Thomas, 79
Fulwell, Ulpian, 97

Gammer Gurton's Needle, 97
gardens and gardening, 157, 160
Perfite platforme of a Hoppe Garden, A,
see Scot, Reynolde
Gardiner, Richard, 160
Gascoigne, George
'Princely Pleasures at the Courte at
Kenelwooth, The', 273
Steele glas, The, 83, 85–6
gavelkind, 247n
genealogy, study of, 232, 234–7
Genesis, *see* Bible
Genovese, Elizabeth Fox, 17n
gentlemen and the gentry
and husbandry, 203–6, 208–10, 228,
281–2
as a 'calling', 47
culture and interests of, 157, 231,
234–7, 267–8
fears of revolt of, 37
landholdings of, 14
see also landlords
Gentylnes and Nobylyte, *see* Heywood,
John
geometry, 54, 171, 182–8, 189
see also surveying and surveyors
georgic
and communism, 129–30
and national prosperity, 207, 211,
215–17, 222–6
and the individual, 206–7, 213–15,
218–22
biblical or Christian, 30–1, 79, 202–3
classical influences on, 198–9, 200–1,
204, 212
definitions of, 198–200, 212
in chorography, 249–52, 256
in rural poetry, 281–4, 288–9, 291n,
293–7
in the sixteenth century, 200–12
in the seventeenth century, 212–28
see also husbandry manuals;
'improvement'; pastoral
Gerard, John, 157
Ginzburg, Carlo, 114n
Glascock, Edward, 169
Gloucestershire, 242

husbandry manuals
  and georgic, 203–8
  and ideals of manorial order, 137–43
  and projects, 151–6, 165–6
  and seventeenth-century agricultural
    revolution, 156–68
  and thrifty smallholders, 143–51
  emergence of, 135–6
  printed form of, 139, 143–4, 145, 146–7
  readers of, 54, 139–40, 204
  see also 'improvement'

'improvement'
  and colonialism, 196–7
  and husbandry manuals, 135–68
  communist endorsements of, 124,
    129–30
  criticism of, 66–7, 72, 73, 75–6,
    169–70, 177–8, 186
  debates over the morality of, 7–12,
    76–9, 151–6
  endorsements of, in chorography, 248–9
  endorsements of, in rural poetry, 299
  etymology of, 136–7
  practices of, 13, 122, 179–80
  religious justifications of, 68–9, 78–9,
    142, 159, 213–17
  satiric attacks on, 89–90, 94–5, 104–8
  see also enclosure; georgic; husbandry;
    individualism; property; surveying
    and surveyors
individualism
  and georgic, 200, 207–8, 212, 213–15,
    218–22
  and improvement, 11–12, 54–7, 136–7,
    147–51, 160–8
  and perceptions of property, 169–70,
    173, 177–9, 186–9, 194–6
  and religious change, 68–9, 213–15
  complaints against, 36–7, 41–2, 72, 126
  in satire, 84–6, 89–91, 94–5, 96–7
  origins of, 7
  'one's own', *see* property
'industry'
  and georgic, 217, 219, 226
  and improvement, 12, 79, 162, 166,
    249, 299

  and poetic labour, 256
  religious anxiety about, 207–8
inflation, 13, 32, 59
'ingenuity', 161
Ireland, 196–7
Ireton, Henry, 164n
Isaiah, *see* Bible

Jackman, Henry, 11, 144
James I, King, 72, 105n
  Book of Sports, 293
  poetry of, 281–2
  social policy of, 279, 280–2
James, Mervyn, 176n
Jeremiah, *see* Bible
Johnson, Robert, 169, 174, 175
Jones, Norman, 68–9
Jonson, Ben, 99, 100, 282n
  Bartholomew Fair, 99–100, 103
  Devil is an Ass, The, 100, 104–9
  'To Penshurst', 285–90

Kay, John, of Woodsome, 204, 208–10
Kegl, Rosemary, 276
Kendrick, T. D., 236
Kent, 118, 246
  Perambulation of Kent, A, see
    Lambarde, William
Kernan, Alvin, 86
Kerridge, Eric, 15n, 137n
Kett's rebellion, *see* revolt and riots
King, John N., 34n, 35n, 63n, 201–2, 270n
Knacke to knowe a Knave, A, 96
'knowledge'
  and estate management, 178, 182,
    281–2
  and improvement, 148, 159, 173
  'to know one's own', *see* property
Kula, Witold, 185n

labourers
  activities and numbers of, 16–17
  as happy workers, 223, 244–5, 257,
    288–9, 291, 295–7
  in improvement projects, 155–6, 167–8
  see also ploughmen; shepherds
Lambarde, William, 247

Inrichment of the Weald of Kent, The,
158
Markhams methode, or epitome, 145
Way to get Wealth, A, 149
Marprelate, Martin, 66
Marsh, Christopher W., 120n
Martyr, Peter, 116
Mary, Queen, reign of, 62
Mascall, Leonard, 145
Massinger, Philip, 101
City-Madam, The, 103
New Way to Pay Old Debts, A, 101
Matthew, Gospel of, *see* Bible
May, Thomas, 212
'merry England', *see* national identity
mid-Tudor reform, *see* Edward VI,
King
Middlesex
Discription of Middlesex, see Norden,
John
Middleton, Thomas, 101
Father Hubburds Tales, 98–9
Michaelmas Term, 101–2, 103
Trick to Catch the Old One, A, 101,
103
middling sorts, 84, 124, 165, 224, 269,
284
Milton, John
'L'Allegro', 2
Of Christian Doctrine, 216–17
Misselden, Edward, 161
Moffett, Thomas, 211–12
monasteries
and land-measurement, 181–2
dissolution of, 28–9
money
and improvement, 142–3, 163, 166–7
in georgic, 224, 225
satire on, 88, 104–5
Montaigne, Michel de, 116
Montrose, Louis Adrian, 264, 267–8,
274
Moore, Adam, 162, 167
Moore, John, 77–8
'moral economy', 17–18, 78
morality plays, 91–7
More, Henry, 280

More, Sir Thomas
Utopia, 10, 23–4, 58n, 114–15
national identity, 6
and chorography, 231–3, 237, 242–3,
257–8
and Elizabethan panegyric, 272–4
and georgic, 222–6
and Protestant reform, 33–4, 38–9, 44, 52
and the English revolution, 121–2
'merry England', 277, 290–1
see also body politic; 'commonwealth'
natural law, *see* nature, law of
nature
as deity, 89, 105, 237, 280, 298
law of, 115–17
study of, 159
new historicism, 3–4
Newdigate, Sir John, 139
Norbrook, David, 203n, 278
Norden, John, 175
'A Chorographicall discription', 248
Delineation of Northamptonshire,
244–5
discription of Middlesex, 243–4
'An Exact Discription of Essex', 250
Pensive Mans Practise, A, 207–8
Surveiors Dialogue, The, 14, 158, 162,
171, 176–9, 192–3, 213, 214
Norfolk, 49, 118, 181
Chorography of Norfolk, The, 247n
'Norman yoke', 121, 128
Northamptonshire, 135
Delineation of Northamptonshire, see
Norden, John

oaks, 260
orchards, *see* fruit, production of
Ortelius, Abraham, 234
otium, 269, 277
Outhwaite, R. B., 14n
Owen, George, of Henllys, 249
Oxfordshire, 237–8
Oxfordshire Rising, *see* revolts and riots

Palladius, 136
Parkinson, John, 157
parks, 260–1

Past and Present Publications

General Editor: JOANNA INNES, *Somerville College, Oxford*

* Published as a paperback
† Co-published with the Maison des Sciences de L'Homme, Paris

Printed in the United States
By Bookmasters